PABLO
AND ME

PABLO AND ME

MY LIFE WITH ESCOBAR

Victoria Eugenia Henao

Translated by Andrea Rosenberg

EBURY
PRESS

1 3 5 7 9 10 8 6 4 2

Ebury Press, an imprint of Ebury Publishing
20 Vauxhall Bridge Road
London SW1V 2SA

Ebury Press is part of the Penguin Random House Group of companies
whose addresses can be found at global.penguinrandomhouse.com

 Penguin
Random House
UK

First published as *Mrs Escobar* by Ebury Press in 2019
This edition published in 2020
First published with the title *Mi vida y mi cárcel con Pablo Escobar* in
Colombia in 2018
by Editorial Planeta Colombiana S. A., Bogotá

www.penguin.co.uk

A CIP catalogue record for this book is available from the British Library

ISBN 9781785039935

Typeset in 11.75/16.75 pt Minion Pro
by Integra Software Services Pvt. Ltd, Pondicherry

Printed and bound in Great Britain by Clays Ltd, Elcograf S.p.A.

To my children, Juan Pablo and Manuela, for their courage and resilience in enduring the atrocious violence their father caused and the terrible periods they spent shut inside as children.

To my daughter-in-law, Ángeles, who is like another daughter to me, a gift from God, for her affection and unconditional loyalty.

To my grandson, Juan Emilio, who gives me the strength and inspiration I need to overcome anything, and for the magical connection he brings to my life.

To my parents, my family, my teachers, my friends and the people who listened to me every night and read my writing, respecting my silence and my tears.

My thanks to them all for their boundless, unwavering love.

Contents

Preface

'How could you sleep with that monster?' one of the victims of my husband, Pablo Escobar, asked me. 'Were you a victim or an accomplice? Why didn't you do anything? Why didn't you leave him? Why didn't you turn him in?'

Those questions are probably ones that thousands of people have wondered. The answer is because I loved him, and while many may find that response inadequate, the truth is that's the reason I remained by his side till the end of his life, even though I disagreed with his actions and decisions innumerable times.

I met Pablo Escobar when I was just twelve years old and he was twenty-three. He was the first and only love of my life. I married him in the Church, believing that marriage vows are to be honoured. I was raised in a male-chauvinist culture in which women were taught to follow their husbands without questioning.

I grew up being moulded by Pablo to be his wife and the mother of his children, not to ask questions or challenge his choices, to look the other way. I finished high school after having my first child, and from then on my life revolved around my husband until the day he died.

I endured affairs, insults, humiliations, lies, loneliness, raids, death threats, terrorist attacks, kidnapping attempts on my children and even long periods of confinement and exile. All for love. Of course, there were many moments when I wondered whether I should keep going. But I wasn't able to leave him, not just because of love but also out of fear, powerlessness, and uncertainty about what would become of my children and me without him. I was even afraid that the most dangerous man in Colombia might hurt me if I left him.

In 1984 – when our situation had become immensely complicated after the assassination of the minister of justice, Rodrigo Lara Bonilla, on Pablo's orders – and during the nine years that followed, I lived in terror. Pablo showed complete disregard for the consequences of his actions, much less for their effects on his own family. His senseless frenzy of activity left no room for any questioning or criticism, and I lacked the strength necessary to leave him even when many others did.

Every single day in the late 1980s and early 1990s was a life-or-death matter for all Colombians; all of us were held hostage by my husband's war, and escaping the brutality unleashed by Pablo was our biggest challenge.

One night in 1988, a car loaded with 1,500lbs of dynamite exploded outside our front door while we were sleeping. It marked the beginning of a fierce narco-terrorist war, with us as the main target of my husband's enemies. Miraculously, we survived, but from that point on we had no choice but to heed Pablo's decisions on how, when and where to move around.

By the time I realised how far removed I'd become from the brutal reality around us, it was too late. I was very young, naive and blind to reality, and so I succumbed; I was often quite comfortable, but it was always comfort born out of the ignorance that comes with having no right to look, think, decide, choose or question.

The last period of Pablo's life was a very lonely one; he was surrounded by many men, but few friends. Thanks to his unfettered greed and ambition, he lost control of everything. He did all his own thinking and planning; he took over our lives and violently took the life of anything that crossed him. I wasn't strong enough to confront him, though I often rebuked him for his actions. He never listened.

The lives of myself and my family were utterly trans-formed after his death. I found myself forced to negotiate with his enemies, coordinate a settlement with the Colom-bian government, legally change our identities, look for a country to take us in, and figure out how to take care of my children and my daughter-in-law. My love for them revealed strength I never knew I had, which allowed me to do things I'd never imagined. But I also realised that no matter what we did, my children and I would continue to be identified as Pablo Escobar's family, and would carry all sorts of social stigmas to our graves.

My son, Juan Pablo Escobar, today Sebastián Marro-quín, decided to show his face to the world in 2009 with the documentary *Sins of My Father*, in which he asked for forgiveness for Pablo's crimes. In publishing his books, *Pablo Escobar: My Father* and *Pablo Escobar in fraganti*, he strove to tell our story with the sole aim of preventing our experiences from ever being repeated. My son's courage inspired me to follow in his footsteps and, with his help I, too, decided to offer an account of all the things I felt and experienced back then.

It took me twenty-five years to stand up, come out of my internal confinement, and conquer my fear in order to describe my life with Pablo Escobar in my own words. Despite all the years I spent with him, it was my research for this book that allowed me to begin to contextualise and really understand what happened in our lives. To accomplish that, I had to overcome my fear of being criticised and rise above the doubts of the many people who asked me to drop the subject and not to continue. In my view, there was no turning back – I wanted to leave those years of silence behind. Telling my story became absolutely essential for me.

Now, with the perspective granted by the distance and wisdom of the passing years, I have watched the film of my life again with great attention, and I am now aware of my responsibilities and irresponsibilities, of all the things I got right and the very many I got wrong.

My research for this book showed me that there were many things I didn't know about my husband, so much so that some elements of the story are completely unfamiliar to me, and others I find frankly horrifying.

When he finished reading the manuscript, my son commented that though he'd thought he knew almost everything about his father, this book has undermined his image of Pablo in fundamental ways. The research and writing process has been painful and sometimes even tearful because it has caused me to question many of my decisions and reflect on the things I did do and those I failed to do. Writing has been a sort of catharsis, a journey into the depths to investigate this story that has devastated the hearts and souls of thousands of families.

During this period, I have begun to review the memories of the people who suffered the horrors of the drug-trafficking war. I feel immense sadness and shame for the enormous pain my husband caused, even as I mourn the agonising consequences his actions have had for my children and me.

Very few people acknowledge me as María Isabel Santos, the name I took after Pablo's death. They see me not as a woman, but as the continuation of my husband's evil. They question me about his actions, regardless of my own endeavours or my struggles as a female head of household. The past continues to pursue us, and Pablo's ghost won't leave us alone. I am, but will hopefully cease to be from now on, 'Pablo Escobar's widow'.

Over the course of this book's pages, readers will find a very different woman from the one depicted in the media, in movies and on TV. I am a human being who has engaged in a process of transformation, aware that my children and I are the perpetual bearers of a last name that is inexorably associated with evil.

Though the law protects my right as a wife not to denounce my children's father, I know this life will not be long enough for me to ask sufficient forgiveness for not having left my husband and denounced his actions. I was in love with him, and because of that, I did whatever I could to take care of my family and my marriage. It will probably seem absurd to ask for readers' understanding while recounting a story that is itself impossible to understand.

Only a person who has loved blindly and unconditionally as I did, as a devoted wife and mother, might be able to view from my own personal perspective how the events I am only now daring to reveal came to pass. With great humility and respect, I ask to be heard as an individual and as a woman. I did not start down this path looking to be exonerated.

Pablo Escobar is not an example to be followed; seeing the false hero recreated in movies and TV series, I have felt compelled to speak up and tell the truth, without sugar-coating anything, to avoid at all costs the chance that his story might be repeated.

In addition, this book is the product of an unprecedented examination of Pablo Escobar's married life, a quarter of a century after his death. And it is the log for a one-way journey into the darkest depths of his soul and of my life with Colombia's most-wanted man, the country's most-despised criminal of the twentieth century. For all of this, for what he did and what I failed to do, I ask for forgiveness.

VICTORIA EUGENIA HENAO

Introduction

My Astral Relationship with Pablo Escobar's Family

by Mauricio Puerta

4 December 1994

'Hello. Who is this?' I asked as I answered my mobile phone.

'This is the widow,' somebody said on the other end of the line.

'The widow? What widow?' I replied, thinking it was a joke.

'The widow of the man you wrote about in *Semana* magazine, saying he was going to be killed.'

This story actually begins about two years earlier, when, while giving astrology classes at the Fundación Santillana – headed by former Colombian president Belisario Betancur – I became interested in studying the birth charts of the country's major personalities, including Pablo Escobar Gaviria.

He was born on 1 December 1949, just one month and three days before me. It was 11.55am when Doña Hermilda Gaviria gave birth to her third son, Pablo. Those bits of information were enough to allow me to interpret the book of his life.

In astrology, the birth chart is like a navigation chart for the soul, like an actor's script – and in this case, the actor was Pablo Escobar. Obviously I'm not going to describe every symbol on his chart, but I will examine those that are relevant to this story.

Pablo Escobar was a Sagittarius with Pisces rising, one of the most difficult combinations in the zodiac. Sagittarius is known as the sign of superior intelligence – in any undertaking. And Pisces is the sign of the deep ocean, where things are done that will never be found out. Sagittarius is a symbol of fire and Pisces is a symbol of water – they were inevitably going to lead to a short circuit at some point.

But he was also born with the most beautiful conjunction of all: Venus (love) and Jupiter (the benefactor) in his eleventh house, that of altruism and aid to other people. At the same time, he was born with the very worst combination: Mars (war) next to Saturn (death) in his seventh house, which is associated with society and known rivals.

He was hardly aided by being born with the Moon in conjunction with Black Moon Lilith in his second house, that of money, and with bloody Mars ruling Aries. That aspect seemed very problematic when it came to seeking economic security. That's how I explained it to Gabriel García Márquez when, years later, he interviewed me for his book *News of a Kidnapping*, first published in May 1996.

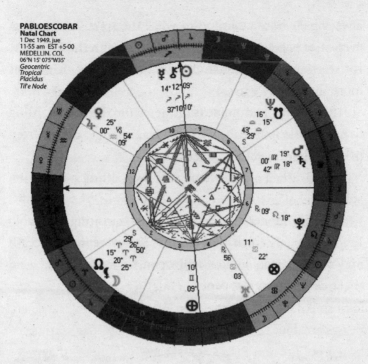

PABLOESCOBAR
Natal Chart
1 Dec 1949. jue
11·55 am EST +5·00
MEDELLIN. COL
06°N 15' 075°W35'
Geocentric
Tropical
Placidus
Til'e Node

3 July 1992

I've kept a detailed diary of my life ever since I was fourteen, which has later served me as an astrologer. The entry
for the day in question reads, 'I met with several friends in
the home of María Jimena Duzán.' As I write this text, I am
linked to the journalist María Jimena Duzán not only by
more than forty years of friendship, but also because she
wrote about the murder of presidential candidate Luis Carlos Galán, who used to consult the stars using the same
astrologer that she did: me. It doesn't seem to have done
Luis Carlos much good. But a script is a script. The friends
in attendance that night were government officials who

always paid close attention to what the stars were saying, ever since negotiating the peace process with the M-19 terrorist group. My friendship with them is one that spans more than thirty years.

That night I had unpleasant news for them. According to my calculations, Pablo Escobar was about to escape from prison. I informed them of as much.

'Why?' asked one of them, who was sitting on a brown sofa.

'Because Jupiter the benefactor is transiting on Pablo Escobar's natal Saturn, and whereas Saturn represents death and confinement, Jupiter will open doors for him.' And that's exactly what happened.

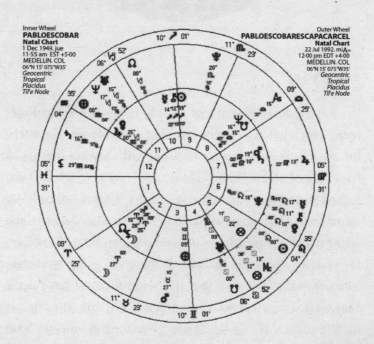

Inner Wheel
PABLOESCOBAR
Natal Chart
1 Dec 1949. jue
11·55 am EST +5·00
MEDELLIN. COL
06°N 15' 075°W35'
Geocentric
Tropical
Placidus
Tií'e Node

Outer Wheel
PABLOESCOBARESCAPACARCEL
Natal Chart
22 Jul 1992. miɅₘ
12·00 pm EDT +4·00
MEDELLIN. COL
06°N 15' 075°W35'
Geocentric
Tropical
Placidus
Tií'e Node

Indeed, on 22 July of that year, 1992, Pablo Escobar escaped from La Catedral Prison, where he was incarcerated. Jupiter, as if presenting an emperor's raised thumb, had crossed over Saturn, whose thumb points downward – just like in the Roman stadiums, where the position of the emperor's thumb decided whether a gladiator would live or die.

It is beside the point here to recount how he escaped and where he stayed during the long months he spent on the run.

4 May 1993

In April of the following year, María Jimena called to tell me that *Semana* was interested in interviewing me to talk about who was going to be the country's next president and what was going to happen to Pablo Escobar. And so, on 4 May, I appeared in the magazine saying two things: first, that the next president would be Ernesto Samper, who would enjoy special protection against hidden enemies because he had Jupiter, the protector, in his twelfth house, which is associated with hidden enemies. But that's another story.

And I also told the interviewers that Pablo Escobar would meet his death before the year was out. What he thought and said when he read the magazine is recounted by his son, Juan Pablo Escobar, in his book *Pablo Escobar: My Father*, first published in 2014. I remember that the priest Rafael García Herreros – a Capricorn – strove tirelessly to get in contact with Escobar and convince him to return to prison, but he never managed it. Upon learning this, I'd mused to myself, 'I'm a Capricorn, and goats never rest till they reach their goal; maybe I can get in touch with him.' So I organised an astrology seminar which I led in Medellín on 10 August 1993. It had been three months since that issue of *Semana* came out, and I figured Escobar had to be curious to know why I'd predicted his death before the year's end. 'Maybe he'll send somebody to look for me,' I thought. But no. Though I promoted the event heavily, I later learned from his widow that they never heard I was giving the seminar.

1 December 1993

Time sped past, and toward the end of the year, on the same day that Pablo Escobar turned forty-four, President César Gaviria invited me to a lunch in the Casa de Nariño, the presidential palace, in honour of the previous year's Nobel Peace Prize winner, Guatemala's Rigoberta Menchú. After all, I'm an anthropologist by profession, and she is an indigenous woman by birth.

The important thing about the timing of that lunch to coincide with Escobar's birthday is that during the fete, Ricardo Ávila, the president's friend and private secretary, complained to me, 'Your predictions are a joke – it's December and Escobar isn't dead.' That's how the account in the newspaper *El Tiempo* from 5 December tells it. In response, I told him to wait a while – the year wasn't over yet. And he didn't have to wait long: the next day, Pablo Emilio Escobar Gaviria was gunned down or committed suicide. Either option would fit with my conclusion.

How had I made my prediction? While interpreting the signs in the stars, I mentioned above that Saturn is death and that the twelfth house is the sector of hidden enemies, but it is also the sector of places of confinement. If he didn't return to prison, he would die. That outcome was dictated by Saturn crossing that part of his birth chart, which it would do approximately every thirty years.

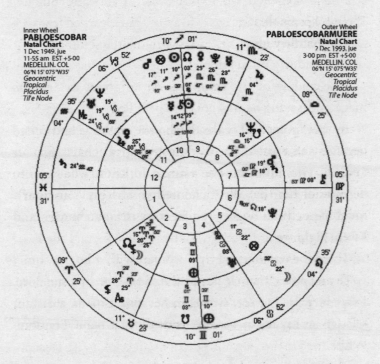

Of course, there were other factors that aided my forecast, but to make a long story short, the most important one was this movement of Saturn through the house associated with prisons, hospitals and cemeteries. I myself had experienced a great personal tragedy six years earlier when that same configuration had appeared in my chart, so it's no wonder I had a foreboding feeling about Pablo Escobar's death.

I spent the next year giving interviews on TV programmes and to authors and journalists who were writing books and articles. And one day my mobile phone rang.

4 December 1994

'Hello. Who is this?'

'This is the widow.'

'The widow? What widow?'

'The widow of the man you wrote about in *Semana* magazine, saying he was going to be killed.'

In that moment, I realised who she was. She had called because she wanted me to do astrological charts for her and her two children. She wanted to know what was to become of her life. She gave me her address – an apartment in northern Bogotá not far from my own home – and I went right over.

The door was opened by a woman with a hoarse, quiet voice and a face that clearly reflected the sorrows she bore. I was surprised to see, sitting in her living room, a distant relative on my mother's side, with the last name Londoño White.

The things I told her about the family's horoscopes and the actions they should take are laid out with great accuracy by her son, Juan Pablo, in the book mentioned previously. The boy, who was seventeen at the time, saw in his chart that if he followed in his father's footsteps, Saturn would also cross through his own twelfth house at some point in his life. It was best not to create the opportunity for his father's story to be repeated.

Astrologically speaking, there was something curious in the birth charts of the entire family, including the deceased. In astrology there is a cross known as the Mutable Grand Cross, composed of the signs Gemini (Manuela, Escobar's daughter), Virgo (the widow), Sagittarius (Escobar), and Pisces (Juan Pablo). All of them belonged to that cross, so the karmic law of Saturn struck each of them equally and in an unmitigated manner.

For this book written by the widow, however, I want to recount what she told me had happened when, a year earlier, her husband had read the issue of *Semana* that contained that fateful astrological prediction.

According to her account, Escobar sent several people out looking for me, without success; they never even learned what had happened to the people charged with finding me. As I said to her when she told me this story, it seemed strange that Escobar hadn't been able to track me down, since he had a massive network of contacts to locate anybody he wanted. Who could hide from Pablo Escobar?

'Events were so set in the stars,' I told her, 'that not even he could go against Saturn's ruling. I even travelled to Medellín to give an astrology seminar, so that when he heard about it he could send for me and I could tell him in person what his horoscope said.'

'We never heard about it,' she replied.

I'm not going to describe the sea of misfortunes across which she'd been navigating in the past year. She will describe them herself in this book, in her own words. Since our astrological interview, life has brought us together unexpectedly on a number of occasions, arranged not by us but by destiny. For example, the invitation I received to visit the Colombian embassy in Panama on 22 August 2015, to promote some of my books and give a talk on the true nature of astrology. When I asked the organiser who else would be lecturing, he told me that Juan Pablo would be talking about the book he'd written about his father, and that his presentation would take in place in the same room as mine, right after mine. Neither he nor I had been aware of this.

When I found out, I changed the subject of my talk. In the standing-room-only auditorium, I projected onto the white wall more or less the same story – but in images – that I've told in this short text, so that Juan Pablo's talk would be a continuation of my own. It had been twenty-one years since we'd last seen each other, and the boy I'd met all those years ago had grown into a man.

We hugged and then called his mother in Buenos Aires to tell her about our meeting after such a long time without seeing each other. In the intervening years, she and I have continued to meet every once in a while. One cold night in October 2017, we even ran into each other on the street in Bogotá. Since she was walking with her editor, she introduced me to him and asked whether I'd write a text about astrology and her family's lives, to be published in the book she was writing.

Well, my dear widow, just as you requested, here it is.

MAURICIO PUERTA*

---

* Mauricio Puerta is a renowned Colombian astrologer. An anthropologist and archaeologist by trade, he is the personal astrologer of presidents, politicians, businessmen, bankers and members of the international jet set.

Chapter 1
The Final Goodbye

It's been twenty-five years since that painful moment, and every time I remember it I get a lump in my throat. It was mid-August 1993, and Pablo and I, our children, Manuela and Juan Pablo, and Juan Pablo's girlfriend, Andrea, were hunkered down in a hideout known as the blue house. My husband and I knew that the final goodbye had to come sooner rather than later: our current situation was unsustainable. Over the previous few days, we'd agonised over the decision for hours, looking for any excuse – my impending thirty-third birthday, for example, or a potential visit from a family member – to avoid the inevitable. Death was peering around the corner at us.

The blue house was in El Poblado, an area of Medellín accessible via the Las Palmas highway that offers a spectacular view of Antioquia's capital city. Pablo had arrived at the beginning of the previous August after escaping yet again from the hot pursuit of both the authorities and his enemies, Los Pepes (an abbreviation of their formal name, Perseguidos por Pablo Escobar, or Persecuted by Pablo

Escobar), who had come within a hair's breadth of tracking him down in one of the three safehouses he was using near Belén Aguas Frías, in the villages south-east of Medellín.

Upon finding that the new hideout wasn't quite ready yet, Pablo hired a handyman to paint the walls light blue, his favourite colour. In his eagerness to make sure the place would be spotless and homely, he loosened his own security protocols and allowed a stranger to do the work for two weeks. In the meantime, Pablo stayed holed up in one of the bedrooms.

By that point, my husband was practically alone; the powerful army he'd once led was no more. After escaping from La Catedral Prison in July 1992, his enemies had assassinated his henchmen one by one; some of his most-trusted men had abandoned him in order to save themselves, and had turned themselves in to the authorities. Now he had Gladys and her husband, El Gordo, a married couple who helped out with some tasks around the house, and Alfonso León Puerta, known as Angelito, one of the last *sicarios* who had stuck by my husband, acting as his bodyguard and messenger.

Manuela, Andrea, Juan Pablo and I arrived at the blue house blindfolded, after hiding out for several weeks in another safehouse in Belén Aguas Frías. Once we were reunited in the new hideout, I was surprised to hear what Pablo had done to get the place painted.

'Pablo, you're crazy, what were you thinking?' I said, and he gave me a mischievous smile.

My husband was always obsessed with light blue. That was the colour of the little bedroom that he had occupied during his childhood on his parents' farm in Vereda El Tablazo, Rionegro, in eastern Antioquia. Traces of the light blue are still visible on its walls. Years later, in the late sixties, when the Escobar Gaviria family moved to Paz de Envigado, where Pablo and I eventually met, Pablo painted his room and the planks he used as bookshelves light blue. Later still, when he had become very wealthy and purchased the Hacienda Nápoles estate, he selected light blue again in painting a section of the estate known as Old Nápoles, as well as for an old Nissan Patrol jeep that he used for driving around in the countryside near the town of Puerto Triunfo. Naturally, his wardrobe also included numerous shirts of that colour. I also remember that he loved the light blues in the painting *La marina*, by the Antioquian artist Francisco Antonio Cano, which I'd purchased and had hung in our apartment in the Mónaco building.

The blue house was to be our final hideout. You had to pass through two gates to get into the property. The first was a sliding gate that opened and closed via remote control and was painted dark green to blend in with the trees and vegetation; once a visitor was inside, he couldn't get out of his vehicle because he'd find himself hemmed in by a huge German shepherd and a fierce white goose we called Palomo. Pablo said the goose was more dangerous than a dog, and we couldn't get close when we fed it because of its extremely short temper. El Gordo had bought it at an outdoor market in Medellín for 30,000 pesos. After a visitor had passed through the green gate and faced off against the dog and goose, a second gate would open; this one was dark blue and ten feet tall. Barbed wire was strung up on posts to keep intruders out.

Our room was dark and unpleasant, furnished with a double bed and two nightstands on either side. There were a number of books, including Og Mandino's *The Greatest Salesman in the World*, Leo Buscaglia's *Living, Loving and Learning*, and Wayne Dyer's *Your Erroneous Zones*. I also had a book on memory exercises that Pablo had given me; I kept it for many years because I was amused by the dedication: 'For my little donkey, Victoria, who can't remember anything but me.' Sometimes, before we went to sleep, Pablo would sit back against the headboard and I'd read him passages, which he listened to in silence.

I was usually exhausted when I went to bed around midnight, but I woke up constantly throughout the night, gripped by fear and the horrible conviction I was going to open my eyes to see a rifle barrel a few inches from my face, as had happened several times before. I continued to be plagued by this nightmare – waking up with a jolt of terror, unable to sleep deeply – until 2015, when I finally managed to overcome my trauma after engaging in more than twenty years of intensive work with specialists in various arenas and participating in numerous spiritual retreats.

Pablo, though, as had been his habit for years, came to bed at dawn, generally after four o'clock in the morning. But now, unlike in previous periods, when his sleepless nights were related to his business dealings or his mistresses, the once-powerful head of the Medellín Cartel had to stay up till dawn because there was no one else to stand guard in his own hideout.

While my husband slumbered, I'd get up at seven o'clock to shower and give Manuela her breakfast. Later, after ten o'clock, I played the role of Spanish teacher so that my daughter, who was nine years old at the time and in the fourth grade, wouldn't fall behind academically. Andrea would teach her maths, geography, history and art. In the meantime, Juan Pablo was being sent copies of the class notes taken by the best student at his old high school along with a list of homework and assignments he needed to complete for each subject. That was the only way I could think to avoid interrupting the children's education entirely; it had been almost six years since they'd stopped attending a regular school.

Educating our children became complicated one day when Pablo summoned me to Hacienda Nápoles and informed me that for safety reasons they wouldn't be able to return to school.

'That just isn't an option, *mister*,' I said, using my nickname for him. 'It's not going to happen; our children's education comes first, full stop.'

But there was no arguing with his reply.

'Tata, you're going to have to accept my decision – or would you rather see your children disappeared or kidnapped or killed?'

It was unthinkable to drop everything and stop Manuela and Juan Pablo's schooling, and it seemed like madness to accept that the war could take away the only place where my children could learn and interact with kids their age. Aghast, I said to Pablo, '*Mister*, pass me the car phone you've got in the jeep. I'm going to figure something out.'

I called the director of the girls' school in the La Paz neighbourhood of Envigado and asked her for help. I knew she had good connections and could make sure Medellín's department of education would authorise Manuela and Juan Pablo to be home-schooled. We presented the necessary documents, and a month and a half later, Manuela had six tutors and was studying English, Spanish, maths, civics, theatre, singing and general humanities. For Juan Pablo, I hired several of my own teachers from high school, who agreed to come to our apartment and give him private tutoring in a number of subjects. Every two weeks they had to fill out forms and submit them to the department of education to make an official record of our academic progress.

Everything had been manageable when we were living a normal life, but when we were in hiding – which was most of the time – things became too complicated, which was why Andrea and I took on the role of teachers. We continued our efforts in the blue house, where I gave my daughter a private class every day.

Once our improvised lesson ended at about eleven o'clock, I'd go to the kitchen to make brunch for Pablo, which was always a plate of rice, fried eggs, grilled beef, fried slices of ripe plantain, arepas, salad – mainly beets, with a little chopped tomato, lemon and salt – and a glass of milk, which he claimed was essential for strengthening the bones. In addition to his usual menu, he occasionally enjoyed eating small portions of rice pudding, bananas, corn pudding and whole-grain arepas with queso fresco and butter.

Pablo was always careful not to overeat and made it a priority not to gain weight, though his method of monitoring it was somewhat odd: after he got up at a little before noon, he'd take a bit of string out of a drawer, measure his waist, and make a knot to mark his size; he'd repeat the process the next day and confirm whether the knot was in the same place. Despite his vanity, the stress and isolation of his final years eventually caused him to become overweight.

Next, Pablo's routine included reading the newspapers *El Tiempo, El Colombiano* and *El Espectador*, which Gladys or El Gordo went out to buy every morning. He'd scan them while keeping an eye on the clock so as not to miss the 12.30 news on television. Annoyingly, he was constantly changing the channel, not wanting to miss any news about himself. Depending on the seriousness of the news, Pablo and I would sit down to discuss what steps to take next.

By that time, the war had changed. Pablo was no longer able to order terrorist attacks, and all the news about him had to do with his prospective second surrender to the authorities and the conditions he was demanding, such as a guarantee that the rest of the family would be permitted to escape into exile in another country.

The blue house had a large car park that could hold up to a dozen vehicles, but because we had so few visitors, we turned it into a sort of multi-use recreation area that also served as a football field and basketball court. The days were long and the nights endless, and we couldn't leave the property, so we had to create a perfect world. Often, taking advantage of the sunshine, we'd put on our bathing suits and shower using a hose that had good water pressure.

Pablo loved moments like that because they helped him relax. It was one way to escape our taxing reality.

Next in his routine, he'd shave as I held up a mirror for him. Then I'd trim and buff his fingernails and toenails. In all the years we shared our lives as a family, I was always my husband's barber. I often told him I knew skilled people who could come to the house to cut his hair, but he never agreed. It was a good thing Pablo's preferred haircut was easy to pull off. I remember once while I was cutting his hair, he combed it out with a little black comb and, pulling a few locks of hair he thought needed to be shorter taut between his fingers, told me, 'Cut right here, sweetie.' I have to admit the final outcome wasn't the greatest; my husband's hair looked choppy and uneven, but he felt comfortable like that.

Up until the very last day we were together, even in the worst moments, Pablo maintained a habit that became an exasperating obsession: he'd spend about two hours bathing and brushing his teeth. Every day. No exaggeration. His ablutions seemed to go on forever; he would floss as if he had all the time in the world, sliding the floss into each crevice several times, and then brush his teeth endlessly with a children's toothbrush.

'There's no need to go overboard, *mister*. Two hours to shower and brush your teeth is too much.'

'I have to take good care of them, Tata, because it's impossible for me to go to the dentist. I don't even want to get a toothache.'

As a matter of fact, Pablo never had problems with his teeth, but I did. On one occasion, at the blue house, I woke up one morning with a terrible toothache. I had no choice but to go to the dentist, and Pablo was forced to reluctantly agree. Of course, going down into the city was very risky, but I also saw it as a chance to get some fresh air, see people, look at something besides the four walls of the safehouse where we were hiding.

Manuela and Andrea both joined me for my visit to the dentist at the San Diego shopping centre in south-eastern Medellín; at least that way they could get a little break from their confinement. The three of us left the house wearing scarves and dark sunglasses and walked with our heads down so nobody would recognise us. While the dentist was working, Andrea took a walk outside with Manuela, but both of them were terrified. During those few minutes of freedom, I was filled with a powerful sense of unease; I was convinced we were going to be kidnapped or shot. I wasn't able to relax at all.

Of all of us, Manuela had the hardest time in hiding. She wanted to go visit her grandmother Nora, her cousins, her little school friends, she wanted to go horseback riding – all the normal things a kid would do. But her father was strict about keeping us away from the outside world for security reasons. Only on rare occasions, when Manuela was reaching breaking point, would Pablo agree to let her go and visit one of her teachers for the weekend.

In the meantime, we all tried hard to make Manuela's life easier. One of the things we did was glue reflective stars to our bedroom ceiling so Manuela could see them when she lay in bed with me and Pablo. She was particularly attached to her father, and sometimes at bedtime she would ask him, 'When I can't see you or you're not with me, Daddy, can I look for you in the stars by looking up at the sky?'

As soon as she was fast asleep, we'd move her to a sort of cot beside our bed. That way she didn't feel alone. In the early morning hours, when the house throbbed with anxiety, Manuela and Pablo would often go to the kitchen to fry up some bologna and eat it with rice and Coca-Cola. She still does that today, and sometimes she asks people who are going to be coming to Buenos Aires from Colombia to bring her some of her favourite brand of bologna, which isn't available in Argentina. She's never forgotten how she used to eat it with Coke by her father's side.

I remember once, looking up at the starry night skies at the blue house with Pablo and Manuela, we found a unique cobalt-blue star glowing in the heavens. Twenty-five years later, that star still accompanies my daughter everywhere she goes, and on sleepless nights on the balcony of her house, aching in the depths of her heart, she always looks for it so she can talk to Pablo.

Though he never said much, I sensed my husband's loneliness. He clearly felt powerless at having been left alone, with nobody he could trust.

When would we need to start running again? We didn't know. We were on tenterhooks, waiting to see if we would be given the option for Pablo to turn himself in. The negotiations were being carried out by one of Pablo's lawyers, who was in direct contact with the attorney general's office and a number of officials from the administration of President César Gaviria. If everything worked out, the rest of us would leave the country.

In those uncertain days, Pablo told me he wanted to arrange for his mother to come to the blue house; he missed her, having not seen her for several months. It was a risky operation, and she'd need to be blindfolded, but he decided to go ahead with the help of two men he trusted implicitly. He started readying a room at the blue house for her to stay in.

When she finally arrived, she brought various platters of Antioquian food, which we ate with gusto. Then we spent several hours talking about everything under the sun, at the end of which Pablo said, 'Mum, we have a very special room for you; we've been getting it ready for several days and hope we can share it with you.'

There was an awkward silence. Doña Hermilda looked him in the eye and said, 'Pablo, I can't stay. I have to go visit Roberto [Pablo's brother] at the prison this Sunday.'

He looked at her in silence, then lowered his eyes and replied, 'Mother, you get to see Roberto more often than you do me. You know full well how complicated things are.'

'Yes, Pablo, I understand, but I have to visit Roberto. My mind is made up; that's what I want.'

I was sitting at one end of the table, and when I heard my mother-in-law's words, I felt my heart break into a thousand pieces. I didn't understand why she couldn't spend a week with her son, knowing the difficulties he was going through.

'My mother can see Roberto whenever she wants, but not me,' Pablo said after she'd left, unable to mask his bitterness.

'That's life, sweetheart,' I said, and then hugged him for a long time.

That episode had a big impact on me, and I'll never forget how my mother-in-law refused to give her son the chance to talk to her about his uncertain future.

DAYS AND NIGHTS WENT BY IN THE BLUE HOUSE AS WE kept waiting for a bit of good news or for the thugs who were hunting us to break down the doors and kill us on the spot. Letters came and went and Pablo was optimistic, but my intuition told me our situation was dire. I told him as much: 'Pablo, they're trying to trick us – they're not going to let you turn yourself in. They won't do that again. I'd rather we stayed here and let them kill us all – our children, you and me. That's the best possible outcome. Let's all just leave this world. We can't keep going like this.'

As the days passed, Pablo was clearly running out of arguments to convince me there was light at the end of the tunnel. He knew I was right in some way: he'd gone too far in La Catedral. Having been allowed to design and build his own prison, he'd taken advantage of the opportunity to pile excess upon excess, and the government had no choice but to order he be transferred to another site. That had led to his escape and the grim situation we were now facing. He was acutely aware that things were getting worse with every passing hour, and at a certain point, deeply worried, he told me, 'Darling, you should go to another country and get married as soon as possible. You need to obtain residence somewhere else and get a new last name for you and our children. That's the only way we can save them. I promise I'll get a boat and come looking for you wherever you are as soon as I get the chance.'

My husband's words sounded dramatic and all too real, but I was too choked up to speak. Deep down, I knew we had to do something – and that meant figuring out a way to survive somewhere else, even if we were no longer together.

I noticed that Pablo started leaving the house more often to gaze at the vibrant beauty of Medellín and the Aburrá Valley. He seemed wistful as he stared off toward the horizon. That was his only contact with the outside world for the little bit of life that remained to him.

But Pablo was also worried about something else: our increasing insolvency. One morning I heard him tell Angelito that he had only a few million dollars in cash left to, as he put it, 'get us back on our feet and win this war'. Given the enormous quantities of money that Pablo dealt with and how quickly he spent it, it wasn't surprising that so little remained. That's the way it always was. With him, money vanished in the blink of an eye.

Even though by that point, in September 1993, Pablo's power was basically a thing of the past, he was still just as dangerous to the government and to Los Pepes, who were searching for him as energetically as ever. That's why the letters were so important: they were his only secure way to communicate with his lawyer and his few remaining men. He had set up a flawless system in which the mail circulated via four or five houses and apartments in Medellín, where they were collected every four hours. At night, someone would pick up all the letters from the established final location and bring them to the blue house. On Pablo's orders, the entire operation took place at night, on a precise schedule. Any delay signalled that something had gone wrong and it was time to run, as had already happened several times before.

It may seem unbelievable, but Pablo received about fifty letters a day, many of them from his lawyer, his brother Roberto, his mother, Manuela's and Juan Pablo's teachers, and his men who were already behind bars. Those messages arrived in different ways, carried by different messengers, and the same route was never repeated twice. That made them nearly impossible to track.

Pablo would sit down at his desk sometime after four o'clock in the afternoon and spend many hours reading them, responding to those that interested him. Obviously, he focussed on the messages from his lawyer, which described the progress the lawyer had made in his negotiations with the attorney general and the administration. Depending on his stress levels at the time, Pablo would engage in another of his old habits: tearing off the corners of the pages, crumpling them into little balls and throwing them out onto the lawn through the window. Sometimes he ate them.

'Don't worry, Ula' – that was Pablo's teasing nickname for me because I was now forced to do the cooking, cleaning and ironing instead of Eulalia, one of our old housemaids – 'my lawyer is helping you all get out of the country. That's one of my conditions for turning myself in. De Greiff, the attorney general, promised to get you refugee status in another country, and then I'll turn myself in.'

Despite Pablo's relative optimism, the days passed very slowly in the blue house and our concern increased as the news from the outside suggested that the Search Bloc, a special operation unit of the Colombian national police, and Los Pepes were searching for my husband more actively than ever. There were raids every day, and we often heard rumours that people close to us had been forced to flee.

At around that time, Pablo surprised me by telling me that one way we might escape our situation was to hide in the jungle; he'd even bought some large parcels of land in a location he didn't specify. He added that he was in the process of setting up electrical grids and that the only person who knew the location was his brother, Roberto, who was in prison and posed no threat. But I was even more surprised when he said that one of his plans was to go off with the guerrilla fighters. Clearly he was very worried and his situation was becoming increasingly grim. My husband was looking for a way out of his predicament, but his announcement worried me. What would happen to Pablo? How many years could he stay in the jungle? Which guerrilla group? All of us in the jungle? These questions joined the many others that plagued me every day.

'Pablo, I'm not the right person to go with you into the jungle. I'm not brave enough to carry a rifle or be by your side in combat. How can we drag two children out there to suffer with us? What's going to happen to them? It's crazy. That's not an option for us.'

As the days continued to pass, we debated the possibilities, but we were unable to come to a decision. I became more and more uneasy.

Amid all this uncertainty, I was about to turn thirty-three years old. It was 3 September 1993. For many years, we'd celebrated as a family whenever one of us had a birthday, but this one was sombre and sad, a portent of bad things to come. We no longer celebrated with huge, lavish parties, with dozens of guests and ostentatious gifts.

Even so, I was pleasantly surprised when I walked into the dining room and discovered a delicious birthday cake made by the renowned baker Pepita, six bottles of Dom Pérignon and several gifts. I asked how the things had arrived, and somebody reminded me that the previous day Pablo had violated his security protocols and arranged for Andrea to go down to Medellín, supposedly to collect the mail, but in fact to bring back all the supplies for my birthday.

According to what they told me, Andrea had left with Angelito, blindfolded just as we'd been when we first arrived so that she couldn't identify our hideout if she was caught. She always grew very nervous passing through military checkpoints, but luckily the soldiers didn't stop them to search the vehicle. Angelito had dropped her off in the car park of a building where Pablo had hidden a car that Andrea was supposed to use to pick up the birthday goodies, and they agreed on a time to meet nearby after she'd left the car back in the car park. Pablo had warned her that Angelito would wait only three minutes; if she wasn't there, he'd leave without her.

Andrea didn't have much time, so she had to hurry. Unfortunately, she hadn't realised the packages – which contained the cake, six bottles of champagne, the mail, gifts and other items – would be so heavy. As the minutes passed, Andrea started to feel anxious; if she didn't meet up with Angelito at the appointed time, she'd be adrift in Medellín.

'God help me, I wasn't going to make it. My arms couldn't do it – I couldn't carry the bags,' Andrea recalled as she described her intense experience.

Apparently, God was looking out for her: 'I was about to pass out by the time I reached the meeting place right as Angelito started the car to take off. When I climbed in, I started to see little lights and then I fainted.'

Luckily, everything worked out, but my birthday had nearly ended in tragedy.

TWO DAYS LATER, WE EXPERIENCED OUR ONLY BIT OF JOY in that final stage of our lives together. And it was all thanks to football, a sport I'd never really liked, though I must admit I was partial to the Deportivo Independiente Medellín team. I'll never forget that day: it was probably the last time I saw Pablo happy. On the afternoon of 5 September 1993, Colombia's national team, playing as visitors, defeated Argentina 0–5 in the final stage of the qualification process for the World Cup, which was to be held in the United States the following year. Gathered in the blue house's little TV room, we treasured that small moment of joy, whooping and shouting as Faustino 'Tino' Asprilla, Freddy Rincón, and Adolfo 'El Tren' Valencia scored their goals.

In those ninety minutes, Pablo was able to forget about our own difficult situation. The relief was fleeting but priceless. We continued to celebrate Colombia's victory for several days after the match.

Nevertheless, all good things must come to an end. A new letter from the lawyer arrived that would determine our future as a family. It was Saturday, 18 September 1993. After reading the message carefully, Pablo suddenly stood up and came over to me, saying we should talk in private in one of the second-floor bedrooms.

I followed him without asking any questions, but my heart started beating faster. It was three in the afternoon on a sunny day.

'Sweetheart, it's time to pack everybody's suitcases – you are all going to live in the Altos building under government protection,'* Pablo said, his voice solemn but somewhat optimistic.

'No, Pablo, I'm not leaving. I'm sure it's a trap,' I replied immediately, as if I'd known in advance that this was coming and was determined to refuse.

'What are you talking about? The most important goal with all these letters and all this back-and-forth was to guarantee your safety, you know that. And I've managed to pull it off.'

'Pablo, please, I don't want to split up. They're trying to trick us with this promise that we can go into exile. As far as I'm concerned, it's all a set-up, a strategy to get to you … They're not going to keep their promise – they're going to kill us.'

Pablo looked like he was running out of patience. He was pale, and it worried me to see that he was restless and having trouble breathing, puffing as he exhaled.

---

* The Altos building was a building owned by the Escobars in Medellín.

'You have to, sweetheart. Whether you want to or not, you have to go. It would be totally irresponsible to let all of you stay here with me. When they find us here, they'll kill us all – don't you get that?'

'It doesn't matter if they kill us all. That's the best possible outcome – they kill us, and all of this will finally be over. Plus, your enemies are going to come after us with a vengeance, Pablo; I don't even want to think about the violence we'll face. They're going to kill us once you're dead,' I said again, but I could no longer keep from crying.

'That's completely irresponsible. We have two children and Juancho's girlfriend in our care. We have to make sure their lives are protected,' he replied, but this time there was deep sadness on his face.

I cried and cried. I'd got married at fifteen in the Catholic Church, thinking it was for life. I was deeply in love with Pablo. I knew that his egregious behaviour over the past few years had unleashed this unfathomable madness, but I was still enormously pained that I had to leave my children's father in order to save them. I understood there was no other option. It was here: the moment of separation, the moment of our final goodbye.

Pablo's next comment sounded like he was wrapping things up: 'Tata, they're going to find a country for you, so don't worry. Like I said, if you can get married somewhere, do it so you can get citizenship. But I swear, when I get out of this, I'll get a boat and cross whatever seas are in my way until I find you, my love.'

For a few seconds, Pablo and I sat in a strange silence that seemed to go on forever. In those moments, I had no idea how I was going to live without him. Where was I going to find the strength to keep going and protect my children? Abruptly, Pablo got right to the point: 'It's time, Tata. Let's not keep debating the subject. Please start packing and go with the kids to Altos, where you'll be safe.'

Before we left the bedroom, we agreed that we'd tell Manuela we were going to take a trip to a really nice place, but that her daddy wasn't coming. Juan Pablo wouldn't be a problem – he understood how complicated things were.

We had to wait a few hours so we could travel at night. As the day wore on, the blue house seemed to become an even sadder place because we knew that fate was pushing us irremediably apart. With the sun setting on the horizon, I felt as if my heart might burst. I couldn't imagine life without Pablo – who would tell Manuela bedtime stories and sing her 'La donna è mobile', Giuseppe Verdi's classic aria?

The nearly twenty years I'd spent by Pablo's side passed swiftly before my eyes as if they were a movie. All my life by his side had been a wild gallop. Things had happened so fast that I'd never had time to think about how to stop this madness. I enjoyed so few years of calm. And so many years fleeing or in hiding. This was the most difficult thing I'd ever had to do, leaving the love of my life right when the world was coming down on him. What a horrible situation. What an impossible choice. Yet I had to summon the strength not to look back and instead look ahead so I could save our children. Still, desperate to prevent our separation, I made a last-ditch effort to bring a halt to our tragedy. I spoke with him again.

'I don't want to leave you all on your own, darling. I'd rather be killed,' I insisted. 'I'd truly rather all of us die together, at the same time,' I told him, with tears welling up in my eyes and my voice breaking. He looked at me sadly, and his eyes grew damp. As I saw it, given our situation, we ran just as great a risk of being killed if we turned ourselves in.

'We had two children together, but one of us has to take charge of them now – educate them, find a place where one day their lives can make sense again,' he responded.

My tears weren't enough. Pablo hugged me hard, but he didn't say another word. We had to split up. Finally, at eleven at night, it was time for us to leave. While Angelito and El Gordo settled the few belongings we could carry with us in the car boot, we said goodbye. We stood beside the car in a sort of line: Pablo gave me a huge hug, long, warm, affectionate. Then he stroked my cheek and hair, like he'd always done, looked at me tenderly, and said in a choked-up voice, 'I love you very much, Tata. Thank you for taking care of our children. Luck will be on your side; things are going to go well for you.'

He fell silent, and then I was the one who hugged him for a long time. The last hug of our lives. Then he bid farewell to Juan Pablo with a heartfelt handshake and a kiss on the cheek. When he reached Manuela, he started crying. We'd never seen him weep before, and that made our goodbye even more heart-wrenching. Then he looked at Andrea, but he was unable to say anything because he was so worked up. Three days later, he sent her an apologetic letter at the Altos building: 'Warm greetings to you, kid. I want to tell you how grateful I am for everything. I didn't have the strength to say it when you left. I appreciate you so much. You can always count on me.'

On our way to the garage, Pablo gave one last instruction: 'The people from the CTI [Technical Investigation Corps] are going to meet you at Altos. Give them these addresses for Los Pepes. They say they haven't raided Los Pepes because they don't have any good intel on them. Now they will.'

We got into the Chevrolet Sprint with Juan Pablo at the wheel, and left. Pablo and Angelito followed behind us in another car until we reached the steep street that leads to the Altos building. Before we split off from each other, he honked a couple of times and then disappeared into the shadows of the night. That was the last time I saw him.

He had seventy-five days left to live.

AFTER SEEING US OFF ON THAT NIGHT OF 18 SEPTEMBER 1993, Pablo and Angelito returned to the blue house. But what happened to him after we left for the Altos building?

I got the answer to that question from Gladys and El Gordo, the married couple that was working for us back then. I interviewed them in July 2017 while doing research for this book. They've been divorced since 1997, but each of them agreed to meet with me independently to give me previously unreported details about what my husband did during those seven weeks they were all together.

According to their accounts, Pablo was deeply affected by our departure.

'It was awful to see him like that, ma'am. He didn't eat for two days, and he stopped shaving. His beard grew really fast. At night he'd go out to stare up at the sky and tug on his beard with his left hand. He looked like he'd lost all hope,' Gladys told me.

El Gordo said that as the days passed, lack of money became a real problem, so Pablo decided not to stay in one place. That's when he got the idea to carry out a hundred quick kidnappings in Llanogrande, a well-known area of eastern Antioquia, and charge 500 million pesos for each person's release. The date was set for 31 December 1993. Pablo told El Gordo they were going to use the ransoms to flee to Bogotá, where they couldn't be found.

El Gordo heard Pablo instruct Angelito to go to Moravia, the landfill where he'd started his housing programme, Medellín Without Slums, a decade earlier, and recruit a hundred young men. At the same time, Pablo asked El Gordo to go with him to scout out a few places in the mountains near Medellín where he could hide the hostages.

The plan was moving forward, but everything fell apart on the night of 6 October, when the Search Bloc killed Angelito and his brother in Medellín's Villa Hermosa neighbourhood. El Gordo told me that Angelito had ignored his and Pablo's warnings and had gone to deliver some money to his brother.

'I told him not to go, that it was dangerous to go to Medellín because there was a 100-million-peso bounty on his head and somebody could turn him in. But he went anyway,' El Gordo recalled.

Pablo was deeply affected by the death of one of his last *sicarios*. He said as much to El Gordo and Gladys: 'It's over, Gordo. I don't have anyone to work with now. They took down my right-hand man.'

Pablo's loneliness grew worse, and El Gordo reported that he started acting oddly. One night, for example, he told El Gordo to put on a hat and a *ruana* (a rustic poncho-like garment), and the two of them went out walking through downtown Medellín.

'I was terrified, but he acted bold as brass.'

Then one day, for the first time ever, the men who were after my husband had the blue house in their sights.

'It was after Angelito died ... There were these two police helicopters circling above the house. Pablo hid in the closet in one of the bedrooms, and Gladys and I went out to work in the garden to throw them off. It was really scary. They hovered up there for half an hour and then left. If the Search Bloc had showed up, they would have found the boss.'

Gladys and El Gordo told me that Pablo's days were monotonous and he hardly left his room. He looked perpetually worried and sometimes sat writing letters at his desk.

El Gordo saw that Pablo was outraged at what was happening to us, but Pablo clearly felt powerless and unable to do anything about it. All he could think to do was to write a letter and ask El Gordo to take it to one of his lawyers, his only contact with the attorney general's office and the government. Pablo told El Gordo to be careful, and El Gordo tucked the letter into his jacket pocket. But something went wrong.

'I got to Parque de Berrío and went up to the lawyer's office on the seventh floor of the building the boss had specified, but when I came out of the lift and walked through the door, I saw four men with guns there. That seemed odd, so I started getting suspicious. Luckily the lawyer was busy with somebody else, so I said I'd be right back. What a scary situation! I got out of there, and to keep them from following me I went into the El Ganadero cafe and had a couple of shots of aguardiente. Then I wandered around for a while and went into a church to make sure nobody was trailing me. Then I headed back to the blue house and told the boss, who put his head in his hands and said, "It's all falling apart."'

The next day, Pablo told Gladys and El Gordo that he was going to another hideout, where El Limón (Álvaro de Jesús Agudelo) was waiting for him.

'It was a normal goodbye, just like any other. But when I shook his hand to say see you later, I sensed I'd never see him again,' El Gordo told me.

Chapter 2

Penned In

When I turned to look back and Pablo honked twice before turning left and disappearing into the darkness of that September night, my intuition told me we'd never see him again. It was a bizarre moment because the hoarse sound of the car horn seemed to be carrying a subliminal message, saying something like 'Goodbye for ever, my love; goodbye for ever, my children.'

In a suicidal act, at eleven o'clock on the night of 18 September 1993, Pablo had accompanied us from the blue house to the Altos building, where several agents from the Technical Investigation Corps (CTI), a division of the attorney general's office, were waiting for us. They would protect us while Pablo went through the process of turning himself in to the authorities. That night, we met four CTI officers who would have direct contact with us: Alfa, whose gestures suggested that he was the group's leader, A1, Imperio and Pantera.

In the building's car park, we got out of the car, which Juan Pablo was driving, and I couldn't help crying, overcome by the feelings of panic and distress surrounding our uncertain future. Holing up in an apartment, far away from Pablo, was our only chance of surviving the hostile persecution we'd been subjected to over the past fourteen months, ever since my husband had escaped from La Catedral.

As we went up to our room on the fourth floor, carrying the few belongings we'd been able to pack, I dreamed that we'd finally be able to travel to another country, walk down the street without constantly turning to look behind us, without bodyguards, without reporters lying in wait; I longed to breathe fresh air, go to a supermarket, go back to being a housewife, to watch my children in a park, feeding pigeons with their friends from school. In other words, to have a normal life again.

Those were our expectations as we entered the apartment in the Altos building, where we'd be living for an unknown length of time. I'll never forget Manuela's and Juan Pablo's hopeful faces looking at me as if to say, 'It's all on you now, Mum.' In that moment we all trusted that the step we were taking was toward life, not toward death.

The apartment was completely empty, so we put our things on the floor. Seeing it like that, without even a chair to sit in, signalled that our stay wasn't going to be an easy one. The apartment was huge – more than 5,000 square feet – which made the lack of furniture all the more stark. Immediately, I went to a neighbour, who lent us a small plastic table with four chairs, and we set them up on the balcony. In the utility room I found two mattresses, which we slept on that night, very uncomfortably. Juan Pablo and

Andrea pulled one into the master bedroom, while Manuela and I bedded down on the other in a bedroom with a view of the guardhouse at the building's gate. The next day I persuaded the same neighbour to lend me two more mattresses.

Our plan that night was to sleep, in an effort to forget our challenging circumstances, but it would soon become clear that my children, my son's girlfriend, and I were hostages of the state, Los Pepes, and my husband. Our safety would now depend on them, and they would decide whether we lived or died. In other words, we were penned in, unaware that seventy-eight terrifying days in that apartment lay ahead.

The next morning and for the first few days, a friendly neighbour brought us food, helping us overcome our culinary challenges, as we had no idea how we were going to get ingredients or cook to survive. Shortly after, she lent us two cooking pots, eight spoons, five towels, and a number of kitchen implements. Later we were able to hire a woman to take care of the grocery shopping. We did our laundry in an apartment that my mother owned in the same building, but which she'd abandoned in February earlier that year after a car-bomb attack.

The apartment was filled with uncertainty. There was no television or telephone, though we'd luckily had the foresight to buy pocket radios, which became our only contact with the outside world. Without fail, every hour we would listen to the news summary on several different stations so we could keep abreast of what was happening in the country; we were particularly concerned with what they said about Pablo because we wanted to know if he was as penned in as we were.

In one of the bedrooms we found a blackout curtain, which, though it was very old, nevertheless darkened the room enough during the day to allow us to rest. We used to gather there to wallow in our bitterness. Altos had broad green lawns, a comfortable gazebo, a semi-Olympic swimming pool, a gym, hot tub, steam room and sauna, but we couldn't use them. Almost imperceptibly, the building turned into a fortress. The CTI agents from the attorney general's office built trenches with dozens of sandbags and placed them on top of the guardhouse roof and at the two corners of the building next to the street. At the same time, more CTI agents arrived from Bogotá, swelling our security detail to forty men armed with rifles, pistols, and machine guns. They patrolled inside and around the building constantly, and a huge, noisy alarm was installed on the roof. Pablo was still public enemy number one, and we, his family, were the only way to get to him.

The siren was employed almost immediately. We started hearing machine-gun fire at all hours of the day and night, and the guardhouse received dozens of threatening phone calls. As a result, we had no choice but to move into the utility room, the safest place in the event of an attack because it was the farthest from the road. Altos was surrounded by very tall buildings, from which we were a perfect target for anybody looking to hurt us. So we were reduced to a small, 65-square-foot room where we had to talk in quiet voices, waiting for the hours to pass while other people decided our future. We all lost our appetites and had to encourage each other to eat at least a fried egg with an arepa and hot chocolate.

Because of the danger lurking around us and our mistrust in the CTI agents, we sought additional protection. We got it from Juan Carlos Herrera Puerta, known as 'Nariz', a childhood friend of Juan Pablo's. We sent him a message delivered by Nubia, the nanny, asking him to come stay with us for a while. Nariz arrived with a backpack containing some clothing and a shotgun with a carry permit, but A1, Alfa, Imperio and Pantera were not at all happy to have a stranger in the house. We argued with them several times because they wanted Nariz to leave, but eventually they decided that Nariz might be of help in emergency situations.

Around then, the few families still living in the building began to leave because of the constant gunfire, threats and raids. In the end, only two women, living alone in separate apartments, and the three of us remained.

For two or three days we had some relief, but one Thursday afternoon the siren went off again after a burst of rapid gunfire and then a loud crash against the building's exterior wall. The CTI agents ran to their posts because it seemed like the building was under attack, and we fled in fright to the dressing room of the master bedroom while Nariz closed the door and prepared his shotgun to repel any intruder. The silence that fell was terrifying, and the minutes seemed to stretch on forever. While Nariz and Juan Pablo whispered to each other through the door, Manuela, Andrea and I prayed.

Finally, the alarm stopped sounding and a CTI agent known as Carrobomba came to the apartment door to inform us that three men had emerged from two cars at the crossroads by the building, and while two of them were shooting, the other had launched a rifle grenade that struck the building facade at around the fifth floor, just above where we were. Luckily, the projectile did not explode.

During that period, the CTI agents took us through various scenarios in which the building might be under attack and we agreed on where each person would be in the apartment if a real emergency ever occurred. We lived with our hearts in our throats; panic was a constant companion. We cried a lot. It was like living on an emotional roller coaster. I often considered leaving Pablo because of everything we were going through, but I couldn't bear to abandon him in those critical moments. After all, he'd given me so much in life; how could I leave him? It was a stew of conflicting emotions: rage and sorrow. I'd have felt very ungrateful if I'd abandoned him.

Our anxiety was immense and the days unpredictable, to the point that we would often sleep almost the whole morning because we'd been awake all night, alert in case something happened. Because of these conditions, Manuela had trouble sleeping and Andrea lost her appetite to such an extent that after a few days she fainted in the bath and we had to rush her to the emergency room at Clínica Medellín hospital, accompanied by Nariz and a dozen CTI agents.

After examining her, the specialist told her she was severely dehydrated, to an alarming degree, and warned her that she could die if she didn't make sure to eat and drink properly. The doctor said it was essential to keep her at the hospital for a few days, but the dicey security situation made that impossible. Very much against his will, the doctor discharged her and prescribed injections, serums, vitamins and pills. Andrea returned to Altos barely able to walk and languished on the mattress for several days while her body recovered. Juan Pablo had to learn to give her the shots and the serum. Today I realise that I always took it for granted that Andrea was there, but during all that time I don't recall ever thinking about the effort she was making as a partner and the many things she was sacrificing to remain with a family that had no future and no hope. All these years later, I reiterate that when women truly love somebody, we're willing to take any risk.

From Bogotá our situation must have looked very grim, because two days after Andrea's collapse, Pantera arrived with a message from the attorney general, Gustavo de Greiff.

'Ma'am, Mr de Greiff has sent me to inform you that he's looking for a country for you. It's not that he's dragging things out; this is a delicate matter, and it's essential to handle it discreetly. That's why things are taking so long. He says you should trust that he wants your husband to turn himself in.'

The message from Pantera – whose real name was Luis Fernando Correa Isaza and who was the regional director of the CTI in Antioquia – calmed me a little, but our quandary remained since I had no way to ask Pablo to turn himself in to the authorities, to plead with him to take into account that, sooner rather than later, Los Pepes were going to kill us. I tried hard to keep Manuela from seeing the fear on my face, and the only thing I could do was cry piteously once my little daughter had managed to fall asleep. In those uneasy moments, I was grateful that Andrea was there – despite the horror – because she was a balm for Juan Pablo, who was overwhelmed by the weight of the responsibility of taking care of three females.

One afternoon, out of the blue, we got a visit from Gloria, one of Pablo's sisters, who brought us a lengthy letter from him that described in very general terms how the negotiations to turn himself in were going and warned us to strengthen our security measures since he'd heard about the constant attacks on the building. Every time someone we knew came to the apartment, we were terrified they'd been followed or that they might be kidnapped or disappeared.

I replied to Pablo with a letter of my own in which I recounted what we were going through: his enemies lying in wait, the discomforts of the apartment, Manuela's despair and her uncontainable sobbing at her confinement, her endless questions: why couldn't we leave, where was her grandmother, why couldn't she see her father or her cousins? It broke my heart into a million pieces, and I was very frustrated at having to see my children trapped in that situation.

We tried to distract Manuela with games, art projects, and storytelling. Sometimes we'd go down to the neighbour's apartment. The three of us would take turns entertaining her, but it was very hard to make her understand how dangerous it was to go out. Whenever a letter from her father arrived, she'd smile. In her innocence, she thought they were bringing good news and that she was going to be free again because Pablo would tell her to be patient, that soon she'd be living in another country where she'd have a new school and would be able to walk in the parks.

In my letters I told Pablo about the security risks we faced, how the CTI agents looked at us, and the constant attacks we were enduring. But nothing seemed to make a difference.

For a few days, Gloria was our only contact with Pablo, and, despite the risk to her own life, she managed to bring messages from him and convey our replies back to him. Whenever she left Altos, I was always very worried about all the things that could happen to her.

It was through one of those letters that we learned about Pablo's dramatic escape from a massive Search Bloc operation carried out by the police and the army, which nearly cost him his life in Belén Aguas Frías, near Medellín. In four pages, with an impressive level of detail, he said he'd fled from the safehouse where he'd been hiding and headed toward a mountainous area surrounded by cliffs, where he'd tried to escape, but he dropped his torch and was left in pitch darkness. Then a torrential downpour began and he had to pick his way over the cliffs, and several times he almost fell into the void. My husband said that at one point he'd wondered if anyone would look for him at the bottom of one of those abysses. The letter was written on pieces of paper taped together with adhesive bandages, and its ragged condition clearly reflected the difficult circumstances he was living in.

Pablo had saved himself yet again. Nevertheless, as always, we would suffer the consequences. One day, out of the blue, several armoured SUVs pulled up in front of the building and at least a dozen armed men spilled out and headed toward the lifts. In a panic, we raced to hide just as we'd practised in our drills, believing we were under attack by Los Pepes. Several seemingly eternal minutes later, we learned that the person who had arrived was Ana Montes, the national director of the attorney general's office and Attorney General de Greiff's right-hand woman.

Montes was obviously not paying a courtesy visit, as she made quite clear when she entered the apartment, standing before me and saying in a scornful tone after a cursory greeting, 'Listen, ma'am, if Pablo doesn't turn himself in within three days, we're going to take away your security.'

Shaken by her threat, I responded that we had no influence over my husband's turning himself over to the authorities, that we were completely isolated from him.

'Ma'am,' I said, 'your best bet is to allow us to leave Colombia and arrange for another country to take us in. I'm sure that once that happens, Pablo will turn himself in the next day. To be honest, though, I've never believed the Colombian government is actually interested in having him turn himself in – what they want is to kill him.'

The tough, brusque official left the building after repeating her threat. My children, my son's girlfriend, and I were left with a new uncertainty, a dilemma that we could not resolve.

Nevertheless, amid the devastating news and our grim situation, bunches of flowers arrived, sent by Pablo to celebrate the Day of Love and Friendship in late September.

There was one bouquet for me, another for Andrea, and another for Manuela. It was ironic for him to send us flowers in that moment: what did we have to celebrate? Plus, he was exposing himself to immense danger. They could have used the bouquets to track him. But it was typical of Pablo to take such a risk.

Things had become so complicated that, desperate, we even considered fleeing the Altos building. Where to? No idea. But just thinking that the attorney general's office might withdraw the protection of the CTI agents filled us with panic. Nothing and nobody could protect us from Pablo's enemies, who would murder us brutally in their efforts to hunt him down.

Fleeing the building was somewhere between risky and insane, but we decided to devise a Plan B just in case. Our first move was to tell Nariz to go through the building and identify the agents' positions, routines, and schedules. We then asked the building's security guards – who'd been working there for years – to wait for our instructions to open the garage door, whereupon we'd exit in the Chevrolet Sprint we'd arrived in weeks earlier.

Our plan was set, but on two occasions, right when we were about to make a run for it, we got word from the attorney general that the arrangements for our resettlement abroad were moving ahead. The messages seemed convincing and even offered us a momentary feeling of calm, but they were placebos; cruel reality always returned to terrorise us again in our daily drama.

Things intensified in October 1993. As the old saying goes, the worst news always comes first, and that happened shortly before ten o'clock at night on 6 October, when Imperio, one of the CTI agents charged with protecting us at the Altos building, rang our bell and Juan Pablo went to open the door. Imperio was smiling. He looked at my son and said, 'Juan Pablo, they've just taken down Angelito. He and his brother were shot by the Search Bloc when they were arriving at a house in the Villa Hermosa neighbourhood.'

Juan Pablo nearly fainted when he heard the news. He knew that Alfonso León Puerta (Angelito's actual name) was practically the last bodyguard Pablo had left. Doing his best to hide his shock, he replied, 'Who's that, Imperio?'

The incident hadn't been reported on the news yet; as a member of the CTI, the agent had first-hand information about what had happened and had come to tell my son. Imperio and Juan Pablo had developed a fairly trusting relationship in recent days, even playing cards together and going down to the building's basement to knock a football about.

When Imperio left, Juan Pablo hurried me into the dressing room and in a low voice told me what he'd just learned.

'No, no, no! What's going to happen to your father?' I said, clutching my head with my hands.

Angelito's death was a harsh blow for my husband, who was more and more alone. And for us it was very bad news because we no longer had a way to communicate with Pablo. The last time we'd seen Angelito had been three weeks earlier, when he'd accompanied Pablo to drop us off at Altos. Angelito was a quiet, shy young man – he had a hard time meeting my eyes. He was unconditionally devoted to my husband, swearing he would stay with him till the very end, and so he'd given up his life.

Pablo's near-total isolation after Angelito's death increased our uncertainty even more, and the messages from Attorney General de Greiff dried up almost entirely. We braced ourselves for a new wave of attacks.

And the attacks came. But we never imagined that the events of just seventy-two hours would be so brutal and have such an impact on the outcome of our tragedy.

On Sunday, 7 November 1993, the circle around us tightened even further with the disappearance of Nariz. Desperate to see his son, that morning he asked us to let him take the weekend off, but we told him we were worried about how he was going to get out of the building. With the security outside, there would be enemies lying in wait. It was a huge risk, but how could we deny him the right to see his son?

Determined to leave, Nariz ignored our advice to do so on foot, crossing a gully behind the building that we'd used previously to evade the authorities, saying he didn't want to get his shoes wet. Instead, he got into the vehicle of two CTI agents who offered to take him downtown. The following Monday he didn't show up. Nor Tuesday. When we called his family, we discovered that he'd never arrived, and all the agents would tell us was that he'd got out of the car halfway there.

We didn't know it then, but Nariz's kidnapping was the first incident in what we would later learn was the beginning of a new phase in the manhunt for my husband. Los

Pepes knew that eliminating the links in the chain that connected us to Pablo would take away more and more of his ability to manoeuvre.

Two days later, we were still recovering from the blow of losing Nariz when armed men burst into the home of Alicia Vásquez, the Altos building manager, in Medellín's Las Vegas neighbourhood, and carried her off.

I remember that she used to come up to the apartment every day to ask if we needed anything, but I didn't dare make any requests, though my eyes must have told her that yes, we desperately needed help to escape from the hell we found ourselves in.

As the days passed, the two of us had become closer, and little by little I had told her our story, the drama that was playing out around us. Alicia felt sorry for us and expressed willingness to do certain favours in secret. One of these was to buy three walkie-talkies so we could communicate with Pablo. We were able to talk to him a couple of times using the devices, but the signal was very weak. In one of those conversations he managed to give us a phone number we could call in case of an emergency. As Alicia became closer to us, she did increasingly dangerous favours, such as carrying letters for Pablo, as well as buying groceries, books, pens and paper, among other things.

The mail we sent Pablo was left in a specific place and then somebody would pick it up. As I understood it, those letters passed through various locations before finally reaching their destination, in order to make sure no one was being followed. My personal correspondence, which had to do with my children's teachers, my family, and my friends – of whom I had very few because I didn't want people to end up in trouble – was sent via Alicia.

A few hours after Alicia's disappearance, I was horrified to learn that Alba Lía Londoño, a high school teacher of mine at the Liceo La Paz who had become instrumental in keeping my children from falling behind academically, had been forcibly removed from her home in the Los Almendros suburb of Medellín by men wearing uniforms from Empresas Públicas de Medellín, the public utilities company. After shoving her into a car, the kidnappers carried out fifty boxes of various sizes from her house and loaded them into a truck. They must have thought Alba Lía was storing secret information for Pablo, but in fact they contained the books and encyclopaedias I'd purchased over the years and which she was secretly keeping at her house.

Alba Lía's children, who were fourteen and sixteen years old, came to the Altos building, frantic, to warn us and ask us to help them find her, but all I could do was hug them tight and ask them to be strong; I knew that Alba Lía wasn't going to reappear. She was one more victim of a war in which her only role had been to educate my children. These events provoked fear, sadness and an enormous sense of powerlessness in me. Death was prowling around our closest allies, and every day we had fewer people we could trust. As recompense for what had happened, I decided to care for Alba Lía's children as if they were my own. I did whatever I could to support them as they grew up and paid for their educations. It was the least I could do; their mother had given her life for my children's education.

Alba Lía and I had reconnected when my family was forced into hiding, making it impossible for my children to attend regular schools because of the harassment, the raids and the risk that they might be kidnapped. Rita – as I called her in order to protect her identity – was a devoted teacher who sympathised with my plight as a desperate mother whose sole desire was a more or less normal life for her children. She took care of acquiring the textbooks so Manuela and Juan Pablo could study, and on two occasions I paid for her to travel to Cuba to receive the most up-to-date teacher training. She had returned to Colombia with suitcases full of texts she thought would be useful in educating my children.

Alba Lía was so close to us that, despite the danger, she was always willing to have Manuela come to her house when Pablo agreed to allow her a reprieve from the constant confinement. The teacher's children would greet Manuela with enormous affection, play with her for hours, and then disguise her in a scarf and glasses, put make-up on her, and take her out in a taxi to drive around the city and walk through the shopping centres or go to the cinema. Today I think about how irresponsible I was; anybody could have recognised her and killed her. But in my desperation, I allowed my little girl to get a break.

The hours of terror were far from over. Alba Lía's kidnapping had occurred at eleven o'clock in the morning, and it was almost six o'clock in the evening when we realised that if Los Pepes had attacked three people so close to us, it was very possible that they'd also move against the only one left: Nubia Jiménez, Manuela's nanny.

Instantly, as we had no phone in our apartment, Juan Pablo ran down to one of the empty apartments in the building to call Nubia and warn her to take her children and hide at once. I went down after him and heard him manage to speak with one of the children, who raced to the building's gate, but he was too late: his mother had just climbed into a taxi. They'd kidnapped her too.

Nubia had worked for us for several years, and given how trapped we were in Altos, isolated from the outside world, I had turned to her and begged her to help us carry letters back and forth so we could communicate with Pablo. She agreed, but she was very nervous, and I've always regretted that I wasn't truly conscious back then of the danger I was putting her in. Manuela wasn't told what had happened to her nanny, and only learned the truth several years later.

In less than seventy-two hours our situation at the Altos building had become quite desperate. Not only had Nariz, Alicia, Alba Lía, and Nubia disappeared, but we also had to protect Alba Lía's two children, who were staying with us. There were six of us, all scared to death, crammed into the dressing room. Things were so tense that Juan Pablo refused to let go of the shotgun Nariz had brought to protect us.

It's no exaggeration to say that those nights in mid-November 1993 were the most agonising ones of my life. To make things worse, the issue of our leaving the country seemed to be at a standstill once more. The national director of the attorney general's office, Ana Montes, sent us a new message, this time via Pantera: they would find a country for us to go to if Pablo turned himself in first. It was the same vicious circle. And we couldn't make a move unless Pablo told us how, when, and with whom.

Once more we were facing the same old dilemma – to live or die – so in the solitude of the dressing room we concluded that the recent events had left us no other option than to look for a place in the world where we could take refuge. In examining our options, Juan Pablo, Andrea and I realised how limited they were; only recently Luz María, one of Pablo's sisters, had been expelled from Costa Rica.

So we turned our eyes toward Germany. Why? We knew that a couple of years earlier, Nicolás, the eldest son of Pablo's brother Roberto, had stayed there for three years without any kind of limitation. In addition, Alba Marina, another of my husband's sisters, had been there for three months. If they could do it, why couldn't we? We decided to buy tickets to travel to Frankfurt as soon as possible and inform Attorney General de Greiff.

In a travel agency recommended by our neighbour, we bought four tickets for a flight to Germany on the afternoon of Saturday, 27 November 1993. The trip was less than a week away, and we needed to move fast. The first thing I did was inform the attorney general's office that we were leaving and request protection for our trip to José María Córdova Airport in Rionegro and then for our layover at Bogotá's El Dorado Airport while we waited for our Lufthansa flight. We were so eager to leave the Altos building and the country that as soon as the tickets were purchased we had our suitcases packed and ready to go, one for each of us.

But it soon became clear that the attorney general's office wasn't willing to allow us to travel until Pablo's surrender was resolved. We discovered this when we got a visit from Ana Montes, who strode into the apartment with a look of fury on her face. Staring at me with a mixture of hatred and indignation, she bluntly informed me that a prosecutor in Bogotá had opened two investigations against Juan Pablo: one for the alleged rape of several young women in Medellín and another for transporting weapons illegally.

Her statements filled me with rage, and I immediately called Juan Pablo in and told him what was happening. He went pale with fury and responded without hesitation: 'Listen, ma'am, I'm the one who's endured harassment from lots of Medellín girls who want to be "the girlfriend of Pablo Escobar's son". I don't need to rape anybody; girls approach me by the dozen.'

The cold, distant official from the attorney general's office replied that the accusations were currently in the process of being verified and that my son's physical characteristics matched those of a man who prior to attacking his victims was identifying himself as Pablo Escobar's son. Nevertheless, she acknowledged that there was not yet any solid evidence for that charge – but there was for the other one, as he'd been spotted entering the building with a box of weapons.

Once more, Juan Pablo responded: 'How about this, ma'am. If you like, I'll stay here and I give you permission to tear apart the apartment – the entire building, if necessary – until you find the weapons you claim I brought in. Go ahead and search it right now, but what if you don't find anything? The only thing here is the shotgun Nariz left.'

Juan Pablo's words were so convincing that the official took a step back, and before she left she told him that she believed him.

WITH THIS OBSTACLE OUT OF THE WAY, THE TIME TO LEAVE the Altos building and move into our uncertain future arrived. Anything that might happen to us was preferable to the torment of that endless imprisonment. Heading to the airport required a complex security operation, and I must acknowledge that the attorney general's office did its job well. Sometime after noon, agents informed us that ten SUVs from the CTI had arrived. We gathered in the living room and hugged each other tight. We looked into each other's eyes. Fear stiffened our spines. We were leaving in pursuit of life, no matter what. Now everything depended on us – or so we thought. Then we went down in the lift from the fourth floor, praying silently that we wouldn't be attacked along our route.

Manuela and I climbed into a white Trooper armoured SUV, and Juan Pablo and Andrea went off in a similar vehicle that was red with a white interior. Leading the convoy was a black Trooper, with no passengers, to confuse our enemies. Inside the vehicle, things were deathly silent. I hugged my daughter and prayed to Mary Help of Christians, advocate for the hopeless, to make sure nothing happened to us.

It was like a scene out of a movie. As we sped toward the airport, I watched a number of police helicopters circling over our convoy. Their doors were open and I could see men armed with rifles and machine guns inside. The noise was deafening, and the other cars on the highway scattered to either side as we came through.

After spending long, tense hours with my heart in my throat, fearing an attack, we finally arrived at the airport in Rionegro without a scratch. A few minutes later, at 1.15pm, we were taking off in an Avianca plane headed for Bogotá. Once we landed at El Dorado Airport, we were led to the VIP lounge in the international terminal, where we were immediately swarmed by authorities and journalists.

The crowd around us was even more absurdly large because the deputy attorney general, Francisco José Sintura, had sent a group of some twenty bodyguards. The DAS (the Administrative Department of Security) sent another fifteen detectives, and four dozen officers from the national police force were posted nearby. Though we were leaving the country, my thoughts were with Pablo, of whom we'd heard nothing for several days. I found it reassuring that at least there had been no mention of him on the news, whether good or bad. I had no idea that my husband had just one more week to live.

For security reasons, we were the first to board the aircraft and were seated in business class. The plane was full and left on time. It climbed swiftly into the heavens, but I kept staring at the door, convinced that somebody was going to burst in and remove us. My paranoia was unrelenting. At a certain point, Juan Pablo and Andrea started guessing which of the passengers might be an undercover police officer. She pointed to several possibilities, and he pointed out two in particular who were seated near us, who ended up being the first to stand up when the plane landed in Frankfurt.

We didn't talk for most of the flight. No questions, only silence. We'd spent the past almost ten years in a sleep-deprived state because our lives had been full of assassination attempts, manhunts and periods of confinement; we'd had to be alert at all times. Exhausted, I closed my eyes but then hastily opened them again, afraid to go to sleep and lose sight of my children.

Once we'd been in the air for more than an hour, I was finally able to breathe a tentative sigh of relief, confident that we were flying toward freedom, toward life. How wrong I was. That illusion would last only forty-seven hours. I didn't know it at the time, but while we were in that plane, hoping to rebuild our lives in a European country, in Colombia a secret plan was under way whose aim was to use us as bait in hunting Pablo.

I only learned in detail about this plan in April 2017 – twenty-four years after my husband's death – when I read the book *Óscar Naranjo, El general de las mil batallas* (The General of One Thousand Battles), a lengthy interview conducted by the journalist and director of W Radio, Julio Sánchez Cristo, with a police official who'd been closely involved in the operation that culminated with Pablo's death.

General Naranjo's account is striking because it leaves no question that we fell into a trap. The text reads as follows:

The ending to this story began in late November 1993, when we learned that the Escobar family intended to travel to Germany and seek asylum there. For three reasons, we believed that would be dangerous for the country and were determined to make sure that Germany would refuse them entry: one, because if his family was safe, he would have nothing to lose and so would harden and be more violent; two, because his family was in fact one of the only ways we had of possibly finding him; and three, because if the family's asylum request was successful, he'd have a refuge abroad that would hamper the operations that were under way. The German ambassador in Colombia played a vital role. He was visited by the head of police, General Gómez Padilla, who persuaded him of how important it was that Germany not grant permanent or temporary entry to the Escobar family. Even as discussions were still ongoing and the two nations' ministries were examining the issue, the Escobars left the country on 27 November, but General Gómez Padilla managed to get two undercover police officers on that flight traveling the Bogotá–Frankfurt route.

We'd been in the air a couple of hours when a young man came up and said his name was Óscar Ritoré and that he worked as a reporter for the TV news programme *Noticias Uno*. How had he found out we were going to be on that flight? I asked him and he gave evasive replies, but it was clear that somebody very high up in Bogotá had leaked the information. The journalist got right to the point and said he wanted an interview with us, that he thought we were in a very difficult situation and wanted to help however he could.

Though none of us had built relationships with journalists over the years, Ritoré's unexpected presence came in handy right then because he could be an ally, a guarantee that nothing would happen to us. We agreed to meet with him once we'd landed in Frankfurt; although we made no promises, we figured that giving him an interview might prove useful to our cause.

The hours passed more quickly than usual, and suddenly the pilot announced that we were landing in Germany. It was six o'clock in the morning on 28 November 1993, and I thought it was strange when the plane touched down, braked hard, and came to a stop instead of taxiing down the runway. Once it was no longer moving, the pilot came on the loudspeaker again: 'Ladies and gentlemen, I apologise for the rough landing and the delay. We are on German soil, and we need to remove some people from the plane and will then carry on to the international terminal.'

When the pilot finished speaking, the two men that Juan Pablo had pointed out stood up from their seats and moved toward us. One of them said, 'Ma'am, we're from Interpol and we're here on behalf of the government to protect you and make sure you don't have any problems.'

I was struck by his claim. The government hadn't done anything to facilitate our leaving the country, so why was it now concerned about our well-being?

With the plane now stopped, I thought, 'That can't be true. The nightmare isn't over.' Frightened, I looked out the window and saw numerous patrol cars pulling up around the plane. In that moment, all my dreams evaporated. The situation became very dramatic. The two armed officers took Manuela by the arm and led her toward one of the police cars. Immediately I lunged toward them, crying, and begged them not to take her because she was only eight years old and still drank from a bottle. Almost at the same time, several other officers did the same thing with Juan Pablo and Andrea and led them off separately to two other cars.

'Officer, you can't take her away from me! Please, I'm begging you, don't take her.' Manuela was screaming and reaching toward me for protection. 'Mummy, don't leave me!'

I sobbed disconsolately. I don't remember exactly if somebody was translating, but my pleading was so impassioned that they must have understood what I was saying. I was shrieking like a crazy person because they were separating me from my children, so one of the officers told me in perfect Spanish to make me be quiet: 'What do you expect, ma'am? Your husband is threatening to blow up every airport in Germany.'

Obviously I had no idea whether this was true, but my priority in that moment was to keep Manuela with me, which I managed after a brief struggle. The Germans must have realised that the girl wasn't to blame for anything and suddenly allowed her to go with me in a patrol car. From the runway they took us to the Interpol offices at the airport, where they interrogated us. While they were getting the logistics in order and tracking down an interpreter, they kept us sequestered in separate rooms, grim places containing only a concrete bunk covered with two foul-smelling blankets. We had to bang on the door so an armed guard could accompany us to the bathroom.

Before we went into those rooms that served as cells, they searched us and our luggage very thoroughly. Juan Pablo was wearing some fashionable loafers with leather tassels, one of which concealed a tiny piece of paper with the telephone number Pablo had given us a few days earlier. They didn't find it.

The interrogation that I endured for more than thirty hours running was one of the most degrading experiences of my life. One official after another asked me every possible thing about my husband: his whereabouts, his fortune, his partners ... but also why we'd decided to come to Germany, who our contacts were in the country and how much money we were carrying. Manuela remained beside me the whole time, sitting on a sofa, and it broke my heart to see her fall asleep holding her bottle. I covered her with a little blanket I was carrying in my handbag.

The Germans assigned us a lawyer who spoke perfect Spanish. We begged her to help us stay in Germany because returning to Colombia would mean certain death. The lawyer was thirty-five years old, with honest blue eyes that teared up when she heard our story, but she looked at me helplessly and said, 'Ma'am, I can't do much for you and your children. I've been forbidden.'

'Please,' I said, 'ask for help from the human rights office. We can't go back to Colombia or we'll be killed.'

'They won't let me, I've been told not to. I can't help you. I wish you the best,' she said, sobbing.

Then we heard a German voice shouting and she had to leave, but not before she squeezed my hands tightly.

The bureaucrat who'd been tapping away on the typewriter suddenly got up and left. The last official, who'd been heading up the interrogation, said he'd be back in a few minutes. Ten minutes later he reappeared and said loudly, 'Ma'am, an aeroplane is waiting to take you back to Colombia. Collect your things and get your children ready. You're leaving right away.'

There was nothing we could do. They practically shoved us out the door, and we had to trot to police cars that took us back to the runway, where a commercial jet was parked that would be leaving for Bogotá in a few minutes. Screaming and sobbing, I told the German police that they were sending us back to certain death, but they didn't care. The lawyer struggled with them too, so they handcuffed her roughly.

'You're condemning two women and two innocent minors to death,' she said, aghast.

We climbed the stairs to the plane, and the flight attendants immediately closed the door behind us. From what I was told, the flight had already been delayed several hours. To make matters worse, the plane was full of passengers who stared at us resentfully, blaming us for the delay, though we'd only discovered we were being deported when the interrogation ended and we were dragged out of the Interpol offices.

Our trip to Germany had been very bold and transgressive. We'd made an end run around the government, Los Pepes and all of Pablo's enemies in an effort to find a solution in those desperate moments where we saw our lives hanging by a thread. I had bet everything on it, but destiny changed the path of events. We faced one problem after another. There didn't seem to be a moment of calm. It was a constant storm that never abated.

A long, tedious silence fell over the hostile atmosphere of that flight I never wanted to take. Again I closed my eyes, trying to rest, but an hour after we took off we heard the slow, friendly voice of the pilot as a map of Europe suddenly appeared on the screens. What the pilot said, of course, had to do with us: 'Passengers, I regret to inform you that our flight will be delayed once more; we are being forced to change our route because the French authorities have forbidden us to enter their air space because we have the wife and children of Pablo Escobar on board. Thank you for your attention.'

I couldn't believe it. We'd just been kicked out of Germany, and now we weren't allowed to fly 10,000 feet above France. I wished for the earth to swallow me up, feeling the reproachful gazes of the passengers search the cabin as they wondered, 'Where are they? Which ones are Escobar's family?'

Hours of tedium and anxiety dragged by. Suddenly my eyes met those of a woman dressed in red and with a red scarf on her head. She was dark-haired and pretty, with a beauty mark on her face and large black eyes that gave off a feeling of peace. I watched as she stood up from her chair and came toward me, holding a small Bible in her hands.

'How are you, ma'am, it's a pleasure to meet you. It's very sad, everything you're going through. My name is Luz

Miriam. This Bible is my gift to you. Read Psalm 23 – it will help you in the dilemma you're facing. Have faith and you'll see everything will be OK.'

The Bible was a special edition with a maroon leather cover, gold lettering and a ribbon to mark the pages. We spoke for several minutes and I told her the reasons we'd been forced to return to Colombia. I must have looked so distraught that she borrowed a pen and jotted down her address and phone number in Bogotá on one of the holy book's pages, in case I needed anything. In that perilous moment, the gift of the Bible and that kind woman's words were a soothing balm, a sign that life would give me another chance. I was grateful someone had spoken to us and said to her, 'Thank you so much, thank you.'

After we said goodbye, I followed her suggestion and read the Psalm she'd mentioned. It read, 'The Lord is my shepherd; I shall not want. He makes me lie down in green pastures; He leads me beside the still waters. He restores my soul; He leads me in paths of righteousness for His name's sake. Yea, though I walk through the valley of the shadow of death, I will fear no evil; for You are with me; Your rod and Your staff, they comfort me. You prepare a table before me in the presence of my enemies; You anoint my head with oil; my cup runs over. Surely goodness and mercy shall follow me all the days of my life; and I will dwell in the house of the Lord forever.'

Reading the Psalm, I remembered that the Lord's mercy had protected us every day. I'm a devout Catholic. I believe in God, in His guidance and His justice. In those moments, I clung to Him; He was the only hope I had left.

I still have that Bible today, and it occupies a special place on my nightstand.

The moment of relief that my encounter with Luz Miriam had offered was a fleeting one; our cruel reality forced us to look ahead to the uncertain circumstances that awaited us. 'What will happen to us when we reach Colombia?' I wondered again and again, terrified. In that moment I had no answer, and of course I couldn't have guessed that as we flew toward South America, in Bogotá the second part of the authorities' secret plan to locate my husband was in motion. The first part had already worked: Germany had forbidden us to enter its territory.

As I mentioned earlier, Julio Sánchez Cristo's interview with General Óscar Naranjo revealed to me in 2017 the truth of what occurred on 29 November 1993, as we crossed the Atlantic on our way back to Colombia.

It's an astonishing account. Naranjo states:

I am responsible for suggesting that they [the Escobars] should go to Residencias Tequendama for security reasons. All based on the premise that they would request protection because Escobar was sure Los Pepes were going to kill them. So we informed them that we'd take care of them, as in fact we did, as long as they agreed to stay in that hotel. The idea was to keep them under watch in a place we could control. Once we confirmed that they were being deported from Germany, we installed wireless microphones that allowed us to listen in on everything they said in the apartment. And we also bugged the phone lines.

It was around eight at night when the pilot announced we'd be landing at Bogotá's El Dorado Airport. At his words, I was overwhelmed by an unbearable sense of anguish and felt like I couldn't breathe. I was very afraid. My legs felt heavy, and for a few moments I put off standing up. I hugged Manuela, Juan Pablo and Andrea tight and recalled a phrase that's very common in Colombia: 'In God's hands.'

Soon after we touched down, the plane came to a stop beside the runway and five minutes later the main door opened and three agents from the attorney general's office came in and asked the passengers to remain in their seats until we'd left. A1 asked for our passports and said he'd get them stamped for us.

We left the plane and found ourselves surrounded by men armed with rifles. It was very cold. A1 came up and said brusquely, 'Ma'am, the only way the government can protect you is if we take you to a hotel owned by the Colombian Armed Forces Retirement Fund. We'll head there now.'

I'd never heard of the place, but I didn't like it from the start. 'No, thank you,' I replied. 'I'd rather you take us to another hotel with good security so you can protect us while we figure out what's going on.'

'Ma'am, we can't guarantee your safety anywhere else. It has to be the place I mentioned – those are the orders I've been given. You don't have a choice.'

We climbed into an armoured SUV and a long caravan of vehicles led us to the city centre, to the Hotel Tequendama, which also has a building of private apartments. Surrounded by armed men, we piled into the lift, which stopped on the twenty-ninth floor. They led us to two rooms at the end of the hall, which were dim and provoked a feeling of melancholy and tedium. I was exhausted and all I could think about was that my children, my daughter-in-law and I were continuing to suffer for Pablo's decisions, and would get no relief. I remember we slept badly that first night, constantly waking up in fright because we didn't know what would happen the next day.

FOLLOWING OUR ARRIVAL, RESIDENCIAS TEQUENDAMA became a sort of bunker. Nobody could enter the floor where we were being held without authorisation from the attorney general's office, and more than a hundred military police officers surrounded the place, patrolling it with bomb-sniffing dogs, while security guards – dressed in plain clothes – used mirrors to examine the undercarriages of any cars entering the premises, searching for explosives.

The next day my sister called to see how we were doing, but my greatest worry was that we hadn't heard from Pablo. I couldn't ask her to find out anything over the phone – I couldn't even mention him. I was sure the phones were bugged. And with all those guards keeping an eye on us, I knew it was impossible for him to get a message to us, much less come to see us.

Soon it was 1 December 1993, Pablo's birthday. Since we hadn't had any communication with him, we decided that Juan Pablo would give a short interview on a Medellín radio station to send him a birthday greeting, tell him that we were OK, and describe our terrible experience in Germany. We knew Pablo would be listening to that station because they'd always been respectful toward us in the past and broadcast his communiqués.

The next day, 2 December, Juan Pablo spoke with a number of journalists who called to request interviews, but he rejected them all. He did agree to receive an envelope that the journalist Jorge Lesmes, from the magazine *Semana*, would send that day with a questionnaire for Pablo. That was the only contact we accepted with a media outlet because Lesmes had spoken with my son in the past and we had a certain amount of trust in him.

At one in the afternoon the reception desk called and told me that three generals – from the army, the navy and the national police – were coming to talk with us. The hotel management had authorised them to reinforce the building's security with another hundred soldiers and lock down the twenty-ninth floor entirely.

During our tense conversation with the unexpected visitors, the telephone rang and Juan Pablo answered. 'Hi, Grandma, how are you? Don't worry, we're all OK, we're OK,' he said briefly, and hung up.

I was struck by his tone of voice and realised he'd actually been speaking with somebody else. The conversation with the generals dragged on, and five minutes later the phone rang again. Juan Pablo picked up.

'Grandma, please, don't call anymore. We're doing OK.'

But this time my son didn't hang up and told me his grandmother wanted to talk to me. I raced to the next room while Juan Pablo said goodbye to the generals.

It was Pablo. I was thrilled to hear his voice, but Juan Pablo rushed in and told me to hang up quick because he was sure they were tracing the call. I understood the warning and said goodbye. '*Míster*, take good care of yourself. You know we all need you.'

'Don't worry, darling, my only motivation in life is to fight for you all. I'm in a cave and I'm very, very safe; we're through the hard part now.'

But he refused to give up and kept calling. Juan Pablo hung up on him twice more, but the telephone rang again and Pablo asked to talk to me or Manuela. Juan Pablo, desperate, yelled at us: 'Hang up! Hang up right now, they're going to kill him! Hang up on him! Ask him please not to call, we're all right! He doesn't need to worry. Hang up now!'

By two o'clock we'd received the questions from *Semana* and Juan Pablo was answering them when Pablo called again. My son put the call on speakerphone and my husband told him to read the questions slowly because Limón – the bodyguard who was watching after him – was going to write them down in a notebook. When they were on the fifth one, Pablo broke in and said he'd call back in twenty minutes. He did, and Juan Pablo kept dictating, but suddenly Pablo said, 'I'll call you right back.'

While that was going on, I was sitting in a little room between the two bedrooms, talking on the phone with my sister. Suddenly I heard Juan Pablo shout, 'My father's been killed? That's impossible!'

Unsure what was happening, I told my sister, 'Find out what's happening in Medellín – people are saying Pablo's just been killed.'

I hung up, ran to find Juan Pablo, and saw that Manuela was taking a shower and singing one of her favourite songs. My sister called again and confirmed that Pablo was in fact dead, and she added that there were several helicopters hovering around the site where he'd been hiding. I wanted to die. I wept inconsolably. The outcome we'd been so afraid of had arrived. My husband was dead, the victim of his own obstinacy, from having ignored his most important security measure: not talking on the telephone. His enemies had caught him at last.

Andrea turned on the radio, and the major news stations were all reporting that Pablo had died in a police operation.

Ten minutes later we got a call and Juan Pablo answered, very upset. He signalled that it was the journalist Gloria Congote, who was working for the TV news programme QAP at the time. Their conversation was brief but dramatic.

'Hello,' said the reporter.

'Don't bother me, we're trying to figure out whether it's true about my father.'

'It's just been confirmed ... the police have confirmed it.'

'Oh?'

'He was at the Obelisco shopping centre in Medellín, downtown.'

'What was he doing there?'

'I don't know. The police just made a statement ... an official announcement.'

'Goddammit. We don't want to talk right now, but if it's true he's been killed, I'm going to kill all those sons of bitches, I'll kill those bastards myself.'

Juan Pablo hung up and we all stared at each other. The threatening tone of his words was most unfortunate, and Andrea and I told him as much.

'It's not an option, son! You can't say that, you're Pablo Escobar's son. You must never, ever use violent words, Juan Pablo. You can't be violent – they'll kill you. I can't bear it, I can't bear all this pain,' I said, desperate and sobbing.

When I heard Juan Pablo's words, the world collapsed on top of me. Oblivious to the consequences, he'd just declared war. His father had just been killed. Didn't he realise our situation? Juan Pablo had lost his temper. He was in so much pain, felt so abandoned, that he'd spoken without thinking. I've never felt as lost as I did in that moment.

But a moment of reflection was enough for my son to regret what he'd said. Immediately he called the journalist Yamid Amat, director of the TV news programme CM&. He explained what had just happened and said emphatically that he was not going to avenge his father's death. Then he called Gloria Congote and asked her to record a brief statement saying that he would not seek vengeance and that from now on he would focus on taking care of his grieving family.

What followed were moments of immense sorrow. My heart was overflowing with sadness; my soul, my entire life were overflowing. I was filled with despair. As soon as I had recovered a bit of strength, I discussed with Juan Pablo how we would break the news to Manuela. After a little while, we did it. There are no words to describe my daughter's pain. Sobbing uncontrollably and writhing on the rug, she kept saying, 'No, no, not my daddy, my daddy's not dead.'

But Pablo was dead, and now our future seemed more uncertain than ever. How were we going to get out of this? What was going to happen now?

Chapter 3

The Negotiation

What do I do now? How do I begin a new life without Pablo? These and many other questions for which I had no answers kept me awake that night. It was 3 December 1993, and we'd just returned from Medellín, where we'd buried my husband's body a few hours earlier.

Because of my maternal responsibilities, I needed to summon strength from somewhere and show my children and Juan Pablo's girlfriend, Andrea, that despite our grief life continued and we had to keep going. But how? I had no idea.

In the silence of my bedroom, I mused that the path ahead of us wasn't going to be an easy one. With Pablo dead, we, his family, had lost all value and were now at the mercy of his many enemies, who wanted us dead. Nor did we mean anything to the Colombian government. Nobody cared about our future.

Two days later, on Sunday, 5 December as we were still trying to figure a way out of our thorny situation, an unexpected visit would be key in starting to sort things out. Our visitor was an old acquaintance, the horse breeder Fabio Ochoa Restrepo, who appeared at Residencias Tequendama in downtown Bogotá. Pablo had held Don Fabio in high esteem, so his arrival was a welcome one, especially since he came bearing a banquet. The food, which he brought from his restaurant, La Margarita del 8, located on the highway north of Bogotá, included – no exaggeration – the equivalent of more than a hundred portions of the traditional Antioquian meal known as the *bandeja paisa*, more than enough to feed us and the dozens of policemen, soldiers, officials from the prosecutor's office and secret agents who were looking after us.

We feasted on beans, ground beef, pork crackling, arepas, sausage, sliced plantain, and egg, a memorable pleasure even if afterwards I couldn't help feeling guilty about the excess. But it was worth it.

Seeing Don Fabio was a delight. We spent the whole afternoon talking about all that had happened to us over the past few years. When he got up from the sofa to say goodbye, though, he told us to be careful, his voice serious and even worried: he'd heard a rumour that Fidel Castaño, the leader of Los Pepes, was insisting to the organisation's other core members that they needed to kill Juan Pablo, Manuela and me to obliterate all traces of Pablo Escobar.

We were quite alarmed by Don Fabio's warning and knew that the security at the hotel where we were staying wouldn't be enough if Castaño decided to order a hit on us. We had the worst of both worlds: we were helpless and at the mercy of both the powerful army that had taken my husband down and of his criminal network.

Even so, after Juan Pablo, Andrea and I discussed various possibilities, we decided our only option was to try to approach Fidel Castaño, with whom I'd enjoyed a brief friendship back in the early 1980s. To that end, I called Elsa Juliana, the young, beautiful wife of one of Pablo's expartners in Medellín, whom I'd lost touch with because of the war, and asked her to come to Bogotá, saying I needed her help urgently. She agreed and came to see us the next day. After I'd explained our dire and pressing circumstances, she agreed to take a message to Castaño.

'Victoria, a letter to Fidel will be enough. I'm sure he'll hear you out. I know the two of you got along in the past. I can get it to him.'

We got to work, and a couple of hours later we'd prepared a short, powerful message in which I pleaded with Fidel to allow us to live: 'You know better than anyone that this is the most painful and confusing period of my life. Given our cordial relationship in the past, I am writing to ask that you spare the lives of my children and me. You know me, you know what I'm like, how I think; you know that for years I begged Pablo not to engage in violence, but he never listened to me. He never understood the danger he was putting his family in every day. My role was always that of a mother who was determined to raise and educate her two children. I am begging for your help: please talk with the bosses of all the cartels. Please, Fidel, my God, they're going to kill us. Please have mercy.'

The effort paid off: three days later, in a gesture I will always be immensely grateful for, Elsa Juliana returned to Residencias Tequendama with a reassuring three-paragraph response: 'Don't worry, Tata, I don't have anything against you or your children. Nothing's going to happen to you on my account. I know what kind of woman you are – you can count on my support in whatever you need to resolve your situation. In the next few days, I'll be sending my brother Carlos to help you with whatever steps you need to take.' He also informed me that he'd instructed his brother to return several works of art that Los Pepes had stolen from us during the hunt for Pablo, including the famous painting *Rock 'n' Roll – La Danse* by the Spanish artist Salvador Dalí. I remember I was overjoyed to learn that the painting was in the Castaños' hands because up until that point I'd assumed it had been destroyed when Los Pepes burned our house in the Diamante neighbourhood in El Poblado, an area of Medellín.

Fidel's letter lifted an enormous weight off of me. It felt like a miracle: one of the most feared and merciless men in the country was not only sparing our lives but also offering the assistance of his younger brother, Carlos, the same man who toward the end of the hunt for Pablo had become the star informant for the Search Bloc, where he was known as 'Alex' or 'the Ghost'.

Fidel Castaño's swift response was unquestionably a good sign, but it was clear our problems were far from being solved. Deep down, I knew very dark days were coming for me, my children and my son's girlfriend, and I didn't have any idea how much time would have to pass for us to escape the endless labyrinth our lives had become.

I'd never imagined that it would one day be useful to have had a relatively close friendship with Fidel, whom

Pablo had once introduced to me as a friend at Hacienda Nápoles. On that occasion, we were in the dining room with Fidel and several drug kingpins whom Pablo had called together so they could work out an arrangement for how much each would contribute to finance the cartel's anti-extradition campaign. During the meal, my husband laid out why it was crucial to have enough money to fight the extradition of Colombian citizens to the United States, and the assembled group applauded. He didn't mention it then, but he'd been paying all the expenses for that effort out of his own pocket for several years, and he thought it was time to get the entire mafia involved.

Fidel Castaño was a courteous, intelligent, and glamorous man who enjoyed art – as did I – good food and fine wines. I didn't see him frequently, but often enough to spend a number of hours talking about our favourite painters, the best techniques, the most enduring artistic movements. The interests that Fidel and I shared filled Pablo with insecurity that eventually turned into unexpressed jealousy.

I recall another occasion when I saw Fidel at Hacienda Nápoles – where Pablo and I were spending a lot of our time at that point. It wasn't uncommon for up to two hundred guests to arrive in a single weekend, and my husband spent most of his time attending to them. The chaos was overwhelming, and even with the estate's massive zoo and gorgeous scenery, I often felt very alone.

On that occasion, Fidel spotted me near the pool of the main house, known as La Mayoría, and asked me to accompany him on a walk to the hacienda's entrance. I agreed, not realising that the round trip would take us a

little over two hours. It was an immensely pleasurable out-
ing because not only did both of us enjoy walking and
physical activity, we also paused to observe the landscape,
the lakes, the exotic animals and the sunset, a real gift from
nature. Upon our return, Pablo was waiting for me, dis-
pleasure etched on his face.

'Where were you, Tata?'

'I took a walk with Fidel because I was bored.'

My husband's irritation was evident, but he said nothing
and continued talking with Fidel while I went to look for
Juan Pablo.

Pablo was your typical macho male, and he was clearly
jealous of Fidel, but he never made a scene or was passive
aggressive. I remember once he must have heard somebody
say that Fidel was planning to visit us at the Mónaco building, which Pablo had commissioned to be built and where
we lived in the penthouse, to see our home in Medellín and
check out my art collection. His only comment was short
and to the point: 'Tata, don't invite Fidel to Mónaco until I
give you permission.'

But how could I brush off Fidel Castaño? Dying of
embarrassment, I ended up telling him he could come,
even though I knew Pablo would be furious with me.

On the appointed Thursday night, I waited for him in
the entrance hall to the penthouse while he came up in the
private lift. He arrived dressed in an elegant black tuxedo
jacket, and I was wearing a dress by the Italian designer
Valentino.

Once we'd said hello, I saw that my guest was attentively
scanning the items decorating the space, including an

Auguste Rodin sculpture, two Chinese-footed candelabras made of wood with two large candles, and an Italian *fioriera* filled with white gladioli that had been brought in from Bogotá that morning on one of Pablo's planes. Then we wandered through the two floors of the spacious penthouse. My collection of paintings hung proudly on the walls, notable among them works by Claudio Bravo, Alejandro Obregón, Fernando Botero, Enrique Grau, Oswaldo Guayasamín, Salvador Dalí and Igor Mitoraj; I also had weavings by Olga de Amaral, sculptures by Édgar Negret, marble and bronze sculptures by Auguste Rodin and the sculpture *La vida* (Life) by the master sculptor Rodrigo Arenas Betancourt, which was in the foyer of the Mónaco building.

When we moved into the dining room, Fidel told me he was very impressed by not only the quality of the artworks but also the care I'd taken in obtaining the certificates of authenticity for each piece.

Pablo wasn't there that night. Over the course of the evening, Fidel and I had a long, stimulating conversation on art, which took us on an imaginary journey through European museums. Castaño told me he particularly enjoyed travelling to Paris because he had a luxurious apartment there whose walls were hung with several of his finest paintings. He added that he usually visited gallery exhibitions and bought a work of art or two on his visits.

My talk of paintings, artworks and museums is not intellectual ostentation, and I certainly have no desire to overwhelm my readers. I will explain elsewhere how I was introduced to that magical world, which for a few years helped lighten the grim situation that surrounded me because of my husband.

Fidel Castaño's visit ended up costing me dearly; Pablo was furious and didn't speak to me for a month. Of course he was overreacting, but knowing his temperament, I decided to send several letters to the safehouse where he was hiding at the time, begging him to send for me so I could explain what had happened. He finally agreed and his men came to pick me up and take me to the farm known as La Pesebrera, in the upper section of the town of Envigado. I found him still very angry and stern, with a cold, distant gaze that was quite intimidating.

It took me a while to break the ice, and I kept trying to explain as best I could, but he seemed absent, his mind somewhere else. Suddenly, two employees called him aside and whispered something to him, and he came straight back into our room.

'Tata, Tata, Tata.'

'What's going on, Pablo?'

'I have to go, a problem's come up – we'll talk another time,' he said, agitated. Before he left, though, he demonstrated that he hadn't forgotten about what had happened with Fidel. He pulled out the jealous husband's classic argument against his supposed rival: 'Tata, you should know that Fidel's gay.'

'Pablo, if Fidel is what you say he is, you have nothing to worry about.'

My argument with Pablo over Fidel Castaño seemed to be over, but there was more to come.

A couple of months later, to repay my invitation to the Mónaco building, Fidel invited Pablo and me to dinner at his mansion, Montecasino. The evening wasn't an entirely pleasant one. Fidel had arranged a very formal affair, and formality and high manners were just what Pablo couldn't stand. Fidel was wearing a black tuxedo, and at least four waiters served the dinner on elegant silver tableware with five forks. Pablo's discomfort finally reached its peak when he was forced to ask me under his breath how to use the seafood crackers to break open the crab claws.

Once we'd finished dessert, our host led us on a sort of tour through his massive residence, which we of course found incredibly impressive. He had original works by Alejandro Obregón, Oswaldo Guayasamín, Fernando Botero, Joan Miró and Claudio Bravo, among others, as well as gorgeous antiques, Persian rugs, and fine Italian furniture. Our exploration of Montecasino ended in a large wine cellar stocked with French wines.

Next, to top off my husband's discomfort, Fidel Castaño said that the evening was to include a steam room and whirlpool tub, which were ready for us. But Pablo was unable to mask his chagrin; he went pale and, after looking at me in surprise, said that we needed to leave soon because we had another engagement elsewhere in Medellín. Weeks later, I learned that this 'other engagement' was just six blocks from our house, where Wendy Chavarriaga, one of Pablo's lovers at the time, had been waiting for Pablo in her apartment.

That was one of the last times I saw Fidel Castaño. By happenstance, I, Pablo Escobar's wife, met only a sensitive, well-mannered man with an immense knowledge of art and a great love of food who never made any reference to his criminal activities in my presence. His other side, a much darker one, I came to know only much later: the drug trafficker who became the powerful head of the para-military group Autodefensas Campesinas de Córdoba y Urabá (Peasant Self-Defenders of Córdoba and Urabá), initiated the first peasant massacres in Colombia, and cre-ated the group Perseguidos por Pablo Escobar, known as 'Los Pepes'.

FAST-FORWARD TO DECEMBER 1993, I REMEMBER THAT though I was reassured by Fidel Castaño's letter promising he would do nothing to harm my children or me, it also raised new doubts. I never heard from him again, although I would later cross paths with his brother Carlos.

My exchange of messages with Fidel was important at the time, but the isolation we experienced at Residencias Tequendama in the days and weeks after Pablo's death was overwhelming. Three of my sisters, close lifelong compan-ions, had left the country with their families because Los Pepes had put out hits on them and destroyed some of their properties. Another sister, who was pregnant, was still in Medellín taking care of my mother, who had fallen into such a deep depression that she wasn't even getting out of bed. Worst of all, many of our friends in Medellín and Bogotá wouldn't come to see us because the government documented all our visitors and they might end up being investigated.

Very occasionally, the telephone would ring and the hotel desk would announce the arrival of people we had no interested in seeing. We didn't allow them up. One day, reluctantly, we agreed to see the Liberal politician José Ignacio 'Nacho' Vives, who said he'd visited Pablo in a hideout known as Filo de Hambre some time ago and offered to help us get asylum in Cuba in exchange for a large sum of money. The former congressman seemed convincing, especially when he took my brother Fernando to the Cuban embassy in Bogotá to prove he had high-level contacts in Havana.

On another occasion, he invited us to lunch at his home and asked me if we liked seafood. I said we did, but I never imagined he would serve us turtle soup. It tasted like swamp water, and Manuela, Fernando and I wished that the earth would swallow us up. We were all immensely uncomfortable, smiling and wanting to run away. Luckily, Juan Pablo rescued that awkward moment: he asked for second and third helpings. In the end, however, the Cuba gambit didn't come to anything.

Nor did I have any luck on my repeated visits to dozens of embassies in Bogotá, hoping that some country's government would take pity on us and give us a visa to get out of Colombia. It was painful to discover that even though Pablo was gone, the Escobars were still pariahs. Over the course of several months, I visited embassies from every continent, from Spain, France and Canada to obscure African nations, and the response was always the same: 'You're the Escobar family. You have no right to enter this country.'

But I refused to give up. I told the consular officials that they were being unjust; my children and I had no criminal record and shouldn't have to pay for Pablo Escobar's mistakes. But the response was as belittling as ever: 'Ma'am, you simply have no right to enter our country.'

I also asked the International Red Cross for help, but they never responded. In my desperation, I even went so far as to call former Colombian president Julio César Turbay, father of the journalist Diana Turbay, who'd been killed after being kidnapped on Pablo's orders. I remember that call as if it were yesterday:

'Mr President,' I said, 'this is Victoria Eugenia Henao, Pablo Escobar's widow. I'm terribly sorry about what happened, but I'm calling to ask you to please help me leave the country, to provide a contact of some kind. They're going to kill my children and me, and we have to get out of here.'

'How dare you call me?' he replied. 'Your husband was the one who killed my Diana. Remember Dianita, remember what happened to her.'

'You're right, Mr President, but I'm not to blame for the crazy things my husband did. Please help me – I have a young daughter and a teenage son. I have to get out of here somehow.'

'Well, all right. Despite the pain your husband caused my family, I'll help you.'

I was grateful for the gesture and hoped that former president Turbay would take pity on us, but I called him several times over the next few weeks and was never able to reach him again.

I spent entire days wandering the city, looking for a way to get my family out. Making things even more urgent was the toll that being cooped up was having on my children: Manuela was calling me constantly, in tears, and Juan Pablo was begging me to come back because he was afraid something would happen to me.

Sadness and pain were part of our daily reality. Out of the blue, the telephone would start ringing and the hotel receptionist would announce the arrival of women who claimed to have come on behalf of Pablo's main lieutenants, the ones who'd turned themselves in to the authorities for a second time after fleeing from La Catedral Prison in July 1992. On some days, an endless string of them would come to visit, so we had to set up a small bedroom to serve as a meeting room. There I talked with the wives or partners of Luis Carlos 'El Mugre' Aguilar, Otoniel 'Otto' González and Carlos Mario 'El Arete' Urquijo, among many others. They brought a deeply worrying message: the capos of the Cali and Medellín cartels who had hunted Pablo were demanding huge sums of money to recoup what they'd spent on the war against my husband.

I was still digesting this new complication presented by Pablo's incarcerated men and their families when we found out that an attempt had been made on the life of my brother-in-law, Roberto Escobar.

The attack took place on 19 December 1993, three weeks after Pablo's death. The fragmentary information that reached us suggested that Roberto had received a letter bomb at the maximum-security prison in Itagüí. Deeply worried, we attempted in vain to get more details by telephone. On the TV news that night, we learned that Roberto had unsuspectingly opened a Manila envelope marked as if had been sent from the inspector general's office; the envelope had exploded, causing serious injury to his eyes, hands, and torso.

The next day, one of my sisters called from Medellín and told me that Roberto had been rushed to the Clínica Las Vegas hospital and was in the intensive care unit. But the hospital lacked the ophthalmology equipment needed to operate on him, so we decided to have him transferred to the Central Military Hospital in Bogotá, which had better technological resources and also offered security services, since there were rumours that the masterminds of the attack had given the order to take Roberto out wherever he was.

Without hesitation, I offered to cover the costs of transferring Roberto to Bogotá in an ambulance plane. Once we were sure he was safely at the military hospital, Juan Pablo and my brother Fernando headed there to see him. When they returned to Residencias Tequendama nearly twelve hours later, I was worried when I saw how upset they were about everything that had happened at the hospital.

According to their account, they'd had to wait in the ICU for almost two hours before a doctor came out and told them that Roberto's eyes would have to be removed because they'd been severely affected by the blast. But Juan Pablo and Fernando refused to sign the authorisation forms for the procedure and instead asked the specialist to do whatever it took to keep Roberto from losing his eyesight. The doctor agreed, and the surgery lasted almost ninety minutes. Juan Pablo and Fernando waited patiently until Roberto, still unconscious, was moved to a room where a guard from the Instituto Carcelario y Penitenciario (INPEC, the National Penitentiary and Prison Institute) was waiting. They said he looked terrible, his face, abdomen, and left hand swathed in bandages.

After a long wait, Juan Pablo and Fernando were allowed to enter the room. Roberto was still groggy from the anaesthesia, but he greeted them and said he could see some light, though he was unable to make out shapes. As the minutes passed and Roberto became more lucid, Juan Pablo told him we'd been very worried because we might be my husband's enemies' next target. Several times, my son asked his uncle for advice on how to resolve the difficult situation, until he finally got an unexpected reply that changed the course of events. Juan Pablo and Fernando said their blood ran cold when Roberto asked for a pencil and a piece of paper and told them to write 'AAA' and go to the United States embassy in Bogotá to ask for help in his name.

The next day, Juan Pablo and Fernando left for the US embassy very early. When they returned a couple of hours later, they looked disconcerted. It may seem unbelievable, but 'AAA' had turned out to be a sort of password that opened the door for my son to talk directly with Joe Toft, the powerful head of the DEA in Latin America.

'I was really nervous. I made my way through the people waiting, and when I got to the little booth at the entrance to the embassy I took out the piece of paper and placed it against the dark glass. Almost immediately, four large men appeared and started taking pictures of us. Then one of them came up and told me to come with him. They didn't ask me who I was or search me,' Juan Pablo reported, still surprised.

My son added that the visit to Toft hadn't done any good; the American told him sternly that the United States could offer assistance only on the condition that we hand over Pablo Escobar's secret files on the Cali Cartel.

'I told him that those files disappeared when my father died because he kept everything in his head, not on paper,' Juan Pablo continued. 'With that, the conversation with Toft was over. All he did was give me his business card and said to give me a call if I remembered anything.'

We still didn't quite understand what had happened with the 'AAA' code, so we looked after Roberto over the next few weeks and visited him in the hospital frequently despite the risk. I took care of all of his expenses, which were substantial, for as long as I could, but the money soon started running out and at some point I told him I wouldn't be able to help him anymore. He didn't like that at all and got really angry, the first in a string of blow-ups that eventually led to our permanent estrangement. It became clear that we were accepted and valued by Pablo's family only as long as we were giving them money; after that, we were their enemies.

Roberto's recovery process after the attack brought about other complications that exacerbated our endless troubles. For example, his girlfriend at the time, who was pregnant, came to live with us at Residencias Tequendama so she could keep up to date on how he was healing; at the same time, his wife, who was living in exile in Argentina because of the war, called constantly to ask after his health. It was horrible being caught between the two of them.

Every day after Pablo's death, a new obstacle arose – it seemed never-ending. That feeling intensified with the sudden arrival at Residencias Tequendama of a woman who identified herself as Ángela and said she had come on behalf of her boyfriend, Jhon Jairo Velásquez Vásquez, alias 'Popeye', who was being held in Bogotá's La Modelo Prison. During our ten-minute conversation, she informed me that Popeye had sent her to summon me to La Modelo to visit the drug trafficker Iván Urdinola Grajales, who had a message for me from the capos of the Cali Cartel.

That brief visit from Popeye's girlfriend left me deeply uneasy, but I knew I couldn't refuse. Though I wasn't yet aware of it, I was about to embark on a long and dangerous endeavour: forging a truce with the heads of the drug cartels that had defeated my husband. Nor did I have any idea that in just a few hours I'd learn that staying alive would depend on handing over spoils of war to Pablo's enemies.

I had little time to ponder whether or not to enter the lion's den. Over the next few weeks, with the help of the prosecutor's office, which took care of getting my visits authorised, I went to the maximum-security wings at the La Modelo and La Picota prisons in Bogotá and at Itagüí in Antioquia. There, it became clear that I was facing a terrifying situation that had to be handled carefully or the winds of war would start blowing again.

The first person I visited was Urdinola, the head of the Norte del Valle Cartel, in his cell at La Modelo. Though he was polite, he spoke very harshly of Pablo, whom he described as the vilest sort of monster. Then he told me it was vital that I go to Cali to speak with Miguel and Gilberto Rodríguez Orejuela, the Cali Cartel heads; Pablo might be gone, he said, but my own fate and that of my children were not yet settled.

To avoid engaging in a fruitless argument, I chose not to respond to Urdinola's comments about my late husband and told him I'd come to talk to him because I wanted to turn a new page with everyone who'd participated in the war and bury the hatchet for good. He agreed and asked about our financial situation. I told him we were having trouble because we were out of cash and couldn't leverage the properties Pablo had left because they had either been confiscated by the government or were in the hands of third parties; though we knew he'd also owned other properties, we had no idea where they were. In any case, I told him, with the government and our enemies breathing down our necks, it was hard to monetise those assets because, for obvious reasons, they were suspected of having come out of the proceeds of drug trafficking.

Once I'd finished speaking with Urdinola, I also took the opportunity to talk with other prisoners, including Popeye, Otto and another *sicario* Giovanni, who complained they didn't have enough money to support their families and pay their defence attorneys during the multiple indictments being brought by the attorney general's office. I was surprised by the men's complaints, since I knew they'd been able to accumulate a good bit of money thanks to their boss's generosity, who'd paid them very well for all their illegal acts. Even so, I understood their concerns and told them not to worry, that I'd take care of it once I was in contact with the Cali Cartel.

That emotionally taxing day ended in a most unexpected manner when I was approached by a tall, thin man whom I didn't immediately recognise. I had seen him only a couple of times many years earlier. Jairo Correa Álzate had worked with Pablo in the Magdalena Medio region and later became his bitter enemy. We spoke cordially for a while without mentioning the past, and it was clear that he was fully aware of what had happened to us in recent years.

'Listen,' he advised me, 'I think it's essential that you go to Cali to settle all this. Don't put it off.'

My conversation with Correa was frank but pleasant. He even offered to have his wife, Claudia, and their young daughter visit us at Residencias Tequendama to spend an afternoon with us. He kept his promise, and Correa's daughter helped Manuela forget her troubles for a few hours.

I continued to have conversations with the prisoners over the next few weeks, but they became more difficult as I had to deal with their foul moods, endure their crude jokes and even contend with lewd propositions. It was awful, but there was nothing I could do about it. And then Pablo's family started making my trying situation even worse.

One day, as I was leaving the maximum-security prison at Itagüí, I ran into my mother-in-law, who said with her usual aloofness, 'Tata, you have Pablo's money – pay those guys. They really need it. Things are rough for them.'

Stung by her comment, I responded in exasperation, 'Doña Hermilda, Pablo never gave me any money to hold on to, much less to pay his men. He did tell me he was going to leave some money with Roberto since, being in prison, his brother was the only one who had protection.'

The widely held conviction that I had the money started to cause serious problems: the phone calls multiplied and the demands increased. Once more, I sensed that my life was in grave danger. I was shocked by my mother-in-law's indifference to our delicate and dangerous situation. What was worse, from the time of Pablo's death until her own, Doña Hermilda never worried about her grandchildren's economic and emotional well-being, nor did she hesitate to cut them out of her will and disown her son Pablo. Luckily, things started to develop in a most unexpected way. On the afternoon of 12 February 1994, the reception desk called up to announce the arrival of Alfredo Astado, a distant relative who for the last several years had been living somewhere in the United States, where he'd fled with his family. I hadn't heard from him much, so his sudden arrival was an ominous sign. We greeted each other warmly but quickly shifted to discussing the reason for his unannounced return to Colombia.

'Jesus, Alfredo, what happened to you? Why are you here?' I asked him, frightened.

The reason was a compelling one: 'Look, Tata, I was at home when I got a call on my mobile phone. I was startled, to say the least, when the caller identified himself as [the Cali capo] Miguel Rodríguez Orejuela. He barely said hello, just told me I needed to come to Cali immediately. Still in shock, I told him I wouldn't be able to go for a couple of months, but he said brusquely that I had four days, otherwise he'd come after me. That's why I'm here, but I don't know why they want me to go to them.'

'What? Noooo, Alfredo, you can't go, don't put yourself in danger. Please, if you go to Cali, they're going to kill you,' I said. But it was no use.

'I don't have a choice, Victoria. Hardly anybody had my mobile phone number, and the Rodríguezes got it anyway. If they found me once, they can do it again wherever I go. I'm going to chance it. I'm tired of hiding. I talked to my wife and told her I was fine with dying if it meant she and our children would have some stability. We've been in hiding for five years, and I don't want to keep running.'

After that dramatic explanation, he fell silent. I was sobbing, but it was clear he was determined to go to Cali as instructed. Anxious about what fate awaited him, he left very early the next morning for Valle del Cauca. We remained in Bogotá with our hearts in our throats, expecting the worst, until Alfredo returned two days later. He immediately described his meeting with the heads of the Cali Cartel.

'As they'd instructed, I got a room at the Inter-Continental Hotel, and a few hours later a man picked me up and took me to a luxurious house in the Ciudad Jardín neighbourhood, where I met Miguel and Gilberto Rodríguez Orejuela and three other people. Miguel took the lead and said they knew a lot about me and that I could help end the war because a lot of innocent people had died. He told me they wanted to end the conflict, so they were asking me to talk to Pablo's widow to try to make that happen. I realised they weren't looking for a fight, so I suggested that I travel to Cali with you and Juan Pablo.'

'And what did they say?'

'As soon as I said that, Gilberto Rodríguez said he'd talk to you, but he refused to talk to Juan Pablo. This is how he put it: "He looks like a duck, quacks like a duck – so he's a duck. He's just like Pablo." Juan Pablo's a minor, so there's no making any agreements with him. He's just a kid. So I think we need to go to Cali as soon as possible, Tata.'

Alfredo's powerful account suggested that there was no time to lose dithering about the situation. The path opening before us was uncertain, but for the first time since Pablo's death we had some possibility for a resolution. My husband's enemies had won the war, and we had no other way to seek a place in this world. Once more, I had to look strong for my children, but inside I was terrified.

NOW THAT WE WERE GOING TO CALI, ANOTHER PROBLEM arose: how to slip out of Residencias Tequendama without being seen by the dozens of soldiers, police officers, DAS detectives and intelligence agents who were guarding us. After discarding several options, we decided that Isa, our psychologist, offered the perfect cover: she could pretend to visit three days in a row to continue the intensive psychological treatment she was doing with us. Luckily, after we explained what was going on and the difficulties we were facing, she agreed to the scheme. The plan worked. We pretended to be holed up for hours teaching me how to manage my depression, and nobody suspected a thing.

At ten o'clock that night, once Manuela was fast asleep, I prepared to leave. Juan Pablo and Andrea were very worried, but they knew this was a step we had to take. I felt raw, not knowing whether I'd ever see them again. The hotel was deathly quiet and, as the minutes passed, I was overwhelmed by grief at my husband's absence and a feeling of powerlessness in the face of an uncertain future.

I closed my eyes and tears ran down my face when I shut the door and headed down the fire stairs, the only way to leave undetected. I descended the twenty-nine floors on foot, my legs hardly responding. Finally I reached the first floor and went down to the hotel's underground car park, where Alfredo was waiting for me in a rental car. I climbed into the back seat, and we managed to get through the security areas in the bowels of the massive old hotel. Once we were out on the streets of Bogotá, the adventure was just beginning. It was incredible: five different government agencies were watching our every move, but that night nobody realised we'd escaped.

It's easy to talk about it now, but at the time I think I didn't fully realise what I was getting myself into. Little did I know that I would soon be face to face with the men who had gone to war with my husband. I was thirty-three years old, a widow with two children, and I was convinced that the only way to save our lives was to get Colombia's drug lords to listen to me, to take pity on us. Bolstered by my love for my children, I was ready to defend them like a lioness defending her cubs.

The eight-hour journey seemed to last forever. I was full of unanswerable questions. Would I come back alive? What would my children's lives be like without me? Would Pablo's enemies go after them next? God, would this nightmare ever end? Would we live to talk about it? I was so anxious that Alfredo looked at me with compassion: 'Tata, God is good. He'll be with you now, too.'

To ease the stress of our long trip and because we didn't have an established time for meeting with the Cali Cartel, Alfredo and I decided to go first to the home of my grandmother Dolores in Palmira. It was six o'clock in the morning, and back at Residencias Tequendama nobody had discovered that I'd sneaked out the night before.

I tried to rest, but it was impossible. We were supposed to wait to hear from Miguel Rodríguez to find out when we'd be meeting him. By mid-morning, Alfredo, who hadn't been able to sleep either, phoned Miguel Rodríguez and told him we'd arrived, but the capo was surprised at how quickly we'd come and said we'd have to wait a few days because he needed to call everyone together, which might take a while.

Alfredo looked at me, startled, and told Rodríguez, 'No, Don Miguel, we can't do that. I brought this woman down here in secret. Nobody saw us, nobody knows we're here.'

'I have to get everybody here. I'll let you know.'

Rodríguez's call came thirty-six hours later. Alfredo wrote down the directions, and we immediately got in the car and headed south out of the city on the Jamundí highway. It didn't take long before we were driving through green grasslands on the way to Cascajal, to a beautiful colonial estate that was now the training campus for the América de Cali football team.

My black mourning garb stood out against the estate's white walls. Miguel Rodríguez met us and told us to wait a moment. We moved off to one side, near a room into which a large group of men was filing. Gripped by a mounting panic, I silently pleaded with God not to abandon me.

'What are all those people doing here, Alfredo?' I asked.

'Don't worry, Tata. They're going to have a meeting, but I'm sure you'll just be dealing with the heads of the Cali Cartel.'

But Alfredo was wrong. A few minutes later, an armed man led us into the large room, where some forty-odd people were sitting around an elegant wooden table. It seemed I was going to be dealing with all of Colombia's biggest drug lords. They signalled for me to sit in an empty chair toward the middle of the table, to Miguel Rodríguez's left. I scanned the scene, terrified. Sitting diagonally across from me and to the right was Gilberto Rodríguez, who was eyeing me with a mixture of contempt and fury. Also present were José 'Chepe' Santacruz Londoño, Hélmer 'Pacho' Herrera, Carlos Castaño, Luis Enrique 'Micky' Ramírez, Gustavo 'Techo' Tapias, Rodolfo 'Semilla' Murillo (brother of Diego 'Don Berna' Murillo who was one of the leaders of the Peasant Self-Defenders of Córdoba and Urabá), and three delegates from the families of Gerardo 'Kiko' Moncada and Fernando Galeano, Pablo's former associates who'd been murdered at La Catedral. Frightened, I noticed that several chairs were occupied by *sicarios* who clearly had no real relationship with the cartel bosses. I sensed that they'd been brought in to intimidate me and send the message that they could recognise me on the street one day. Alfredo Astado sat at one corner of the table.

The next four hours were eternal and agonising. Pablo's enemies gloated over having taken him down, complained about his brutal tactics and laid out a litany of grievances that ended with a single demand: Pablo's money should be divvied up among them as compensation for what they'd spent hunting him.

The whispers suddenly ceased when Gilberto Rodríguez gestured that he wanted to speak.

'All right, gentlemen, this is Pablo's widow ... We're here so each of us can make his demands and set his price. We all know the harm that bastard caused us, and that's why we've come to hear from his widow. Say what you have to say, ma'am,' the capo told me, visibly angry.

'Look, gentlemen, this is one of the most painful moments of our lives.' I scanned the entire table slowly with my eyes so that none of the capos would feel I was scorning him. 'I'm ready to do whatever I have to do to bring this conflict to a reasonable end. In being here, I am hoping that we can find a way to make peace and that you will spare the lives of the Escobar family, my family, our lawyers, our friends, Pablo's employees, my children, and myself.'

Without responding to my remarks, Gilberto continued to act as a moderator: 'Let's see what each person has to say.'

Miguel Rodríguez spoke next, attacking Pablo quite harshly. He claimed the war had cost each of those present more than US$10 million and they expected to get it back.

He then explained that another reason for the meeting was to find out whether Pablo Escobar's family was truly ready to end the violence and seek peace. 'By the way, ma'am,' he added, 'don't bother asking for anything for the siblings of that bastard husband of yours. Roberto, Alba Marina, Argemiro, Gloria, Luz María ... and their mother too – they're going to destroy you. We've listened to the tapes we recorded during the war, and almost all of them were calling for more and more violence against us.'

'You may be right about that, Don Miguel, but I refuse to negotiate unless Pablo's family is included. Pablo loved them dearly, so they must be included in these arrangements.'

Miguel was silent, and the other men present seized the opportunity to offer their own complaints about Pablo.

'That bastard killed two of my brothers. How much is that worth, besides the money I spent trying to kill him?' one said.

'He kidnapped me and I had to pay him more than two million dollars and hand over a bunch of properties for him to let me go. And as if that weren't enough, my family and I had to flee,' another cried.

'Ma'am, your husband burned one of my estates and also tried to kidnap me, but I escaped and had to leave the country for several years. How much are you going to give us in recognition of that harm?' another said.

The list of claims grew and grew, but the next one was the most painful one yet. It came from a capo from the Medellín Cartel. He was clearly furious and gritted his teeth as he said, 'I want to know, I want you to answer me this: if it was our wives sitting here with that bastard husband of yours, what would he be doing to them? Answer me!'

'I can't imagine, gentlemen, I have no answer,' I said, my voice trembling and a strange sense of fear spreading through my body.

All of them were staring at me intently, scrutinising me. I wished I had wings so I could get away, vanish into the stratosphere, but the reality of my situation compelled me to stay.

'God is very wise, gentlemen, and only he can know why I'm here sitting before you,' I replied, no longer shaking.

The last one to speak was Carlos Castaño, who, after talking about Pablo in the foulest terms, said, 'Ma'am, I've met bad men on this earth, but never anybody like your husband. He was a bastard, and I want you to know we raised heaven and earth looking for you and Manuela. We wanted to chop you up into little tiny pieces and mail them to Pablo in a burlap sack. You were the only thing he really cared about.'

I can't even express how agonising it was not only to listen to all their insults and threats but also to find out about the many terrible things my husband had done to them. But the torment was far from over. Gilberto Rodríguez spoke again and started in on the one thing I love most in life: my children.

'Look, ma'am, everyone here is willing to make peace with everybody but your son.'

I'd known that this moment was coming, but I wasn't prepared. The mere mention of Juan Pablo filled me with fear, and I couldn't help starting to cry. Even so, I didn't stay silent.

'Don Gilberto, peace without my son isn't peace. I'll vouch for his actions – I'll stake my life on them. I swear I won't allow him to go off course. If you want, we'll leave Colombia for good, but I promise he'll stay on the straight and narrow.'

'Ma'am, you have to understand that there's a reasonable concern that Juan Pablo is going to end up amassing a lot of money and might go crazy one day, arm a paramilitary group and go to war against us. That's why we're only agreeing to let the women live. There will be peace, but your son must die.'

That death sentence took my breath away. My mind racing, I decided that the best outcome would be for them to kill us all so we didn't have to suffer anymore. Why keep on living if they were going to kill my son? But Miguel Rodríguez stepped in to ease the tension, calming the waters by explaining why they'd agreed to allow me to attend this meeting with the entire mafia.

'You're sitting here now because we used to listen in on your conversations and you were always trying to resolve matters; you never told your husband to continue the war or try to kill us. In fact, you were always asking him, begging him, to make peace with us. At one point you even sent a messenger to try to arrange a meeting with us to talk about making peace, but we heard that Pablo didn't let you come. Still, how could you have supported such a brute unconditionally? How could you have written that bastard love letters, despite how often he cheated on you? We ought to make our wives listen to you on those tapes so they can hear the kind of support a wife is supposed to offer her husband. I want you to give our wives classes on how to love and take care of their husbands even when we're unfaithful.'

The other capos nodded their heads in agreement. Then Miguel Rodríguez brought the meeting to an end with a firm verdict, as if he were a judge: 'We need you to talk to Roberto Escobar and Pablo's men in prison and make them pay. Roberto owes us two or three million dollars, and the prisoners about the same. You owe all of us together something like one hundred and twenty million dollars – go ahead and start thinking about how you're going to get it to us, but it has to be in cash. We'll give you ten days, and then we expect you to bring us a concrete, feasible proposal.'

Despite his harshness throughout the meeting, at various points I felt that Miguel Rodríguez was looking at me with compassion, even empathy. That observation offered me some comfort just when I was feeling acutely hopeless.

As the meeting came to a close, I ventured to say a few last words: 'All right, gentlemen, let's trust in everyone's good judgement so that we can restore peace and calm for our families. I will work on your request and return in ten days with a payment proposal.'

WE INITIALLY HEADED FOR PALMIRA TO CHECK IN WITH my family, but out of fear that something might happen, we pushed on to Bogotá without stopping. I felt powerless: with all the hate arrayed against him, it was clear that Juan

Pablo had no chance of surviving. I wept inconsolably most of the way back, my soul aching. An abyss was yawning at my feet. When we finally reached Residencias Tequendama, I wasn't able to tell Juan Pablo that his life wasn't included in the agreement with the Cali Cartel. Several days passed without my working up the courage to inform him what was going on; all I could do was give myself over to God and beg him to open the capos' hearts so they would listen to me, so they'd believe I was willing to die if my son strayed from the path.

We urgently needed to assemble the jigsaw puzzle of Pablo's properties, so I summoned the lawyer Francisco Fernández. Though he seemed well aware of how complicated my current situation was, he agreed to represent me, and the first thing he did was visit Attorney General Gustavo de Greiff to discuss my options.

Upon his return, the lawyer painted a challenging picture.

'De Greiff says the Cali people are asking for direct retribution because they spent many millions of dollars on the war, and he says that if the family doesn't pay, they'll have all of Pablo's lieutenants in prison killed,' he said. 'He also says Los Pepes have a lot of power and the government can't give itself the luxury of allowing former members of Pablo's terrorist wing to be massacred.' I was terrified, absolutely convinced that we needed to meet the Rodríguezes' demands.

I didn't have much time before I'd have to return to Cali with a list of assets, so we started making an inventory of Pablo's properties and the few works of art I still possessed.

Juan Pablo, seven lawyers from Fernández's firm, a couple of accountants and I spent hours gathering information. I also went to the prisons and asked Pablo's men what they knew, since we weren't aware of all of the holdings Pablo had acquired around the country. The task was even more complicated because my husband had purchased more than a hundred safehouses deeded to trustworthy associates who looked after them.

We managed to produce several spreadsheets for me to take to my second appointment in Cali so that each capo could choose the property he wanted. We couldn't take the risk of lying or hiding anything; it was well known that Los Pepes already had all the information, since many of them had been friends or associates of Pablo's.

Nevertheless, by an unexpected route, a more complete list of Pablo's properties made its way into the hands of the Cali capos before I headed back to meet with them again. I was startled to learn that Pablo's family had sent the list behind my back, putting us at a substantial disadvantage. But that wasn't all. Days later, I found out that my sister-in-law Alba Marina Escobar had gone to Cali to meet with the capos and give them Pablo's will in the hope that they'd get involved in the distribution of the Ovni, Dallas and Mónaco buildings, which my husband had signed over to our children when he was still alive.

To this day I question the way Pablo's siblings – my children's aunts and uncles – behaved. While I was pleading for their lives, they were constantly undermining ours. What's worse, they attempted to make the cartel bosses lose trust in me and kill my son.

In the middle of the tensions with my husband's family, two men claiming to represent the Moncada and Galeano families summoned me to a number of meetings in Bogotá because they wanted to decide what properties, works of art and antiques I should hand over to them as a settlement.

Andrea, my son's girlfriend, would help me elude the CTI agents guarding us in the Santa Ana neighbourhood, where we'd moved in March 1994, and drop me off near the address I'd been instructed to go to, almost always at eight o'clock in the evening. She'd hang out in a nearby shopping centre, but pretty much every time the place would close while I was still in the meeting and she'd end up having to drive around until I called. Andrea would cry disconsolately, worried about the danger I faced at each meeting with the capos or their representatives.

In the meantime, I'd be having a terrible time in the meeting; the pressure was very intense and they did nothing but insult Pablo and call him a monster. They drank whisky constantly, and when they offered me some I'd tell them I didn't like spirits and only drank water. I remember they clearly believed people's gossip and had completely fantastical notions about the value of our assets. At one point, one of them said to me, 'I know you have two hundred million dollars' worth of artwork stored in a warehouse in New York.'

Knowing it wasn't true, I looked at him and said, 'Sir, if you show me where they are, I have no problem handing them over, but let's come to an agreement first: you get a hundred fifty million dollars, and I get fifty. I'm looking forward to hearing from you and completing these negotiations.'

These meetings were intensely complicated and traumatic, full of insults and attacks. They were so brutal that one day, on my way back from the bathroom, one of the bodyguards actually came up to me and said, 'Ma'am, I'm so sorry about all the things they say to you. I'm going to see what we can do to get you out of here.'

The pending matters my husband had left behind occupied a substantial portion of my time, and I spent my few spare moments trying to take care of my children and daughter-in-law. In addition, I had to keep on top of the household. Though the attorney general's office and the army did provide protection, they took no responsibility for feeding the close to fifty men who guarded us. The apartment in Santa Ana functioned as a sort of restaurant, what with providing meals to some seventy people a day, including the members of our security detail, our domestic help and the visitors who arrived – lawyers, teachers, negotiators or relatives. And I also had to try to alleviate my children's depression. During the time we lived there – around nine months – Juan Pablo left the house only five or six times. On some weekends we would take Manuela to Fabio Ochoa Restrepo's restaurant and ranch, La Margarita del 8, to ride horses; those outings distracted her a little from the sadness and loneliness she felt.

As a result, despite our still-intense grief, we decided it was time for Manuela to finally receive her First Communion. We'd put it off several times before, but now we went ahead and set the date for 7 May 1994. My entire family and some of the Escobars were in attendance, but it was a tough day because Manuela cried the whole time, and her sadness brought all of us down. It wasn't easy to navigate our circumstances. Being there for my family, cooperating with the attorney general's office, dealing with the neighbours who didn't want us living there, taking on the negotiations with my husband's enemies, going to all kinds of meetings in the most unexpected places – it was all mentally draining. The pressure I faced sometimes surpassed my capabilities but, even so, I've never so much as taken a sleeping pill. Fulfilment has come from my children's love and my quest to build a better life for them.

A couple of weeks after the first meeting, I returned to Cali with my brother Fernando and the lawyer Francisco Fernández. We had the list of Pablo's properties with us. I was ready to hand it all over, not hiding a thing, so they'd spare our lives.

In the room at the América de Cali training grounds in Cascajal were the same narcos as before. I found it comforting to know that they were willing to set aside their initial demand that I give them only cash; they must have learned that my husband had spent almost all of his cash on the war. They also must have known that Pablo wasn't the sort to stash money in safehouses and instead spent money like it was going out of style.

It was a long, tedious meeting. One by one, the drug lords selected from among the sixty-two assets listed on the document I'd brought. Unlike at the first meeting, though, it seemed like another good sign that they were agreeing to receive half of the debt in confiscated assets and the remaining percentage in properties that could be leveraged, free of any judicial constraints. There was a reason they were now willing to accept 'problematic' assets: their high-level government connections would help them 'launder' Pablo's assets, leaving his heirs high and dry. Which is apparently what happened.

In this critical meeting with Pablo's enemies, I relinquished a nine-hectare lot that Alex or the Ghost – as they'd called Carlos Castaño when he'd been a member of Los Pepes – demanded on his brother Fidel's instructions. The large, valuable property butted up against Fidel's Montecasino estate, which would allow Fidel to expand his economic power. I also handed over at least a dozen empty lots in downtown Medellín; years later, they were developed with high-end hotels and fancy shopping centres. The list of assets also included the Miravalle high-rise apartment buildings in El Poblado, which Pablo had acquired back in the 1980s. The complex had more than ten unoccupied apartments, which the capos divided up among them. My mother-in-law, Hermilda, lived in a penthouse there that she passed down to one of her daughters.

The inventory also included an estate in the Llanos Orientales, as the savannahs of the Orinoco watershed in eastern Colombia are known. I'd never heard Pablo mention the place. It sprawled across 100,000 hectares and was highly coveted by my husband's enemies because it had a landing strip, among other reasons. The plundering of Pablo's assets additionally involved planes, helicopters, dozens of vehicles including Jaguars, BMWs and Mercedes-Benzes, high-performance motorcycles, motorboats and jet skis.

And although I handed over many properties, they were nowhere near enough to cover the astonishing sum of 120 million dollars that the capos were demanding.

As if he could tell what I was thinking, Carlos Castaño suddenly interrupted a long silence and tossed me a lifeline.

'Ma'am, I have one of your Dalí paintings, *Rock 'n' Roll*, which is worth more than three million dollars. I'll return it to you so you can pay these people back,' he suggested.

I looked into Carlos's eyes and remembered his brother Fidel's promise to return the artwork, but I also saw that the capos were expectantly awaiting my reply. In an instant, something Pablo used to say came into my mind: 'When I die, give my enemies half of the money you have left so they don't kill you and our children.'

'Carlos,' I said, 'please tell Fidel thank you for keeping his word, but my wish is that the two of you should keep that painting as a contribution to the cause. I'll make sure to get the authentication papers to you as soon as possible.'

The capos didn't conceal their surprise at what I'd just said. Castaño, who was even more surprised, said, 'Thank you, Doña Victoria, thank you so much for your kind gesture. My brother will be grateful.'

After that, the tone of the tense meeting changed. For the next three hours, the huge table was transformed into something resembling a register of deeds office that took care of transferring my husband's assets to his enemies, who did not mask their triumph but were still conscious of the formidable opponent they'd gone up against.

'Regardless, there won't be another beast like Pablo Escobar born in the next hundred years,' Miguel Rodríguez said as he ended the meeting.

On our way out, the capo said he wanted to show me something and led me to a remote area of the grounds.

'Look at all this we've got on tape. We had your husband's estate bugged for years, and even so we almost didn't catch him.'

I was taken aback by the sizeable room full of hundreds of audio cassettes and Betamax and VHS tapes, which contained Pablo's phone calls that had been intercepted by the Cali Cartel as well as video recordings they'd made of our family home. It was impressive to see how they'd tracked us day after day, and I wondered why they hadn't been able to catch us, given all the information they had.

Once again, on our way back to Bogotá, I did nothing but cry. My debt to the major capos was paid, but the matter of my son, Juan Pablo, was not yet resolved. His life was still hanging in the balance. But this time, halfway home, something unexpected inspired a bit of optimism: Alfredo got a call from Miguel Rodríguez.

'Pablo's widow is no fool. She scored a huge win today,' he said. 'With that Dalí business, she's got none other than Carlos Castaño in her corner, one of the most violent, dangerous men in the country.'

The words of the Cali capo were significant; they indicated I was on a good path. I'd promised Colombia's drug lords that I'd take responsibility for paying, and I was keeping that promise.

Somewhat relieved by the positive change in attitude among the Cali Cartel, I continued my talks with Carlos Castaño, who was following the process of relinquishing Pablo's assets every step of the way. At one point, he told me it was vital to discuss matters and come to an agreement with one of the chief leaders of Los Pepes, Diego Murillo Bejarano, known in Medellín by the aliases 'Don Berna' and 'El Ñato'. Because our meeting would have to be secret, we agreed to take advantage of one of my upcoming visits to Medellín.

And so a few days later I traveled to Medellín with CTI agents from the attorney general's office to take care of some legal matters. I stayed at a friend's country house, but once again was faced with the challenge of sneaking out without my escorts noticing. Luckily, the house had several exits and I managed to slip out after telling the agents I was very tired and was going to rest for a couple of hours. Carlos Castaño picked me up in an armoured SUV, and after criss-crossing through the streets of El Poblado for twenty-five minutes, we reached an imposing estate.

As we climbed out of the vehicle, my legs started shaking again as if the temperature were below freezing. I felt like I was walking in slow motion, and deep down I was reluctant to go into the room where Don Berna was waiting. How could I look into the eyes of another of the men who'd headed the hunt for my husband?

'Good afternoon, sir,' I said when Castaño and I finally entered the spacious home.

'Afternoon,' he said drily, almost contemptuously.

Our eyes met, and for a moment it seemed as if his were shooting flames. Then he fired the first volley: 'You lived with that monster for so many years, you must be just like him.'

Don Berna was obviously very angry with Pablo, and he gazed at me with hatred, with the fury of the recent past. But I was in no mood to put up with much: for many days now, I'd been enduring all kinds of insults, until a strange swell of inner strength told me I couldn't keep quiet any longer.

'Please don't attack me and treat me like this,' I cried.

'I just don't much feel like negotiating with you, ma'am. That man caused so much harm ...'

Don Berna seemed to be in a foul mood. Frightened, I looked over at the picture window and saw that there were about twenty men armed with high-powered rifles slowly parading around the swimming pool. I said, 'Wars are merciless things. You people killed my brother, and he was innocent. He never participated in any fighting or the drug trade and he was a really hard worker.'

'That was a mistake.'

'Regardless, that's not going to bring my brother back.'

'Your husband is the one who's responsible for everything.'

'Responsibility is a shared thing in war. All of this is completely insane; it shows an utter lack of conscience.'

The conversation wasn't going anywhere, and Carlos Castaño must have realised it. He stepped in to calm the waters.

'Listen, we're here to put an end to these problems once and for all, but it seems like you're looking to keep this war going. So look here, Doña Victoria, let's settle this, and as for you, brother, what would it take to fix things?'

'First, I'd dig that bastard up and kill him again. But I'll sign on to the payment agreement everybody's drawing up. I'll join them,' Don Berna replied.

The situation was very dicey. This man had assumed enormous power in Medellín and the Aburrá Valley after my husband's death. Luckily, Carlos Castaño was there too, and I decided to take advantage of his presence.

'Don Berna, I'm here acknowledging that you won the war. I ask that you spare the lives of my children, Pablo's family, my family, my husband's employees, the lawyers and me. And I'm here to offer compensation for a substantial portion of the damages incurred,' I said, my voice trembling.

With a gesture, Castaño signaled that the meeting was over, that this crucial summit with Don Berna had been a failure. I was crestfallen as I left, and scared, especially when the bodyguards looked me up and down as if to say, 'If we ever see you on the street ...'

Castaño reproached me as soon as I got into the SUV. 'That was really bad,' he said as I wept in despair.

'But he was awful to me, didn't you hear him?'

'Sure, Doña Victoria, but he's one of the people in charge now.'

Worried that the peace process had failed, I returned to my friend's house, where the CTI agents remained unaware that I'd sneaked out.

Very early the next day, I got a call from Castaño, who sounded nervous: 'It's not looking good. Don Berna is furious with you, really offended that the big boss's wife came and yelled at him. He's not happy at all.'

'Carlos, what should I do? Please, I don't want any more problems,' I said, convinced that death was close by yet again. In those moments of terror, it was clear to me that I had to weigh every sentence, every word, because I had everything to lose.

'Give him a gift.'

It worked: I gave the lawyer Fernández instructions to find Don Berna and work out what the capo wanted from the list of assets. Through Fernández, I apologised to Don Berna for having upset him.

'Don Berna is very satisfied and says we can put the unpleasantness behind us,' Castaño reported, and I was finally able to breathe more easily.

One enemy had been placated, but there were more, such as Commander Chaparro, another of Pablo's powerful opponents, with whom I had to go and negotiate in the Magdalena Medio, his base of operations. Because my meeting with him was essential to the arrangements that were moving forward, the attorney general's office authorised me to travel in the company of Carlos Castaño. He picked me up in an armoured car and we headed to Guaymaral Airport, in northern Bogotá, where a helicopter was waiting to take us to an estate on the border between the departments of Caldas and Antioquia.

As the aircraft sliced through Colombia's western skies, Castaño and I discussed how hard the war had been and the long road that still lay ahead of us.

'Don't worry, Doña Victoria, I'll be with you, just as I promised my brother Fidel I would be.'

I thanked him, and our conversation continued. Eventually, he offered up a revelation.

'The truth is, ma'am, we were all demoralised by the end. We'd killed 99 per cent of Pablo's people, but we couldn't get to him. We almost threw in the towel. Even some of the lead members of Los Pepes started saying if they hadn't got anywhere by December, they were going to give up the hunt. And as if that weren't enough, the police officers leading the Search Bloc had already been given an ultimatum.'

We arrived at our destination by mid-morning. From above, I saw about forty armed men arrayed in a sort of circle so that the helicopter would land in the middle of them. My heart caught in my throat. They looked like a firing squad awaiting the fateful instruction to 'Ready, aim, fire!' and mow down their victim. That's how I felt.

When we got out of the helicopter, the sun was beating down with all its might. It burned. I took a moment to catch my breath and pray: 'Lord, if they disappear me today, what will happen to my children? My mother? The rest of my family? What will become of them?' It was a horrible situation. I had to summon strength I didn't even have to keep them from seeing my panic and fear.

We approached the group of armed men. A small man stepped forward and came toward us. Castaño introduced me to Commander Chaparro, who in turn introduced me to his son, who was carrying a powerful rifle and offered me a chilly, aloof greeting. After a few minutes of small talk, Castaño got to the point: 'Commander, she's ready to settle all these problems and establish peace. Give her a price for all the harm you suffered.'

'What value can I place on my son's death, Carlos? And what about all those times Pablo tried to kill me? All the people who disappeared?'

'Of course, Commander, but I'm here so this nightmare can finally come to an end. Nobody wants any more fighting, and this woman is fully committed to resolving this terrible situation. All she talks about is peace, pretty much nonstop.'

Once the tension had eased a little, I offered my own thoughts: 'Commander Chaparro, I can offer you two estates, one with a landing strip and another along the river, as well as some equipment from Hacienda Nápoles, including the bulldozer and the generator, which are good-quality machines, quite expensive.'

Chaparro was silent, and I saw that he was looking at me, watching me, as if trying to figure me out. I spoke again: 'Commander, many people want part of what Pablo left behind, and I have to accommodate everybody. Please understand that the assets I'm offering are of substantial value.'

My plea did not fall on deaf ears. Commander Chaparro agreed, and a firm handshake between us sealed the deal.

Feeling more confident, I took the opportunity to ask after the whereabouts of Manuela's nanny, Nubia Jiménez, and our teacher, Alba Lía Londoño, who had been kidnapped by Los Pepes in early November 1993, when the hunt for Pablo started to pull in the people closest to us.

'Ma'am, take a look at all this land here. The disappeared are buried all over the place. There's no way I can give you their bodies – it would be impossible to find them.'

Chaparro's brutal words brought me back to my harsh reality, and I cried for a good while. Then I looked over the vast property, unable to comprehend how much pain, how much uncertainty, how much sorrow was interred there. What was I going to tell the teacher's and the nanny's children? How could I tell them that the bodies would never be found? I remember it took me weeks to work up to it because I felt utterly torn apart. I would think about my own children and feel reluctant to face the pain of theirs. I couldn't tell them what I'd learned. There were no words for it. I didn't want to tell them their mothers were never coming back.

Suddenly the helicopter's engines roared to life. Commander Chaparro shook my hand and I thanked him for having mercy on us. For a moment I felt like I was going to pass out, like I didn't have the strength to climb into the helicopter. But I managed it and, once we were aloft, I looked out at the sky and thanked God for allowing me to return home and giving me the wisdom to handle all of the meetings successfully. We had overcome another imposing obstacle.

In the meantime, I continued to make my rounds at the prisons, including La Picota in southern Bogotá, where I went to talk with El Arete, Tití and El Mugre, accompanied by a couple of CTI agents from the prosecutor's office. After I'd heard their problems and promised to solve their money issues, another young man approached. He'd also been one of Pablo's men, and he was bearing more bad news.

'Boss lady, ma'am, Don Leonidas Vargas wants to see you in his cell to settle one of the boss's outstanding debts.'

Surprised, I agreed, and the young man led me down a series of corridors. On the way, I grew increasingly miserable as I observed the lamentable condition of the downtrodden souls who were clearly mistreated, isolated, without a future. I was so wrapped up in pondering those dismal scenes that I didn't even realise the messenger had entered one of the cells. We'd reached Leonidas Vargas. I remained standing outside.

'Don Leonidas, Pablo's widow is here.'

'Show her in.'

When I walked in, I found a short, pale man who spoke with great precision even though he was clearly of humble rural birth. He greeted me amicably, and after a few minutes he told me that Pablo had owed him a million dollars and he wanted to get the money back.

'Let's figure out a way to settle this that'll be best for both of us,' he said politely, but with the unmistakeable tone of a person who's willing to go to any lengths, however nasty.

Somebody had already told me that Leonidas Vargas was a serious man but also easy to anger, so it was important to pay the debt without putting up too much of a fight. But there was a problem: we didn't have any money. There was a solution in sight, however, since the prosecutor's office had recently agreed to return one of Pablo's planes, confiscated ten years earlier.

'Don Leonidas, would it be at all useful to have one of Pablo's planes?' I asked.

He said it definitely would, so we agreed to have the aircraft appraised. Luckily, it turned out that the plane's value was almost the same as the debt. After verifying that the plane was airworthy, he accepted it in payment. In fact, he even came out ahead, as we also gave him US$300,000-worth of replacement parts for the plane that had been stored in a hangar at Medellín's Olaya Herrera Airport.

But the negotiations were far from over. That became clear one day when Miguel Rodríguez called to tell me that Pablo's siblings had come to see him to ask that he and his brother Gilberto intervene in the execution of my husband's will. They were trying to get around Pablo's wishes; he'd signed some assets over to Manuela and Juan Pablo while he was still alive. Before we hung up, Rodríguez asked me to allow the Escobars to participate in the upcoming meetings to discuss the subject. I refused.

'No, Don Miguel, if you recall, you yourself told me they were out to destroy me. I don't want to meet with them. I'm offended that they've been going behind my back trying to get you to take away the things left to my children by their father.'

'Do it for me, Doña Victoria. I've bent over backward to support you during this process. It's your turn to listen to me.'

'All right, Don Miguel, I'll do it for you,' I replied, remembering how grateful I'd been for the compassion he'd shown regarding our situation.

Ten days later I was seated at the table once more, but there were notably fewer people in attendance this time because several capos had decided they'd now been adequately compensated. Still, this meeting would include a new ingredient: a discussion of my son's fate.

Only a few minutes in, Gilberto Rodríguez made their position clear: 'Don't worry, ma'am. There'll be peace after this, but we are going to kill your son.'

Terrifying as it was to hear Juan Pablo's death sentence reiterated, I now felt, unlike in the previous meetings, that I could appeal to reason and persuade the Cali capos that my son had no intention of prolonging the war and that I would ensure it stayed that way.

'Gentlemen, please, let me say it again. All of you gathered around this table are extremely formidable men. I don't understand why you're bound and determined to take his life – he's just a teenager. I'm putting in a lot of energy and assets to reach a peace agreement; in recognition of my efforts, I ask that you give my son another chance.'

Absolute silence fell. The capos whispered among themselves for a bit and then some of them went to another part of the house to talk in private. Finally, half an hour later, I received their verdict.

'Doña Victoria, we will expect you and your son back here in ten days to decide whether he gets to live,' Gilberto Rodríguez announced.

It was done: we had to come back to Cali, and we had to brace ourselves for the worst. The countdown had begun, so I called on my loved ones who are no longer here on earth and asked them to protect us and help soften our enemies' hearts. It's an old custom of mine that I've turned to in critical moments of my life, and it must have worked; after all, we're still alive.

With the passing days, the tension in the apartment in Santa Ana increased. Not only did we have to continue to endure our neighbours' hostility, but it also broke my heart to witness Juan Pablo's sense of powerlessness as he felt death bearing down on him. We were living in such uncertain times that, incredible as it may seem, at seventeen years old, not yet an adult, my son sat down at the computer and composed a will. Despite everything, deep down I still harboured the faint hope that my son's willingness to come before Pablo's enemies voluntarily would earn him a second chance. I prayed to God every minute not to snatch Juan Pablo away from me, the boy who had been forced to leave school at seven years old, to leave his cousins and friends, endure being confined in hideouts and being pursued, and all the other adversities that my husband had experienced in his last years. I learned to take each day as it came, and to bear the unbearable. And now I was realising there was no reason for my children to endure this inherited suffering.

As always, we took advantage of the cover of darkness and headed for Cali at four o'clock in the morning with my brother Fernando, who was driving a white Toyota SUV. It was an uneventful trip, and as we drove the 300 miles, we discussed how we might convince the cartel lords to spare Juan Pablo's life.

We reached the city at a little before six o'clock in the evening and took a room in a hotel owned by one of the capos from the Cali Cartel. Following the instructions we'd been given, we didn't check in at the desk. Once upstairs, we spoke only in whispers, afraid that the two rooms we were occupying were bugged. We didn't order any food from the restaurant out of concern that they might poison us, and we drank only tap water.

As the hours passed and our meeting with the capos approached, Juan Pablo couldn't help being gripped by a profound feeling of uneasiness. At about eleven o'clock at night, he got down on his knees for a long while, prayed the rosary, and cried. I am pleased that my son has maintained that habit even today, along with the faith with which he kneels before God each day to give thanks for the chance he was granted to remain alive and fight to achieve a better future.

The next day we went to Palmira to see my Aunt Lilia and other relatives and wait for the call from the cartel that would tell us where we needed to go. The day passed uneventfully until ten that night, soon after we'd returned to the hotel, when we got a call from Hélmer 'Pacho' Herrera, who told me he was having us and Pablo's siblings over for lunch to talk about the estate and the distribution of the assets.

'Don Pacho, don't worry about that. Pablo left a will, so we'll work that out on our own as a family. We're here because Don Miguel Rodríguez called us to talk about establishing peace, and he just needed Juan Pablo, my son, to come with me to resolve the situation,' I said curtly. Herrera merely said he'd see us the next day.

Frankly, it didn't sit well with us, given the circumstances, to think about having a meal with in-laws who'd caused us significant problems and the capos who'd ended my husband's life.

At a little before two in the afternoon, a man who said he'd been sent by Miguel Rodríguez picked us up in a Renault 18 with tinted windows. Ten minutes later, we entered the underground car park of an old building in downtown Cali. On our way there, seeing Juan Pablo's terrified face, my brother Fernando tried to calm him down.

'Don't worry, it's going to be OK,' he said over and over, in vain.

The driver went up with us to the top floor and gestured to a nearby waiting room before leaving again. As we headed there, I noted with relief that we hadn't been searched and there were no armed men standing around.

To our great surprise, already seated in the waiting room were my mother-in-law Hermilda, my sister-in-law Luz María with her husband, Leonardo, my brother-in-law Argemiro, and Nicolás, son of my brother-in-law Roberto. Everybody was so caught off guard that we barely said hello and the two groups sat at opposite ends of the large room.

Things were extremely awkward. Luckily, our lawyer, Fernández, arrived with the list of properties and Pablo's will. A few minutes later, a servant in an elegant black suit led us to a larger room that contained a pair of three-person sofas with chairs on either end and a glass table in the middle. Just as we sat down, Miguel Rodríguez, Hélmer 'Pacho' Herrera and José Santacruz Londoño walked in. Gilberto Rodríguez wasn't there.

Juan Pablo, Fernando and I sat on the sofa to Miguel Rodríguez's left. Though he said nothing, he somehow calmed my nerves because he seemed to be on my side, my guardian angel. Pacho Herrera and Santacruz sat beside

Rodríguez, and across from us were the Escobars and the lawyer, Fernández. In the long silence that fell, I had time to reflect on how absurd it was that the meeting to determine whether my son would live or die had been postponed – on my mother-in-law's request! – in order to discuss Pablo's estate first. It was shameful that my in-laws had gone to the Cali Cartel to settle a matter that concerned only the Escobar Henaos.

Miguel Rodríguez was the first to speak.

'We're here to talk about Pablo's inheritance,' he said without preamble. 'I've heard the demands of his mother and siblings, who want the assets he gave his children while he was alive to be included among the assets to be distributed.'

'Yes, Don Miguel, we're talking about the Mónaco, Dallas and Ovni buildings. Pablo put them in Manuela's and Juan Pablo's names to prevent them from being seized by the authorities, but they belonged to him, not his children. That's why we're calling for them to be included in the inheritance,' said my mother-in-law. You could have cut the tension in the room with a knife.

Then it was my turn: 'Doña Hermilda, from the beginning when Pablo built those buildings, it was very clear that they were for his children. He left plenty of other assets to the family. You know that's the case, even though you've come here saying things that, with all due respect, aren't true.'

Two schools of thought quickly emerged among the capos in that bizarre summit: Pacho Herrera expressed support for my mother-in-law and Pablo's siblings, while

Miguel Rodríguez was on the side of my children and me. He said as much in a statement that he intoned as if he were a judge issuing a ruling: 'Look, I myself have corporations set up in my children's names, and those corporations have assets that I, in life, decided were for them. Pablo did exactly the same thing. So the assets he wanted his children to have will not be touched. End of discussion. The assets for my children belong to them, and the assets that Pablo chose for his children belong to them. Divide up the rest of it among yourselves in accordance with the will.'

Nobody spoke. The Escobars went pale, never having imagined that Miguel Rodríguez would take our side. I observed the behaviour of Pablo's family, their uneasy glances, their discomfort with their dead brother's children. Silently, I begged the universe to allow Pablo to look into his family members' eyes, even if it was just for a moment. As a mother, I knew in my heart that I was defending what was rightfully my children's. But as the saying goes, 'Anything that's going badly tends to get worse.' And that's what happened after Miguel Rodríguez spoke, thanks to Nicolás Escobar, who asked a question that ended the meeting: 'Hang on, Tata, what about the ten million dollars my uncle owed my father? We all know my father was the one who supported Pablo financially.'

After that ridiculous remark, Don Miguel looked at me, a snide look on his face, then smiled and winked in a sign of disapproval. It was clear that Juan Pablo, too, was irritated by his cousin's comment and couldn't resist the urge to respond: 'Just listen to this guy. Nobody believes that,

Nicolás. You say the birds are shooting at the hunters now, huh? Turns out your father took care of mine? You've got to be kidding me.'

Smiling, Miguel Rodríguez, Pacho Herrera and Chepe Santacruz got up and headed toward the door without saying goodbye to the Escobars.

I sprang up from the sofa and went after them, asking for five more minutes so they could talk to Juan Pablo. I signalled for him to come over. It was time. The capos nodded, headed to another room, and sat down with their arms crossed, as if to say, 'Speak now or for ever hold your peace.' Juan Pablo got the message.

'Gentlemen,' he said, 'I came here because I want to tell you I have no intention of avenging my father's death. What I want to do, as you know, is leave the country to pursue an education and seek opportunities that aren't available to me here. I don't want to stay in Colombia and I don't want to bother anybody, but I feel unable to leave. We have no way out. I understand full well that if I want to stay alive, I have to go.'

I'll never forget how pale my son was as he uttered those words. It pains me to recall his grief and desperation. But things started looking up when the capo José Santacruz Londoño spoke: 'Kid, what you have to do is not get involved in drug trafficking or paramilitary groups or things like that. I understand what you must be feeling, but you must know, as we all do, that a thug like your father will never be born again.'

'Don't worry, sir, I've learned a lesson in life. Drug trafficking is a curse.'

'Just a minute, young man,' replied Miguel Rodríguez, his voice rising. 'What do you mean, drug trafficking is a curse? Look, I have a good life, my family lives well, I have a big house, tennis courts, I go for a walk every day ...'

'Don Miguel, please understand, life has shown me something very different. Because of drug trafficking, I've lost my father, family members, friends, my peace and freedom, and all of our worldly possessions. Please forgive me if I've offended you, but I can't see it any other way. That's why I want to take this opportunity to tell you that I'm not going to create any kind of trouble. I realise revenge isn't going to bring my father back. Please help us leave the country. I feel absolutely helpless in finding a way out. I don't want you to think I don't want to leave. The airlines won't even sell us plane tickets.'

Sounding oddly like a judge and counsellor, Miguel Rodríguez spoke: 'Ma'am, we've decided we're going to give your son a chance. We understand he's just a boy and should continue being that. You will have to answer for his actions from now on with your life. You have to promise you won't allow him to go astray. We'll leave you the three buildings so you can get by. We'll help you get them back. To do that, you'll have to donate some money to the presidential campaigns. Whoever wins, we'll ask him to help us, and we'll tell him that you contributed to his campaign.'

Pacho Herrera, who hadn't spoken, now chimed in. 'Don't worry, man, as long as you don't get involved in drug trafficking, nothing's going to happen to you. You don't have anything to be afraid of. We wanted you to come here so we could make sure you had good intentions. The only thing we can't allow is for you to have a lot of money, so you don't go crazy out there where we can't control you.'

Miguel Rodríguez brought our brief twenty-minute conversation to an end. 'Don't worry anymore. You can even stay and live here in Cali if you want. Nobody's going to do anything to you. We have mansions, cars and security we can lend you, ma'am – you have nothing to worry about. If you want, go visit my wife's clothing store. Wait to see what happens now with the new president who's coming, and we'll help you,' the capo said. Then he said goodbye rather amicably, called the driver and instructed him to take us to his wife's shop. I was grateful for the gesture and the Cali capos' kind intentions, but there was no question that creating a new life for ourselves would require us to leave Colombia.

A few minutes later, we arrived at a high-end shopping district and I went into a clothing boutique that the driver pointed out to me. Behind an elegant desk I found Miguel Rodríguez's wife, Martha Lucía Echeverry. Slim and beautiful, she welcomed me warmly. I felt that she was looking at me with compassion, as if to say, 'I totally get what you're going through.' I tried to be friendly too and looked at a few of the elegant garments she was selling, but I didn't have the heart for it – I felt like a zombie, overwhelmed by the immense sorrow in my heart. I was there for close to an hour, and I hope she was able to understand that I was in no state for clothes shopping. When I left, Juan Pablo was waiting for me; he'd bought a tartan plaid terrycloth bathrobe.

After the endless fight to keep him from being killed, it was clear my son was going to live. I decided that from then on, as much as possible, I would take advantage of any opportunity for us to be together and celebrate life. We had begun to surmount the main obstacles that stood in our way. Carlos Castaño, who'd been keeping a close eye on the process of distributing Pablo's estate, confirmed as much. He was so kind to me that on one occasion, as we were travelling by plane to resolve an issue with one of Pablo's properties that I was supposed to give to another capo, he made a statement that turned out to be prophetic: 'Don't worry, Doña Victoria, we're fixing your problem now, but it won't be long before we all kill each other, just like what happened with Pablo.'

A few days later, I was surprised to get a call from Ismael. He'd been a big shot in the Medellín Cartel because he was Kiko Moncada's right-hand man, but I'd never heard from him before. He asked me to come me to his office, which was very close to the Centro Andino shopping centre in Bogotá. I went with my brother Fernando and found him in a well-appointed office, beautifully decorated and with an expensive bottle of whisky on the desk that he chugged down over the course of our six-hour conversation. It is no exaggeration to say that Ismael spent 80 per cent of the time criticising my husband for the horrors he'd perpetrated during the war, for abandoning his values, for allowing his men to exert too much of an influence, for his terrorist attacks.

'Your husband was insane! Totally insane!'

As the night went on and Ismael continued to down large glasses of whisky, the moment of truth arrived.

'Listen, ma'am, you're going to die if you don't give me what I ask for,' he said.

My brother pounced like a wild animal: 'You're going to die too, Ismael. Or do you think you're going to live forever?'

My brother's unexpected fierceness caught Ismael so off guard that he lowered his eyes and said nothing. That's why I loved Fernando so much: he was great company, a peaceable man who always supported us no matter what. I feel his absence keenly today – he eventually died as a result of his drug addiction and terminal illnesses on 16 June 2014.

After two or three more meetings, Ismael ended up with the assets he was demanding from Pablo. I handed them over without complaint because he not only had a lot of influence in the cartel but was also extremely dangerous.

At the end of our final tense meeting, Ismael apologised to me for the death of my eldest brother, Carlos, whom Los Pepes had killed on 2 June 1993, as he arrived in Medellín from Cartagena. He told me the two of them had been friends and that he knew Carlos hadn't been involved in any of Pablo's activities. He also told me that when he found out Carlos had been kidnapped, he'd made several calls trying to prevent him from being killed, but before he was able to contact the right people, it was too late.

BY THE TIME LATE AUGUST 1994 ROLLED AROUND, WE HAD been immersed in these exhausting negotiations for eight months. We'd already handed over all of the assets Pablo had left behind except the Dallas, Mónaco and Ovni buildings, which, according to our agreement, belonged to my children. At least until the government confiscated them.

Once we'd resolved the matter of distributing Pablo's assets, both to the cartels and to the Escobar family, we had to focus on our own future, which would inevitably involve leaving the country. It was our only option. But where to? Though there were a number of possibilities on the table, they were very uncertain. We were busy discussing them when I was summoned to Cali again out of the blue: questions had come up about the paperwork for an aeroplane and a helicopter belonging to Pablo.

As always, I headed out immediately and arrived at the América de Cali headquarters in Cascajal, where I found some forty people – the same ones, I think, who'd been there at the very first meeting. Luckily, the insults and death threats were now a thing of the past, and we were able to resolve this matter relatively easily. After we'd done all the relevant calculations, it turned out that we had paid out more than our obligations required, and the capos agreed to pay back the difference by returning a couple of planes to help ease my financial situation, which was looking grim. For the first time, they gave me phone numbers I could use to call them and finalise the details of the handover, which never actually took place.

Once we'd resolved the issue that had brought me there, we all stood up. Miguel Rodríguez wanted to say one more thing. 'Ma'am, we want to thank you for keeping your word of honour during this process. We feel that you respect us and you have earned our respect.'

Nobody said anything more. I shook hands with each capo, and they quietly acknowledged the care I'd taken throughout the negotiation process.

Before we left, we gathered in a sort of circle and Miguel Rodríguez, more relaxed now, recalled an incident that had occurred during the most intense period of the war with my husband: 'If we'd ever ended up meeting as you requested several years back, we would have avoided so much suffering and death.'

'You're right, Don Miguel, but we all know my husband wouldn't let me.'

Miguel Rodríguez was referring to my decision, while Pablo was trying to win his wars, to do something to end them in a less destructive way. But how? The answer, I'd decided, lay in an aunt with whom I'd always been close. She'd once told me she knew someone close to the Cali capos. Without thinking twice, I'd asked her to talk to her friend and request a meeting with the Cali Cartel to discuss how we might stop the conflict.

My aunt had gone pale at my suggestion; she'd been dubious that she was capable of such a thing. I had tried to reassure her, 'Of course you're capable. You're capable of much bigger things than this, even. You're a fighter; no situation has ever been too much for you.'

I had convinced her, and her effort was a success: her contact spoke with the Cali capos, who were willing to meet with me as soon as possible. Receiving that news had made me enormously happy; I'd felt like I could touch the sky. But then I'd had to convince Pablo, who was hiding out on an estate in eastern Antioquia. Despite the trying circumstances, I'd made the difficult trip there so he could see his children and spend a few hours with them.

I'd figured the best approach was to wait for my aunt to give the news to Pablo, who had no idea what was happening. Deep down, I'd been worried about what he'd say, since I'd taken it upon myself to get in touch with the Cali Cartel without saying anything to him. My aunt had arrived at about seven at night, and I'd given her a big hug so I could whisper in her ear, 'Auntie, we have to pray to God that Pablo listens to us.'

'It's OK, sweetie, he'll listen.'

We had slowly approached Pablo, who was staring off at the horizon from the deck. He was wearing white trousers, a white shirt and special tennis shoes with grippy black cleats in case he needed to make an escape.

'Pablo,' my aunt had said, 'Tata and I were thinking about how we can end this nightmare, and she asked me to speak to this man I know from the Cali Cartel to see if they'll talk to her. And they've agreed to have her come talk to them.'

Pablo had simply stared at me with a look on his face I knew all too well: disapproval.

'Tata, you're nuts. My enemies are going to send you back here wrapped in barbed wire. You can't go to Cali – you're too naive; you don't have a wicked bone in your body. I can't believe you even suggested it. You're crazy! Totally nuts! Over my dead body.'

Even today I regret that Pablo didn't understand that it actually would have been possible to stop his war with the Cali Cartel. It was unthinkable to him that his wife would attempt such a thing. Was he afraid they'd kill me, or was he so chauvinistic that he couldn't conceive of having his wife negotiate with his enemies? I don't know. The saddest part of this painful story is that it was only after his death that I was able to go to them – but despite his assumptions they didn't kill me, my children or my daughter-in-law, and many years later we found a new life.

Chapter 4

Pablo's Women

Talking about my husband's affairs for the first time is especially painful for me because it undermines my status as a wife, my dignity, my self-esteem and my self-respect.

In some cultures it's no big deal if a husband is unfaithful; affairs are widely known but never discussed. They're an open secret in thousands of families. As women, we were raised not to see or speak, to be there, silent, fulfilling our duties as wives and mothers. We lived in a role of resignation, where the accused was offended by recriminations that he always emphatically denied, and so eventually the fights ended. We didn't have the right to object or lash out; for many women, doing so would have meant certain death.

Even so, I understand that this chapter is an inevitable one in a book about my life with Pablo Escobar because everybody knows about his numerous relationships with all sorts of women throughout his life. As such, I know my readers would not forgive me if I failed to address the adultery I endured for years, even if it makes me dizzy and pains my heart, my skin, my soul … my life.

Recounting this is all the more agonising because now, years later, I've learned that my husband had many more dalliances than I was aware of at the time. I heard about them while doing research for this book, when I returned to Medellín and other places in Antioquia to interview a number of people who were close to my husband, who kept their mouths shut back then out of fear or gender solidarity.

In other places in this book I talk about the Pablo Escobar who caused immense harm, who committed crimes, who destabilised a nation, who defied an empire, but here I will address the man, the father, the lover.

MY FIRST MEMORY OF HIM DATES BACK TO 1972: I SEE A young man riding through the streets of the newly built La Paz neighbourhood in Envigado, on a striking red and white Vespa that a neighbour sold him for 3,500 pesos and that he agreed to pay in monthly payments of 300 pesos. His success with women is obvious: lots of them smile at him and gesture to him to take them for a spin. He's a real lady-killer, gregarious and romantic, and the girls talk about him all the time and call him 'the guy with the motorbike'.

At the time, to be honest, I wasn't interested in knowing who he was, though the neighbourhood gossip made it inevitable that I would find out eventually: his name was Pablo Emilio Escobar Gaviria, he was twenty-three years old, he was studying in the public high school at the University of Antioquia, and it was clear from a mile off that his life was very different from mine, as I'd just turned twelve and had to ask permission to leave the house. Pablo had a complex about being short – he was just five feet five inches tall – so he would get really offended when his friends called him 'midget' or 'shrimp'.

My family, the Henao Vallejos, was the wealthiest one in the neighbourhood, which we'd moved to in 1961 from Palmira – a small, affluent town in the department of Valle del Cauca in south-western Colombia – after my parents decided to put down roots in Antioquia because they were tired of constantly travelling all around the country for my father's work. That endless pilgrimage meant that most of their eight children were born in different towns and cities throughout the country.

My mother, Leonor, who'd been called Nora since she was a child, had set up a small shop in part of the common area of the house, where she sold a little bit of everything: clothing, fabric for school uniforms, office supplies, appliances and perfumes. My father, Carlos, was a snack distributor for a company known as La Piñata, so people around the neighbourhood called us 'the Piñatos'. Thanks to my parents' hard work, their children – three boys and five girls – grew up surrounded by creature comforts and studied in private schools. I took swimming and guitar lessons, got new shoes two or three times a year, and one of my aunts used to bring us clothing from New York fairly regularly. And during our end-of-year holiday, we generally travelled to Palmira, where my grandmother Dolores and my Aunts Lilia and Fanny lived.

The Escobar Gavirias' situation was quite different. They arrived in the neighbourhood in 1964, three years after us, and their roots were in the countryside, where they'd barely eked out a living, and during the period of political violence in the mid-twentieth century had been forced to move around Antioquia to avoid getting caught in the middle of the conflict. The mother, Hermilda, was a schoolteacher, and the father, Abel, was a farmer. They had four daughters and three sons, of whom Pablo was the youngest.

The new neighbourhood came with a school, so Doña Hermilda was hired immediately as a teacher thanks to the intervention of the former minister and renowned Liberal politician Joaquín Vallejo Arbeláez – Pablo's godfather – who persuaded the Antioquia Ministry of Education to give her a job. But the family income wasn't nearly enough, so Don Abel worked in the neighbourhood as a security guard. Every night, members of the Community Action Board would sell Pablo's father a pack of Pielroja cigarettes on credit and give him a thermos of coffee and some bread.

As I continued to often see Pablo around, I started to notice that he was interested in me. First it was a seductive glance, then a wink and later a brief hello every time he saw me. But he must have realised it wouldn't be easy to get near me, so he asked Yolanda for help. Yolanda was a young woman from the neighbourhood whose family was close to the Escobar Gavirias; though Yolanda and I weren't good friends, we had known each other a long time. And it worked: pretty soon, Yolanda became the go-between for our future relationship.

One day, after she'd already started playing that role, Yolanda told me what Pablo had said when talking about me: 'Yolanda, Tata has people who really love her. Will you help me go out with her?'

But Yolanda warned him what might happen because the eleven-year age difference between us was too pronounced.

'Pablo, remember that Mario [my second-oldest brother] has a short fuse. I'll talk to him if you want – he's my maths teacher, and I'll tell him you're interested in her. Plus Mario admires you but, don't forget, Victoria is really young and you're way too old for her. Look, Pablo, I don't want to have problems with the Henaos – they're family friends. You have to talk it over with her mother, but you should know that she's a firecracker too.'

He rejected her arguments and kept pushing. 'The age thing doesn't matter. We wouldn't be the first couple like that, or the last. She's going to be the mother of my children. I want her to be my wife, and we'll have five.'

Yolanda thought Pablo was getting ahead of himself since we'd never even spoken, but she soon learned that he was quite serious. Far from resigning himself to keeping a distance, one day, when I'd just turned thirteen, he came up to me for the first time and said, 'Tata, come on my motorbike and I'll take you for a ride.'

'No way, Pablo! My parents won't let me get on anybody's motorbike,' I replied, trying to make it clear that I followed the house rules to the letter.

But he refused to give up, and with some regularity, when I was walking through the neighbourhood at night to order the milk for the next morning, he'd emerge from the shadows and ask if he could walk with me. I'd nod and we'd change routes so people wouldn't see us walking down the main street. During the short walk, he'd talk about how pretty I was, my sexy smile and my legs, which he claimed to admire. No surprise there: hot pants were in fashion at the time and looked pretty good on me, since I was slim as a result of hours and hours spent skating and swimming.

Weeks later, the compliments still continued, but now the gallantry was accompanied by a pink box of Adam's gum and a large bar of Jet chocolate, the wrappers of which I saved for years. By then I'd started to like Pablo a lot, but I didn't dream of bringing him home since at my age I wasn't allowed to have a boyfriend.

As the weeks passed, it was only a matter of time before something happened between us, and Pablo did his best to hurry things along, aided by Yolanda, who gradually gained enough of my mother's trust that I was allowed to go out with her on Saturdays, from seven to nine at night. Once we were on the street, Yolanda would go with me to meet up with Pablo in secret at nearby ice cream parlours, such as La Iguana, which later became El Paso, La Esvástica, which had booths for two, El Trianón and others. Our chats were pleasant, if short, and it was clear that Pablo was an agile conversationalist and a dynamic storyteller.

Since Pablo was bent on winning me over, the gifts soon started to arrive. The first was the large, square watch he wore, but I never wore it for fear of my parents noticing, so Yolanda kept it for several months. Then he gave me an LP by the Spanish singer Camilo Sesto and dedicated one of its songs, 'Amor amar', to me. One of its verses seemed to anticipate the future: 'My love, if your pain were mine and mine yours, how lovely it would be, my love, to love. I don't have today or yesterday, but I will have a tomorrow where I can fly ...' I loved it.

I remember that on Valentine's Day that year I was mad at him and we didn't talk for several days because his infidelity was already common knowledge. He was constantly looking at and seducing the neighbourhood girls, and I was very jealous. But Yolanda showed up with a stunning pearl and turquoise ring.

'It's from Pablo, Tata. He told me to give it to you so you wouldn't think he was trying to get out of giving you a gift.'

The ring was beautiful, and according to what Pablo told Yolanda, he'd bought it in the Medellín's La Perla jewellery store for 1,700 pesos – US$77 at the time – a huge sum.

In those few months of courtship, I discovered a romantic man with poetic airs and a sexy smile, one who was affectionate and immensely thoughtful, frequently sending me gifts and flowers. Gradually I began to fall in love, until I was completely smitten. The age difference between us made our budding relationship very appealing because he wasn't a teenage boy, full of insecurities and digressions, but an older man who made me feel like he was after more than a short fling.

But lies don't last for ever, and after a while some of my sister Luz Marina's friends saw me out with him a few times and ended up reporting back. Everybody in my house found out about it immediately, and my mother stopped letting me go to the dairy store, my only chance to see Pablo. I became really unhappy and couldn't understand why my mother was being so adamant, unable to accept that somebody was interested in me and that I wanted to know what it meant to fall in love. A strange rebelliousness came over me, and for the first time I was unwilling to allow my parents, and especially my mother, to interfere in my relationship with Pablo.

After that we couldn't see each other on weekdays because I wasn't allowed out of the house unless accompanied by a sibling; in addition, Pablo often sent word through Yolanda that he was travelling for business. She wasn't specific in the details, and of course I didn't remotely suspect that my beau had already become involved in the dark underworld of crime.

The spell cast over our relationship led Pablo to defy my family, and in early 1973 he took a step toward formalising matters. I heard about it one night when my brother Mario came to my room and said we needed to talk.

'Tata, you know I'm fond of Pablo, but it's my duty as your brother to warn you he's not right for you. We go out with women all the time. He's not the best man for you. Forget about him.'

I listened in silence, but in my naivety, I was not saddened by his remarks – I remained unfazed. It was clear my brother was upset that his friend was courting his sister, but even so he was gentle in trying to push us apart. Mario wasn't wrong: right around then I heard all kinds of details about Pablo carrying on an affair with the rector of the Liceo La Paz, where I studied. But I excused it, believing it was because we didn't yet have a formal relationship.

Pablo knew full well that if he wanted something serious with me, he needed my family's approval, so he took advantage of his friendship with Mario to pave the way, though he was aware of my brother's opposition. He invited him out for a whisky at the La Iguana ice cream parlour and they talked for more than two hours, after which Mario returned home and sought out our mother.

'I talked to Pablo, and he says he wants to be Tata's boyfriend. So I want to warn you, the guy never goes to bed, he doesn't sleep – he perches on the bedrails like a vulture.'

'Oh, God. What next. And what did you tell him?'

'I suggested he look at my other sisters, since they're older, but he said no, he wants Tata. So it's your call, but we're going to have to keep our eyes on that girl at all times. Pablo's serious – he wants to visit her here at the house.'

And that's how we began. On Tuesday, 1 May 1973, a holiday, he asked me to be his official girlfriend and clinched his commitment with a gift: Claudia de Colombia's newly released single 'Nuestra historia de amor'. Then he told me confidently, 'Darling, you'll be mine for all my life. I'll never give you up for anything or anybody.'

Excited – and naive – I swore I would be his love all my life, unconditionally. We sealed our relationship with a passionate kiss and a long embrace. My die was cast.

At last we were boyfriend and girlfriend, and my family's doubts had posed no obstacle to my pretender. They saw all sorts of flaws: he was eleven years older than me, he dressed badly, he looked very short next to me, he used Lechuga hair tonic to tame his curls. The list of cons was a lengthy one, but I didn't care.

My mother imposed harsh restrictions on seeing Pablo, demonstrating that we hadn't won yet. The primary obstacle was that we could only meet on Saturdays from seven to nine at night. It was a nightmare: I was on the arm of a very attractive man, but we had to go out when the clubs were just opening. It was a miracle he became my boyfriend, given how the neighbourhood girls would line up to go out with him. When the eagerly awaited day arrived, I would always start getting ready very early. My sisters thought it was hilarious how I would lay out my clothes on the bed to make sure the colours went together: the bra underneath and the blouse on top; then underwear and trousers or a skirt; then the stockings stretched out as if they were my legs and finally my shoes. Obviously I would switch things out several times, obsessed with finding the perfect combination. I was meticulous – I wanted Pablo to see me as put together, attractive and sexy. I think I succeeded, because my beau always went crazy when he saw me.

During that happy period, a unique individual appeared in my life. Marquitos was a friendly young man we used to see around the neighbourhood with his camera. It was common to see him wandering around snapping photos – he was part of the landscape – but after I started going out with Pablo, I noticed he'd started taking photos of me wherever I went. At first I felt uncomfortable and even found it odd, but I relaxed when I learned that my romantic boyfriend had hired him. Later, Marquitos fell in love with me and decided to confront Pablo.*

---

* Marquitos is still alive, and I ran into him one day in Medellín while doing the research for this book. He told me he remembered me fondly, and that in the middle of the war Pablo had sent him a message asking him to destroy all the photos he'd taken back then. And he'd obeyed.

Meanwhile, Pablo used to cruise through the neighbourhood on his new 1963 Lambretta motorcycle, but since
I was his girlfriend now, I took it hard and started throwing
jealous tantrums and fighting with him because I'd seen
him talking to other girls. It was mortifying to realise that
he liked being seen as a ladies' man. But as a true male
chauvinist, he hated it when I danced with other men, even
my brothers, and when he got angry about that, he'd give
me the silent treatment. I remember once he went off on a
trip for a few days, and though I was sad, I ended up going
to a party at school, where I danced with another boy.
Innocently, since I'd done nothing wrong, I wrote him a
letter and told him what had happened. As a reply, he
mailed me an envelope containing the ripped-up pieces of a
wallet-sized photo I'd given him and a sheet of paper with a
message that said, 'This is what you're worth to me, Tata.'

I had to wait several long weeks for him to come looking
for me. It was the first time we'd been driven apart by his
jealousy, but in the end he gave in and brought me a bicycle
as a present, a yellow Monareta with lights, a basket, a horn
and fat tyres.

'Tata, look what I bought for you. I brought it from
Ecuador.'

'Pablo, do you think that bike is going to erase the pain
you caused me? Keep it.'

'Tata, please, listen to me. I love you. You're the most
important thing I have in life.'

His seduction efforts paid off, and he ended up wearing
down my resistance. After we apologised to each other for
the fight, we agreed to continue our relationship, and then I

went home with the bicycle to show off the gift my boy-friend had brought me.

Over the next few weeks, we had some very happy moments. He made me feel like a princess in a fairytale, and I was convinced he was my longed-for prince.

The spell on our relationship that I've referred to was real, and it elevated even the most mundane acts such as driving a car. Pablo taught me to drive in a massive 1954 Ford, one of the first cars in the La Paz neighbourhood. It was an enthralling experience that included not only the tutelage I needed but also a high dose of flirtation.

He knew how to treat a woman, and he must have had a lot of patience because at first the car stalled out whenever I shifted gears.

'Relax, don't worry, it'll start up again in a minute.'

My sister Luz Marina and her boyfriend, Óscar, came to the driving lessons too, but they didn't want to join in and sat in the back of the car. At first we would practise pretty close to home, in a nearby neighbourhood known as Los Periodistas, but later Pablo took me to drive high up in the mountains, full of curves and with dangerous drop-offs. At a certain point he would let go of the wheel, and while I drove, scared to death, down the Las Palmas highway, try-ing to keep the car from stalling, he would caress me, gently stroking my hair.

Obviously the car would end up stalling, and then Pablo would pull up the handbrake and play driving instructor: 'Darling, first gear; darling, second; darling, third,' he'd say with inimitable sweetness. Never, during those lessons, was

Pablo crude, pushy or impatient. We never fought because of that ... It was pure romance.

Once I'd got over my fear of driving in such places, Pablo's secondary intention was revealed: ending our lesson at El Peñasco, a cosy, romantic, exotic nightclub perched on a rock on a mountainside, with a beautiful view of Medellín. Though it was very cold, we stayed outside, hugging and kissing passionately.

Thanks to Yolanda's ability to convince my mother to let me go out with Pablo for a few hours, we were able to make a few trips to the dance club Carrusel, across from the Centro Automotriz in Medellín. Our personal Cupid would claim we were going for a walk in Sabaneta Park, but we would actually go to Carrusel, where Pablo would order half a bottle of aguardiente and I would get a soft drink. We'd arrive at five in the afternoon, and I'd be back home at eight.

But nothing is perfect in life, and my parents' resistance to my boyfriend did not abate. My mother was particularly hostile; she couldn't stand his rudeness and his slovenly dress. Pablo had no interest in making sure his clothing matched, and he always used to roll up his sleeves and leave his shirts untucked. And as if that weren't enough, it was common to see him walking through the streets wearing a rustic white wool poncho. My parents didn't miss an opportunity to criticise him.

'Sweetheart, there's no need to get all dolled up – it looks like you're dating a truck driver anyway,' my mother once complained.

'Tell him to leave the poncho at home. He can't come here looking like that,' my father said on another occasion.

'You'd better show my daughter respect. You're not getting past that door,' my mother told Pablo one Saturday night when he dropped me off.

Pablo was the opposite of what my parents wanted for me, but I was happy with him, and that was enough. Until, of course, he started to make a hash of it, like in the second half of 1974, when he simply disappeared. I was totally out of sorts because nobody knew where he was, not even Yolanda, the first person I asked; she told me she didn't know anything, just that he'd gone off with Rodrigo, one of his friends. That first absence hit me hard, and for several days I cried endlessly and, anxious at not knowing where he was, ate large quantities of Del Valle dulce de leche sweets, one of the many snacks my father distributed.

Years later, Yolanda confessed that she'd lied to me on that and many other occasions when I asked her about Pablo's repeated absences.

'I didn't say anything because he told me it was better if you didn't know where he was going. I remember once he came back from one of those trips and asked me, "How's my doll doing?" "She's a mess, you're a real jerk, Pablo," I told him, and he made excuses: "It's not my fault, Yolanda, I have to make a living. I have to help my mother, my siblings, and down the road I want the best for her."'

Since Yolanda and his closest friends apparently had no idea where Pablo was, I had to go to his parents' house to ask. They told me they didn't have any information about his whereabouts either. In any event, it was normal for them to deny everything when I called. Even Teresita, the Escobars' housekeeper, who practically raised Pablo, was hostile toward me and always rude when she answered the phone. It was quite obvious that my boyfriend's family didn't support our relationship, as Doña Hermilda told Yolanda several times.

'That girl's a drama queen, she's not wife material,' Yolanda told me my future mother-in-law had said.

I finally got some word about Pablo a few weeks after his disappearance when one of his friends showed up one afternoon to talk to my mother.

'Doña Nora, I've got a letter from Pablo to Tata; I want to ask your permission to give it to her,' I heard the messenger say.

I noticed that he was speaking quietly, as if something was happening and they didn't want me finding out. After a long time, the man came out and handed me a white envelope that contained a sheet of paper with a handwritten paragraph. It was Pablo's handwriting. Maybe he'd heard I was falling apart and sent the letter, which read:

Victoria Eugenia, out of the deepest loneliness and nostalgia, full of sadness and convinced that you no longer remember me, I turn to your heart, which I knew to be full of tenderness and nobility, to search there for a dream that might give meaning to my life once more. If you forget me now, I would think that your affection was not sincere, that you are forgetting me because you want to, but I will not forget you because I can't. If you don't forget me now, I promise to gather up all the nobility in the world and bring it to you, and if one day my affection became a source of suffering for you, I would leave without a word, carrying with me only the beautiful memories I have of you.

I love you.
Pablo.

It made things worse, because I didn't understand what was happening. The message was beautiful and reassured me that our love was still strong, nothing more. The uncertainty came to an end just a few weeks later, when Pablo returned and I received him with open arms. I didn't ask any questions; it was enough to have him near. I noticed he looked pale, quiet, worried, and all he said was, 'My love, I was looking for work opportunities. You know I have to find a way forward so we can get married.'

He didn't say anything else. I stroked his face and hair, as if telling him, 'Rest in my arms, have faith that you're going to find success and we're going to be very happy.'

Since I didn't know at the time why Pablo had disappeared for two months without warning, I also failed to understand the implications of a comment my mother made a few days later in the same room where a year earlier my brother Mario had asked me to think things over before dating Pablo. She looked serious, upset, and asked a question I'll never forget: 'Sweetheart, are you ready to spend your life taking meals to Pablo in prison?'

'Yes, Mother, I am.'

My mother remained silent at my reply, which I gave without hesitation. It was clear she knew the reason for Pablo's unexpected absence, but she didn't say anything to me about it. I learned the truth afterwards, as occurred many times over the course of my tortuous life with Pablo. What had happened was that he'd been arrested while driving a stolen Renault 4 and been incarcerated in La Ladera Prison, in Enciso, not far from downtown Medellín. He'd been released when the evidence incriminating him disappeared.

Now that I'm recalling these events to tell my story, my late mother's words echo in my mind. I swear I don't know where my answer to her question about bringing Pablo meals in jail came from. Maybe it was naivety, inexperience, the love I felt for him. Today I see it clearly: in that moment, I let myself be carried away by my emotions. I was blind and deaf. Why did I ignore my mother's warnings, which turned out to be correct? How did I not see that a tragedy was approaching? At my young age, I wasn't able to perceive what was to come.

Immersed in my boyfriend's infidelities, I was ashamed that I lacked the strength to leave him. Gradually a language developed between us that is very likely seen in other couples in the same situation. Being with a man I loved but who was a womaniser, I came to accept that many situations are never to be spoken about. 'There are some things you can talk about and others you can't' was a rule that shaped me even before I reached adulthood. I still remember what Pablo always said: 'Don't ask, Tata, you don't know anything about all that.' That sentence marked my life for ever, though later, when times got hard, I refused to stay silent and would respond, 'I don't know or understand anything, according to you, Pablo. The only thing I understand is that we're being forced to live in hiding underground. I understand that perfectly well, because the price we have to pay to be with you is intolerable.'

My relationship with Pablo wasn't exactly a bed of roses, as many people believe. The path was full of thorns, and my parents didn't help much; every day they came up with something else to keep us apart, though the only thing they achieved was making Pablo do the impossible to get closer to me. Seeing him, meeting up with him, gazing at each other from a distance – it was less an act of defiance than it was torture for me. I felt I should leave him because of my family's disapproval, even though I loved him. The days were endless and grey, and in my long silences I wondered, 'Where is the love of my life? Will we ever be together? Will there be a place for us? Will we have a family?' I'd lost the ability to listen to my parents, something that I now regret. If only children listened more; the wisdom that parents gain with experience is invaluable. I certainly was incapable of valuing it.

At the time, one of the two television channels we received was broadcasting the Venezuelan soap opera *Esmeralda*, which I found fascinating. It made me imagine an intense romance with Pablo in which love would ultimately prevail. The show starred Lupita Ferrer as Esmeralda and José Bardina as Juan Pablo Peñalver, a couple forced to overcome all sorts of obstacles. I remember I admired the male protagonist so much, I decided to name a son after him if I ever had one.

The drama of having a boyfriend I wasn't allowed to see because of my parents' fierce opposition came to an unexpected head in March 1976, when Pablo sent word via Yolanda that he was going to be travelling for two months and was waiting for me at the El Paso ice cream parlour to say goodbye. I asked my mother to let me see him for half an hour, but she said curtly that I couldn't go out because I had homework to do and needed to be up early for school the next day.

'Mum, please, I won't see Pablo for two months.'

'Victoria, I said no!'

Sobbing, I started washing up the dinner dishes, trying to figure out how to go and meet Pablo. Suddenly a wild impulse took hold of me and I pulled my hands out of the soapy water, removed my apron, ran out of the house and arrived at the ice cream parlour to give him a furtive kiss. He looked really upset, and we had a short conversation that would transform our lives.

'Tata, what's wrong? Why can't we see each other?'

'My mother won't let me.'

'What is her problem with me? Let's leave here, darling, I want to marry you,' he said, and suggested that we travel to Pasto, a city in southern Colombia.

A short, complicitous silence was enough. I didn't go back home that night. I went off with him and we spent the night in the home of Pablo's cousin and closest associate, Gustavo Gaviria, and his wife, who promised to keep our secret since we knew there would be an uproar as soon as my absence was discovered.

Which is exactly what happened. Very early the next day, Pablo and Gustavo learned that my mother was weeping hysterically and people were out looking for us like a needle in a haystack. They also heard that not only was La Paz in an uproar, but most of the neighbours were blaming Pablo and accusing him of not doing things in the right way. In addition, my brother Mario was in a frenzy, searching for Pablo so he could give him a thrashing for having carried off 'the little girl' of the family, as he always called me.

'He's my friend, but I'm never going to forgive him for this,' Yolanda told me my brother said.

'What will the neighbours say? Whatever happens, she can't marry that man. This is the limit,' my mother told Yolanda in despair.

At mid-morning we left for Medellín's Enrique Olaya Herrera Airport to catch a flight to Cali, which was unfortunately delayed by three hours because of bad weather. We were incredibly nervous, convinced that at any moment my family was going to show up. I considered changing my mind and going back home.

'Pablo, what are we going to do? My parents are going to punish me, this is crazy. I should go back.'

'No, darling, I'm going to marry you. Don't worry, I'll never fail you, I promise,' Pablo replied, and gave me a kiss that made me melt and fall back into his arms.

I was a fifteen-year-old girl, and I can't deny that his powerful embrace gave me enough of a feeling of security that I was able to endure the long wait and the anguish I felt over the decision I was making, ignoring the lessons and values my parents had taught me. But once I'd recovered from my panic, we decided to hide in the bathrooms and peek out every once in a while. Fortunately, nobody appeared, and we were finally allowed to board the plane.

In the meantime, my frantic parents and siblings went from house to house looking for us, until Gustavo went to find my mother and told her, 'Doña Nora, I don't want any trouble with you. I'm here to tell you that Pablo stayed at my house with Tata last night and they've left for Cali.'

Alarmed, my mother immediately called her mother, Dolores, in Palmira and asked her to go to the airport – which wasn't far from the city – and to prevent me from leaving for Pasto with Pablo. At the same time, Segundo and Alfredo, two of Pablo's best friends, headed there in an SUV with the idea of catching up with us.

From the moment I fled my family home with my future husband, everything was a whirlwind. I found myself sitting on an aeroplane, without any idea of the destiny that awaited me. Pablo looked happy and worried all at once, and I felt a combination of uncertainty, anxiety and terror about the adventure we were beginning. I also thought about how I was losing my good reputation with my neighbours in La Paz and was overwhelmed by a sense of unease at not knowing whether I would ever go back to school, see my family or hang out with my friends again. The impulse to be with Pablo hadn't allowed me to think; I'd listened only to my heart. I loved him and wanted to be with him. That's all.

We arrived in Cali, and when we walked into the waiting area in the domestic terminal, we were surprised to see my grandmother Lola and my Aunts Lilia and Fanny waiting for us with worried faces. When we reached them, my grandmother hardly said hello before she grabbed my arm and said to us, 'Come here, sweetie. What's wrong with you, Pablo? What's this madness all about?'

With his usual gift of the gab, Pablo explained why we'd taken the extreme step of running away.

'Doña Lola, the situation became more and more difficult. Doña Nora is very obstinate and does everything she can to keep us apart. She wouldn't let me say goodbye to Tata even though I'm going away for two months. That's why we're here, because I want to be with her for the rest of my life.'

My grandmother seemed to understand and suggested that Pablo make his scheduled trip and work things out once he came back. But he refused.

'No, Doña Lola. We've come this far, and I'm staying until this is all resolved. I want to marry your granddaughter.'

Silent and very frightened, I listened to them go back and forth. To top things off, my Aunt Lilia's eyes were shooting daggers at me. I felt awful. My future was being decided at that moment by adults without my having a say.

But Pablo spoke so convincingly that my grandmother told us to come to Palmira and stay at her house. She was sure she could persuade the bishop to authorise our marriage. It didn't seem impossible that she'd pull it off, either; we knew she lived next to the cathedral and had won the priests' affection by visiting prisoners and doing works of charity.

Things were looking up; Pablo and I had an ally in our adventure.

Right at that moment, as we were walking toward the exit, Alfredo and Segundo appeared, a look of alarm on their faces.

'Pablo, please listen. Mario is furious and we want to help you. We've got to call Tata's family in Medellín. They're distraught and Doña Nora is irate,' Segundo said.

Realising how anxious his friends were, Pablo agreed and we all headed to a phone booth on the second floor of the airport. Alfredo spoke with my mother.

'Doña Nora, I'm here with Tata and Pablo. Don't worry, I'm going to stay with them till things are resolved. Doña Lola is with Tata, everything's going to be OK, don't worry, I promise I'll call and keep you updated.'

As we'd anticipated, things were looking very complicated, but even so we went to my grandmother's house in Palmira. I stayed there with her and my Aunt Lilia, who made her disapproval clear from the start. At bottom, I understood her behaviour. My aunt was unmarried, devout, and very concerned with upholding the law. She was so rigid that even after the marriage had been agreed to, when my mother called her and asked her to buy me a ring and a dress, my aunt refused, saying I didn't deserve anything. For their part, Pablo, Segundo and Alfredo occupied a separate area of the main house, known as 'the nook'.

The next day, at Pablo's insistence, my grandmother took us to the home of the bishop of Palmira, Monsignor Jesús Antonio Castro, a good, kind man with whom, over the next few days, we had three hour-long interviews. We met in a spacious office that he presided over in a large armchair. It was a magnanimous place where God's presence was palpable.

'Victoria Eugenia, are you ready to get married?' the bishop asked, a little confused when he learned I was just fifteen.

'Yes, sir, I want to get married,' I replied, frightened, my voice trembling, after glancing at my grandmother, Alfredo, Segundo and Pablo.

But the process wasn't going to be as fast as we thought; we had to wait for a few documents to be sent down from Medellín that were needed to legalise our union. Two weeks went by before we had the paperwork in order, whereupon the bishop granted us permission to marry.

The wedding was held at six o'clock in the afternoon on Monday, 29 March 1976, in the Santísima Trinidad church in Palmira. By coincidence, the priest who married us was the same one who'd baptised me years earlier. My parents weren't in attendance, much less my siblings. Nobody from Pablo's family was there either. Alfredo and Segundo gave us our only wedding gift: a card expressing a heartfelt sentiment. 'For the regrettable mistake you've just made,' it read, in their usual jesting tone.

I, the runaway bride, was wearing the same clothes I'd had on the day I escaped: army-green polyester trousers and an orange sweater. I think I looked pretty. He was wearing jeans and a long-sleeved light-blue shirt with the sleeves rolled up.

The temperature was in the mid-thirties for the ceremony, though I was so frightened I didn't notice the heat. My happiness was bittersweet because I was overwhelmed with fear at what would come afterwards: the disapproval of my parents, my siblings, the entire neighbourhood. I had my heart in my throat. At some point during the Mass, Pablo, who looked very happy, gazed into my eyes, smiled, and said, 'We'll be together for ever, my love.'

Despite the turbulent way things had unfolded from the moment I had fled with Pablo, my grandmother and my Aunt Fanny, who were always loving and never reproached me for tricking my parents, cooked a delicious dinner for us after the ceremony. In the airy dining room, we spent hours telling stories and recounting memories, until the magic moment came, at midnight, for us to leave. Since we were married now, my grandmother let us use 'the nook'. Kissing and hugging and wrapped in the night's spell, with a splendid moon hanging in the sky above us, Pablo and I crossed the house's romantic, flower-filled patio. It was a night of unforgettable love that remains tattooed on my skin as one of the happiest moments of my life. I wanted time to stand still, for the intimacy we were enjoying to last for ever.

AFTER WE WERE MARRIED, PABLO POSTPONED HIS TRIP TO Pasto because we had to return to Medellín. Resigned, we stayed there in a room lent to us by Alba Marina, one of Pablo's sisters who was already married and lived in a house in the La Paz neighbourhood. My mother, who made no effort to hide her deep resentment, lent us an old double bed that my father had made when he was still living in Palmira and owned the city's most renowned carpentry shop. Despite our meagre circumstances, I thought being married was the best thing that could have happened to me. My love for Pablo was vast, and I adored his laughter and his sense of humour. Our relationship was full of continual surprise and delight. I wanted to be a woman in every sense of the word, but reality reminded me that I was still a girl.

Scared to face my new reality, I refused to leave the house for two weeks. When I finally did, I found that my day-to-day life was going to be very complicated: not only did I have to deal with the disapproval of my entire family, but it was also hard to return to high school and endure people's scornful looks. The full weight of conservative, Catholic Antioquian society fell on top of me. I'd lost my reputation because I'd left the family home and impulsively wed an older man.

My married life began with me going to school in the morning and coming home in the afternoon to do homework, cook, clean, wash the dishes and mend Pablo's clothes. It was nothing exciting, but I was thrilled with my new role. What I did find difficult was that almost immediately Pablo started going away frequently, supposedly for work. What kind of work? I didn't know. What I did know was that his efforts to make a living were accompanied by the same old womanising. The gossip about his affairs was constant and, I must admit, deeply painful for me. I remember I used to cry all night, waiting for dawn to come.

I was hurt by his infidelity, but I didn't have the courage to leave him. The story I told myself to get through it was the old standby, 'Men are all the same.' Then I'd think, 'I'm not going to leave him over that.' Indeed, when we got married, because his history suggested that cheating was a possibility, I'd decided not to follow him, track his phone calls, or check his shirts for lipstick. He who seeks shall find, as the saying goes, and I preferred not to find anything.

Feeling powerless in the face of my husband's behaviour, I sought advice. Yolanda had played the role of Cupid perfectly, but given my new circumstances, I went to somebody who would serve as a shoulder to cry on, a pillar of support in the worst moments.

I'd first met her when I was eight years old, and from that moment I called her Aunt Inés, though she was no relation but a schoolteacher who was well known around La Paz and a close friend of my mother's. We didn't see each other for many years because of the war and then my forced exile, but in August 2017 I visited her at her house in Medellín. Even at eighty-eight years old, she still clearly recalled the good and bad moments she'd shared with us. Aunt Inés always loved and defended Pablo, so she was vital in helping me endure my situation back when we were first married.

The best way to get through it was for me to sleep over at her house, sharing a bed with her. That's what we'd do whenever Pablo was late, and she'd keep me company in my long hours of sleeplessness and weeping. Forty years later, when we spoke in 2017, she still remembered those nights. 'Remember, Tata, how when Pablo was late, you'd be really sad and we'd talk about how you were going to greet him, how you'd talk to him, how you had to pretend you hadn't noticed, how you were going to hide your anger?'

'Of course. He'd show up and make me slide over to the edge of the bed and say, "There's room for all three of us." And he'd be smiling, even though he was coming from another bed, another tryst!'

Scenes like that one played out over and over, but Aunt Inés always said the same thing, based on her age and her experience at the time of what it meant to endure a bad marriage. That seemed to be 'normal' back then. I remember I always used to ask her what to do, and in my naivety I'd accept her advice as the best possible course of action.

'Don't be silly, child, don't let him get away, spoil him to keep him by your side,' she would say. 'Don't lose your temper. It's your duty as a wife to wait for him and take care of him when he comes home. Divorce? No way. You have to stay – he loves you, he'll never leave you. You have to accept that this is a chauvinist culture and that marriage includes some unhappiness. It kills me to see you like this.'

I did what she said. As she recommended, I made my best effort as a woman, a lover, a wife, a mother, to keep Pablo by my side. Sometimes she'd even help me write him love letters to seduce him. Though my husband had many notches in his womanising belt, it's true that he never left me. He never even suggested we split up so he could go off with another woman, and in the final moments of his life, it was us, his family, that he turned to.

Seducing women was part of who Pablo was, a sort of challenge to himself that led him to flirt shamelessly, even sometimes to be completely disrespectful. Like one night when we went to a gala at the Inter-Continental Hotel in Medellín. I danced with the husband of one my sisters, and then with one of my brothers. Pablo got angry and refused to talk to me for the rest of the evening. Since I couldn't dance and he wouldn't sit with me, I decided to leave on my own. What choice did I have? But Pablo seized the opportunity to let loose. He invited Mónica, a pretty young blonde, to dance, and during a slow song he gave her a kiss. But he hadn't figured on one my sisters still being there, and she flew into such a rage that she slapped my husband hard across the face. The woman turned out to be the wife of one of his employees.

The next day my sister told me what had happened at the party, and I saw red. My heart shattered, I went to the betrayed husband and told him that his wife had been kissing my husband and that they'd probably spent the night at the Inter-Continental Hotel. The man was furious and immediately went home and gave his wife such a beating that she had to go to the hospital. I will never forgive myself for responding that way to my husband's shameful behavior. The situation could have ended in tragedy. I never did it again.

That day, I once more berated Pablo for what he had done, but he smoothly deployed the same claims as always: I was the love of his life, our marriage would last for ever, and I should be aware that there were lots of ill-intentioned people out there who didn't want us to be together.

After two months at Pablo's sister Alba Marina Escobar's house, we moved to a house Pablo bought in the Los Colores neighbourhood with one of the new UPAC loans created under the administration of Misael Pastrana Borrero. There we attempted to live a normal life and I continued my studies at the local high school, but Pablo soon went back to his womanising, often coming home at daybreak, or not coming home at all. It was really hard on me because I was frightened of living in such a large house in a neighbourhood with many undeveloped lots. I had to ask my mother to let my little sister, who was thirteen, come and live with me because Aunt Inés couldn't always keep me company.

A few days later, I got a huge surprise when a truck pulled up in front of the house full of huge pieces of Louis XV furniture that Pablo had bought. It was completely over the top! Those pieces were our first bedroom, living room and dining sets. When he saw them arranged around the house he was really happy, though they were clearly too big for the space. I thought they were beautiful, though I never understood Pablo's priorities. We had these massive pieces of furniture, but he never thought it necessary to buy a refrigerator, so I had to go to the supermarket every day to buy food. All in all, my sister and I enjoyed the furniture. We'd pretend to be wealthy, important women. And then we'd turn the stereo all the way up and start dancing. For me, a fifteen-year-old girl, it all seemed like a game, and Pablo made sure the fantasy made me feel like a pampered child.

My life continued in a seemingly normal manner. My sister and Aunt Inés helped alleviate my stress over Pablo's erratic behavior. School offered a kind of respite because my classes and assignments kept me distracted for a good part of the day. In addition, there was no school bus, so I used to go to school in a pale yellow and white Nissan Patrol SUV that my husband lent me almost every day.

But on 7 June 1976, the last day of the first semester, something happened that, without our realising it, would change our lives for ever. Early that morning, Pablo received a phone call and, without any explanation, rushed out in his Jeep, forcing my sister and me to take a taxi to school.

At one o'clock that afternoon, when our classes were let out, we went to my mother's house and found her distraught.

'What's wrong, Mum?'

She stared at me and her eyes grew wet. Then she took a deep breath and said, 'Honey, Pablo's been arrested along with Mario, Gustavo and three other people.'

'What? What happened?'

'They got caught with twenty-six kilos of coca paste.'

Coca paste? What's that? It was the first time I'd heard of it, but nobody could tell me any more about what had gone down. Shaken by my husband's sudden arrest and unaware of the full extent of what had happened, that night my sister and I went back home and before bed we lit several candles and prayed to Mary Help of Christians.

The days after Pablo's arrest were very hard for me. We fell behind on the mortgage, and I couldn't visit him because he and the other arrestees were still being held in DAS cells in Medellín. So I fretted. One day I received a message that Pablo had written on a paper bag. It was the first sign of life I'd received from him. 'My love, I want you to know I'm all right. Don't worry, everything's going to be OK. I've gone through darker times than this before.'

And so I had no choice but to hang my head and return, defeated, to live with my parents in La Paz. Soon after that, the bank repossessed the house because of the outstanding mortgage payments. Luckily, I was welcomed warmly, but my mother – like any mother in such a situation – started to distance herself from her incarcerated son-in-law.

'Victoria, be careful about having a child with that man, that's the last thing you need.'

'Relax, Mum, I'm not pregnant,' I replied confidently.

But she had her doubts. She gave me a box of birth control pills and made me take one in front of her every night.

Finally Pablo and the others were sent to Bellavista, a notoriously dangerous prison in Bello, in southern Medellín. The next Saturday, at four o'clock in the morning, my mother and I were ready to go and visit them. It worked well to go that early; we had no problems getting in, despite the overcrowding, foul smells and grim atmosphere.

I felt mixed emotions at seeing my husband again after all those days apart. The evidence clearly showed that he was involved in illegal activities, but I ignored it because deep down I was delighted to see him. In addition, with his customary verbal agility, he said he was innocent and summed up his situation with another sentence he would often use to avoid giving further explanations: 'Tata, some friends from Pasto called me to help them out of a jam, but it didn't work out and I got caught. Look what I got myself mixed up in trying to help a friend out.'*

---

* We soon learned what had actually happened: secret agents from the Administrative Department of Security (DAS) stopped a truck in Pasto, near the border with Ecuador, that was carrying a package of coca paste hidden inside the spare tyre. The driver called to report the situation, but he told Pablo that the detectives would let him through in exchange for US$5,000 in cash. Pablo agreed, and they arranged to meet at six o'clock in the morning on 7 June, at a food stall in Medellín's La Mayorista wholesale market. When Pablo, my brother Mario and Gustavo Gaviria showed up, they fell into a trap because the agents' plan was to arrest the entire group and confiscate the coca paste. After his arrest, Pablo was assigned the prisoner number 128482. His mug shot from the arrest became infamous because he is smiling in it.

And then he changed the subject.

Days later, I went back to visit them, but this time I was accompanied by Nohemí, Gustavo's wife, and my sister-in-law, Alba Marina Escobar. I remember it was awful getting in there; while we were waiting in line, I started vomiting because of the horrible odours. I didn't know what was happening to me, but over the following days I discovered, to my great fright, that I was expecting a child. Far from being happy, I went into a panic because of what my mother would say. I didn't tell anybody, and the next week, when I went to see Pablo again, I gave him the news along with a warning, 'Pablo, this has to stay between us. If my mother finds out, she'll kill me.'

He was delighted to learn he was going to be a father, but he was constitutionally incapable of keeping a secret. Ignoring my fears, he immediately told his mother, who had gone to visit him, and my brother, with whom he was sharing a cell. It was only a matter of hours before everybody knew, and I dreaded the reactions to come. I looked so worried, Doña Hermilda came up with a plan to avoid my mother's wrath.

'Don't worry, Tata, here's what we'll do: you tell your mother to go to my house because I need to talk to her. Then I'll tell her she's going to be a grandmother.'

I reluctantly agreed, and two days later my mother and I arrived at my mother-in-law's house. After a warm hello, we sat down in the living room and had some coffee.

'Doña Nora, just think ...' Doña Hermilda began, but my mother interrupted.

'I think, Doña Hermilda, that this little girl is pregnant.'

That stopped us in our tracks. My mother's intuition was impressive.

'You're right, Doña Nora.'

'Let's go, child,' my mother said, and stood up from her chair.

We left the Escobars' house and headed toward our own, which was two seemingly endless blocks away. I couldn't breathe, I was so worried, and the night seemed particularly cold and sad. My mother couldn't hold it in any longer: 'This is the last straw, Tata. You're completely irresponsible. I don't know when you're going to learn to listen. It's just unbelievable the pain and suffering you're going to cause me if you stay with this man.'

I sobbed disconsolately and felt deeply ashamed.

'I swear, Mum, I never imagined this was going to happen to me.'

At Pablo's insistence, I went back to my daily routine and back to school, but this time I had two reasons to be ashamed in front of my classmates and teachers: I was pregnant and my husband was in prison.

Meanwhile, the torture of visiting Bellavista didn't last much longer. Pablo arranged to be transferred to the Yarumito Prison in the town of Itagüí, a sort of country house that was so laidback that it didn't even have guards. The change was a good one, and my mother-in-law was able to visit every day to take them breakfast and lunch.

But Pablo couldn't sit still, and two weeks later I got a call from the prison telling me he'd escaped. They claimed he'd disappeared during a football game with the help of some of the other players, whom he'd asked to kick the ball really hard and far away so he could go after it. They had, and on one of those occasions, he'd failed to return to the football pitch.

The worst part was finding out that Pablo had only escaped to seek shelter in the arms of Noemí, the widow of a friend who'd died a couple of months back, and with whom he'd been having an affair since we first started dating. I couldn't believe it. He was completely shameless. She was thirty years old and he was twenty-six. It made my soul ache to find out about that infidelity, and for days I wanted nothing to do with him. I felt helpless; I'd given him my purest love and he'd cheated on me with a woman twice my age. I admit I was afraid of losing him because she was very mature, with a lot of experience, and I thought he'd be reluctant to give up that relationship. And once again I asked myself, 'How can I leave? How can I stay?' I was outraged by his lack of respect for me, but I couldn't see a way out. All I could do was lean on my parents and siblings for support, because deep down I didn't want to leave him.

More than twelve hours later, Pablo reappeared at the prison as if nothing had happened. He showed up after his mother, Doña Hermilda, had scolded him over the phone, telling him to stop making me suffer and call me. When he did, I managed to convince him that he'd made a mistake and asked him to go back to the prison for the sake of the baby that was now on its way. As a result of that brief escapade, he was transferred to the Itagüí prison, which was a little larger and had stricter security measures.

When things had calmed down again, we went to visit him and I chided him for his actions, but he simply replied that he hadn't found anywhere else to hide. But somebody told me later that my husband's lover had a lot of money and that he'd planned to ask her for a loan. I have to admit that Pablo was a snake charmer, a professional swindler who deftly used flowery language, and so he managed to convince me that his relationship with Noemí had been only a meaningless fling. In the end I succumbed to his nuzzles, his passionate kisses and his caresses, which washed over me like ocean waves. Our love story ended up continuing despite the betrayal.

The turmoil was constant with Pablo. One day I got out of school and went to have lunch at my mother's house, but I found her agitated, sad and worried because she'd heard that soon Pablo, Gustavo and Mario were to be transported to a prison in Pasto, near the border with Ecuador. Without thinking twice, I told her I was going to Itagüí to try to say goodbye. She agreed and gave me a small bag with some shirts and trousers and a bit of money to take to them. I didn't have time to change my clothes, so I went still in my school uniform. When I reached the prison door, I found a line of soldiers forming a security barrier. I approached and asked one of them to let me in so that I could deliver the package. Unfortunately, right at that moment the bag broke and several items of clothing and the money fell out, which caused a bit of a commotion since the three prisoners were just coming out. Everything happened really fast, and I grew afraid when one of the soldiers prodded me with his rifle as I bent down to pick up the things that had fallen. I only caught a glimpse of Pablo aboard the SUV that would take him to Olaya Herrera

Airport. Since I'd gone there in my mother's car, I followed them and managed to position myself on one of the balconies of the airport terminal. Finally, Pablo walked up the stairs to the plane and from a distance, his hands cuffed, was able to say goodbye.

It was awful. Even today it's painful to recall the events of that day. I felt powerless, desolate, without a husband, without a place to live, without a compass. I was fifteen years old and two months' pregnant. I was very sensitive. I went back to my parents' house with my heart in tatters and crying inconsolably.

A few days later I decided to go to Pasto to visit Pablo. It was a long trip by air and land. My mother-in-law offered to go with me, and for that first visit we left at midday on a Friday after school finished; we went by plane from Medellín to Cali and from there by overnight bus to Pasto, where we arrived early on Saturday. I was tired and overwhelmed with morning sickness. We went to the market to buy the things Pablo liked and prepared a lunch to take to him. Then we ate with him inside the prison. We carried on a conversation that was brief but painful and sad. We didn't know how long he'd be incarcerated, so I felt only a vast uncertainty. Pablo must have noticed my distress and made a futile effort to placate me.

'Don't worry, Tata, this nightmare will be over soon. Don't freak out,' he said calmly, with the same attitude he always had, even when he was in hot water up to his neck.

In the afternoon, when the visit ended, I cried at having to leave him and return to Medellín, and at the hard trip that awaited me.

Over the next few weeks I repeated the routine, some-times accompanied by Doña Hermilda. I loved going to see him, but it was hard on me because I was pregnant and the visits were taxing: standing in line for hours, exhausted, nauseated, surrounded by foul smells and vomit. There were 500 of us trying to visit the prisoners, and the search we endured before entering was humiliating. To top it all off, Doña Hermilda wasn't very nice to me and was always rather hostile, making rude comments and saying things with double meanings. Complete torture. She made it clear what she thought about me: I wasn't the woman for her son.

The strain of going to Pasto so often, combined with the anxiety and fatigue, eventually took its toll on me, and one day the gynaecologist forbade me from travelling because I'd lost nearly a stone since getting pregnant and the baby's life was at great risk. I told Pablo, but he didn't understand the seriousness of what was happening to me.

'You don't want to visit me, you're not putting in the effort,' he said plaintively in the courtyard of the prison where we were walking.

Despite the doctor's warning, I kept going to Pasto, though the conditions did improve dramatically when Pablo managed to persuade them to allow him to leave the prison on the weekends so we could stay at the Morasurco, Pasto's finest hotel, in a suite with two bedrooms, a living room, a dining room and a kitchenette. He and I would occupy one room while my mother-in-law or whoever had accompanied me would occupy the other. In those fleeting moments, I felt fulfilled. It was pure romance. I remember that on one of those weekends I was turning sixteen, and I celebrated my birthday in the hotel with Pablo. I was deeply touched when he dedicated the song 'Muñequita negra', performed by the Mexican singer José Alfredo Jiménez, to me. The lyrics were beautiful, and Pablo was humming along: 'Sleep with me, sleep in my arms that long for you because they are your shelter / Close your eyes, hush your mouth, and all curled up like I said sleep soundly. / Forget that the world will be cruel to you and believe instead that never in your life will you have to suffer.'

Finally, in November 1976, five months after his arrest, we were delighted when Pablo was finally released, cleared, he said, of all charges.

'Now we really can start a new life, darling, I'll be the best husband and a great father, I promise,' he said when he returned to La Paz from Pasto.

Nevertheless, things were still very uncertain: my doctor ordered that I go on complete bed rest because I was very weak and the baby might die if it was born right then. So we decided to move to my parents' house, where they gave us the master bedroom. I was in bed for the next month and a half, attended by my one-in-a-million mother, who took good care of me, though she took no pains to hide her dislike for Pablo. She was so mistrustful of him that one day she asked if he'd threatened me, unable to understand why I refused to leave him. My answer was simple: 'Mother, I'm with him because I love him.'

Still, living at his in-laws' house with his pregnant wife wasn't an option for Pablo, who was noticeably uncomfortable, though he maintained a cordial relationship with my father, mother and siblings. The situation was resolved two months later, in January 1977, when he rented a tiny apartment in the La Candelaria neighbourhood, near the park in El Poblado. We moved one weekend, and of course the Louis XV had to come with us; it was an absolute nightmare trying to find places for them. The only way was to put the dining set in the living area and the living room set in one of the bedrooms, where it blocked access to the closet. Paradoxically, though we lived in a rented apartment with many limitations, Pablo had a brand-new, burgundy Porsche with a tan leather interior in the garage. How had he acquired such an expensive car? Was it his? I had many such questions, but I knew it was best not to ask. Those kinds of contradictions were endemic with my husband, who just twenty days before I gave birth bought the refrigerator we so desperately needed.

I should note that at the end of my pregnancy Pablo was very attentive to every detail. I think he appreciated that I'd been very good to him when he was in jail and that my health had deteriorated because of the sacrifices I'd made to visit him in Pasto. In the run-up to the birth, we enjoyed a few weeks of calm and quiet.

Then came 24 February 1977, and the birth of my first child. I was in my fourth year of secondary school, and I went to school that day because I had maths class and an English test with a fearsome teacher. When I got up that morning, I felt definite signs that the baby was on its way, but I didn't want to miss the test and get a zero. I was so thoughtless! It shows how immature I was, that I wasn't able to make my own health a priority.

Somehow, I got a 6 on my English test, just enough to pass. When the teacher – we called him 'Molars' because he had huge teeth that seemed to stick out of his mouth when he talked – gave me my grade, I struggled to my feet.

'Teacher,' I said, my voice cracking with the continual contractions, 'I have to go. My water broke.'

'You can't ask for a pass yet, Victoria,' he replied as if failing to understand what I'd told him.

My twenty-five classmates started to object loudly and made the teacher see that there was a puddle next to my desk. One girl offered to go to the office to ask them to let me leave because I was about to give birth. Finally I was given permission and walked two blocks to my mother's house, but I had to stop every ten seconds because of the agonising pain of the contractions. When I arrived, my parents and siblings were waiting along with my grand-mother, who'd come up from Palmira to welcome her great-grandchild. We headed to the El Rosario Hospital in downtown Medellín, but first I asked if we could collect Pablo from the La Candelaria apartment. It all happened very quickly; half an hour after we arrived, the baby was born, and by one in the afternoon I was already calling my school friends to give them the news and tell them to come visit me and my new son, Juan Pablo.

I was discharged two days later and we returned to the apartment in La Candelaria. From the start, I told Pablo I was determined to finish high school because I had just two years left till graduation. I went back to school three weeks later since my mother would take care of the baby while I was studying.

In the meantime, Pablo would go out on his motorcycle with his friends and bring me roses, and on the weekends he'd spend time with Juan Pablo, talking to him, singing him songs, affectionately calling him Juancho or Grégory,* and taking him for drives in a convertible.

But nothing's perfect in life, and Pablo also tended to disappear a lot, claiming he was going to work. Of course, his 'work' included spending a lot of time with women, both day and night, but he did make an effort to be there for our day-to-day domestic life.

ALMOST IMPERCEPTIBLY, OUR LIVES BEGAN TO CHANGE because of the gradual improvement of the economic situation of Pablo and his cousin Gustavo. At some point I noticed that my husband's fortune was growing and poverty was fading into the past. In early 1978 he paid 3 million pesos – US$76,000 at the time – for a house in the Provenza neighbourhood, an up-and-coming area above Calle 10, in the heart of El Poblado. The place had a pool, several bedrooms, a garage, and a huge hall with enormous stained-glass windows. That's where our beloved Louis XV furniture ended up, and since there was a lot more room, I arranged them as best I could.

---

* Pablo called his son Grégory because they used to watch movies about the Russian czars together; my husband was fascinated with Grigori Yefimovich Rasputin, a Russian mystic who had a huge amount of influence at the end of the Romanov dynasty. Pablo used that same nickname when he sent letters to his son while in hiding.

Once we'd moved to our new home, Pablo set up an office in the first bedroom, by the front door, where he and Gustavo started to receive visits from all sorts of people. Assuming they were involved with his 'business', I stayed away from that area. My brother Mario must have foreseen that those 'visitors' were going to cause us problems, so he suggested to Pablo that he move the office somewhere else, arguing it was a bad idea to mix business with one's personal life. My husband agreed, and three months later they moved to an old house on Calle 9, an ugly, tacky place they referred to as Los Tamales de Aliria.

I'm not going to get into how Pablo became a millionaire here because I will address that subject elsewhere, but I do want to emphasise how the size of his fortune was always matched by his drive to be surrounded by women. He was with some for fun, because they offered him pleasure and companionship; others he seduced just to further his business interests; and he carried out intense romances with others because they were strategic keys to accessing state secrets. But I can firmly declare that none of them posed any danger to our marriage.

Starting in 1978 and over the next ten years, Pablo became fabulously wealthy, and his economic power allowed him to venture into the world of automobile racing and participate in the Renault Cup series of 1979 and 1980. Later, he started a variety of social programmes to help the most under-served classes and encouraged sports by building dozens of football fields. Besides creating the empire known as Hacienda Nápoles in Antioquia's Magdalena Medio region, he couldn't resist sticking an oar into politics too, where he dreamed of going very far – and actually did, at least until it all blew up in his face. In all of these endeavours, inevitably, my husband was always in the company of women.

Pablo's business ventures prospered noticeably, but I was completely unaware of where the money was coming from. I was still a naive teenage girl in a sexist social context where a woman's role was merely to look after the children and the home, not to have opinions about what the man of the house was or was not doing to provide for the family. The bonanza allowed me to finish my education, travel to many places in Colombia and around the world, and attend the best interior design and fashion shows in Italy and France, since my dream, which alas I have never realised, was to be a well-known and well-respected professional.

From the start, I believed that Pablo was involved in smuggling, and I didn't consider it a bad thing; it was a common activity among residents of the neighbourhood who were trying to eke out a living. Even my mother used to travel to the town of Maicao, on the border with Venezuela, and bring back perfume, fabrics and other goods to sell in her shop. That had always been a lucrative business that skirted the margins of the law, but it was accepted because the authorities never cracked down on it. Even today smuggling doesn't have the same connotations as drug trafficking. Pablo never told me seriously, openly, that he was involved in trafficking narcotics. And I don't actually know when he switched.

Pablo never wanted me to be in his workforce. I wasn't made for that kind of role. It was a strict, unbending

Several months after our wedding, in 1976, we were able to go on our honeymoon in the San Andrés Islands.

In 1976, Pablo was in prison in Pasto, a city near the Ecuadorian border. I was pregnant at the time and went to visit him on weekends, when we would stay at the Hotel Morasurco.

I was still in high school when I became pregnant with Juan Pablo. I was sixteen years old.

At high school in La Paz. I was thirteen years old and already dating Pablo.

Despite the difficult conditions, Pablo and I had a good relationship while he was in prison in Pasto. I don't know how he did it, but he managed to get released at the weekends to be with me.

View of Hacienda Nápoles soon after construction had begun. The first building to go up was La Mayoría, as Pablo named the main house.

Hacienda Nápoles and the zoo were dreams come true for Pablo. He used to spend hours watching the exotic birds and animals.

My husband bought six giraffes for his zoo at Hacienda Nápoles. But it was the only species that never adapted to that habitat; all of them ended up dying.

The Chilean comedian Lucho Navarro, during Juan Pablo's birthday celebration at Hacienda Nápoles.

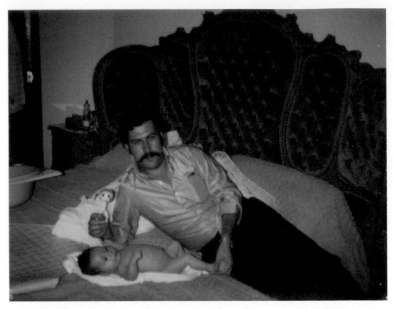

Pablo with a newborn Juan Pablo, on the bed from the set of Louis XV furniture that he bought after our wedding.

At a car race in Medellín when I was twenty. Pablo taught me to drive and encouraged me to race.

At Bogotá's International Autodrome, Pablo raced in the famous Renault Cup. I used to travel to races with him on the weekends.

I kept one of my first art purchases on display in the living room of our house in El Diamante; it was a triptych by Luis Caballero.

Pablo was very active in his role on the Envigado town council. From there, he went on to run for a seat in the House of Representatives.

In 1982 I accompanied Pablo to a number of political events associated with his run for the legislature. This photo was taken just after he'd given a speech in Envigado.

It was exciting to see Pablo in his role as a patron of athletic facilities.

Pablo insisted that I graduate from high school after the birth of Juan Pablo. We celebrated at my mother's house in La Paz.

Sitting in the chamber where the House of Representatives meets was a thrilling experience. On my left is the singer Rafael Urraza.

As a couple. Fleeting moments that
I tried to enjoy to the fullest.

Pablo in a motocross race in Puerto Triunfo, in the Magdalena
Medio region.

Wanting to provide houses for the people who lived in the Moravia landfill, Pablo purchased a plot of land and built three hundred dwellings in the initial phase.

Pablo gave the welcome speech at the Starry Paintbrush auction I organised as a fund-raiser for Medellín Without Slums, at the Hotel Inter-Continental in 1982.

1 December 1979: for Pablo's thirtieth birthday, I gave him this vintage car.

In 1980, on one of our trips to the United States, we went to a theme park in Miami.

I was once invited to Bogotá to attend an exhibition by the master artist Fernando Botero. There we exchanged a few words with then President Belisario Betancur.

In 1982, soon after Pablo's election to the House of Representatives, we traveled to Brazil with around twenty members of our family.

In the penthouse at the Mónaco building. I was twenty-four years old.

In 1987, after Juan Pablo's First Communion at the Colegio San José, we went to the hideout known as El Paraíso. This photo was taken there with Pablo, my mother-in-law, Hermilda, and my father, Carlos.

The living room of the penthouse at the Ovni building. Juan Pablo and my younger sister. On display were several of the most important works in my art collection.

Auguste Rodin's sculpture *The Lovers* occupied a very special place in the Mónaco building.

The master bedroom in our house in Medellín's El Diamante neighborhood. I was twenty-one years old. Los Pepes ransacked it and burned it down in 1993.

In the sitting room on the second floor of the penthouse in the Mónaco building, I displayed my valuable collection of pre-Columbian art.

division of roles: on the one hand were him and his business dealings, and on the other, all of us, his family. In those first years, I never thought that his activities were particularly dangerous or wrong; they simply weren't a topic of conversation, whether out of indifference or ignorance. In my world people didn't talk about drugs, definitely not cocaine, and much less the Medellín Cartel. Smitten as I was with Pablo, I was unable to see what the future might hold.

As I was saying, 1978 marked the start of Pablo's meteoric economic rise, and out of nowhere he became a highly visible figure. The first thing Pablo and Gustavo did was get involved in motocross competitions, participating in several races on the Furesa track near SOFASA, the Renault assembly plant in Envigado. For several months he used his powerful 200cc IT motorcycle, but he'd soon discover another, more exciting adventure: car racing. That hobby became a passion that lasted almost two years. Back then there were informal races on the outskirts of Medellín, like on the new Vía Las Palmas highway or the ascent up to Santa Elena, where drivers sought to set records, especially in races against the clock. Pablo would drive his powerful Porsche, and it was obvious that he was drawn to extreme speeds.

As usual, one thing led to another, and Pablo and Gustavo's interest in racing didn't stop there. That year, for the first time, the organisers of the prestigious Renault Cup – held every Sunday in the international autodrome in Bogotá and sometimes in Cali and Medellín – allowed rookie drivers to enter the races. Pablo and Gustavo, but especially Pablo, went all out: they acquired a fleet of Renault 4 cars; they rented the top floor of the Hilton, in downtown Bogotá, for all of 1979; and for most of that year they would arrive in Bogotá on Saturday by helicopter, stay in the Hilton, compete on Sunday, and return to Medellín on Monday morning. We sometimes travelled there together by helicopter or plane, but it was much more common for the two of them to be in Bogotá on their own.

That was all well and good, but of course things had to include the usual ingredient: women. They used to show up to watch the two young men who were competing in one of the Renault Cup categories. One of them was a singer on the musical TV programme *El show de Jimmy*, and her friendship with Pablo meant that on the weekends when we didn't go to Bogotá, they'd organise hours-long parties in the Hilton attended by dozens of women.

The participants also had reinforcements. For instance, Héctor Roldán, owner of the Roldanautos team, which won the rookie championship in November 1979 with the driver Álvaro Mejía. As I learned much later, Pablo and Roldán, who were old acquaintances, gave free rein to their insatiable lust for women and hosted memorable bashes in the Hilton.

They remained close for a long time; indeed, in 1984, when I was pregnant with Manuela, my husband had the gall to suggest that his friend be our daughter's godfather. The idea infuriated me: 'Pablo, as long as I live, Héctor Roldán will never be my daughter's godfather. In case you don't know, a child's godparents have responsibilities in case the parents are ever not around. And you choose

Héctor because he brings you aeroplanes full of women. It's completely disrespectful.'

Pablo reluctantly backed down, and we chose another of his friends, Juan Yepes, his teammate in the Renault Cup. He was already known as John Lada because he was the first person to import Lada SUVs from Russia to Colombia.

At the start of the 1980s, Pablo Escobar was an immensely wealthy man and he was beginning to become powerful. Almost imperceptibly, that mix of money and power pushed us into a whirlwind that made it impossible for us to perceive the misfortune that was approaching.

Many of the facts I recount here I learned only recently, when I traveled to Colombia to do research for this book and talk to people who were close to us back then. And I got multiple surprises, such as when I discovered that Aunt Inés had hidden numerous examples of Pablo's cheating to protect my feelings. I also found out that he ordered his men, sometimes under threat, that they'd better not tell me anything about his affairs.

Now that I'm talking about people's complicity and silence in protecting Pablo's betrayals, I bitterly recall the role played by Alba Marina, his sister, who was in charge of organising his parties, looking after his lovers and buying them gifts. I was indignant to discover that she had been helping him out, but I was even more devastated by what happened in Residencias Tequendama four days after Pablo's death, when the Escobars came to visit us. At one point, Alba Marina paused and said, 'Victoria, I want you to know something: I always told Pablo's girlfriends that he adored you above and beyond any fling.'

What a sweetheart, my sister-in-law. I never would have thought she'd have the brass to look me in the eyes and say something so insolent. But that wasn't all. Despite my grief and forgetting my status as wife and mother, my in-laws started bringing up all kinds of dalliances that I hadn't known about. Their discussion was so appalling that Doña Hermilda actually stepped in: 'Show some respect to Tata. That's enough.'

A deathly silence fell, and the visit ended a few minutes later.

In those early years, though, the flood of money brought along with it an immediate change of status that was apparent on 27 February 1979, when Pablo bought a beautiful house in the El Diamante neighbourhood of El Poblado, which cost 4 million pesos.* It was my dream house: a spacious, elegant two-storey structure on nearly half an acre of land. In the centre was a pool of water with a fountain that contained a sculpture called *The Kiss*. Raúl Fajardo, a prominent architect of the period and the owner of the property, told Pablo that the artwork wasn't included in the deal, but I told my husband not to buy the house if they kept it. *The Kiss* stayed.

Hacienda Nápoles came into the picture when Pablo and Gustavo, who had established a solid family and business relationship, hit the big time. My husband's dream of having a large piece of acreage sliced by rivers and

---

* We left the El Diamante house to one of my sisters years later – along with various paintings and sculptures that I'd acquired – and she lived there until early 1993, when Los Pepes burned it down and she was forced to flee Medellín.

mountains became a reality when they found appropriate properties in Antioquia's Magdalena Medio region, right beside the future Medellín–Bogotá highway.

Nápoles became the epicentre of Pablo's new life. For good and for ill. And there's more. From the very start he set out – and managed – to lead a sort of double life on the estate: one with his family and another with his buddies and his mistresses of the moment. Of course, in addition he also had his business, which he always kept away from me. Though we, his family, had a space there, the other women secretly dominated the estate. To meet with their lovers, Pablo and Gustavo had the nerve to build an apartment that they camouflaged behind the stables, very close to the main house; they also built several cabins in more remote areas, which they used to escape to even when we were there.

There's no denying that Pablo did his own thing at Nápoles. Like the weekend when Héctor Roldán showed up in his aeroplane with a dozen gorgeous women. I'm sure they weren't expecting that I would be there and make a huge stink about it.

'I don't want to stay here one more minute, Pablo. What you're doing is completely disrespectful.'

But he, as always, had an excuse ready: 'Honey, Héctor brought these girls so the boys could have a little fun. It has nothing to do with me. Those women are for my friends, and I can't tell them not to bring them.'

I didn't say anything, but it was obvious he was lying. If I hadn't been there at that moment, they would have thrown a huge party.

My husband's shameless behaviour pushed me to the brink when we went to a farm near Doradal to visit some friends. Sometime after eight o'clock, the power went out and we sat chatting by candlelight in the living room. I was so engaged in the conversation that I didn't notice Pablo had disappeared. The electricity came back on a couple of hours later, and the lively gathering continued. I didn't realise at the time that the blackout had been planned and that Pablo had asked the host to flip the breakers because one of his lovers was waiting for him in one of the bedrooms.

Money made Pablo's life start to spin faster and faster. He'd been surrounded with women when he didn't have a cent in his pockets, and now that the world was his oyster, his quest for entertainment, partying, and women became frenetic.

As his fortune grew, it became necessary to hire bodyguards: first Pinina and then Chopo, La Yuca and Pasquín, who became our shadows. With time, dozens were recruited to make up the powerful army of young men – from the most impoverished areas of Medellín – who would risk their lives for my husband.

At around that time we also met Ferney, a mysterious man from I don't know where who became something like Pablo's private secretary. He was a miracle worker, always resolving every difficulty, but I later learned that among his many other duties he was also responsible for looking after Pablo's lovers: he bought them expensive gifts – sometimes even importing them from abroad – organised serenades for them, sent them flowers, accompanied them to the beauty parlour, gave them money and entertained them while they were waiting for his boss.

I also began to notice the presence of another figure around my husband: Jerónimo, a handsome lad of seventeen who lived in La Estrella. I trusted him because Pablo used to tell me what good company Jerónimo was and said that was why he took him everywhere. Much later I found out that in fact he was in charge of finding women for my husband, and the two men were so close that sometimes they even shared the women in the same bed.

They'd met one night at the La Turquesa ice cream parlour when my husband went to visit Luz Ángela, a gorgeous green-eyed blonde, possibly the most beautiful women in town. It wasn't the first time Pablo had gone there, and this time he showed up in a convoy of three cars with a dozen men surrounding him. Pablo had the bar shut down and paid all the customers' tabs just to impress Luz Ángela.

Seducing her became a sort of challenge for my husband, who started going to La Estrella several times a week, almost always after midnight. She played hard to get, which drove him crazy, to the point that one Saturday he ordered Ferney to go to the main park in Envigado and hire every musician he found and bring them to La Turquesa, where Pablo was meeting Luz Ángela. After a long wait, Ferney showed up with a bus full of musicians, who all took turns playing boleros, rancheras and vallenatos until four o'clock in the morning. Then everybody went out to nurse their hangovers in a restaurant in the neighbouring town of Caldas, where Pablo again paid all the customers' tabs. The image he was seeking to project, as a rich, powerful man who liked to have a good time, must have worked: Luz Ángela fell for him, though not for long, since the romance lasted only a couple of months, and though Pablo had been really into her, he went straight out to find another woman to replace her.

Wanting to up his game from womanising out on the town, Pablo decided he needed a bachelor pad. He bought a luxurious penthouse for the purpose, in a building on Avenida Colombia in Medellín with ice-skating rinks and bowling lanes on the first floor. That first hideaway would be known among Pablo and his men by the code name 'Frost', and it was just a hundred yards away from the main entrance to the headquarters of the army's Fourth Brigade. Since at the time there was no warrant out for Pablo's arrest, the soldiers let him through when the adjacent streets were blocked by military checkpoints. He was seen as just another resident of the neighbourhood who used to take beautiful women home to his apartment.

So Pablo's partying became a daily occurrence, and he was seen as a king in the places he frequented because of the way he haemorrhaged money. He eventually became the most popular patron of the Génesis and Acuarius nightclubs, trendy hotspots at the time. Whenever he arrived, he'd be seated at a table that provided a panoramic view of the establishment, and if he spotted a beautiful woman, he'd tell Jerónimo or Ferney to bring her to his table to he could say hello and chat her up. After a short conversation, his target would go back to her table and Pablo would send over a bottle of champagne or whisky, knowing that the girl would come back later to thank him for the gift. Once that happened, everything was set. Pablo's next move would be to put his arm around her, leave with her and then invite her back to his apartment.

In that period of his new life as a rich man, Pablo was a show-off and liked to be noticed. Once as they were leaving a club, he was driving his powerful Renault 18 and made his bodyguards chase him. It turned into a sort of cat-and-mouse game as my husband tore down Medellín's dark, empty streets, driving up on the pavements, going the wrong way around the roundabouts and committing all sorts of infractions. He would do it to impress whatever woman he happened to be with at the time. Then, when he figured he'd been sufficiently impressive, he'd head to Frost.

It was also common for Pablo on his nights out to be surrounded by all kinds of women, who'd get to party for free because he was covering their tabs. Hours later, some of them, the most beautiful, voluptuous ones, would be invited back to his apartment. Of course, there always had to be musicians, and he'd frequently hire classical quartets, mariachis and guitarists. The penthouse my husband had bought had never seen such a swarm of activity, and the parties generally went on till four or five in the morning.

Jerónimo once told me that Pablo wasn't a big drinker, though he did love Alexander cocktails, a concoction of gin, sweet cream and crème de cacao, and his bartender Eduardo, the only person who was always at the apartment, made a delicious version.

When a party was at its most raucous, Pablo would request a song he loved, 'Eye of the Tiger', the hit song commissioned by Sylvester Stallone as the soundtrack to the movie *Rocky III*, the famous cinematographic saga of the boxer Rocky Balboa. Whenever the song came on the apartment's powerful stereo system, Pablo would leap up and start dancing.

In that intimate atmosphere ripe for romance, it was inevitable that Pablo would end up seducing some young woman. Though he wasn't the most attractive guy, he had a gift with the ladies because he was charismatic and charming. And he had a lot of money. At that point, he'd dismiss his bodyguards and other guests and stay in the apartment with his new lover, Jerónimo – who would almost always bring along a girl from his neighbourhood or Pablo would find him one – and Eduardo, the bartender. But that wasn't all, of course; there's always more to these stories. In an utterly shameless act, Pablo had ordered that hidden cameras be installed in all of the bedrooms and bathrooms to film his female guests in their private moments. There was also a secret room from which he could watch everything that happened in the apartment. Once he and Jerónimo were alone in the apartment, they'd watch the recordings together.

Since he was partying every day, Pablo sometimes opted to travel to Guayaquil, one of the most dangerous lower-class areas of downtown Medellín, usually accompanied by Gustavo. They would walk through the streets and then go into a little bar to drink and listen to music, mainly tango. After his second beer, Pablo would ask to hear his favourites: 'Sangre Maleva' performed by Alfredo de Angelis's orchestra; 'Cambalache' by Carlos Gardel; 'El Sueño del

Pibe' by Osvaldo Pugliese; and 'En Casa de Irene', a classic by Gian Franco Pagliaro. Pablo and Gustavo loved tango songs because the lyrics reflected the hardships they'd experienced in their youth because of their families' difficult economic circumstances.

Despite his wild partying during that period, my husband would come back home with a copy of *El Colombiano* newspaper under his arm and go to bed only after reading the headlines and the main articles. Jerónimo told me he was obsessive about always going back home to sleep – because he had a home to go to. That's why he never stayed at Frost later than five o'clock in the morning and would leave even if the party was still going on. On Pablo's orders, Jerónimo or the bartender would stay there until the apartment had emptied out.

DURING THAT PERIOD OF NIGHTCLUBS AND CAROUSAL, I now know that Pablo had numerous girlfriends with whom he enjoyed a week or two, even a month or two, but never took them seriously.

All of that would change one night in mid-1981, when he met Wendy Chavarriaga Gil.

According to what Jerónimo told me years later, a very wealthy man and compulsive card player known in Medellín's underworld as El Tío asked Pablo to meet with a young woman who'd come in from the United States and was proposing a good business idea. My husband agreed and told El Tío he'd wait for her in the bowling alley on the bottom floor of the building where he had his bachelor pad.

Pablo wasn't expecting his guest to show up with another woman in tow, a dark-haired twenty-eight-year-old, six feet tall with green eyes and a gorgeous body. That was Wendy. The meeting lasted just twenty-five minutes and the two women left after discussing the business at hand. Of course, Pablo wasn't one to waste an opportunity, and when Wendy excused herself to go to the bathroom, he went to spy on her through the one-way mirrors. Pablo was stunned by Wendy's beauty and the way she carried herself, and he immediately called El Tío and asked him to set up a date with her. No sooner said than done, and a few days later they met up again. There followed a relationship that really was serious, one that blew Pablo away and lasted several years, but that would eventually end in tragedy.

From the start, Wendy was different from the other women who'd been with my husband. In general, they were young women from the lower middle class who were looking to improve their economic situation. In contrast, my husband's new conquest was wealthy, with a luxurious apartment in one of the best spots in El Poblado. Pablo was so aware of it that one day early on in his relationship with Wendy, he told Jerónimo, 'I'm a champion.' She was the first woman he didn't have to give anything – no car or apartment or money. She had it all, though to speed his conquest along he gave her a Renault 18 anyway.

Pablo was so smitten with Wendy that he used to go to see her almost every day in Altos de San Lucas, where she lived alone, and would leave at four or five in the morning. His bodyguards, who had to wait down in the street till he came out, found this routine extremely boring.

The height of my husband's brazen behaviour was that his lover lived just two blocks from our house, near the Club Campestre in Medellín, but he led his double life so skillfully that I didn't figure it out for a long time. I remember he used to come back every evening at seven o'clock and we'd sit down for dinner with Juan Pablo, who must have been around four years old at the time. It was a sort of ritual to share that time as a family. After the meal, Pablo would go to our son's room to play with the sophisticated toys he'd given him – aeroplanes, racing cars and helicopters, almost all of them imported from abroad. He'd explain what they were for and how they worked, and since we were travelling to Nápoles by helicopter back then, it was clear that Juan Pablo was starting to understand.

But that peaceful scene would be interrupted by Pablo, who'd invariably say he had to go because he had important meetings at his office or somewhere in Medellín. Juan Pablo would cry whenever his father started to leave, but Pablo would soothe him with the promise that he'd be back soon. For my part, I was very sad that I couldn't share an evening with my husband, watch a movie, talk ... It gave me an empty feeling that accompanied me for years.

'Ma'am,' said Jerónimo, a direct accomplice in my husband's womanising, 'I think that was the only time we ever doubted his authority. It was hard for us to see how you remained ignorant of his betrayals, but we couldn't say anything because he'd forbidden it.'

The people around Pablo prevented me from finding out what he was up to for some time, but despite his skill at hiding his double life from me, I ended up learning about his cheating on multiple occasions. My woman's sixth sense was triggered one time when I went to visit him unannounced at his office at *Antioquia al Día*, his newly launched news programme, in the Los Balsos area of El Poblado. When I arrived, I was struck by the elegance of the whole place, especially my husband's office, which had clearly been decorated by someone with excellent taste. My intuition told me that one of Pablo's girlfriends must have been involved. I wasn't wrong, though as usual I confirmed it only much later.

At that time, my husband had begun his political career and was campaigning to be elected to Congress. He'd been told that an effective way of achieving that goal was to have his own news outlet, which is why he started *Antioquia al Día*, a news programme that aired every afternoon in a slot rented on the TV channel Telemedellín.

Intrigued, I started trying to figure out who had done the decor and who owned the building that housed the *Antioquia al Día* offices, and I became all the more suspicious at the evasive answers I got. Eventually, by asking questions and putting things together, I learned that the building belonged to a woman known as Wendy Chavarriaga, whom Pablo paid rent, which she in turn handed over to her nieces and nephews. But I wasn't able verify that they were having an affair.

My suspicions continued and were finally confirmed when a beautiful woman began appearing very close to my candidate husband at the public rallies for Liberal Alternative – the movement backing Pablo in his quest to reach the House of Representatives – in Medellín and the other communities in the Aburrá Valley. Tall, dark-haired, with green eyes – it was Wendy Chavarriaga.

One of my sisters, who knew about the relationship but hadn't said anything to avoid hurting me, was involved in an incident with Wendy during a rally in Envigado's main square. It occurred one Saturday afternoon when Pablo and congressman Jairo Ortega were giving a speech from the balcony of a house. I was there, but I must have been distracted just then because I didn't notice a thing. My sister saw that Wendy and her sister were behind Pablo, clapping enthusiastically when the attendees applauded for my husband. In a furious whisper, my sister said to her, 'This is my sister's place. If you don't leave here right now, I'll throw you off the balcony.' Wendy didn't say a word, and left. Of course my sister didn't actually intend to harm her, but she was upset that her brother-in-law was showboating with a lover while his wife looked on.

In the end, I learned the full truth about Wendy and Pablo when somebody gave me the details about the intense affair they were carrying on. The thing that hurt me most was knowing that my husband seemed to have fallen for her hard. Unable to bear it any longer, I gave him a piece of my mind.

'Pablo, you're young and have the right to be happy; you go ahead with your life and whatever relationship you choose. I'll be the mother of your children, but not your wife. Don't worry about me – there's only one Victoria Eugenia Henao on the planet. You just choose and I'll understand. You have free rein, you don't have to stay, it's not necessary, Pablo.'

Despite my enormous pain and indignation, I never let myself look weak in front of him, and on several occasions I asked him, 'Have you ever seen anybody die of love, Pablo?'

I was determined to force him to make a decision, but I should emphasise that, though he was an irredeemable cheater, he never assaulted me either physically or verbally and we were always able to communicate despite how painful it was to talk about infidelity. Of course, it was a fruitless conversation because he had an answer for everything and his sentences were repetitive and melodramatic: 'No, darling, you're wrong ... Don't fill your head up with gossip. I'm not going to leave you for any reason. Lots of people would like to see us split up, but it's not going to work.'

Of course I didn't believe him and stopped talking to him for several days, but he kept proclaiming his innocence and trying to convince me that I meant a lot to him. He was so insistent that one day he invited me to a party at the house of one of his friends and gave me a song and dance about how going was very important to our future. I reluctantly agreed and we went to El Pomar, an estate in the upper section of Envigado that belonged to Pablo Correa, a wealthy drug trafficker. But the party was ruined for me as soon as we arrived because Wendy was there, looking stunning as usual in a yellow miniskirt that was causing a sensation. Pablo remained by my side the whole time, showing me through his actions that I came first, before Wendy or any other woman. She, for her part, spent the party flirting at every table in the room, trying to get my husband's attention.

It was a horrible experience. Immensely uncomfortable, I wondered for the millionth time what I was doing there, why I put up with Pablo. But things didn't end there. To escape the grotesque scene, I went to the bathroom and was confronted with the sight of numerous women of all ages snorting cocaine off the counter.

I fled in horror and told Pablo, 'Get me out of here right now. I can't stay here a minute longer.'

He must have seen the fury on my face, and we immediately got in his car and left, followed by three cars full of bodyguards.

'Pablo, if that's the kind of place you need me to be, forget about me. I'm not the right person. If I have to be in that awful environment in order to be with you, you should just be with Wendy. She's more your speed. Don't count on me for that.'

'No, sweetheart, I promise, I'll be wherever you want.'

Those few words were enough to calm the waters. Pablo wanted to hang on to every single one of his women, and he succeeded. Despite his constant affairs, he managed to remain as romantic as ever, the thoughtful husband who brought me yellow flowers every time he cheated, the passionate man I used to see when we were alone.

In the meantime, the congressional campaign was sailing along and the regional elections were right around the corner. Pablo was showing signs of fatigue because of the pace, as he was constantly visiting neighbourhoods, giving speeches and talking to people, so he suggested we go to Miami for a few days. We stayed at the Omni Hotel on Biscayne Boulevard, a posh area of the city, which had a massive shopping centre on its ground floor. That worked well for us because Juan Pablo could amuse himself there while I went upstairs in the afternoons to take a nap. At the time we were trying to wean our son off bottle feeding, and Pablo decided to suggest that the boy say goodbye to his bottle because it was going on a trip on a helium balloon. Not really understanding what was happening, Juan Pablo agreed, we tied the bottle to a balloon and it soared slowly up into the sky. When he realised the bottle was gone and wasn't coming back, he sobbed for a while but then calmed down and never asked for it again. The strategy worked.

It was a fun trip, until eventually Pablo said he had to go to New York to meet with some Puerto Ricans about a business deal. I didn't think much about the matter and he returned three days later, bearing a gift: a beautiful round compact made of sapphire-encrusted gold, engraved with my name. I still have it. It survived the bombs, the life in hiding, the war. Months later I realised that he'd lied and that in fact he'd gone to meet Wendy, and that she was the one who chose the compact for me.

On the subject of the United States, I want to mention another trip Pablo took there before his visa was revoked in 1983. It's relevant because in gathering the information for this book, in April 2017 I went to the town of Carmen de Viboral, forty miles from Medellín, to look for Quijada, Pablo's personal accountant in the United States, whom I hadn't seen for more than thirty years and with whom I'd never discussed my husband's affairs.

It wasn't easy to get information out of Quijada; he seemed both wary of me and remorseful about having facilitated Pablo's cheating on the dozen or so trips he made to the States. If he was able to sneak off to New York to see Wendy even when he was holidaying with us in Miami, it's not hard to imagine he also did so when he was visiting the States on his own. And of course Quijada turned out to be full of surprises, describing several episodes that illustrate how my husband would go crazy on his US visits.

Once we'd established some trust, Quijada recalled one occasion when Pablo had rented six suites at the Omni for four nights, where he stayed along with several American drug traffickers. The men selected beautiful Latina women from photos and had them sent over from a club in Kendall. The prettiest one was always for Pablo.

Quijada described another scandalous episode in the same hotel, where Pablo and several of his Colombian partners, including Gustavo Gaviria and Gerardo 'Kiko' Moncada, rented an entire floor for a week. At night they'd gather in the largest suite for their parties. Each day, Quijada said, about forty women from every nationality would show up and be examined as if they were in a beauty pageant. The ones they liked were allowed to stay, and the rest were sent home with US$200 in their purses, until the group was down to twenty. Then they'd engage in a sort of seductive game in which they'd pay the girls US$20 to remove each item of clothing they were wearing, and once they were naked, the men would make them dance together until the final act.

On another occasion, Pablo traveled from Medellín and arrived at Tamiami, the small private airport in Miami, in his newly acquired Learjet. There he picked up three people and they flew to Orlando, where they stayed at the Marriott. Five women were there with them for the three-day trip. And the men were more than generous: the women were charging two to three thousand dollars to provide company, but received five.

Though I'd managed to drag these details out of him, Quijada tried to defend himself, claiming he was only following my husband's orders. It was true, but it was also true that money could buy anything, even the silence of the hotels, which would fill their coffers at the expense of rowdy guests who brought in women of dubious reputation and nobody would say anything in exchange for fat tips. Obviously the bills were huge; Quijada was paying out between ten and fifty thousand dollars a week for the services obtained in that hotel.

Some time later, at the peak of his empire, Pablo bought a gorgeous mansion in North Bay, Miami Beach, next door to the famous pop group the Bee Gees. It was a one-storey ranch, fully furnished and decorated, with a huge pool and a cabaña from which you could see the port. It cost him US$700,000 and was his for five years, until 1987, when the American authorities confiscated it. Quijada recalled that Pablo had thrown at least seven huge parties there that had lasted till ten in the morning of the following day. At all of those bashes, he said, Pablo and his buddies were always accompanied by beautiful women.

'Ma'am, the boss only had weekend flings. They were temporary, paid for. He didn't get involved with any women here.'

I believed Quijada, but the problem was that Pablo didn't seem to have a limit when it came to women. He exhibited chauvinism in its fullest expression, combined with the power conferred by money.

I don't want to go on too long about my husband's excesses in the United States, so I will merely note that he and his buddies frequented the most famous hotspots and shows during the early 1980s. I couldn't help blushing when Quijada told me that Pablo had hired five dancers from the legendary Parisian cabaret Crazy Horse to come to Medellín for a few days. The same thing happened with three young women from the Folies Bergère, the classic temple of nightlife in the French capital. He also brought in several voluptuous women from Big Fannie Annie, one of the most famous nightclubs in the United States. And of course there were also stunning girls brought from Brazil, one of whom Pablo had fallen for on a trip with his friends to Rio de Janeiro; there, Quijada told me, he'd met a gorgeous girl who then visited him in Medellín, and he later went to see her in his Learjet. Other Brazilian girls, some of them very famous, were brought to Hacienda Nápoles for a week to celebrate one of Pablo's birthdays.

Obviously, Quijada was in charge of buying the gifts in Miami that Pablo wanted to give his girlfriends. Pablo would request rings, bracelets, earrings, necklaces and watches, which the employee would buy at the high-end jewellery store Mayors, on the first floor of the Omni. On my husband's instructions, Quijada ignored the price of the baubles, which could cost between US$25,000 and US$250,000. And since he liked to be 'thoughtful' with his conquests, he also requested dozens of pairs of tennis shoes, jackets, skiing caps, trousers and perfumes, all for women.

Every two months, Quijada would send five suitcases to Colombia full of gifts that Pablo would use to wow his lovers.

While all this was happening, life was smiling on my husband, and on 14 March 1982, he was elected as a substitute to the House of Representatives. That Sunday afternoon, we met at the headquarters of the Liberal Renewal Movement with congressmen Alberto Santofimio and Jairo Ortega and waited for the final tally of the votes, but since the process was going so slowly, I told him I'd rather go home. I remember that before I left I heard people saying that it would be necessary now to make room for Pablo at baulking media outlets and in Bogotá's elitist political circles.

It was at this point that, to the misfortune of myself and my family, Virginia Vallejo appeared.

Writing about her provokes a combination of pain and indignation at the suffering her romance with my husband caused me and the harm she's inflicted on me since his death.

Though she has declared herself 'Pablo's biographer', she doesn't actually seem to know his story and so frequently relies on clichés and draws unfounded conclusions. One clear example is her claim in an interview that after Pablo's death my children and I were ashamed to use the last name Escobar but not ashamed to live off of my husband's millions in Argentina. That sentence, full of hatred, resentment, and lies, shows that she was never interested in knowing why we felt we had no choice but to change our names or in finding out what happened to us. Had she done so, she would certainly think differently. That truth will be thoroughly apparent in this book.

Through the years, the media have obsessed over Virginia and Pablo, publishing endless photos, videos and interviews with the two of them together. It's true they had an intense romantic relationship, but it's also true that at that time – the early 1980s – he also had another well-known lover, Wendy Chavarriaga, and sporadically – according to Jerónimo and Ferney – was also with Alcira, winner of the Miss Coffee beauty pageant; Miss Antioquia; Luz Ángela, who'd been crowned Miss Medellín; and a volleyball player from Caldas. And another woman was about to come along too, who would make history with him: Juliana, Miss Livestock. All at the same time. And on the other side of the table was me.

Into this mix, Virginia appeared. I met her one night in early September 1982 in the Bogotá Hilton, at a meeting between Pablo and Jairo Ortega and Alberto Santofimio Botero. My husband had listened to Santofimio, who'd told him about Virginia and how influential she was in the capital city's political, social, and journalistic circles.

Virginia, Santofimio, Ortega, Pablo and I sat down in a lounge in the hotel and I merely listened without offering an opinion. That was to be expected. At my young age – twenty-one years old – I didn't know the ins and outs of political matters.

My first impression of her was a favourable one, that of an intelligent woman with experience with the media and apparent contacts in high society and the celebrity world. I wasn't at all wary of her as a woman. Pablo knew perfectly well that she could be his ticket into the Bogotá elite, the class that ruled the country; he was obsessed with getting a place at the table with the bigwigs of the traditional political parties, and she was the perfect vehicle for achieving this.

After that first meeting, almost immediately the two of us started participating in political events together, mainly in Medellín, each of us playing her individual role. The campaign certainly hadn't made a mistake in contacting her: she fulfilled her role to perfection, and Pablo's star soon began to rise. That process was helped along by the lengthy interview Virginia conducted with him in Moravia, which gave him the opportunity to explain the scope of his project Medellín Without Slums, which sought to relocate thousands of residents in that impoverished area of the city and give them a house in a new subdivision. My husband was pleased because the programme lasted half an hour and was seen all over the country. He didn't tell me about it, but I knew that as a thank-you he gave a large sum of money to alleviate the dire financial straits of the production company Virginia was part of. I later learned that though Pablo didn't give her watches or jewels, he did provide resources for her to acquire better TV cameras and editing equipment. She, for her part, brought him a pure-bred German shepherd and explained that a dog would never betray him, but he gave it to Ferney because he didn't like that breed.

There's no denying that Virginia was a sexy, beautiful woman with a lovely smile and an intelligent mind, but she seemed obsessive about applying face powder every five minutes because she couldn't stand it when her skin was shiny.

As the weeks passed, I sensed that Pablo might be having an affair with Virginia. Their consultations became more intense, and it seemed odd to me that she was appearing at so many political events, public and private alike, that he was attending in both Bogotá and Medellín. I also noticed they seemed a bit flirty with each other, and then Pablo started dropping whatever he was doing whenever she arrived. I remember once we were on a farm in Rionegro when she appeared with a black briefcase, and he got up from the table where we were having lunch and they left together. As if that weren't enough, he used to send his plane or one of his helicopters to pick her up in Bogotá and then put her up in the Inter-Continental Hotel. Something was going on.

Around then, in early 1983, my husband, who was now a representative with parliamentary immunity, hardened his opposition to the extradition of Colombian citizens to the United States. During the campaign he'd talked about repealing the treaty signed between Bogotá and Washington in 1979, and now he seemed determined to wage a frontal assault on the extradition law.

The place he always went to discuss the subject was the new nightclub Kevins, opened in February 1983 by José Antonio Ocampo, better known as 'Pelusa', a good friend of Pablo's. The modern, luxurious club, located very close to the Inter-Continental Hotel, immediately became my husband's favourite spot, and he'd spend time there with his little girlfriends and have meetings with all kinds of people.

Other establishments he frequented nearly as often were Acuarius and Don Mateo, which were also very popular.

It was in Kevins that Pablo organised the infamous first national forum against extradition, which was attended by more than 300 people from all over the country. It took place in the second week of April 1983, and sitting at the main table were, among others, the priest Elías Lopera, the former magistrate Humberto Barrera Domínguez, Virginia Vallejo and my husband. I didn't attend, but there was plenty of talk about it on the news, and for the first time a national publication, the magazine *Semana*, did a story about the event along with a profile of Pablo. The article was titled 'An Antioquian Robin Hood', and it was the first time that the Bogotá media noticed my husband, even as they wondered where his fortune had come from.

As I later learned, the meeting at Kevins was a success, but several of the attendees commented on how Virginia and Pablo were flirting. My hunch about there being something between them would soon be confirmed when Pablo suddenly cancelled a visit to Hacienda Nápoles with Gustavo, our children and several guests, and said that he and his friends were going on a political trip to a number of communities in the Magdalena Medio. No wives allowed, of course.

Sceptical of his excuse, and convinced they were actually going to Nápoles but didn't want us there, I decided to show up unannounced at Nápoles with the wives of Pablo and Gustavo's friends. Everything was ready for the trip, but at the last minute I backed out, afraid to find out the answers to my questions. Would I leave Pablo if I caught him red-handed? What would become of my reputation if I made a stink? I realised I wasn't going to leave him even if I caught him cheating again. I preferred to preserve my role as a wife and as a woman.

In the end, the committee of betrayed women, including one of my sisters, went out to the estate, where they arrived after eight one Saturday night. Needless to say, I paid the expenses for their journey and provided the cars needed for the trip. Upon their arrival, they found a pathetic scene: Pablo's friends were around the pool with several women in tiny bikinis, and my husband was with Virginia on the second floor of the house – in our bedroom. Our bedroom!

Pablo came down after hearing the commotion, and Virginia stayed upstairs, on the balcony. Knowing he'd been caught red-handed, my husband went straight to my sister.

'Please don't say anything,' he begged her.

'Don't ask that of me, Pablo. Tata's going to find out. You can kill us if you want, but she's going to find out.'

I was horrified to hear my sister's brief account when she telephoned from the estate, but the call suddenly cut off because Pablo hung up the phone.

In any event, she managed to tell me what I needed to know. I couldn't believe Pablo had gone so far as to violate the intimacy of our family estate.

Amid the uproar that night, the men started disappearing, including Pablo, who went off with Virginia, but they hadn't counted on their wives tracking them down several hours later, dancing at Nebraska, a well-known spot in the neighbouring town of Doradal.

Pablo arrived at our house in Medellín two days later, and he obviously found me very angry and hurt. I didn't even want to look at him. I couldn't understand how he could have started having an affair with a woman right when he and I were assiduously going through fertility treatment, trying to impregnate me through artificial insemination. At that point, I'd had at least three miscarriages, so we'd consulted the best gynaecologist in Medellín, Byron Ríos, who set up a strict regime of appointments several times a week. Pablo always arrived right on time, and his love and his determination to have another child were obvious. How was it possible that a man who was making such a genuine effort to expand his family could so shamelessly cheat on me with another woman?

The days passed quickly, and once more I let this new betrayal pass. Kevins now weighed on our lives because everybody knew Pablo used to go there sometimes with Virginia, sometimes with Wendy, and other times with various other women. On a couple of occasions, when they announced a concert by a famous performer, I'd go to Kevins with some of my female friends once Juan Pablo, who was six, had fallen asleep. I was looking for a bit of distraction, but it was futile because somebody would tell me that Pablo had been there and had taken off out the back door when he'd heard I'd arrived. Hours later he'd come back home as if nothing had happened, and as always he'd tell me he'd been working.

Of course, sometimes I also got to go to Kevins on Pablo's invitation, but he must have noticed that I went reluctantly unless an outstanding singer was performing. Plus, when it came time to dance, he'd always claim his knee was hurting. If he saw a pretty woman, though, he'd head out onto the floor. And my husband was hardly a good dancer; he had a rather crude style.

In the midst of that complex situation, we received the good news that the treatment had worked and I was pregnant again. Pablo was delighted when I told him, and hugged me tight.

I followed my gynaecologist's instructions to the letter, and during the first few weeks of the pregnancy I didn't experience any problems. Pablo made an effort to be there and take care of me – but it was obvious that he was still up to the same old tricks, because he continued to come home late, offering the threadbare excuse that he'd been working to provide everything we needed.

But I was really upset when I found out that Virginia and Pablo were regularly having dinner together, just the two of them, at Kevins. Once more, I was devastated. During that stage of my pregnancy, I was particularly sensitive and my emotional state wasn't great. I felt an overwhelming rage, and though my doctor had forbidden me to drive, I raced to Envigado to seek out Aunt Inés, my shoulder to cry on, to ask for her advice and to tell her how hurt I was by Pablo's infidelity and selfishness. On my way there I got a huge scare because I almost ran over a young man. When I reached Aunt Inés's house and told her what had happened, she was alarmed to see me so desperate and managed to persuade me to let her drive on the way back home. In her usual conciliatory tone, once again she told me to be patient, that this wasn't Pablo's first affair and wouldn't be his last, and that she was sure I was the only woman Pablo loved.

'Sweetie, don't worry about the other women. The power of money gives him a lot of opportunities, but you will still be his wife and the mother of his children. Focus on taking care of your pregnancy.'

Though her words did pacify me, a few minutes after getting home I noticed I'd started spotting. Frightened, I called my doctor, who ordered me to bed, but there was nothing to be done and a week later I miscarried again.

Pablo showed up a little while after the event, as if nothing had happened.

'I'm here for you, Tata. Tell me what hurts.'

On those long nights of tears and loneliness, I often used to listen to the songs of Helenita Vargas, the popular Colombian singer whose lyrics reflected my own emotions. She was my idol, my companion in suffering, in despair, in desperation. The song 'Usted es un mal hombre' (You're a bad man) hit the nail on the head: 'Few people know you the way I know you, I know you / Few have tasted that sour bile inside you / Few guess that you feel arrogance rather than love / God is witness to my disillusionments over all these years.' My reverence for Helenita was such that I even hired her at least eight times to sing at family gatherings. I also attended her performances at various nightclubs in Medellín.

Virginia, Wendy and Juliana. Those women were my husband's lovers during that period of his life – he was thirty-four years old, with access to the power granted by money, the impunity granted by politics and the pleasure granted by having three beautiful women in his bed.

We already know how Virginia and Wendy met Pablo. Years later, Ferney told me how Juliana had come into my husband's life: he discovered her when she was in the running for the Miss Livestock competition and he spotted her on TV, riding a float in a parade through Medellín. Eager to meet her, Pablo told Ferney to look for her and persuade her to come and see him, which occurred soon after.

Thus began a wild romance that lasted several years, even after Pablo went into hiding. According to Ferney's account, Juliana's mother – a very beautiful older woman – played a key role in their relationship. She accompanied her daughter everywhere and even had the gall to tell my husband, right in front of me on a walk at Nápoles, to help promote her at a national level. He did so and had a massive billboard with Juliana's image on it installed next to the highway.

I began to sense that something was going on with another woman and decided to go to the farm known as El Paraíso, in Loma del Chocho in Envigado, where Teodora, the loyal maid, gave me all the gory details about Pablo's affair with a girl with long, wavy blond hair. When I complained to Pablo, he denied it as usual and flew into a rage when he found out who had told me. Teodora was fired, but she managed to survive even though she'd broken my husband's rules for his employees about keeping quiet.

Brazen and flirtatious, Juliana was able to win Pablo over from the start. He let her visit him in his office constantly, attend meetings with his business partners and even live with him for a while at El Paraíso, where he was hiding from justice. Ferney also told me that once when she and Pablo were at Nápoles, they were informed that the army was on its way, and she didn't hesitate to ask for a gun in case of a confrontation with the soldiers. Once again, one of Pablo's lovers took on a role that freed me from doing things I'd never have wanted or been able to do. What's more, as my son Juan Pablo revealed in his book *Pablo Escobar in fraganti*, she and her mother were with my husband at Nápoles at the critical moment when Minister of Justice Rodrigo Lara was killed on the night of 30 April 1984.

For all of these reasons, Juliana's loyalty was more than repaid by my husband, who flooded her with gifts such as cars, apartments, jewellery … Whatever she wanted, he would give it to her.

Faced with so much evidence that my husband was still carrying on as always, at a certain point I decided to revolt, to punish him somehow. I did it one day when I learned that there was going to be an important art exhibition in Bogotá that would be attended by the great artists Fernando Botero, Édgar Negret and Alejandro Obregón, among others, with lunch included. Without thinking twice, I broke Pablo's security rules, slipped away from my bodyguards, and took a commercial flight to Bogotá, accompanied by my hairdresser and another female friend.

As was to be expected, Pablo noticed my absence within a few hours, whereupon he called his bodyguards together and yelled at them for having failed to carry out his instructions not to leave me alone at any moment. His men searched for me in Medellín, unaware that I was in another city. The next day I called my mother, and she told me Pablo was going crazy looking for me and asked me to come back right away. I was worried Pablo would be angry, imagining his irate face, but I also felt relief because it was the only way I could show him that his wife had other worlds in which to learn, enjoy myself and interact with others. I managed to escape on other occasions too, going to exhibitions and art salons that provided contact with people who are still part of my life today, and who were vital to my survival.

On that particular occasion, I returned the same afternoon and told Pablo I was home, but he didn't come back, instead sending me a letter saying that he was furious, that he wanted nothing to do with me, that I should go back to the oligarchy since I thought I was one of the elites. In closing, he told me to forget about him for ever. I remember how a chill ran through my body, and I was struck by two sudden emotions: satisfaction at what I'd done because I'd demanded respect, but at the same time the fear and pain of losing him for good.

A few weeks passed, and he still refused to see me. He kept seeing Juliana, and they were involved in an accident together when the helicopter they were in crashed on a farm in Cupica Bay, in Chocó on the Pacific coast. One of my husband's men, alarmed, called to tell me that the craft's tail rotor had broken and it had plunged toward the earth from 3,000 feet up, but the skillful pilot had managed to manoeuvre it over to some trees, which had softened the impact before the helicopter tumbled into a swamp. My informer didn't tell me that Pablo was with Juliana at the time, so I naively tried to get in touch with him to find out if he was hurt. When I finally spoke to him, we forgot that we were fighting. He told me we couldn't see each other because he was near his father's farm and he wanted to go and visit him instead because his father was also quite worried about the accident. He was lying yet again, because the truth was that Juliana had broken her arm and Pablo had taken her to a hospital in Rionegro for treatment.

As the days passed and Pablo returned home, things settled down again, though the ghost of infidelities past still lingered. It was true that Pablo was still with Virginia, Wendy, and Juliana, and he was the one who set the parameters for their relationships and they obviously accepted them. I don't know whether they knew about one another. What I do know is that whatever the case, he fulfilled his obligations to his family and was present whenever he was needed as a husband and father.

There's an old saying that goes, 'The pitcher goes to the well so often that it finally breaks.' To mine and Pablo's delight, in September 1983 I became pregnant once more. As I mentioned above, there had been complications on at least four previous occasions and the pregnancies had failed. But this fifth time was the charm, and by the grace of God Manuela did arrive, even if, as we will see, it was in the midst of enormous difficulties.

But all of our lives, including those of the family, Pablo's lovers, and indeed the entire country, would be changed abruptly and for ever on the night of 30 April 1984, when hitmen assassinated the minister of justice, Rodrigo Lara Bonilla, in Bogotá, apparently on my husband's orders.

I will describe those painful events elsewhere in this book; at this point it is only relevant to mention where everyone was at the time of the murder. In her book, Virginia claims she was travelling in Italy at the time. According to the account of Malévolo, one of Pablo's employees, Juliana and her mother were visiting my husband at Hacienda Nápoles when news of the crime was reported on the television. As for Wendy? I have no idea. I was with Juan Pablo in my mother's apartment in Medellín.

The assassination marked the start of the war, and it changed all our lives for ever. After this event, Pablo's political career stalled and eventually a warrant was issued for his arrest as the government sought to extradite him to the US. As a result, he was often on the run or in hiding, which had a huge impact on us as a family. It also led to the end of some of his affairs – and not in ideal circumstances.

First I'd like to address Wendy Chavarriaga Gil and her sad end. In mid-2012 I travelled to Medellín from Buenos Aires to deal with some legal matters related to the estate of Don Abel, Pablo's father, who'd died in October 2001. One of those appointments was in the chambers of a judge, who adopted a very hostile attitude as soon as he saw me, to such an extent that at one point he told me scathingly that I looked just like the actress from *Pablo Escobar, the Drug Lord*, the series that was being broadcast at the time on the Caracol channel. I knew about the programme, but I hadn't had any interest in seeing it. But the judge's remark made me anxious, and that night I tuned in.

Imagine my horror when I was faced with the following scene on-screen: Wendy was pregnant and, appallingly, Pablo was trying to hire a nurse who would put her to sleep and remove the baby, a boy who was five months along. I had no idea these events had taken place. At first I thought what I'd just seen was the product of a screenwriter's imagination and not an episode from real life, because up until then all I'd known of the situation was what Popeye had publicly stated: that he'd killed Wendy on my husband's orders after Pablo found out she was collaborating with the Search Bloc.

Unsettled, I decided to look into whether the story of the brutal forced abortion was true and whether Pablo had committed such an atrocity. I racked my brain to recall which of his men might still be alive who had been accompanying him at the time, but it wasn't easy to find somebody who knew first-hand what happened. Once again I found myself faced with the silence of those who'd promised Pablo that they wouldn't tell me about the awful things that were happening around me. So I returned to Argentina with my questions unanswered. A couple of years later, on another trip to Medellín, when I ran into Yeison, one of Pablo's men from that period who'd been part of his praetorian guard, the ones who were with him on his nights on the town, at his raging parties in the apartment known as Frost. We talked for a long time, and finally I decided to ask about Wendy and what I'd seen on TV.

'Ma'am, why do you want to know, what good does it do? It's been so long, it's pointless,' he replied, unable to disguise his shame.

Firmly, I told him I did want to know. He sat thinking a while longer, then sighed. 'Yes, ma'am, that's what happened. I was there.'

His tale was a chilling one. I couldn't hold back my tears when he started describing how, despite Pablo's warnings, Wendy had fallen pregnant, but she'd hidden it from him because she was planning to escape to the United States to have her baby. But Pablo ended up finding out, and one night he called her over to Frost, gave her a long embrace, and then several of his men – including Yeison, La Yuca, Carlos Negro and Pasquín – held her down so the nurse could give her an injection to knock her out.

Several hours and three beers later, Yeison continued his story. Wendy woke up and went crazy when she realised what had happened, to the extent that with an agile movement she leaped up and tried to hurl herself out of one of the windows, but Pablo's men reacted quickly and managed to grab her before she fell.

Yeison paused, then gestured that the story wasn't over yet. While he pondered what to say next, in that moment, as a woman, as a mother, I felt deeply angry at this confirmation of my husband's barbarous act, which he had committed so that he wouldn't have any children outside his marriage.

The relationship between Pablo and Wendy was, unsurprisingly, over after the abortion. But some time later, Popeye came to talk to Pablo, told him that he'd started seeing Wendy and asked him for permission to continue. My husband replied that he didn't have a problem with their relationship, but he did warn Popeye to be careful because he wasn't the kind of man she was generally interested in. The romance worked pretty well for a while, but Pablo's men soon saw that something wasn't right. It seemed bizarre that Wendy would send Popeye nude photos and he'd put them out on a table so everybody would see them.

The Wendy situation took an unexpected turn one day when Jerónimo caught her rifling through his papers in an apartment where they were hiding out in Caracas, Venezuela. Wendy, Popeye, Yeison, Jerónimo and two more of Pablo's trusted men had been forced to flee to the neighbouring country after a terrorist attack in Medellín.

Concerned about Wendy's suspicious behaviour, Jerónimo let Pablo know what had just happened with his ex-girlfriend, now Popeye's girlfriend. My husband called his old contacts at Empresas Públicas de Medellín and asked them to tap Wendy's calls. A few days later he received a cassette containing several conversations in which she was talking with officers from the Search Bloc; the calls made it clear she was collaborating with the authorities to help them locate my husband. The events that followed have already been described by Popeye many times. That was the sad end of a beautiful woman who got involved with the wrong man. She didn't deserve what happened to her.

My husband's romance with Virginia Vallejo didn't end well either, though at some points their over-five-year relationship seemed like something out of a soap opera.

For instance, in 1987 the tabloids started talking about how the famous TV anchor Virginia Vallejo and the 'businessman' Pablo Escobar were getting married. One of the headlines read, 'Virginia Vallejo weds a millionaire'. That millionaire was Pablo Emilio Escobar Gaviria, my husband, who was married to me by law and in the eyes of God. How was he going to get married without divorcing me?

I remember that during that year, Pablo wasn't under legal pressure because the Supreme Court had ruled in favour of a lawsuit against the extradition treaty with the United States and the government had no choice but to cancel its warrants for the arrest of Pablo and several of his partners with the aim of extraditing them. As a result, for three months during 1987, Pablo lived with us in the Mónaco apartment building.

The tabloid announcement of the impending matrimony of my husband and Virginia left me in a state of shock. It was deeply humiliating because my former schoolmates and some of my friends started calling to ask if the news was true. With little success, I tried to answer sarcastically and just said that Pablo slept at home every night and hadn't yet told me about his upcoming nuptials. I felt powerless, irate, disconsolate, frustrated as a woman. The sensationalist press continued to speculate about the juicy topic for several weeks.

An article published in a tabloid specialising in celebrity romances said of Virginia, 'According to a source close to the well-known TV presenter, Vallejo is now preparing her trousseau, on which she has spent nearly a million pesos.'

Of my husband, it claimed, 'Escobar Gaviria, of hardy Antioquian stock, is considered one of the richest men in Colombia. Now thirty-eight years old, he went into business at thirty-three and has interests in numerous Colombian companies.' And it concluded, 'Virginia has taken advantage of her public image and her beloved's money to launch a political career.'

At first I was wary with him, but when the news of the wedding started to take off, I questioned him firmly. But Pablo, the sly old fox, still defended himself: 'Look, sweetheart, don't listen to that stuff. All those people want is to hurt our marriage. You're the only one I love, and I'm not going to leave you for anything or anybody.'

How could I believe him when the media were saying the opposite? Until one day, tired of my nagging, he flew into a rage and said he was leaving.

'Tata, you're being melodramatic. You're bugging me over something that's not even real. They're making it up because I'm a public figure. You're being silly.'

And he took off for two weeks. Totally shameless. There's another old Colombian saying that applies here: 'My neighbour got mad because she stole my chicken.'

But he didn't disappear entirely: he still called frequently, claiming that he missed me.

'Tata, I need you, you're really important to me, darling. You're my reason for being in this world.'

Finally, one night I heard the sound of several vehicles approaching the house and the front door opening, and then Pablo walked into the bedroom. He didn't let me say a word, came over to the bed and hugged me, telling me I was the best gift life had ever given him. I fell for his sweet words again. That night once more my love for him overcame my reproaches.

In those moments I also remembered the day he brought home a bottle of Ballantine's whisky with a wind-up dancer inside it. He liked making her dance. That's how I felt, like that dancer spinning whenever Pablo wound her up.

Pablo and Virginia's affair ended abruptly. It can't have been easy for her to accept her lover's rejection, given the way, one night, he instructed his men to deny her entrance to Hacienda Nápoles. According to what I was told during my research for this book, she arrived in an SUV with her driver and one of the guards told her she couldn't go in. It was about eight o'clock at night and she was wearing an elegant gown and high heels.

In tears, she went to the farm of Alfredo – Pablo's friend – five miles from Doradal, where she and my husband had been a few times.

There, she asked Alfredo if he knew why there were orders not to let her in, and he replied that he had no idea. Of course he did know: Pablo had confirmed that she'd cheated on him with Gilberto Rodríguez Orejuela, one of the capos from the Cali Cartel. Then Virginia asked if Pablo was at Nápoles at that moment, and Alfredo said again that he didn't know.

Realising that Virginia had nowhere to go, Alfredo invited her to stay the night and return to Bogotá the next day. He also offered her something to eat since he was in the middle of cooking with a group of friends who'd come to visit. She accepted and after eating some grilled beef with potatoes went to lie down. She left at seven the next morning, a mix of rage and sadness on her face.

As I've described, Pablo took full advantage of the power money gave him, indulging in the company of many women with whom he carried on affairs throughout his life. But there was another, smaller group of women who were useful not just for romance but also for his business and protection.

Those women were ones who held important positions in the government agencies charged with prosecuting him. According to Ferney, Pablo had an affair with one of the secretaries of the minister of defence, General Miguel Vega Uribe, who held that post between 1985 and 1986, under the Belisario Betancur administration. An army colonel who worked for my husband took the young, beautiful woman that Pablo was romancing out to Hacienda Nápoles. Naturally, he soon had access to precise information about the planned dates and times of military operations against him. That's how Pablo was able to avoid raids for years: he had privileged information.

A high-level staffer at the Ministry of Justice also fell into Pablo's nets, and the two had an intense relationship that he leveraged for vital information. For example, one Friday she went looking for him at a farm in Doradal and told him an operation had been planned against several cocaine processing labs near Nápoles the next day. Thanks to that information, Pablo's men were able to move all the materials and avoided losing a huge amount of money.

During my research for this book, I confirmed that my husband had female informants in many places, including the F-2, the national police's intelligence service (which would later become the DIJIN), Interpol and the Administrative Department of Security (DAS).

SECRECY, SAFEHOUSES, MANHUNTS, RAIDS AND THE THREAT of imminent death became our new lifestyle starting in 1984. It became harder and harder to be at my husband's side, and after a while we would go two weeks, a month, two months without seeing each other because he was in hiding somewhere. Sometimes he managed to send letters in which he'd explain that things were very complicated and then claim that he'd send for us once things had settled down. When one of his men would finally show up and tell us that Pablo was waiting for us, I'd go, frightened but eager to see him, with Manuela and Juan Pablo, who were still very small, to whatever hideout he was staying in. But it was very frustrating because we often got only half an hour with him before he'd say we had to go because 'the law' might come. Agonisingly, we didn't have a choice and would return, dejected, to Medellín.

Of course the danger was real, which is why Pablo had to change hiding places so often, but even in the worst circumstances he never resisted the temptation to be with other women. Jerónimo, Ferney and Yeison told me much later that my husband always arranged to have female company.

In concrete terms, you could say that Pablo was a fugitive from justice for eight years, and during that time he hid at countless houses, apartments and farms, staying as long as his safety required. When it came to women, though, he pushed the limits, even if it put his life in danger. He spent five months in hiding at a farm in San Pedro de los Milagros, on the road to Santa Fe de Antioquia; we went to see him three or four times during that period, but he spent the rest of the time with women hired in Medellín, who agreed to the conditions in exchange for a hefty sum. They'd be brought to the safehouse blindfolded so they didn't know where they were. When they left, several days later, they'd be blindfolded again.

Because of several young women, Pablo nearly got snared in a massive police operation on the El Oro farm, a beautiful place on the banks of the Cocorná River, in the Magdalena Medio, in late 1989. He escaped by fleeing through a newly planted field, but my brother Mario wasn't so lucky. He was killed by bullets fired from a helicopter.

Months later, in July 1990, Juan Pablo, Manuela, myself and two bodyguards were staying in a rented house in Lausanne, Switzerland, where we'd travelled to get away from Pablo's enemies and the harassment of the authorities. Pablo remained in Medellín, in a spacious apartment on Avenida Oriental, a central area a few blocks from the headquarters of the city's police force. Obviously he was keeping himself busy, this time with Sandra, a beautiful young woman who was with him for several months, until December 1990, when we returned from Europe unexpectedly upon discovering that there were several men tailing us.

From then on, we stayed with Pablo almost all the time because he'd started negotiating with the government to turn himself in. I will tell that story elsewhere, but in the end my husband was able to impose his conditions and on 19 June 1991, just hours after the Constituent Assembly eliminated extradition from the new Constitution, and he was safe from being extradited to the US, Pablo retreated to La Catedral, the prison he'd built on land he owned up in the hills in Envigado.

Finally, after seven years of constant running, I was suddenly filled with a pleasant sense of calm. I thought I was going to recover my femininity, my place as a wife, as a mother, as a companion, as a lover. I thought he'd be in prison for many years and that he'd repay his debt to society.

As the saying goes, a new broom always sweeps well, and at first I visited my husband every Sunday with Manuela and Juan Pablo. My romance with Pablo was more intense than ever, and we quickly converted his large prison bedroom into a setting that was conducive to love: a romantic fireplace, large candles in every colour and scent, a large waterbed, several paintings by famous painters, the finest quality bedding and pillows, a well-stocked refrigerator, and champagne ... lots of champagne. And best of all: a spectacular view of Medellín. The nocturnal light show allowed us to see the full sweep of our beautiful city.

Three weeks. That's how long it lasted, my illusion that my life with Pablo would regain some degree of normality.

Naive as always, I started going up to La Catedral several days a week. And while Pablo was meeting with somebody or playing soccer, I'd take the opportunity to organise, rearrange and mend anything in his room that needed attention, but I also looked through the many letters he'd started receiving. They were messages from women all over the world, many of them with photos showing the senders in various poses, many of them naked, and the common denominator was that they were offering themselves to him in exchange for money. I was even more surprised when I read shocking letters from women recalling their recent intimate encounters with him in great detail and inviting him for an encore whenever he wanted; others wrote flowery missives dreaming of another night of passion in La Catedral.

It was horrible. I remember I waited for him and threw a fit, decrying his lack of respect and his failure to recognise the effort and sacrifices I'd made in order to be with him. His response was a repeat of the ones he'd given before.

'Tata, I can't help it if women visit the men who are looking after me and protecting me.'

'You're a liar, Pablo, I don't believe you. Don't touch me, I want to go back to Medellín, I don't want to be with you any more.'

I left. He came out after me and asked me to talk to him, but I ignored him. Deep down, I knew that as the days passed, La Catedral would become a temple of perdition.

The next day, predictably, he sent me a bouquet of yellow flowers with a card that read, 'I'll never trade you for anything or anybody.' His standard show of repentance.

Though I considered it, I never stopped going to La Catedral because Manuela and Juan Pablo would ask me to take them to see their father. When we arrived, I'd notice a smirk on the faces of my husband's lieutenants. It was obvious that he had plenty of female companionship.

What could I do? Once more I was trapped with no way out. Remembering Aunt Inés's words, I decided to win my husband back. Rather than kicking up a fuss about his betrayals, I attempted to seduce him instead. I was determined to be more romantic than the women who went after him for his money, and with the help of a philosophy professor, a good writer and an even better poet, with whom I was taking classes at the time, I started sending Pablo up to six messages a day. They were beautiful letters and their one sincere, heartfelt aim was to outdo any beauty queen who visited La Catedral. If I lost him, I thought, it wasn't going to be because of my lack of romanticism, consideration, and attentiveness. I was thirty years old, but I acted like a teenager, and even consulted a sex therapist because I wanted to excel in bed. My sole intention was to preserve my marriage at any cost.

The strategy worked for a while, and Pablo made the effort to respond to all of my messages and began a game of seduction that was a raging success. And since everything was going his way right then, he decided to have El Mugre, one of his most trusted men, build a pigeon coop at La Catedral and acquired a quantity of messenger pigeons. Pablo would write tiny love notes, which the birds would bring without fail to the Torres de San Michel building, where we were living at the time.

Distressed by Pablo's constant womanising, one day I received some relief from one of his lawyers, who went up to La Catedral and later met with me to sign a few documents. While we were having coffee, he told me that he'd talked to Pablo about male infidelity. He summed up my husband's attitude in a single statement: 'All men cheat, but you should never take your clothes out of the closet. In the end, the only things that matter are your wife and children. Everything else is money. And you can use money to buy whatever you want.'

That may have been what Pablo thought, but he did just the opposite. At La Catedral he returned to his old predilection for beauty queens, who visited in droves during the year he was there. Jerónoimo was with him for much of that time and witnessed several occasions on which groups of women arrived to satisfy the base impulses of my husband and his confederates who were incarcerated with him.

Once, Jerónimo told me, a truck concealing no fewer than twelve beautiful women was stopped at a military checkpoint, the last one before reaching the prison. There, the officer on duty filled out a form with the vehicle information, such as the license plate, the driver's name, and the type of cargo it was carrying. Needless to say, he was writing down made-up information because in fact the hidden compartment was full of eager young women who were after a bit of adventure and a lot of money. The soldier circled the truck several times and suddenly stopped, looked at the back of the vehicle, and shouted, 'Do me a favour and at least wear less perfume next time, goddammit!'

A bad beginning makes a bad ending, and the La Catedral adventure lasted only a year. My husband squandered that opportunity to rehabilitate himself and repay his debt to society. His actions there were so extreme that in the end he was forced to flee after he got on the government's nerves for the last time and they ordered that he be transferred to a military base.

Pablo escaped on 22 July 1992, and that day marked the start of the final countdown. He found himself without money, without men, without the ability to move around. He even gave up his womanising. In other words, Pablo was forced to become faithful to me because of his enemies. All he had left were his wife and his two children, and we never abandoned him.

The big question that many people still ask is why I stayed when I found out about all these affairs, why didn't I leave? First, because of my love for my husband. Pablo really was the love of my life. Second, because of my unconditional love for my children. And third, because I'm not sure I was ever really there. By this I am referring to how much real time I spent with Pablo and how much time I spent on the run or in hiding. My husband was very busy waging a war that demanded a great deal of physical, economic and mental effort, and which he always kept me away from. And the time he had left over was taken up with the countless stories I've just told. What, then, was the space we occupied as a couple?

All the women who passed through my husband's life left a mark on our story. What might have been a tragedy back then, with the passage of time and in the solitude of my exile, seems faintly comical today. These days I often feel that, rather than lashing out at them, I should be grateful to those women for entertaining him and giving him the pleasure he needed to endure the torturous life he led. That gave me the space to focus on being a mother, on raising and educating our children, and, most importantly, on saving their lives.

Chapter 5

Get Ready to Be First Lady

On the night of Wednesday, 26 October 1983, the plenary session of the House of Representatives lifted my husband's parliamentary immunity, thereby ending his political career, which had lasted just fifteen months and six days.

Learning of the vote on the TV news, I felt sad for him, as he'd genuinely come to believe he had a future in national politics and even in running the country. Now none of that would be possible. I tried to sleep a little, figuring he'd be home late as usual. At midnight he opened the door to our house in Medellín's El Diamante neighbourhood, fury on his face. Up until that day, he'd been the king, and now someone was daring to attack him? He paced back and forth, snorting and puffing, and then tore off the corner of a piece of paper and chewed it, an infallible sign that he was fuming with rage.

'Pablo, what are you thinking?' I asked.

'Don't worry, darling, nobody's going to stop me ... or my name's not Pablo Escobar.'

I was unsettled by his response, which he followed up with his battle cry: 'I've gone through darker times than this before.'

Losing parliamentary immunity, which meant being pushed out of Congress, and left vulnerable to justice, was one of several items of bad news he'd received in the past two weeks: first, his role as a drug trafficker had come to light and been brought to public attention; second, the United States had cancelled his visa to travel there; and third, a judge had reopened an old case in which he'd been implicated in the murder of two DAS detectives.

Being forced to retire from Congress was a hard blow not just for my husband but also for me; though in many ways we lived in different worlds, it was clear that everything around me was falling apart. I had no idea how to explain the unexplainable to my friends. What was going to happen with my son's schooling? How could I explain to my seven-year-old boy what we were going through? What words would I use? It wasn't a small issue.

Amid all that uncertainty, 1983 drew to an end and we went to spend Christmas and New Year at Hacienda Nápoles. It had been almost two months since he'd left Congress, and Pablo, at least externally, acted as if nothing was out of the ordinary. He even brought in a huge truck with a container full of fireworks that he'd had shipped from China. My husband's favourite activity during our stay at Nápoles that Christmas was setting off fireworks. At midnight as 31 December turned to 1 January, he raised a toast for the coming year (1984) to be a lucky one and told us not to worry, everything was going to be OK.

Pablo's words sounded hopeful, marked by the confidence with which he'd solved his problems in the past. I was feeling sensitive that New Year's Eve because I was just four months along in a hard pregnancy. Manuela was on her way. I couldn't hide my worry because it was obvious our situation was going to get more complicated. Still, I didn't want to ruin the night, so I toasted with all the guests and silently asked God to help us and show Pablo the light so he'd return to the righteous path.

But that New Year's was different. Those of us present noticed his long silences, his solitary walks around La Mayoría, as we called the main house on the estate.

In the second week of January 1984, we returned from holiday and Pablo immediately met with Neruda, his most trusted adviser when it came to giving speeches or writing messages. After several hours, they finished a letter that was then released to the public on 20 January. It contained his resignation from politics, from public life, relinquishing the power he'd gained when he became a 'father of the nation', as Colombians call members of Congress. His short message left no doubt about how hard it was for him to give all that up: 'I will continue to battle against oligarchies and injustices, and against partisan backroom deals, which continually work to undermine the people, and especially against political intriguers, who are fundamentally indifferent to the people's suffering and opportunists when it comes to bureaucratic wrangling.'

Ending his political career that way was very hard for my husband, who had real aspirations to go far in that world. I know for a fact that from a very young age he had a special interest in helping the poor and working for social causes. That tendency may have originated in an event he described to me many times over the course of our life together and that marked him permanently: owing to his family's economic hardships, he and his brother Roberto had to walk more than four miles to school every day, often in the rain, barefoot and undernourished. One of the Escobars' neighbours had two children studying at the same school and he used to take them in his SUV, but he never offered Roberto and Pablo a ride. Pablo never forgot that gesture of indifference. In gathering information for this book, I was told that when he'd attained enough power, he ordered two of his bodyguards to visit his old neighbour: 'I want that family to walk for the rest of their lives. Don't kill them or hurt them. I just want you to burn any car they have. If they buy another one the next day, burn that one too; and if their insurance gives them another, burn it. I want them to walk more than I did.'

BY THE TIME I FIRST HEARD ABOUT PABLO ESCOBAR BACK in La Paz, he was already popular not only for his ladykiller qualities but also for his leadership in the neighbourhood. He used to talk to the residents and ask them how they were doing and how they thought the neighbourhood could improve. His room was next to the front door of his house, and people who urgently needed help used to come and see him. 'Pablo, my mother is dying,' someone would say, and he'd rush to their aid. 'Pablo, my brother was in an accident,' another would say, and he'd look for help immediately. He also encouraged the other boys in the neighbourhood to plant trees so the shade would cool the houses because the metal roofs made them unbearably hot.

To expand my book research, in 2017 I returned to La Paz and met up with several people who knew Pablo as a young man nearly fifty years ago. I spoke for a long time with William Uribe, president of the Community Action Board, the same one who'd looked after the neighbourhood security and used to give Don Abel, Pablo's father, coffee and food when he was working as a night watchman. Don William recalled that Pablo had been sixteen years old back then and because of Pablo's influence in the community, Don William had persuaded him to work as the secretary of the Community Action Board.

Regarding that time in Pablo's life, I also spoke with Martha Paz, a young woman who dated him for a while. She mentioned an event that took place one night at the La Esvástica ice cream parlour in Envigado, when Pablo was leaving with some of his friends, including the brothers Mario and Rodrigo Leal. They were discussing the consequences of the recently begun workers' strike by employees of the Coltejer textiles factory when Pablo broke in: 'Those people are going to suffer a lot and go hungry because of that strike. One day when I have lots of money, I'll pay workers what they miss out on during strikes.'

At Pablo's words, the other boys laughed and one said, 'Keep dreaming, Pablo, it's free.'

But Pablo insisted: 'Look around. You see the houses in our neighbourhood? Money's going to flow through here like a river.'

I don't know if Pablo was aware as a youth that he had leadership skills, but in 1979 he was elected council member for Envigado on a list presented by the political party headed by the Antioquian Liberal politician William Vélez. Aunt Inés, my solace and also Pablo's political mentor, congratulated him for having gained a seat on the town council. Marginalised communities had rewarded my husband and his uncle Hernando Gaviria for their efforts in creating the movement Civismo en Marcha (Public Spirit on the Move) to promote social and ecological projects in the Aburrá Valley.

Martha Paz also recalled that in speaking on the council, Pablo always talked about the importance of building athletic facilities that were well lit and accessible to the public. Pablo attended the council meetings for a time, but one day he decided to give up his spot to his substitute and never returned; he'd set his sights on a seat in the national Congress.

Pablo's political life took off in early February 1982, during a lunch at my mother's house. Promptly at noon, Aunt Inés arrived with the mayor of Envigado, Jorge Mesa, and a little later Pablo walked in with his friend and business partner Carlos Lehder.

We sat around the table and after a few minutes the conversation turned to the year's turbulent political agenda; Congress was going to be replaced in March and a new president elected in May. Aunt Inés and Mesa knew the ins and outs of electoral campaigns very well: she'd already left a mark on her community by getting homes for thousands of people and improving the health, work and educational conditions of those who needed it most. And Mesa came from a family that had been pulling the political strings in the region for years.

The conversation continued over lunch and I listened in silence. Suddenly Mesa looked at Pablo and got right to the point: 'Pablo, I think this is your moment to launch a run for Congress. This is a great opportunity for you to get into politics. You'll clean up – I know how committed you are to the city's lower classes.'

My husband smiled and looked down, a characteristic gesture of his that indicated shyness. Then, in his typically teasing Antioquian manner, he replied, 'Is that how you see it, Mr Mesa?'

'I do, Pablo. It's a hard decision, but if you want my advice, it's best not to think about it too much.'

My mother, who never held her tongue, especially not when it came to her son-in-law, stood up, her famous stern look on her face, which meant she was going to say something very harsh.

'Pablo, have you forgotten who you are and what you do? If you get involved in politics, there won't be a sewer in the world where you can hide. You're going to put us all in danger, you'll hurt all of our lives. Think about your son, about your family.'

Everybody at the table looked at one another in silence, and Pablo stood up, paced around the table, and replied, 'Relax, Mother-in-law, I do things right; there's isn't anything in politics that could compromise or harm me.'

Lehder just sat there, impassive, but Mesa insisted that my husband had a lot of guaranteed votes because people were grateful to him for financing the construction and lighting for football, basketball, and volleyball facilities and the planting of thousands of trees in impoverished areas of Medellín, Envigado, and other towns in the Aburrá Valley.

They were right about that. I used to accompany Pablo to the openings of these sports facilities and – despite the paradox they embodied, funded as they were by his illicit dealings – I was very happy that the objective of the projects he financed was to guide young people away from vice and trouble. It was comforting to hear the excitement of all those people shouting and chanting my husband's name, and I could tell it made him feel confident to have me and our son Juan Pablo at his side. Sometimes he would ask me in a quiet voice what I thought of how he was doing, and I'd wink approvingly. I felt even more proud when people would put up massive billboards that read, 'For good deeds that last, young athletes congratulate Pablo Escobar.'

Near the end of lunch, as my mother served a delicious dessert and coffee, Pablo, who could no longer hide his interest in going into politics, asked Aunt Inés for her opinion.

'I'm happy, Son ... I know you'll go very far.'

It was settled.

'Pablo, man, that's awesome, I know you're going to be huge,' Lehder said, and lifted his cup of coffee in a toast.

Jorge Mesa shook Pablo's hand and announced that he'd include my husband on the second line of the list for the House of Representatives headed by the Antioquian politician Jairo Ortega in the name of the Liberal Renewal Movement (MRL). He also noted that the MRL was allied with New Liberalism, the party that advocated the ideas of Luis Carlos Galán and promoted his candidacy to the presidency. Pablo was pleased; on several occasions, he'd told me he admired Galán's oratory skills and his liberal policy proposals.

It was a given now that Pablo was going to make a run for Congress but, deep down, I was very anxious. He was entering unknown territory, a world that wasn't his.

The lunch guests left after three in the afternoon, and I stayed with my mother, who looked concerned. 'Honey,' she asked, 'what's going to happen now that Pablo's taking this step?' My mother's fears filled me with worry; everybody in the family was well aware of her uncanny accuracy at predicting events, so I returned home very pensive. At the same time, though, being just twenty-one years old, I was intrigued by the idea of my husband becoming a politician.

Pablo was serious about being a candidate, and three days later he held his first rally in La Paz's main park, where he gave a speech from the hood of a Mercedes-Benz. Five hundred people attended, including his friends from childhood and later nights out on the town; wanting to impress him, I called my old classmates and neighbours and invited them to attend. In his address, Pablo talked about how the neighbourhood had welcomed him as a teenager and he promised to work for a better future for the poor people of Envigado and Antioquia. In closing, he said something that filled me with emotion: 'I am proud to be part of Envigado because it has given me the best thing I have: my wife.'

The rallies became frequent affairs, and at one of them I met Jairo Ortega, who from the start struck me as a conservative, prudent, cautious man, too quiet for my taste.

There were just five weeks till the election, which was to take place on March 14, 1982, and even as my husband was busy planting trees and opening sports facilities, he was becoming more and more confident on the stump. I remember one Saturday afternoon I went with him to a campaign event in Caldas, Antioquia, and in the middle of his speech he started railing against the extradition treaty with the United States and urged the government of then-president Julio César Turbay to withdraw from it.

For more than a year, in private and in public, Pablo had been talking about the need to end extradition to the United States. He was so obsessed that he even ordered hundreds of bumper stickers that said 'No to Extradition!' I helped him put up a good many, but the truth is I didn't know much about the issue. So one night I asked him, 'Pablo, what does that word mean? Why are you fighting against extradition when it doesn't affect you?'

He paused for a long moment, as if considering how to respond, and adopted a professorial tone: 'Look, sweetheart, extradition is like handing your child off for another parent to discipline. It's not right. That's what the Colombian government is doing: turning over its citizens so they can be buried alive in the United States and die like rats.'

I understood.

In his fight against extradition, Pablo and Carlos Lehder were on the same page. My husband used to talk about the subject in almost all of his speeches, strongly condemning the sending of Colombian citizens to the United States: 'A nation's greatness is not born in the farce and hypocrisy of the Colombian oligarchy. It is unjust that people who committed a crime in this country be tried in another and sentenced to punishments that don't even exist in Colombia.'

In the meantime, Lehder was combatting extradition from Armenia, the city where he grew up and where, in 1981, he'd founded his own political party, the National Latin Movement, with a nationalist bent. Pablo used to say that Lehder was good at extemporaneous speaking, but he found the speeches interminable and boring, lasting up to three hours. Lehder also had a newspaper, *Quindío Libre*, which published dozens of articles against extradition every week. At the time, a series of full-page ads against extradition published in the country's major newspapers were getting a lot of attention. Lehder had paid for them.

In the meantime, Pablo's campaign was sailing along and more and more people were coming to the demonstrations. But one night Luis Carlos Galán led a rally in Berrío Park in downtown Medellín and not only rejected the MRL's support but also called for the shuttering of the campaign headquarters and the destruction of the billboards and all other materials advertising Pablo and Jairo Ortega's support for his presidential candidacy. 'The lists headed by Jairo Ortega do not represent my presidential campaign in Antioquia because that group did not respect our commitments to the Colombian people, political renewal and moral rehabilitation, which we cannot abandon in any sense for any reason. We'd rather lose those votes to avoid losing our moral authority in defending the restoration of the country's democracy,' Galán said.

The next day, Galán sent Ortega a letter justifying his decision: 'We cannot tolerate links to people whose activities go against our core tenet of restoring Colombia's moral fibre and politics. If you do not accept these conditions, I cannot allow your candidate list to have any ties to my presidential campaign.'

Galán was alluding to my husband, of course, and Pablo was agitated and angry when I arrived home that night. It was like he'd been slapped in the face. How would Pablo Escobar take being expelled from a movement by the party leader? Accustomed as he was to doing whatever he wanted, to buying permission, to defying any circumstance that posed an obstacle to reaching his goal, what had just happened was a severe blow to his ego.

But Jairo Ortega was a sly old fox when it came to politics, and he wasn't about to be scared off. Two days later he called Pablo to a meeting in Medellín and introduced him to Alberto Santofimio Botero, a politician from Tolima who was leading Liberal Alternative, which also planned to put up candidates for the House and Senate. After an hour-long conversation, they agreed that Ortega and Pablo would be included on Liberal Alternative's list of House candidates. The new alliance was sealed at a public event in Medellín, where Santofimio and Ortega went up on stage wearing jackets and ties, with red carnations in their lapels.

Pablo was beside them, but in a short-sleeved shirt, though he had a carnation too.

Ortega's skill had a huge impact on Pablo; the manoeuvre revitalised his campaign and kept it from losing momentum. My husband even believed the alliance with Santofimio would open new possibilities for him.

The next day, Liberal Alternative published an ad in the local papers welcoming Pablo into the fold: 'We support Pablo Escobar's candidacy for the House because his youth, his intelligence, and his love for the most vulnerable make him deserving of the envy of cocktail-party politicians. He has the support of all the liberals and conservatives in the Magdalena Medio, as he has been the Saviour of this region.'

I met Santofimio soon after. He was very courteous with me and made an effort to honor me as Pablo's wife. Though he thought I was too young to be in that environment, he treated me with respect. During the short time I knew him, I valued his intelligence, his erudition and his ability to captivate the masses with his masterful oratory. My husband was impressed with Santofimio, as he told me on a number of occasions: 'The man's a powerhouse, darling. The two of us are going to go far in politics because we've got similar ideals. I'm really excited about that. I've got a feeling that at some point the doors of the Casa de Nariño [the presidential palace] are going to open for us.'

'You think so, Pablo? What makes you think that will happen? Santofimio has been building his political career for years – it's not something that happens overnight.'

'I know, my love, but we're moving entire communities. Nothing's going to stop us, you'll see. Oh, I did hear that Santofimio was arrested over some kind of trouble, but he was exonerated, and that's enough for me.'

Pablo and Santofimio continued to grow closer, and when they appeared together in public, they stood out for their speaking skills and their warmth toward the gathered people. Beside them, Jairo Ortega seemed to fade away because of his quiet, aloof style. Pablo was diligent about giving speeches. He'd come home with the texts, almost always written by Neruda, and stand in front of the bathroom mirror and read them several times until he'd memorised them. Then he'd recite them out loud while moving his arms and gesticulating as if he were at a rally. It worked for him; he was persuasive and came off as a good orator.

A few days later, the party opened a campaign head-quarters in downtown Envigado, on the third floor of a building across from the Ley supermarket. I remember I used to go with my old schoolfriends to see Pablo and hear him talk about his proposals. I liked being there because once the event was over we'd meet up and he'd ask my opinion about his speech.

'What did you think, my love? What didn't I say?'

We would discuss my husband's words for a while and then enjoy delicious snacks and a rum and Coke or two. Of course, my friends and I would have to keep an eye on my husband so he didn't end up hooking up with a campaign groupie. We'd joke about surrounding him so girls couldn't get near him.

Pablo never forgot that Luis Carlos Galán had declared him undesirable, and I noticed that his speeches were beginning to reflect a great deal of resentment toward Galán: 'I'm telling you, the aristocracy and Galán's movement will tumble. The public has to know that there are people who hypocritically preach morality. With the support of all of you, we will crush the political puppets manufactured by the Colombian oligarchy.'

As the campaign went on, the personal relationship between Santofimio and my husband became all the closer, and our new best friend started travelling frequently to Medellín on Pablo's planes. It became standard for him to visit Nápoles after campaign tours. Santofimio enjoyed the beautiful landscapes of the Magdalena Medio and he loved to sit out and eat chicken sancocho stew cooked over an open fire. I enjoyed seeing him smile; he always seemed to be in a good mood and ready to chat about any topic. Many photos from that period show Santofimio and Pablo cruising down the Claro River on airboats, which are powered by aeroplane engines attached to enormous propellers. They'd also go to the Blue Pool, a gorgeous spot at Nápoles where my husband used to take his best friends, TV anchors, and beauty queens. I remember going there only once with Santofimio and Pablo, where we enjoyed a sunny afternoon with delicious food and several bottles of champagne and whisky.

But as the days passed, Pablo started to resent Santofimio's frequent travel in his planes, including back and forth between Bogotá and Medellín. Finally, one day he told one of his pilots to do something to make the politician stop

using his planes and go back to commercial flights. Pablo
didn't tell me what happened, but the pilot later said they
pretended to have an emergency mid-flight, and Santofimio never got on one of Pablo's Learjets again.

With the regional elections right around the corner,
Pablo increased his visits to every corner of Medellín. He
included the landfill site in Moravia, an impoverished area,
on his agenda. One night he came home quite upset and
told me that at least sixty shanties made of cardboard and
scrap wood had burned down because of the constant fires
produced by the toxic gases emanating from the mountains
of rubbish. He described walking through Moravia's filthy
streets and seeing the suffering of dozens of families who
had nowhere else to go. He was so horrified by what he'd
seen that he'd ordered his men to buy blankets, mattresses
and basic necessities and distribute them to the residents of
the slum. Unsatisfied with that gesture, however, he told
me he wanted to give houses not just to the residents of
Moravia but to the whole city. 'Darling,' he said, 'I don't
care how much it costs to get all those poor people out of
poverty.'

I'm sure he meant it: he seemed deeply affected, and
though giving houses to all of Medellín's poor might sound
a little crazy, I think he believed it was possible because he
had so much money – even though he'd acquired it through
illicit means – and he didn't mind giving it away.

And so Medellín Without Slums was born. The project
took shape quickly. Pablo purchased a huge lot in the Buenos Aires neighbourhood, on the way to the airport in
Rionegro, with the goal of financing an initial construction

phase of 500 houses and getting up to 5,000 over the next two years.

One day, at the house, he told me he'd received a report from the departmental Ministry of Health that said that Antioquia had a high number of people with cleft palates, a congenital defect that marks a person's life for ever. He told me he thought it was horrible for a person to have to live like that, so he was going to help them. He hired a prominent plastic surgeon from Medellín to head a team of specialists to assess cases. The idea took off, and soon four surgeons arrived from Brazil and Spain and operated on dozens of children with the condition. In addition, many people came to us about serious illnesses, and several times Pablo agreed to pay for costly treatments and surgeries to help them.

On another occasion, after a charity telethon was held in Medellín, the regional director got upset because the money collected had to be sent to Bogotá, where the national organisation would determine how the funds should be distributed. A prominent anchor told the director he could get him more money if he didn't care where it came from. The director replied that he wasn't interested in where donations came from, and so my husband contributed a large sum of money to that year's telethon.

On 5 March 1982, as the preparations were beginning for the land where the Medellín Without Slums houses were to be constructed, the campaign finished with a large rally in front of the Liberal Alternative headquarters in Envigado. Buses chartered by the party brought voters from the towns of Barbosa, Girardota, Copacabana, Bello,

Itagüí, Sabaneta, La Estrella and Caldas. That night, besides Pablo, the main speakers were Jairo Ortega, Orlón Atehortúa, Raúl Ossaba, María Alzate de Escobar and Fernando Avendaño. (Avendaño, known as the Animal Guy, was in charge of collecting the animals that Pablo purchased for the zoo at Nápoles.)

I went with Pablo that day, and I remember that his brief pep talk was focussed on the need to change political habits:

> This is the night things change ... We're not going to allow our candidate lists to be corrupted by tyranny or incompetent or outmoded elements. The primary ideology of our movement is public-mindedness, nationalism, and social, ecological and athletic programmes. We want to reach the hearts of housewives to ask them not to buy foreign products, to support our domestic industry, which creates job growth and progress.

Finally, on 14 March 1982, we were delighted when Pablo was elected to the House as a substitute member. After four in the afternoon, once the polls were closed, I accompanied him to the Liberal Alternative headquarters in Envigado to meet with Ortega and Santofimio and get updates on the vote count. But as the hours passed and the results were only trickling in, I told my husband I was going home and would be waiting by the phone. Around eight o'clock at night, the National Civil Registry confirmed that the candidate Pablo Escobar had won a seat in the House of Representatives.

It was a big surprise. I was young – twenty-one years old – and I didn't know much about politics, but I loved what I'd seen so far. Naively, my first thought was to imagine what I would wear on 20 July, when the new representatives were sworn in. But I was also haunted by worries about how to act, how to respond if I was asked about current affairs in the country. That night, I impatiently waited once more till after midnight for Pablo to return home. When he did, his face was all lit up. After a bite to eat, he sat on the edge of the bed and said, 'Honey, get ready to be the First Lady of the nation.'

I hadn't seen him like that for ages. He was aglow, going on and on about the projects he wanted to push forward in Congress, including that the government should fully fund education in the public universities and build hospitals to treat under-served populations at no cost.

As we lay there, he hugged me tight, with an unusual fervour that expressed his joy, and then whispered in my ear, 'Tata, the day of the swearing in, I'm not going to wear a suit and tie; I'm going to Congress in my shirtsleeves.'

I didn't say anything, but I thought a person should attend such a solemn occasion dressed in his finest.

A couple of weeks later, the National Electoral Council certified the election results and the then-government minister, Jorge Mario Eastman, issued the credentials acknowledging the new legislators, my husband among them. From that moment on, Pablo Escobar had parliamentary immunity.

At the beginning of April, Pablo suggested we spend ten days in Brazil to celebrate his election and relax. He explained that he was going be very busy in the coming weeks: the first and second rounds of the presidential election would be in May and June, he'd be sworn into Congress in July, and the government would change over in August. It was obvious that politics was all he could think about, although I assumed that his occasional lovers still had a special place in his private day-planner. What's more, his cousin Gustavo Gaviria was still heading up his businesses, which were raking in vast sums of money.

Following the Antioquian custom of prioritising family above all else, on 12 April 1982, we took a commercial flight to São Paulo and from there to Rio de Janeiro. Pablo had managed to persuade everyone to come along: my mother-in-law; his siblings and their spouses and kids; my mother, sisters, brothers-in-law, and nieces and nephews; Gustavo Gaviria and his wife, children, and parents ... More than twenty people! It was a difficult trip because we had to rent a bus to go anywhere and finding a large enough table at restaurants was practically impossible.

But the worst part wasn't the crowd of people my husband had invited but rather the shame I had to endure when the men would take off at night to see strippers and prostitutes in the best bars in Rio. Because of their endless partying, almost all of the couples, including Pablo and me, ended up fighting, so we headed back to Colombia but ended up having to spend a night in São Paulo. I was deeply hurt and felt demeaned as a woman. 'Why did he invite me?' I kept asking myself. 'To celebrate what? If he wanted to have fun with his buddies, why didn't he do it alone?'

Pablo wanted to make me believe I was important to him, but his behaviour was very selfish, as I wrote to him sitting alone in our room in São Paulo's Hotel Maksoud Plaza: 'I want very few things from life, among them the person I adore, but I want life to teach him to hold on to me.' I never knew whether Pablo even read my letter because he only got back in at dawn, by which time we needed to leave for the airport.

Back in Medellín, in the third week of April 1982, my husband, now a representative to the House, stayed long hours in his office working on political matters. Whenever he came home, I noticed, he'd talk about his and Gustavo's intense interest in the outcome of the presidential election on 30 May. The candidates at the time were Alfonso López Michelsen, Liberal; Belisario Betancur Cuartas, Conservative; Luis Carlos Galán, New Liberalism; and Gerardo Molina, from the leftist Democratic Front. I was concentrating on the preparations for Pablo's swearing in on 20 July and on family matters that took up quite a lot of my time, so I didn't pay much attention. But it was becoming common for Pablo to be at the centre of any problem, and a few weeks later, major media outlets reported that the Liberal campaign had received donations from people of dubious repute. Though I asked several times what was going on, Pablo told me not to worry, he'd explain later.

However, it seemed like the scandal might get bigger, so I decided to talk to a few people who'd worked with Pablo on his congressional campaign and soon had a fairly clear picture of the situation. I was terrified. According to what I learned, Pablo and Gustavo had agreed to contribute money and logistics to the López and Betancur campaigns to get assurances on the topic that concerned them most: extradition.

Pablo was tasked with approaching the Liberals, and his first move was to organise a meeting with the candidate and the campaign's national director, Ernesto Samper Pizano. The appointment was arranged thanks to the intervention of Santiago Londoño White, Antioquia coordinator and one of my husband's acquaintances. From what I heard, the private meeting in the Medellín suite of the Inter-Continental Hotel was less a gathering of Liberal supporters than it was a summit at which Pablo and his partners – Carlos Lehder, Gonzalo 'El Mexicano' Rodríguez, Rafael Cardona, Alberto Prieto, Pablo Correa, Gerardo Moncada, Fernando Galeano, Santiago Ocampo, the Ochoa brothers and Héctor Roldán – were presented as wealthy businessmen who were ready to help. One of the attendees told me that López was there for just ten minutes before leaving Samper as his representative. Samper said several times that he was in favour of legalising marijuana. As the meeting wrapped up, the attendees extravagantly bought 60 million pesos' worth of raffle tickets for a car, one of the campaign's fundraising efforts.

While my husband was rubbing elbows with the Liberals, Gustavo Gaviria was in charge of working with the Conservatives through Diego Londoño White, campaign treasurer in Antioquia. According to close associates of my husband, El Mexicano had his twin-engine Piper Cheyenne II plane painted blue and lent it to Betancur, the Conservative candidate, for the final stretch of the campaign.

In the end, on Sunday, 30 May, Belisario Betancur won the election by more than 400,000 votes. According to analysts, the second-place candidate, Alfonso López, lost because the dissident Luis Carlos Galán siphoned off a lot of his votes.

On Monday, 19 June, the day before Pablo was sworn in, our house in the El Diamante neighbourhood was absolute chaos. While I packed our suitcases for Bogotá, people kept trooping in and out: family members, neighbours from La Paz, and even strangers drawn by the commotion. Everybody had opinions on what we should wear, what would look best. One of my sisters and I insisted to Pablo that he needed to wear a tie, but there was no persuading him. In preparation for that day, on my most recent trip abroad I'd bought him two lovely Italian neckties, and for myself I'd bought a red and black velvet Valentino dress.

'Pablo, who do you think you are? You think they're going to change the protocols just because you were elected congressman?' I asked, but he didn't listen.

As always, we stayed at the Hilton in Bogotá. My husband couldn't stop beaming. On Tuesday, 20 July, we arrived at the Capitol in a luxurious army-green Mercedes-Benz limousine that Carlos Lehder lent to Pablo. Immediately, it was clear the new congressman couldn't do whatever he wanted; the guard refused to let him in as he wasn't following the dress code. Pablo kicked and argued, asking for the guard's help getting around the rule, but it was no use. In the end, he had to give in and borrow the guard's tie. It was mustard-coloured with light blue and red stripes. Hideous. Finally we were allowed in, but I couldn't hide my anger at Pablo's stubbornness and my own lack of initiative since I could have brought one of the new ties in my handbag.

Entering the halls of Congress was an unforgettable experience. I was dazzled and very excited, especially when I saw I was the only woman who'd accompanied her husband to the swearing-in ceremony. I felt very important, and Pablo looked proud to introduce me to his peers. I finally believed that Pablo's political career had become a reality. There is one photo of the swearing-in ceremony that perfectly illustrates Pablo's frame of mind. While all of his colleagues took their oaths with their right hands raised and their fingers pressed together, he raised his right hand in a triumphant V for victory.

The day after we returned to Medellín, I started looking for the best consultants on protocol and public image; I also decided to study English and French, as I imagined I might find myself travelling around the world as the wife and companion of Congressman Pablo Escobar.

In October, three months after the ceremony, Congress selected a committee to travel to Spain to observe the election that would choose that country's new head of state. The senators were Santofimio, Raimundo Emiliani Román and Víctor Cárdenas, and the representatives were my husband and Jairo Ortega. Being part of that 'exclusive' group was evidence that Pablo was beginning to wield influence over the decisions of the Colombian Congress.

Pablo was very excited about the trip to Spain and agreed that I could pack his best clothing, including a dark suit, a long-sleeved shirt, a trench coat and a tie. It was a big shift since up to that point he hadn't cared about protocol and what people thought.

On the day of the trip, though, there was nobody in the world who could have convinced him to wear appropriate clothing, and instead he donned sneakers, jeans, a printed shirt and a flashy watch with two faces: one showing Colombian time and the other Spanish. In the suitcase he also packed a pair of elevator shoes somebody had brought him from New York that made him look two inches taller. As always, much later I would discover that those shoes had been a gift from the TV host Virginia Vallejo.

Santofimio, Ortega and my husband travelled from Bogotá to Madrid on Monday, 25 October 1982, in first class on an Avianca jumbo jet that made a brief stop in San Juan, Puerto Rico. Three days later, on Thursday, 28 October, the three men witnessed the landslide victory of Felipe González, the Spanish Socialist Workers' Party (PSOE) candidate, and that night they headed to the Westin Palace Hotel in downtown Madrid to greet the winner. Pablo told me by phone that they'd been allowed in easily because Santofimio had known González for years, and the two had even spent time together in Bogotá when the Spanish politician was travelling there. Afterwards, they went to a party organised by the bullfighter Pepe Dominguín, and at dawn they found themselves at another celebration with the Colombian journalists Enrique Santos and Antonio Caballero.

When he came back from Spain, Pablo told me he wanted to make his mark in the House of Representatives, so he intended to put more focus on the role he'd given

Virginia Vallejo in September, to burnish his public image and open doors for him in Bogotá's closed-off political class.

At the same time, Pablo foresaw that reporters would seek him out for his opinions on various topics, so he asked Neruda for advice and got two recommendations: to learn basic economic concepts and to read biographies of the writer Gabriel García Márquez, who had just been awarded the Nobel Prize for Literature. My husband followed his advice to the letter. He also hired somebody to record the TV and radio news programmes and create a summary of the day's most important events because he wanted to keep abreast of what was happening in Colombia and around the world.

Life seemed to be smiling on my husband, who every day became more convinced he was destined to occupy an important position in the country's political life. The good thing about that dream was that I was apparently included; he often told me to get ready to be the First Lady of the nation. But his ego was growing, and he started asking regularly, 'Tata, what have people been saying about President Reagan, Pope John Paul II, and me?'

IN EARLY 1983, PABLO STARTED FOCUSING ON MEDELLÍN Without Slums, using Virginia Vallejo to record an episode of the programme *¡Al ataque!* [Charge!] with him, in which he explained his plan to give houses to the residents of the Moravia landfill site. Then, on Sunday, 13 March, my husband hosted a bullfight in the La Macarena ring, which was filled to the rafters. I was there with Juan Pablo and my father-in-law, Abel, and it was exciting to watch each bullfighter approach the stands and offer his performance to Pablo, who looked pleased but a bit embarrassed. He was never a big fan of public accolades, though in private it was obvious he enjoyed receiving applause. That afternoon included performances by the mounted bullfighters Alberto Uribe Sierra, Andrés Vélez, Dayro Chica and Fabio Ochoa, and the toreros César Rincón and Pepe Cáceres, who fought eight bulls from the ranches of Los Guateles, in Spain, and Rocha Hermanos, in Colombia.

Despite the success of the events organised to promote his social programmes, my husband became the target of attacks from the senator Rodrigo Lara Bonilla and the newspaper *El Espectador*. Filled with a swelling sense of power, though, he dismissed the vehemence with which Lara, the right-hand man of New Liberalism leader Luis Carlos Galán, talked about what he called 'dirty money' in politics and football, and the way the Bogotá newspaper criticised the emergence of dubious characters in the country's political and economic sphere, especially in Antioquia. Though no one mentioned Pablo by name, he got the hint. One day at a public event, he started ranting about the newspaper, calling it a 'journalistic enterprise that distorts the news, injecting a morbid and damaging venom into it and attacking people'. He continued, 'I hadn't wanted to be too hard on *El Espectador*, but you've seen the attacks and slanders they have been launching against our programmes recently.'

Confident of his influence, Pablo insisted all the more strongly on fighting against extradition. He put all his energy into organising a summit of 'businessmen' from all over the country in the newly opened Kevins nightclub in Medellín. And so in the second week of April 1983, no fewer than 300 people descended on the locale to participate in the first meeting of the National Forum of Extraditables. Virginia Vallejo, acting as the host, explained the reasons for the gathering and then turned the floor over to Pablo, who opened the event with a brief statement: 'I want to ask all of you, in the name of citizenship, sovereignty and human rights, for your help in combating the extradition treaty.'

The discussion lasted more than three hours, with many attendees arguing in favour of the idea that Colombians should be tried in their own country and not handed over to foreign courts. Somebody even requested the floor and said that the group should demand that the government intervene to prevent Colombian citizen Carlos Arango, who'd been convicted in Florida for homicide and cocaine trafficking, from being executed in the electric chair.

The following Tuesday, 19 April 1983, Pablo arrived home with a broad smile on his face and holding a copy of issue 50 of *Semana* magazine, which contained an article titled 'An Antioquian Robin Hood'. He was beaming with pride that a national media outlet had mentioned him for the first time, and he told me that a reporter from the magazine had attended the extradition forum and interviewed him afterwards.

'You see the way the mass media construct myths, darling? I wish I actually were Robin Hood so I could do more good things for the poor.'

The article was mentioned on several radio stations, and one journalist asked him whether he felt like Robin Hood. Pablo replied, 'Not at all, but it's a label I like a lot ... Anyone familiar with the story of Robin Hood knows quite well that he fought for and defended the lower classes.'

Public recognition of my husband was on the rise, and he took advantage of this new popularity to keep opening sports arenas built with money he'd donated. On 15 May 1983, I went to watch him to take the opening kick in front of 12,000 people for the inaugural game at the football stadium in the Tejelo neighbourhood of Medellín. Three weeks later, in early June, he also performed the ceremonial kick-off for a night game between the reserve team of the Club Atlético Nacional and amateur players from the Moravia neighbourhood, for the grand opening of a football field with modern lighting.

But my husband's lucky streak came to an end on 8 August, when President Belisario Betancur upended his cabinet and switched out eight of his ministers. One of the new ministers, Justice Minister Rodrigo Lara Bonilla – the first member of New Liberalism in the administration – didn't like Pablo, as was clear to me that night.

Over the next few days, Pablo grew irritable and restless, and he started doing something out of character: if he got home and found me watching the news and Lara was on explaining the measures he planned to take to combat dirty money in politics and football, he'd rant angrily about the minister and shut the television off. When I asked him what was wrong, he'd say it was better if I didn't watch the news because the programmes presented false information.

One night, Pablo was with me when the 9.30pm news showed a press conference with Minister Lara. A television screen in the minister's office was displaying a close-up image of my husband, which made Pablo so incensed that he almost hurled the TV to the floor. For years, Pablo was constantly turning off the TV when they started talking about him, the things he was doing, the manhunt, the rewards on offer.

Very worried, one night Gustavo Gaviria came over to talk to Pablo and was so upset that he said what he was thinking right in front of me: 'Pablo, man, let's leave the country, let's disappear. It's risky being here now. We've got plenty of money – we can hide anywhere we want. Listen to me.'

'No,' Pablo replied, 'there's no going back. We've got economic power, and now we're going for political power. Leave Colombia? Not on your life.'

Pablo was unfazed by the warning of his cousin, partner and friend, but it was clear that Minister Lara was gearing up for a fight.

As was usual in our relationship, I found out about what was happening around him little by little – sometimes, as in this case, through the media, and at other times from his men, who would sometimes let slip a bit of information here or there when I was nearby, although they were forbidden to tell me anything directly.

And so 18 August 1983 arrived, when the congressmen Ernesto Lucena and Jairo Ortega, from the same party as Pablo and Santofimio, participated in a debate on dirty money with Minister Lara during a House session. That night I turned on the TV news and heard a journalist reporting that my husband hadn't attended the debate. But Carlos Lehder had, in his role as editor of the newspaper *Quindío Libre*, occupying a spot in the box reserved for reporters. A photo of the event showed him smiling and defiant.

I felt a twinge of worry when Representative Ortega said to Lara, 'I'd like to ask you a very respectful question, Minister. Minister Lara, are you familiar with our fellow citizen Evaristo Porras? Do you know how much the individual in question donated? Was it a cheque for a million pesos?' He then pulled a copy of the cheque out of his pocket, exhibited it to those in attendance, and said it had been given to Lara in a room at the Hilton.

The revelation of the donation put intense pressure on Lara. At first he claimed not to recall the event, but the following day he called a press conference and admitted what had happened: 'I could have made any claim to justify the cheque's existence, I could have said I'd received it as payment for professional honoraria or any other kind of business, but the truth is that it was an exchange made with Roberto Bahamón related to a deal involving my family.'

Then the minister went on the offensive and said that the cheque incident was part of a mafia conspiracy and

accused my husband directly, naming him as a drug trafficker, backer of paramilitary groups and a wanted man in
the United States. Agitated, he made the following
statement:

> I know what's coming for me for denouncing the
> mafia, but that doesn't scare me. If I have to pay for it
> with my life, so be it. This is an escalation of drug
> trafficking, attempting to take out a cabinet minister
> because he's dangerous to the mafia's pernicious
> purposes, and it will then move on to other national
> figures in an effort to undermine the country's
> morals.

I was horrified by Minister Lara's words because they posed
a point of no return with my husband. Alone in my house,
I knew very difficult times lay ahead, but I never dreamed
that the clash between the two men would soon change our
lives for ever.

Pablo wasn't about to keep quiet, and the next day he
called a press conference in the Congress and another at
the offices of his newspaper, *Antioquia al Día*, in Medellín,
to respond to the minister's charges. 'Everybody knows
how much I've invested in agriculture, industry, livestock,
and construction. I've always asserted that my money has
no ties with drug trafficking.' Then he pulled out his passport and said that, contrary to Lara's claims, he wasn't
under investigation in the States, displaying his visa as
proof. He gave Lara twenty-four hours to present evidence
of his accusations. He went on to attack Lara for his lies:

The minister of justice has lied six times: he lied to the country when he said he didn't know Mr Evaristo Porras; he lied to the country when he said he hadn't received personal cheques from Mr Evaristo Porras; he lied to the country when he said that Pablo Escobar had founded MAS [Muerte a Secuestradores, Death to Kidnappers]; he lied to the country when he said that Pablo Escobar had a criminal record in the United States; he lied to the country when he said he wasn't going to resign.

The tug of war between minister and congressman dragged on, and the tension was palpable at home even though Pablo insisted that everything was under control. I remember that during that period my mother once came to visit just as Pablo was finishing reading the newspaper. Never one to hold back, she said, 'Son, if you have a tail made of straw, don't swish it next to a candle.'

'No, don't worry, nothing's going to happen.'

'You're hard-headed, and you're not considering what's best for your family. You'll remember what I said.'

As always, my mother was right, and on 25 August 1983, a week after the debate against Minister Lara, *El Espectador* published the news that would lead to my husband's political demise. In a front-page headline, the paper recalled that in June 1976, Pablo and five other people had been arrested in association with a shipment of cocaine.

From there, things happened at a dizzying clip. The minister got his second wind and ordered the grounding of nearly a hundred private planes and helicopters operating throughout the country that were suspected of being used for drug trafficking. Several of Pablo's aircraft were included. In addition, the judge of the Tenth Superior Court in Medellín, Gustavo Zuluaga, reopened the closed investigation into Pablo over the deaths of two DAS detectives who'd been after him. And as if that weren't enough, the United States revoked his entry visa.

With dark days now upon him, my husband knew he had only hours to step down from Congress and give up his seat, but he held out till the last minute. In the second week of September 1983, he refused to sign a pre-written letter that Santofimio brought to his office, in which he resigned from Liberal Alternative and his seat in the House of Representatives. It was simple: Santofimio was the head of the party and needed Pablo to step down to avoid a larger political scandal. But he was forced to leave empty-handed; my husband told him angrily that he was accustomed to writing his own statements, without anybody's help.

That was an awful period. With his credibility destroyed and accused of being a drug trafficker, now even his freedom was at stake. He looked increasingly worried. He was tormented by the idea of extradition, as he expressed to me one day: 'Three life sentences, Tata? A hundred feet underground? A living death? They're never going to get me for that, I swear.'

I was frightened to see him so shaken. I thought to myself, 'My God, what's going to happen now?'

But fate is the one at the controls, and in September 1983 I discovered that I was pregnant. We'd been trying unsuccessfully for six years, with four miscarriages and an ectopic pregnancy, but it seemed that my second baby was now on its way. It wouldn't be easy, but I was ready to go overboard taking care of myself in order to make this new dream a reality. When Pablo found out, he was thrilled. He was convinced he could resolve everything that was going on, so I didn't worry. The truth is that I was completely unaware of the actual situation.

The next weeks and months were very complicated indeed. On 26 October, a majority of the House of Representatives finally voted to revoke my husband's immunity.

The power of the state had come down on him, but he mistakenly believed he could overcome it. Being kicked out of politics was a devastating blow to my husband. He'd never imagined that his power and ability to intimidate would end up destroying him. His participation in the world of politics was fleeting, just as his crime-ridden life was fleeting. In the end, my mother had been right on that day in 1982 when Pablo agreed to go into politics and she warned him, 'If you get involved in politics, there won't be a sewer in the world where you can hide. You're going to put us all in danger, you'll hurt all of our lives.'

Pablo hadn't listened.

Chapter 6

The Hacienda Nápoles That Nobody Knows

The first time I went to see the land Pablo had just bought turned out to be a terrifying experience.

It was a Saturday morning in February 1979, and I flew there in a small, flimsy Hughes helicopter with one of my sisters, Gustavo Gaviria and his wife. After less than an hour we landed in a muddy corral, and when we got out my boots sank into the muck so far that Pablo had to come and retrieve me.

I was furious. My husband had an impish look on his face. We reached a rustic house that was hidden in the forest, very basic, with red window frames, white walls and a concrete floor. Since there wasn't really anything to see – just jungle everywhere you looked – we stayed in the house waiting for nightfall. To make things worse, there was no electricity. Several of Pablo's employees lit a bonfire and prepared beans, rice, pork crackling, beef, green plantains and arepas.

The dim light of the candles illuminated huge insects and snakes prowling outside the narrow windows, but they didn't come any closer because the men had placed lit wicks in jugs of diesel around the perimeter. Even so, I had a horrible night because the place scared me – I felt like I was in danger, like I could get bitten by a snake and die. I was shouting and unable to sleep in the unbearable heat. Pablo became irritable because he thought I was being melodramatic and immature.

I prayed silently, begging for dawn to come so that one of the worst nights of my life so far would be over. Luckily, the sun rose before six and I felt my soul return to my body.

Where was I? Pablo told us we were at the Valledupar estate, more than 2,000 acres owned by Jorge Tulio Garcés, who'd sold the property to Pablo and Gustavo for 35 million pesos – US$820,000 at the time. Fully in character, my husband told what sounded like a fantastical story, claiming that a highway would soon connect Medellín and Bogotá, and that the area, Puerto Triunfo, would become a tourist site right in the heart of Colombia.

'This land will be priceless, I'm telling you, Tata. It's got plenty of water, mountains, jungle ... It's paradise, you'll see,' he said.

Pablo seemed to have fulfilled a dream he'd mentioned to me many times: to own a piece of property like the one he'd just found. I remember he and Gustavo used to travel around in the first helicopter he bought, spending many weekends visiting different parts of Antioquia – Santa Fe de Antioquia, Caucasia, Bolombolo – but they hadn't found one they really liked.

But one day Alfredo Astado went to his office and showed him a classified in *El Colombiano* newspaper selling a farm in the town of Puerto Triunfo, near the future Medellín–Bogotá highway. Astado explained it was a beautiful area of the country and was guaranteed to thrive because the highway construction was about to start.

I didn't say anything, but I thought he was nuts. It never would have occurred to me to buy anything in that hot, dry wilderness, and deep down I thought Jorge Tulio Garcés had been lucky to find someone willing to invest in such a hostile place. It was gorgeous, I won't deny it, but my husband and his partner would have to spend a lot of money to transform such an inhospitable environment.

Over the next few weeks, Pablo was visibly excited about not just building a house but also buying more land. In mid-1979 they bought Hacienda Nápoles, right next to Valledupar, and another eight properties totaling 4,700 acres. When I asked him how much they'd cost, he told me they'd got them at a great price: all together the land had cost 90 million pesos (US$2,100,000).

Since the estates all had different names, Pablo chose one to use for all of them: Nápoles, in honor of Al Capone, the American gangster, whose parents had been from Naples. My husband admired Capone, and I sometimes saw him reading books or magazine or newspaper articles about him.

I started visiting the area fairly regularly, right at the time they started building a huge bridge across the Magdalena River that would connect up to the highway. Pablo, my sisters and I spent several weekends watching the piles of the new structure being installed, and it was fun to cross the river on the barges used for automobiles and livestock.

Overnight, all kinds of earth-moving machinery appeared at Nápoles, but Pablo and Gustavo didn't tell their wives what they were planning to do. They kept us completely sidelined, and as the months passed I realised that a hundred men were building a two-storey house and a pool.

The result couldn't have been worse. The photos that everybody's seen of the main house and pool at Nápoles are pretty and colourful. But what's not so obvious is that both were a monument to bad taste. I'll explain why.

I'll start with the two main bedrooms, located on the second floor. Ours was about fifty square feet with a bathroom, totally out of proportion with the rest of the house, which was 8,600 square feet in total. Gustavo's was the same size.

I never understood why Pablo and Gustavo had their builders create such tiny bedrooms, only big enough for a couple, not taking into account that both of them had children at the time. It was obvious they were thinking about themselves and not their families. Because of our bedroom's terrible design, we put a cot by our bed so Juan Pablo could sleep near us, and sometimes he'd bring a friend. It was extremely uncomfortable, and every time I got the chance I complained to Pablo about the complete lack of common sense of the moron who'd built the house. Much later, we sealed off one of the doors to our room to build a space large enough for a crib, but the bathroom continued to be shared by everybody.

On the first floor they built eight identical bedrooms big enough for eight people each, but just one bathroom. Behind the house were three five-car garages. The space that could be called the common area consisted of a TV room that could fit up to thirty people. Beside it was a saloon with ten four-person tables, a bar lined with large bottles of whisky and arcade games of the era such as Donkey Kong, Pac-Man, Galaxian and Space Invaders.

Viewed from a distance, the house looked rickety because the columns were too skinny and a bit crooked. It looked like it was propped up on stilts that might topple at any moment. The pool was extremely dangerous, and on one occasion I almost drowned in it. In the middle they'd built a concrete structure with the idea of setting up a refreshment stand with a bar and concrete chairs where six people could sit in the water. But there were several accidents because people would hit their heads on it when they were swimming underwater and attempted to come to the surface. It happened to me once, and I almost passed out from the blow. Ultimately, Pablo ordered the whole thing torn down and dropped the idea of the refreshment stand.

I guess Pablo assumed from the start that a lot of people would come to Nápoles, and that's why the storerooms he had built for our stocks of staple foods were so large. They were nearly as vast as warehouses, and as if that weren't enough, the kitchen contained three enormous walk-in refrigerators large enough for eight people to stand in.

Even as the house, pool, bar, gas station, Latin America's largest motocross track, helipad, landing strip and many other over-the-top structures were still being built, my husband announced one day that he wanted to build a zoo. He'd visited the Veracruz estate – owned by his friends the

Ochoas and located in the town of Repelón, in northern Colombia's Atlántico department – and was smitten with the beauty of some of the exotic animals he'd seen there.

The project became an obsession. The first thing he did was tell Alfredo Astado to look for a zoo in the United States where he could buy zebras, giraffes, elephants, flamingos, camels, buffalo, hippopotamuses, kangaroos, ostriches and exotic birds. To compose this list, Pablo consulted *National Geographic* to find out which animals would adapt most easily to the habitat in the Magdalena Medio region. Lions and tigers were left off because he thought they were dangerous and would have to be kept in captivity. The most important thing to him was that his animals would never be confined.

In the meantime, Pablo told all the street vendors and beggars he ran across to bring any rare animal species they found to his office and he'd compensate them handsomely. There followed such an endless procession of pilgrims to his door that Gustavo, furious, would simply point toward Pablo's office and say, 'The animal department's down there, to the right.' Eventually my husband called it off because people would bring him sick and malnourished animals that were in bad shape.

The method that did work was Astado's: he arranged an appointment with the owners of a zoo in Dallas, Texas, and twenty-four people went on Pablo's invitation, including all of us members of the family. When we arrived in the Dallas/Fort Worth Airport, we were surprised to find eight gleaming limousines waiting for us on the Tarmac, sent by the Hunt brothers, who owned the zoo. One of the vehicles was empty and Juan Pablo asked to travel in it alone so he could watch cartoons on the TV.

Pablo was excited about the variety and beauty of the animals we saw, especially the giraffes, kangaroos and elephants. He wanted to buy them all – he was like a kid in a toyshop. After he'd finished choosing, he added up how much they'd cost and whispered to me, 'Sweetheart, Gustavo's going to be pissed when he finds out I spent two million bucks on animals.'

I believe that trip was the happiest one he ever took. In that zoo, Pablo's face beamed with wonder and admiration. He hugged me several times and told me he was picturing how his animals were going to look at Nápoles. He was so delighted with everything that he even agreed to climb up on the back of one of the elephants, where he remained for almost ten minutes.

Once we'd visited the whole zoo, Pablo paid the US$2 million in cash and said he'd send for his animals very soon.

Two weeks after returning from Dallas, my husband organised the first trip to bring the largest group of animals into the country. They arrived via a rented ship that docked in the port city of Necoclí, on the Caribbean coast 250 miles from Medellín. From there the animals were transported by truck to Nápoles in what turned out to be a complicated operation. Concerned about how long and risky the retrieval trip had been, Pablo decided to switch to secret flights. For the task, he chose Fernando Avendaño, who thereafter came to be known as the Animal Guy.

Pablo couldn't stop talking about it. As the Animal Guy later told me, he'd hired several Hercules planes, which landed at Medellín's Olaya Herrera Airport a little after six o'clock in the evening, when the runway lights had already been turned off, to transport the animals. At the time Pablo owned two hangars next to the main runway, so Avendaño was able to land with such precision that he didn't even have to turn off the engines. Several employees then emerged from one of the hangars in trucks and cranes and unloaded the crates of animals with impressive speed.

The zoo Pablo had dreamed about was almost ready, but he wanted more animals. He bought two black parrots in Miami on a business trip. He told me they cost US$400,000, and he didn't flinch at the price because they were very exotic. Then on a leisure trip to Rio de Janeiro with his pals, he came across a blue parrot with yellow eyes, a protected species under Brazilian law. Since he couldn't export the bird legally, Pablo arranged for the pilot of his Learjet to smuggle it into Colombia after he bought it for US$100,000. The parrot travelled in the plane all by itself, Pablo told me in a mischievous tone.

The last animals to arrive at the zoo were two pink dolphins brought from the Amazon and released into one of the estate's many lakes. They were very pretty, and I used to go and play with them even though they gave off an unpleasant odour. There was just one species that didn't adapt to the Nápoles habitat: the giraffes. The six that Pablo bought at the Texas zoo – three females and three males – rejected their food and refused to eat out of the feeders installed up in the trees. In the end, sadly, they all died.

Everything was ready for the zoo opening, but something was missing: the entrance. In record time, a large gate was built and painted white with the word 'Nápoles' on the main columns in blue. On top, they perched a single-engine Piper monoplane, registration number HK-617. The history of that plane, which was white with two blue stripes along either side, is full of lies and half-truths. One version claims that my husband used the aircraft to transport his first load of cocaine, but that's not actually the case. The truth is that the little plane belonged to a friend of Pablo who crashed while landing at Olaya Herrera Airport and abandoned it because it was too badly damaged to salvage. The pieces lay there for some time until Pablo spotted them and, without really knowing what he was going to do with them, asked his friend if he could have them. Once they were his, he ordered them brought to Nápoles, where the plane was restored, but without an engine.

The bullet-riddled car that visitors saw at the estate also became legendary. The most common story was that the famous American bank robbers Bonnie and Clyde had died in the vehicle in May 1934. Nothing of the sort. That car was actually constructed from two separate vehicles: a Toyota SUV in which my husband's younger brother Luis Fernando had been killed in a crash, and a 1936 Ford that had been given to Alfredo Astado. Alfredo had built a single car from the chassis of the Toyota and the body of the Ford. One day Pablo went to Astado's house and, not finding him, told his men to take the vehicle to Nápoles to put it on display. The next week, my husband went to the spot where they'd placed the car and ordered several of his men to shoot it up, with the idea of simulating the 167 bullets that struck Bonnie and Clyde's automobile.

With the entrance now finished, Pablo opened the zoo to the public. It was an immediate success: not only was it free, but visitors could also drive through it in their own vehicles. In short order, families from all over the country came to the estate to enjoy the exotic zoo my husband had created in the heart of Colombia.

Pablo was ecstatic. At some point I asked him why he wasn't charging people to visit the zoo, even a nominal amount. His response was firm: 'Sweetheart, this zoo belongs to the people. As long as I'm alive, I'm never going to charge an entrance fee. I want poor people to be able to come and see this spectacle of nature. The day I die, you can start charging.'

But it wasn't all sunshine and rainbows. After the zoo opened, the main house at Nápoles turned into a hotel, but one with no rules. Anybody who wanted could stay there, and on the weekends it wasn't unusual for there to be 300 'guests'. In the kitchen there would be snaking lines of people, plates in hand, waiting to be served beans and shrimp or beans and fish. The caretaker did the grocery shopping, and the cooks' menus were an insult to gastronomy. There was somebody to wash and iron the guests' clothing. And very soon the ample parking area was turned into rooms full of bunks, with not nearly enough bathrooms. Around the pool were placed large boxes of swimsuits in every size, personal hygiene kits, nappies, bottles, and various brands of powdered milk, and if somebody asked for a glass of aguardiente, the anise-flavored spirit common across Colombia, they'd get an entire bottle. And so on.

The pool would be crowded with up to fifty people, and we'd have no idea who they were or where they were from. The same thing happened in the dining room – we'd be eating with dozens of strangers, many of them young women who'd gaze as Pablo as if he were some kind of god and hit on him right in front of me. I'd be left with a bitter taste in my mouth because after dinner he'd pull out his well-worn excuse about having a meeting to go to, which would generally end at four o'clock in the morning.

During that period, Pablo and I shared very few intimate moments. With all those swarms of people around, I, Pablo's wife, the supposed hostess at the estate, often felt like just another guest.

Despite everything, even with Pablo frequently away, I tried to enjoy the moment and sought distraction with my friends from school and my sisters. We'd set up races on the motocross track, ride motorcycles along the unpaved roads on the estate, and spend hours with the zoo's animals. I tried hard to entertain my guests, often inviting to bring them to Nápoles by helicopter, plane or car and asking what schedule suited them best. Some would say they needed to be back at work at seven o'clock in the morning, so at 5.30 the planes would be ready on the landing strip to take them back to Medellín.

At night, after putting Juan Pablo to bed, I'd leave him with a nanny and we'd go down to the games room and enjoy ourselves. We'd often be joined by the pilots of Pablo's planes, and would play arcade games for hours, but sometimes Pablo would come back and, if he saw me happy, he'd give me a silent, frosty stare in front of everybody, making a jealous scene in his own inimitable way. He wasn't one to throw fits or speak harshly to me, and in fact he never did, but his look would make it clear that he was furious.

I'd follow him to our bedroom, where he'd start haranguing: 'Those pilots have no respect. You're a lady, Tata, you have no business being there.'

'Pablo, what do you want me to do? Sit locked up in a bedroom somewhere? My family and friends are here, and the one who should show some respect is you. If you want to live like a free man, do it, but leave me alone in Medellín,' I'd retort.

As I've said, in designing and building Nápoles, Pablo and Gustavo did whatever they wanted. But in September 1982 I tried to put my own two cents in and asked my husband to allow me to build a gazebo because I wanted it done by his birthday. He said yes and immediately hired a prominent architect from the city, who designed a beautiful wooden structure with a thatched roof. It could hold 150 people and had a dance floor and two relaxation rooms. We'd go down three times a week by helicopter to oversee the construction, which was completed in just two months.

Once the gazebo was done, I started decorating it with Aunt Inés and four landscapers, but I made the mistake of leaving late one night, forgetting that the guerrillas set up checkpoints in an area known as Monteloro on the road to Medellín. I was anxious to get home to see Juan Pablo, so we took the risk, but Aunt Inés and I became frightened when numerous armed men came out and stopped the vehicles on the road, including several intercity buses.

The bodyguards and I had agreed that they'd deny knowing me if anything happened, and that's what we did. The guerrilla soldiers brought everybody out of the cars and buses, and Aunt Inés and I managed to go unnoticed because we hid behind a house. Then the attackers burned the buses and I panicked, thinking that they were going to kill us.

We had been in the rebels' hands for about five hours when one of them said we could go. We got back to Nápoles at two o'clock in the morning, and I called Pablo to tell him what had happened. He ordered that security be reinforced at the estate and said a helicopter would come pick us up at seven o'clock in the morning. I'd barely escaped a kidnapping.

And so things went. After celebrating my husband's birthday in the new gazebo, the new year came, with a month-long celebration from mid-December to mid-January. Pablo hired the Venezuelan Pastor López and his band, and they'd play from nine at night to nine in the morning the next day. One night almost a thousand people came to dance, but we didn't even know a lot of them.

Life at Nápoles was lived at a frenetic pace. The landing strip looked like an airport, and on a normal weekend, there would be up to a dozen aircraft parked there. Pablo had a lot of friends, and at that time he was not being pursued by the law. Even my brother Mario got caught up in the atmosphere of excess; he had a plane too and was always flying around: 'I'm going to have breakfast in Bogotá, and

I'll be back for lunch. I'm going to bring Pablo some of those cheese and guayaba treats they sell at the airport.' Nicolás Escobar, the son of my brother-in-law Roberto, was at Nápoles one day and got a craving for a particular hamburger sold at the Oviedo shopping centre in Medellín, and he immediately had employees fetch one for him by helicopter.

My husband devoted a lot of time to the zoo whenever he was able to be there. I often saw him visiting the animals at all hours to see what they needed, what kind of food they liked. That desire to take care of his animals could also lead to excesses, such as feeding the flamingos king shrimp for six months when he noticed their pink plumage losing its colour. Or the day he ordered his men to buy three tons of carrots to feed to the elephants because he was worried about their lack of appetite. The idea didn't work, and the pachyderms languished for a long time, even though my husband tried to tempt them with chopped sugarcane and different kinds of grasses.

Nápoles became so renowned that on 31 May 1983, my husband authorised Naranja Postobon, the soft drinks arm of the Ardila Lülle corporation, to film an advert there. The filming took two days and made use of Pablo's Twin Otter plane and our amphibious and safari vehicles. The commercial starred a large number of children alongside the elephants, ostriches, giraffes, antelopes, cranes and kangaroos. Juan Pablo and one of my sisters participated too. After they left, my son was angry because the other children had damaged several of his motorcycles and racing cars.

Days later an impressive floral arrangement with chocolates and a bottle of spirits arrived at our house, sent to Pablo by the soft drinks company.

In that golden period, many famous people passed through Nápoles. These included the diva Amparo Grisales, who at one point was filming a movie in the area and came to visit us with the other actors. Pablo gazed at her blissfully; as I learned afterwards, they'd already met at a party in Medellín while I was travelling in Europe.

Nápoles also frequently welcomed the famous Argentine singer-songwriter Leonardo Favio, who went out partying with Pablo on numerous occasions. It was always hard for me when he came because my husband would disappear for days at a time, and when they left the estate they'd go around in a luxurious Porsche. Another frequent visitor was the ranchera singer Helenita Vargas, who charmed guests at several parties at the estate. As I've already mentioned, she was my idol because I identified with her songs' heart-wrenching lyrics. I also remember the Argentine star Leo Dan, who livened up long parties at the estate with the most famous starlets of the era.

And how could I overlook Virginia Vallejo, whom I never saw at Nápoles but whose romance with my husband she describes at length in her book. The two even met at the estate, and their intense emotional relationship blossomed from there.

In the time that he had it, Hacienda Nápoles was everything to Pablo, who wanted to do many things, almost all of them at once. One day, while flying over the Claro River in a helicopter, he even decided to build a dam. He was convinced the water from some of the rivers in the region could generate energy for part of the country.

In his enthusiasm, he contracted people for the massive project who were not remotely qualified and made him spend a lot of money. He also hired 700 workers. But the project crashed and burned after my husband consulted the engineer Diego Londoño, who brought in experts who warned of the danger of a catastrophe since the area was not appropriate for a dam. Worried, Pablo had no choice but to call the enterprise off.

Much has been said about the evil things that happened at Nápoles; I did not witness those. I sometimes didn't visit for long periods and, when I was there, Pablo made sure I didn't witness the darker events.

Twenty-five years after Pablo's death, the estate is now a tourist attraction in the Magdalena Medio. There, life overcame war and thousands of families earn a living from the zoo, the natural attractions, the climate. These days, 12,000 people visit the estate every weekend, paying 85,000 pesos (US$29) each.

My husband put all his efforts and endless amounts of his illegal money into building something that would outlast him. And he succeeded. The only thing he didn't manage was to be buried at one of the prettiest spots on the property and have us plant a kapok tree on top of him, as he instructed us several times.

Chapter 7

Looking for a World That Wasn't Pablo's

One of the several wars I've experienced in my life started at dawn on Tuesday, 13 January 1988, when Manuela, Juan Pablo and I were sleeping in the penthouse of the Mónaco bulding in Medellín and were awakened by what at first seemed to be an earthquake but was actually a car bomb going off.

It was 5.13am. The shockwave tore through the building, located in the Santa María de Los Ángeles neighbourhood near Medellín's Club Campestre. Behind it, the chapel where we went to pray nearly every Sunday and where we had only recently baptised my daughter, Manuela, was badly damaged. At least five houses in the neighbourhood disappeared because the car bomb opened a crater some twelve feet deep and thirty-three feet across that killed three people, seriously wounded ten more and left a hundred injured.

The attack greatly damaged my art collection. Valuable works were destroyed by the expanding wave that stretched more than half a mile out around the explosion, while others were riddled with shrapnel, although some were completely unharmed. The powerful boom made the whole city shake.

In those ill-fated moments, I remembered my mother, who as usual seemed to be able to prophesy the future. That morning she'd called me from San Andrés, where she was holidaying, and told me, 'Darling, help me rest easy this last night here. Please go stay at my apartment – I've got a bad feeling … Something's going to happen to you.'

'Relax, Mum,' I replied, 'it's too late at night to be going out with a two-year-old baby and a nine-year-old boy. God is good, nothing is going to happen to us, don't worry.'

She was right, but we survived thanks to the grace of God.

After the bomb, my relationship with art was hit hard. I'd been exploring that sophisticated world since I was eleven years old, and had visited the most exclusive galleries in Medellín and Bogotá and abroad in order to acquire a large number of paintings and sculptures, almost all of which were on display on the two floors of the penthouse of the Mónaco building, my home.

But I didn't just want to buy art. During that period I also visited the studios of dozens of artists and learned to interpret their works, to connect with their essence. In doing so, I also frequented the sumptuous mansions of upper-class families in Medellín, Bogotá, Rome, New York, and Paris, where I discovered incredible museum pieces. To get up to speed, I took several courses on art history and purchased specialised books that gave me the tools to communicate more easily with that insular coterie.

Even as a child, I'd been struck by the beauty of certain objects, maybe because I was raised in a family environment that prized creativity and detail. Of course I knew nothing about aesthetics, much less about art, but as I grew older I became interested in painting, reading, etiquette, languages and athletics. The image I sought to project to others sent the clear message that I was looking to transform my story.

Practically from the start of my relationship with Pablo, his absences shaped the rhythm of my life. I had to get used to his lies, his activities, his coming home at daybreak and his disappearances that lasted days and even weeks. That reality, which caused me immense pain and indignation, forced me to create a world that would minimise my suffering. Art held a central place in my daily life, and I must acknowledge that my husband's money and that of some of his friends helped me to obtain a brief role in that world.

In the beginning, while courting me, Pablo gave me a guitar and later an organ that sparked my interest in music. Later, in 1977, shortly after Juan Pablo's birth, my husband met the Antioquian artist Pedro Arboleda, whose work focussed mainly on painting nude women, women coming out of the shower and women promenading in sun hats. Pablo was fascinated by Arboleda's work and bought several paintings, including a still life, which we hung in our newly rented apartment in the La Candelaria neighbourhood. I always thought that, rather than having a genuine interest in Arboleda's works, what Pablo was really interested in was being around his models. Even so, we formed a close bond with the painter that I have maintained to this day.

It was around that time that the International Furniture Centre, located in an industrial area of the town of Itagüí, in the Aburrá Valley, started to take off. The business had been founded in the early 1970s, and from the very start its owners gave space to small galleries that exhibited works by young artists. I loved the place and in short order acquired works by renowned Antioquian painters such as Pedro Nel Gómez, Débora Arango, Francisco Antonio Cano and Ricardo Gómez Campuzano. I also bought an oil painting by the Argentine artist Delia Cugat; I was struck by the movement in it and its interesting use of light. The painting was of a woman with dogs, and in the background was a light-blue and white ribbon with a sun embroidered in the centre. It was the national flag of the artist's home country, which I would coincidentally come to know well years later, when I was forced to flee Colombia.

Buying the house in El Diamante from the renowned architect Raúl Fajardo opened unimaginable horizons for me in my burgeoning contact with the art world. The comfortable structure had a reflecting pool and in the middle of it a beautiful bronze sculpture of a couple kissing, the Antioquian artist Salvador Arango's *The Kiss*. Though Fajardo initially said that the work was not included in the deal, I told Pablo not to buy it if they removed the sculpture. In the end, *The Kiss* stayed and, weeks later, I decided to meet the sculptor, visiting him at his studio in a place known as Las Letras de Coltejer, in eastern Medellín.

That first conversation with the great artist was unforgettable, and Arango ended up becoming my mentor, friend and travel companion for several years. He was an honest, unbiased guide who didn't take advantage of my naivety and lack of experience. Being with him was enriching, and through him I learned much about the contemporary art scene.

One thing leads to another, as the saying goes. One day I went to visit a friend and was struck by the good taste and elegance with which she'd decorated the house's large terrace. I asked who had designed the space and she pointed me to Julia Acosta, an expert on interior design and art from Medellín. I asked for Acosta's telephone number and invited her to come see me. The next day I met a friendly, cheerful woman who immediately started wandering slowly through my house, not saying a word. Once she'd finished half an hour later, she said coldly and with great professionalism, 'Look, Victoria, the first thing you have to do is bring in three or four trucks.'

'Why so many trucks, Julia?'

'You've got to empty everything in this place out and take it to the dump. It's all hideous, including that tacky Pedrín lamp.'

Pedrín was well known in Medellín for his unique, exotic lamps.

'What? That can't be right. Even the Louis XV furniture my husband gave me? That has to stay,' I said unhappily.

'It's horrible. And those porcelain figurines, just god-awful. Where did you get all that stuff?'

I was willing to change a lot of things, but I told her there was no way she could remove the living-room furniture; it would be the end of my marriage. She agreed, and thus began a great friendship. Julia ended up being vital both in decorating many of the spaces we lived in and in shaping my future art collection.

Having decided what to do with the furniture – we moved it to the study – we started visiting interior design and decor stores, and Julia occasionally invited me to exhibitions at the few art galleries Medellín boasted at the time. It was very satisfying, and I had soon bought my first work by the master Alejandro Obregón, an oil painting with a colourful bird on a yellow background called *Carnivorous Flowers*. I also acquired a watercolour by the painter Fernando Botero and three charcoal drawings of nudes by Luis Caballero, who was famous in the Medellín art world because in 1968 he'd won the city's first Ibero-American Biennial of Painting.

Julia also took me to the homes of some of the most prominent families in Medellín to see their private art collections and exquisite decorative objects. It was incredible to discover the Antioquian 'aristocracy's' interest in travelling through Europe and the United States to educate themselves and keep on top of the latest trends in art and decor.

One of those visits took us to the huge, beautiful home of the Echavarría family, located diagonally opposite the Oviedo shopping centre. I was impressed by the grandeur of their artworks and historical objects, which had been in the family for centuries. But the new generations that would inherit them were less interested in the pieces, so there was a possibility that I could buy some of them.

Julia and I went to the house several times. We could only visit at two in the afternoon and tiptoe through the house because at that hour the grandmother would be resting in her room – she was in delicate health and wouldn't have been pleased to see strangers wandering around. The situation was a bit awkward, and I disliked the sensation of being both guest and intruder at the same time, nor was I sure about breaking up part of the history of such a pedigreed family.

Over the course of those visits, I acquired several prized items: the medal awarded to Simón Bolívar after his victory in the Battle of Boyacá, in 1819; the original sketch for a sculpture of Bolívar on horseback that the governor commissioned from a famous Italian artist to be erected in Medellín's Bolívar Square; and a painting of a violin by the master Francisco Antonio Cano, painted in homage to the Antioquia Symphony Orchestra. With those objects of great historical value in my home, I made a sort of secret pact with the grandmother of the Echavarría family and promised to preserve them as genuine treasures.

In my effort to expand my horizons in the world of art, it wasn't long before I took the next step: meeting Bogotá's most prominent art dealers through Julia, who introduced me to them at their respective galleries. I will not mention their names out of respect because they are honourable people. In addition to establishing a business relationship with them, I was also genuinely interested in learning about art.

Thanks to my frequent visits to the capital city to talk with dealers, people started whispering that an investor from Medellín was buying works by contemporary artists of the era. Overnight, artists and Bogotá's most prominent gallery owners became interested in meeting me, inviting me to exhibitions, dinners and cocktail parties. Things were easier for me then because at the time Pablo was still seen as a politician and businessman, and his problems with the law had not yet come to the fore.

These visits to Bogotá galleries once led to an odd experience involving one particular artwork. It happened when the wife of one of the dealers offered me a painting by the Bogotá artist Alberto Iriarte, known in art-world circles as Mefisto. She and I had met a few times, and though I thought it was a strange offer, she was asking so little money that I leaped at the chance to buy. Both of us were pleased to seal the deal.

But things didn't end there. A little while later, a gallery owner called to ask me to resell the painting, but I told him no. What had actually happened was that the woman sold the work – which her husband treasured immensely – as retribution for her spouse's continual infidelities.

In the meantime, I eagerly cultivated my relationship with the great Salvador Arango, from whom I commissioned several works, and he also connected me with a number of artists in Bogotá, including Armando Villegas, Manuel Estrada and Édgar Negret. Whenever I travelled, I took the opportunity to visit them in their studios, so each meeting was a master class in art history told in the first person. It was a happy time for me in which I learned a lot.

Negret in particular was very generous, opening up his studio and home in the Santa Ana neighbourhood, in northern Bogotá. It was an impressive place because in addition to his collection of Latin American art, his own works, which were full of colour and magic, were on display.

Days later, Julia gave me some good news: the master Alejandro Obregón was willing to receive us in his home in the walled city of Cartagena. When we visited, I was struck by how charming the place was. It was a typical Cartagena home, full of interior courtyards, with beautiful roofs and terraces. Many of his works and several by other contemporary artists were hung on the walls in the spacious colonial mansion.

It was an unforgettable afternoon. Obregón made every effort to make us comfortable, and talked at fascinating length about his processes as a painter, his rejection of academicism and how no artist had influenced his own style. Despite his kindness, however, he refused to sell me any of his pieces, saying that a renowned gallery in Bogotá represented him. I returned to Medellín frustrated but grateful to have seen into a world that few people could access.

Being in constant contact with dealers and gallery owners, visiting them, buying artworks, attending exhibitions – it all gave me some of the greatest satisfaction I've ever experienced. Back then it wasn't unusual for me to receive packages in the mail containing 8"x10" colour photographs of works for sale, not just in Bogotá but in other parts of the world, with information about the artists and the works' value. It was an excellent system. Clients could pay for the art in monthly instalments, and the work would be delivered once we'd paid in full.

One morning I received an envelope containing the images of a painting that left me dumbstruck: *Rock 'n' Roll – La Danse*, 33"x46" in size and signed on the right-hand side by the Spanish artist Salvador Dalí. It was extraordinary. I was struck by the dynamism of the couple in an endless desert, sexually charged and dreamlike. I found it incredible that at twenty-two years old I could have a work of art like that in my home. But I pulled it off and, twenty-four months later, when I made the final payment, the painting was already hanging in the library, in a place of honour where it could be seen from various spots in the room. I couldn't believe it. For a while it was my big secret; I didn't tell anyone I'd bought it, and Pablo didn't notice because he was busy and never paid attention to the paintings in our home.

I didn't know it then, but the Dalí would play a key role in my life in the years to come.

Little by little, as I learned and grew, I became intensely interested in the painter and sculptor Fernando Botero, who was taking the world by storm with his art and whom I admired for his moving life story. I remember having read several articles that discussed the financial hardships he and his family had faced and how he'd overcome the endless criticism he received for the style he chose to employ in his work.

Since I was on the radar of people who sold art, I was able to travel to Bogotá to see Botero paintings as they arrived in Colombia and choose which ones to buy. In that way, I acquired a number of his paintings and sculptures, but my favourites were his bullfighting paintings; nevertheless, their high prices made them out of reach for me. As I mentioned, I bought art in instalments because I was doing it all without Pablo's support, since he wasn't interested in art, just in objects and old cars. If my husband had understood what art meant, I'm sure my collection would have been five times larger than it ended up being.

My love of Botero was so widely known that two major Bogotá dealers invited me to the opening of an exhibition of his best works in the Quintana Gallery, which was the most famous gallery in Bogotá at the time. The event was a huge deal and drew the crème de la crème of Bogotá society. President Belisario Betancur attended as a special guest.

At some point during the evening I was introduced to Fernando Botero. Excited, I told him how much I admired his work and his path as an artist, and I added that my big dream was to acquire more of his paintings and sculptures because I wanted to build a good collection. He was very polite and after we had been chatting a while he gave me a couple of posters and signed them at the bottom: 'To Victoria, from Fernando Botero.'

That night I also spoke with President Betancur, with whom I exchanged opinions about the greatness of Botero's works and other topics; we were united in our shared admiration for the artist and foresaw an unstoppable career that would be a watershed in the history of Colombian art.

This immersion in the art world also took me to Europe, and the first city I visited with Julia was Florence, Italy. I was awestruck by the squares full of sculptors and painters and spent several days studying their creations. I went to

Pietrasanta three times and visited Botero's studio, though we didn't cross paths because he was travelling at the time. I did, however, meet the Polish sculptor Igor Mitoraj. In Rome I was introduced to a woman from an eminent family – she was wearing two seven-carat diamonds and her casual clothing came from Armani and Valentino – who was an agent for painters and sculptors. She lived in a penthouse next to the bell towers of the basilica, and since she knew I was an art collector, she sent an elegant limousine to pick me up from my hotel.

On one of my trips to Rome she invited me to a party at her apartment where there were going to be several artists, dealers and gallery owners in attendance. The view of the Eternal City was incredible, and the terrace was decorated with dim torches. Listening to the conversation of such a distinguished, sophisticated group made me feel like I was in a magical space that could never be replicated.

My trips to Europe sometimes lasted two weeks and on other occasions up to two months, almost always with Pablo's approval, though deep down it was clear that he took advantage of my absences to sow his wild oats. As for my son, Juan Pablo, I never worried when I was away because my mother always looked after him. She understood my eagerness to learn and was always willing to help me raise my child. After all, she had taken care of him while I was finishing high school.

In the meantime, in mid-1982, Pablo's economic success swiftly led us to more and more ambitious projects.

First came the construction of a building on two large lots near the Club Campestre that the engineer Diego Londoño White sold to my husband. Pablo didn't say anything to me at first, but I ended up finding out when two architects had already prepared the initial design for the future construction. I asked my husband about it, and he replied that he was planning an eight-storey apartment building, and that we would live in the top two and rent out the other six.

From that point on, I took charge of the entire project and began to develop it alongside Julia and two architects, one of whom told me he'd shown my husband more than twenty blueprints, but all he'd wanted to see were the plans for the master bedroom and asked that they install a large window in the dining room that would offer a view out over Medellín.

As the months passed and the construction advanced, Julia and I started thinking about how to set up the penthouse, which would be two storeys and nearly 5,000 square feet. I remember we settled discussions about the living room, dining room, foyer, bedrooms, library, TV room, pool and lounges fairly easily, but we focussed particularly on where we would hang the pictures and place the sculptures I'd purchased, in addition to those I planned to acquire in the following months. I decided that each artwork would have its own space, so we sought the opinions of interior designers and art lighting specialists. In searching for the best pieces for the building, I travelled all over the country with Julia in Pablo's Learjet. In my research for this book, I spoke with one of my husband's pilots, who told me that Pablo became suspicious of all the trips I was taking and ordered that my calls and Julia Acosta's be intercepted. The wiretaps were active for a month, but in the end he realised that his suspicions were unfounded.

As the building started taking shape, the architects and I realised we should take advantage of a Medellín planning department policy that, with an eye toward city beautification, incentivised developers and property owners to exhibit artworks on building facades in exchange for a tax break. I decided to seek out the prolific Antioquian sculptor Rodrigo Arenas Betancourt, known for his monumentalist works. After contacting him through Salvador Arango, I went to visit him at his studio in a rather distant, dodgy area of Medellín. Artists need large spaces to work in, and his finances didn't allow him to rent the space he needed closer to downtown.

Arenas Betancourt turned out to be a fascinating, affable, astute man who immediately understood my idea of creating a sculpture to be displayed on the exterior of the future building, which was slated to be finished in three years – that is, in 1985. I explained that I wanted the piece to depict a family: a woman, a man and a small child. As we drank cup after cup of coffee, the artist picked up a pencil and on a large sheet of white paper he began to trace the first outlines of a man holding a woman and the woman holding a boy. It was incredible – the master sketched it just as I had envisioned it. The massive piece, titled *Life*, was completed on time. It cost me 20 million pesos – US$310,000 at the time – and experts have said that today it would cost nearly 400 million pesos.

Every building has a name, and I had no problem coming up with this one: Mónaco. Why? Because just a few months earlier I'd been to the Principality of Monaco for the first time and had been amazed by its grandeur, its elegance, its architecture. The building's name was displayed on the facade in large letters made of red acrylic. As the construction proceeded and the sixth and seventh floors became habitable, though still unfinished, I decided to use the space to store the artworks and sculptures I'd bought. It was more than large enough for the ones I already owned and those to come.

Having learned of my eagerness to acquire the best of the best, a dealer in Bogotá called to tell me about the Chilean painter Claudio Bravo, renowned, he claimed, for the realism of his work, and said he'd mail me photographs of a few oil paintings that were for sale. The photos arrived, and I was struck by one in particular: *The Monks*.

I loved that painting, in which a monk and a little boy seemed to be speaking through their gazes, and I immediately decided to buy it. We agreed on the price and the number of payments, and some time later the painting – 8 feet tall by 6.5 feet wide – was sent by boat from Europe to the port of Barranquilla and from there by truck to the Mónaco building.

Soon after we'd negotiated *The Monks*, the same dealer in Bogotá offered me *Bacchanal*, another Claudio Bravo painting, and sent the photographs. We tried to negotiate, but I thought it was priced too high and said I'd think about it because it wasn't easy to pay in instalments. The days passed, and then something strange happened: a woman with a very refined manner of speaking called to offer me the same painting. She said she lived in New York and that if we reached an agreement she'd send me the painting in a month at the latest, including the certificate of authenticity.

Immediately, I thought it might be a scam – the woman was asking for half the amount the dealer had demanded for the same painting – so I asked her to send me documentation, photos and any paperwork she had available to prove that the painting was genuine. Several weeks later, my doubts had been dispelled and I arranged to obtain the full amount of money, since the painting was a bargain at US$140,000.

The amazing thing about this story is that once we were installed in the Mónaco building, the Bogotá dealer called me again and told me he knew I had the painting and offered me double what I had paid. I refused.

In my mad push to buy works of art, I once lied to Pablo. He'd given me an armoured Mercedes-Benz, a beautiful blue car imported from Germany, but I had a hard time driving it because it was so heavy. It also looked like a tank and the windows didn't roll down, and of course it was very uncomfortable because having the air conditioner on all the time turned it into an icebox. Pablo understood my reasons and gave me permission to sell it – under one condition: that I save the money in the bank. Of course, I ignored him and used the money to buy another Claudio Bravo painting.

When a person is constantly making deals, more and more tend to appear. That's what happened the day I was offered a huge old house for sale on Calle 10, above Avenida El Poblado, a place that wasn't a hot area in Medellín at the time. I bought it for a very advantageous price, thinking it was the perfect place to put a new building. The architects and the decorator moved quickly in drawing up the blueprints for the project, which soon took shape and which I called the Ovni building.

Eight storeys tall, it would contain primarily offices and a very large apartment on the top floor. In thinking about the future, I decided it would be a good idea to have an alternative place to live. The sobering events that took place soon after would prove me right.

As with the Mónaco building, we needed to exhibit a work of art on the Ovni's facade, and I commissioned the piece from Salvador Arango, who designed a huge sculpture appropriate to the name of the building, which means 'UFO', and titled it *Man with Rocket*.

Art is not free of the fraud and deception that arise in business of all kinds. Indeed, I have to admit that on three occasions I was conned by dealers who stole a large amount of money from me. In one of those episodes, I delivered 90 per cent of the agreed-upon amount, but the piece was never delivered. I also almost got tricked by the owner of a major art gallery in Bogotá, who sold me a painting by Fernando Botero, but I realised that the price we'd agreed on was much higher than the market rate. Furious, I demanded that he return my money, which he eventually did. Those experiences were very unpleasant ones, and I decided I would never tell Pablo about them. Not only did I not want to cause problems, I wanted to protect the world I'd built and keep it as far as possible from the other part of my life.

My everyday life was very busy in the early 1980s. It energised me to know I was doing things that were important for my family and me, but it was also comforting to see Pablo fully engaged in his project to give houses to the people living in the Moravia landfill site. Medellín Without Slums, the foundation my husband created for that purpose, organised all sorts of fundraising events, and its March 1983 bullfight in the La Macarena bullring in Medellín had been a huge success.

Thinking about how to help my husband's cause, one night I decided to propose a charitable art auction. Having extensive contact with galleries, painters and dealers and having even attended a few auctions myself, I knew how effective such events could be, so I suggested it one day when my husband came home at dawn. He stared at me in confusion.

'What's that, Tata?'

'People auction off art to help foundations, assist after tragedies or contribute to social causes like yours. I'm sure you'll be able to build more houses for the poor.'

Pablo must have found my suggestion strange, but he didn't say no. The next day I took on the enormous task of organising the event, hiring ten people to lobby for the works to be presented at the auction, provide assurance that the paintings would be well cared for, and acquire insurance to cover transporting them. In the meantime, I contacted a few dealers in Bogotá and asked them to help me obtain major pieces to present at auction. I was lucky: several members of Bogotá's upper class who owned valuable paintings contributed them. In the end I managed to pull together 170 paintings, sculptures and antiques by twenty-five artists, including Fernando Botero, Darío Morales, Édgar Negret, Alejandro Obregón, David Manzur, Enrique Grau, Débora Arango and Rodrigo Arenas Betancourt.

The auction was going to be quite an event. It would take place in the Antioquia Ballroom of Medellín's Inter-Continental Hotel and was called Paint Brush Made of Stars after a Neruda poem. When I told Pablo the details, he was flabbergasted. I'd finally managed to overcome his scepticism, since he admitted he'd assumed the auction would be a flop.

The photos of that memorable night show Pablo standing in front of a lectern beside the Botero sculpture *Pedrito on Horseback*. The Antioquia Ballroom was bustling with 200 people, many of them members of the upper crust, businessmen, tycoons and regular people, but also a number of 'entrepreneur' friends of Pablo's.

My husband opened the auction and invited the attendees to purchase pieces to contribute to Medellín Without Slums. Then he added, 'Victoria, thank you for all your effort, thank you for what you've achieved tonight, thank you because the families of Moravia will have more houses … Thank you for making this auction a success.'

In the end, the art sale exceeded my expectations and most of the pieces were acquired by buyers who paid a total of nearly half a million dollars. How, at just twenty-two years old, did I manage to organise such a large, successful art auction? Certainly, having Pablo behind me helped. At the time, in 1983, he was already a representative and was enjoying renown as a businessman with a great deal of economic power.

Thanks to the auction's success, I was able to propose an idea that had occurred to me some time back but that I'd kept to myself to avoid having Pablo rebuff me. I decided to talk to him about the importance of making his office space comfortable, pleasant and modern because he spent a good part of the day and night there. I must have been convincing, because he listened to me and didn't object to buying some paintings and a couple of sculptures for his office in El Poblado. A few weeks later, he had a bronze torso by the Polish sculptor Igor Mitoraj, a painting by Francisco Antonio Cano, three by Obregón and one by Grau behind his desk.

A little while later, as the architects and I had planned, the Mónaco building was almost finished. It was the first half of 1985. In the last phase, when only some final touch-ups were needed, the decorator, Julia Acosta, asked me not to go to the building because she wanted me to be surprised when I saw its finished form. For two and a half months, close to twenty-five people worked day and night until it was finally ready.

On the night of the viewing, my two children, my family and I got all dressed up. The building was incredible. I really felt like I was in the Principality of Monaco, but unfortunately my prince was in hiding at the time.

I knew he'd show up one night or early one morning, at the most unexpected moment, and that's exactly what happened. It was a short visit, no more than two hours long, but I was used to it by then. When an employee announced that my husband was down in the lobby, I thought he'd enjoy seeing *Life*, the massive piece by the great artist Rodrigo Arenas Betancourt, which stood more than thirty feet tall.

I waited for him in the penthouse by the lift doors, and when I saw him I felt a rush of happiness and gave him a huge hug. I was nervous about how he'd react to the piece because it had cost a lot of money, time and effort and I didn't know if he'd be as impressed with it as I was. I wanted to show him the Chinese tapestries, the wall hangings, the antiques, the furniture by famous Italian designers ... But most of all I wanted him to see my collection of paintings and sculptures and to tell him that an influential Bogotá dealer had told me a few days earlier that mine was the most important art collection in Latin America at the time.

In fact, Pablo looked very surprised and immediately told me that the sculpture down on the ground floor was impressive. We walked down the hall of the first floor of the penthouse and came to a sculpture by Auguste Rodin and then an oil painting by Alejandro Obregón. While he studied the painting, I told him that all the artworks in the building had come with a certificate of authenticity.

As we passed the swimming pool, the first one ever built on an upper storey in Medellín, he remarked in amazement that the architects had done a fantastic job. On one of the walls of the enormous reflecting pool, my husband stopped to stare for a while at one of the suns painted by the great Édgar Negret. Then we strolled through the two terraces. The first held a dining room for eight decorated with a still life of lemons in greens and ochres by the painter Alberto Iriarte. In the second was a living room with leather furniture and a painting of navy blue flowers by Obregón on the far wall.

As he always did, Pablo stroked my hair with his hands as we walked through the building's seventh floor. With our arms around each other, we entered the gym, which contained modern exercise machines and the posters that Fernando Botero had dedicated to me when I went to his exhibition in Bogotá.

Pablo said he was happy that his family was living in such a palace. The remark made me wistful, and I replied, 'Pablo, will this nightmare be over soon so we can go back to living together in peace and enjoying this space?'

'Yes, darling, I'm working to resolve these problems and come back to all of you.'

I led him by the hand toward the main living room, but before we entered I showed him *Bacchanal*, the Claudio Bravo painting. He looked at the piece, took a few steps back, and stared and stared at it in silent admiration. Then he asked how I'd bought it and I told him I'd tell him a story about the piece later.

In the main living room, we sat on a modular sofa large enough to seat thirty, and Pablo seemed to be in a trance as he gazed at the artworks displayed there: on the coffee table, a marble sculpture by Auguste Rodin, a small sculpture by Fernando Botero and a red horizontal sculpture by Édgar Negret, *The Metamorphosis*. On one wall hung the painting *Levitation*, by Enrique Grau, and on another a painting by Alejandro Obregón.

We moved on to the library, a cosy, inviting place, where a niche contained the original study for a sculpture of the liberator Simón Bolívar on horseback by an Italian artist; in addition, there were several works by the painter and sculptor Francisco Antonio Cano on one of the columns.

We'd started up the stairs toward our bedroom when Pablo stopped to examine *The Monks*, the extraordinary Claudio Bravo piece that made us feel like we were being watched because the monk's eyes kept staring at us. Further along, in the hall leading to the bedroom door, was a console table with the sculpture *The Bather* by Edgar Degas, the master of French impressionism.

We entered our imposing bedroom and Pablo lay down on the bed to look at every detail. He studied everything around him and his gaze paused on a chest of drawers topped by a crystal vase by the Italian designer Alfredo Barbini, several art books and *Reclining Woman*, a small bronze sculpture by Botero. The visual tour ended when Pablo got up from the bed and headed to a case with glass doors and special lights that illuminated my priceless collection of pre-Columbian gold pieces. He pulled out the figures one by one and examined them carefully before returning them to their places. Several times he asked me where I'd got such a beautiful collection, and I told him art dealers had sold it to me.

We went out to the sun room off the main bedroom, which was decorated with a breakfast table and the sculpture *The Lovers* by Auguste Rodin.

On the wall before Manuela's room was a Botero painting of horses from 1954, early in his artistic career, when he hadn't yet adopted his signature style. We entered the girl's room and Pablo loved how much light it got and the sweet, childlike atmosphere the decorator had achieved. He also liked the Botero pastel of a white toy poodle in a pale pink dress and another, ochre-hued oil painting of a dog, which hung on the walls. He went to the crib and gazed at the wall behind it, which contained a mural painted by Ramón Vázquez depicting guardian angels watching over children.

From there we went to Juan Pablo's room, which Pablo also loved. Next to the door was a Botero sculpture of the artist's son Pedrito, cast in epoxy resin after the little boy died in an accident. On a table was another Botero sculpture, *The Doll*, cast in bronze. Hanging on the headboard of the bed was a screen-printed image of a condor in red ink, by Alejandro Obregón. And on Juan Pablo's bookshelf was a bronze statue of the liberator Simón Bolívar and the medal he received for his victory in the Battle of Boyacá. In the bathroom was a massive red sculpture, set into the wall, by Édgar Negret. On a wall as you exited the bathroom was a pastel drawing, by Botero, of Pedrito holding paintbrushes in his hand. That piece was destroyed by the blast of the car bomb that detonated in front of the building in January 1988.

We went down the stairs and were greeted by an Olga de Amaral tapestry that filled the space with light; then we entered the main dining room, which held a still life by Botero and another by Claudio Bravo that depicted some lemons that looked so real that you wanted to reach out and pick them up. A few years earlier, when Pablo saw the first design of the building, he'd asked the architects to install a huge picture window in the dining room with a view of Medellín. But his wish was never fulfilled because once I had my hands on that massive Botero sculpture, it was clear we needed to create a special niche where we could exhibit it.

Pablo and I had been walking around Mónaco for more than an hour, but that wasn't all. In the spacious guest room, a coffee table displayed a bronze torso by Darío Morales, and a wooden table held a Botero sculpture and, beside it, Rodin's *The Age of Bronze*. On one wall of the room was a large self-portrait by Pablo Picasso, and on another, a pencil drawing by Enrique Grau.

Then we headed to the auxiliary dining room in the kitchen, whose walls were hung with two paintings by the great Francisco Antonio Cano: an oil painting of horses and dogs with a gorgeous landscape in the background, and another of a violin that I bought from the Echavarría family.

Pablo's visit ended as abruptly as it had begun two hours earlier. Claiming as usual that he couldn't be in one place too long, he said he needed to go. His children and I were left behind, living in a palace in which I truly believed we would remain for a long time.

But that dream ended at dawn on 13 January 1988, when the car bomb went off and seriously damaged the building, forcing us to leave for ever. A few hours after the explosion, the army occupied the building and stayed there for more than five months. No government authority ever informed us of what condition the interior was in, much less provided an inventory.

Despondent, without any information, three days after the explosion I asked one of my sisters to try to get into the building to see what condition the penthouse and the priceless works I'd used to decorate it were in. Most of all, I told her to try to find a way to get anything that hadn't been damaged out of the building. Luckily, when my sister returned she had some good news: many paintings had disappeared in the explosion and others were damaged by shrapnel, but the most important ones were in relatively good shape. This was also the case with the other decorative objects and the furniture. In addition, in a bold act, my sister had managed to take several photos of the destruction. I asked her how she'd been able to get in with the soldiers there, but she just said it was better if I didn't know. She added that the soldiers would let her enter again, but only after ten o'clock at night.

And so it was. Incredibly, over the next four nights, my sister and two employees went to Mónaco in a small truck and removed the most valuable pieces they found. The first thing she did was rescue the Salvador Dalí painting, which fortunately had not been damaged. Very carefully, by torchlight, she pulled the canvas from the frame, folded it, and hid it under her clothing so the soldiers wouldn't find it if they searched her on her way out. She also managed to retrieve Claudio Bravo's *The Monks*, but it was in bad shape, torn in dozens of spots by shrapnel from the car bomb.

She rescued a few other pieces from my collection of paintings and sculptures, and we initially hid them in the wine cellar of a trusted friend in Medellín, but we couldn't leave them there long. Preserving the artworks in the middle of the war became an enormous effort because Pablo was still in hiding. My children and I couldn't move around as we had previously because my husband had turned us into military targets. So, finding people who could be entrusted with such a treasure was extraordinarily complicated. It wasn't an option to give everything to just one person. And even when I found a place for some of the art, I ran into another problem: who would transport it? We usually relied on drivers who carried the pieces without realising what they were, but we'd have to wait a month or two to find out whether a delivery had arrived safely.

That's what happened with Bravo's *The Monks*, which left Medellín and arrived in Bogotá some time later, where a dealer did me the favour of handing it off to an esteemed art restorer who spent six months reconstructing it.

In the meantime, the Dalí was hidden away in a modest house in Medellín until the war abated a little and I was able to send it to our old place in El Diamante, where another of my sisters was living at the time. There it remained safe for a couple of years.

Anxious to preserve my art, I developed a complex system. I rented a warehouse in Bogotá, as far away as possible from our enemies, and had workers build a couple of false walls to conceal a well-ventilated secret chamber containing numerous paintings and sculptures that, years later, after my husband's death, would be vital to our survival.

Despite my precautions, some items from the collection that didn't fit into the Bogotá warehouse ended up being lost. For example, a person who'd promised to safeguard a few paintings sent me a message some time later informing me that the transporter had never arrived. An art dealer stored ten paintings and sculptures in his home, but one fine day he simply disappeared. I tracked him down several months later and he claimed he'd had to hand the art over to Los Pepes, my husband's enemies, who'd threatened to kill him. These incidents filled me with a sense of powerlessness and grief, but I couldn't do anything because I had no way of determining what had actually happened.

It may have been reckless to believe that the war had put only Pablo, me, and our children in danger. On 2 February 1993, a Los Pepes commando unit headed by Carlos Castaño showed up at the house in El Diamante, where my sister had been living since we left the Mónaco building. She wasn't in at the time, so her life was spared, but Castaño must have spotted three of my most treasured works of art: *Rock 'n' Roll - La Danse, The Monks* - which had been taken there after its restoration - and the Arango sculpture *The Kiss*. Elsewhere in the house were small sculptures by Fernando Botero, Igor Mitoraj and Édgar Negret, along with paintings by other artists.

Without hesitation, Castaño's men set the house ablaze and within minutes it and all its contents had been reduced to ashes. At the time, I was hiding out with Pablo and my children in a modest house in the Prado neighbourhood, very close to the city centre. Hours later, when I heard the news, I cried disconsolately. All signs indicated that the paintings and sculptures had been consumed by the flames. Pablo must have seen how upset I was and immediately called us all into the courtyard and asked us to form a circle. He stood across from me, with Juan Pablo to his left and Manuela to his right, and said, gazing into our eyes, 'Look, sweetheart, do you know where the most important Dalí of your life is? The most important Dalí is our family, which is priceless ... Don't worry, I'm going to give you whatever Dalí you want.'

Because of the endless manhunt, my husband's enemies lying in wait and the ever-present possibility of a raid that could cost us our lives, I gave the authenticity certificates for all of my artworks, even those that had been destroyed by the Mónaco car bomb and the El Diamante fire, to an art dealer for safekeeping. I wanted to preserve the documents, which were of enormous value to me. But the unthinkable happened: the dealer panicked at the thought that the certificates might be found during a raid, and he burned them because they were in my name. Most of those documents had the artists' signatures, which was unusual at the time. A work of art without a certificate of authenticity is like a person without a birth certificate. When I heard the news, in my loneliness and total isolation, I wondered again and again how that dealer could have committed such a sacrilege.

Getting replacements for those certificates meant knocking on doors that were now closed to me because we were in a state of war. In the case of one work, it took me more than twenty years to get the artist to sign a new document. The task required immense persistence, with the artist refusing several times, until one day he finally agreed to certify that the work was his.

The unrelenting hunt for my husband ended on 2 December 1993, when he died on the roof of the house where he was hiding in Medellín. Far from solving our problems, though, his death would soon bring me more and bigger difficulties, as I have previously explained; Pablo's enemies turned their gaze on me and demanded I pay US$120 million that they claimed they'd spent hunting for Pablo.

With the attorney general's authorisation, I went to the La Modelo and La Picota prisons in Bogotá, accompanied by officers from the Technical Investigation Corps, and met with several drug-trafficking capos and with Pablo's old lieutenants, who invariably started asking for money.

One of the first inmates I visited – because he sent several messages to Residencias Tequendama demanding it – was Iván Urdinola Grajales, one of the capos of the Norte del Valle Cartel, with whom I engaged in an intense conversation in which I was obviously the one with everything to lose. He surprised me with the news that he had the sculpture *The Kiss* in his possession. He said it had survived the fire and a friend from Medellín had given it to him, but he was prepared to return it to me. Then he asked if I had any paintings for sale, and I told him I did, an oil painting by Obregón. We agreed on a price that he promised to pay after I sent it to him; naively, I believed him. Time passed and *The Kiss* never arrived, much less the money for the painting. That was how Urdinola charged me for his part in the war against Pablo.

In the prisons I also had to come to agreements with some of Pablo's employees, delivering works of art and sculpture to them to pay the supposed debts. But the hardest part of that period came when I had to go to Cali to negotiate directly with the heads of the Cali Cartel and with the commanders of the Self-Defenders, who were after all of my husband's assets and my celebrated art collection. At the first meeting, as previously recounted, they demanded I draw up a complete list of properties, but they were clearly interested in having me hand over paintings and sculptures right away.

'Go and get them, quick,' one of the capos said.

'Gentlemen, quick isn't an option – I've been in isolation a long time and I don't know if the people who were keeping them are still alive. Believe me, it won't be easy,' I replied.

Disheartened, I returned to Bogotá and started looking for some of the people who had my art. I was lucky that they returned it to me. Over the following days, I managed to hand over the first piece, an incredibly valuable Botero still life. I also managed to go to the warehouse in Bogotá where I was storing several works and handed them over to reduce my debt.

But it was Dalí's *Rock 'n' Roll – La Danse* that was to play a crucial role in the difficult negotiation process with Pablo's enemies. As I mentioned, weeks after my husband's death, I received a message from Fidel Castaño in which he assured me he wasn't going to have me or my children killed and revealed that the Dalí painting hadn't been destroyed in the fire at the El Diamante house. I was thrilled, because he also promised that he and his brother Carlos would return the piece to me.*

---

* In later enquiries, I confirmed that the Claudio Bravo painting *The Monks* and the sculptures by Botero, Negret, and Mitoraj had been burned in the fire that destroyed the El Diamante house in February 1993.

In one of our meetings in Cali, Carlos Castaño announced in front of everyone in attendance that he'd taken the painting – valued at the time at US$3 million – so he could give it back to me. But on an impulse that I later thanked God for, I refused to accept it and asked him and Fidel to keep it as a sign of peace. The capos looked favourably on my gesture, and a week later I gave Castaño the painting's certificate of authenticity. The last I heard of *Rock 'n' Roll – La Danse* was that Castaño called several Bogotá art dealers and asked for their help selling the piece to a foreign collector. Today I take comfort in the knowledge that after so much turmoil, the Dalí is safely held in a museum in Fukushima, Japan.

My relationship with art was always motivated by the desire to learn; I never saw it as a way to elevate my status or enter elite circles that I always knew were out of reach. I don't pretend to be a connoisseur of art, because I'm not. I still go to exhibitions, museums and lectures throughout Argentina because I'm interested in learning.

I feel no frustration, but I am nostalgic. I was able to own incredible works of art that I truly thought would be with me all my life. But it wasn't to be. My readers will think, with some accuracy, that the old saying 'Live by the sword, die by the sword' applies here. That may be true, but in my defence I will note that though I used Pablo's ill-gotten wealth to purchase art, I was able to buy many sculptures and paintings because I paid for them in installments and by playing an intermediary role in buying and selling art for others who trusted my judgement. I plunged into an exciting world that gave me immense satisfaction but, in the end, it was devastating to let go of such a dream.

Chapter 8

The Wars I Lived Through
with Pablo

1984

I didn't say anything to my mother at the time, but my thought in that dramatic moment was that Pablo might have been the one who ordered the crime.

It was 9.30pm on 30 April 1984, and the TV news programme *Hoy* was reporting that the minister of justice, Rodrigo Lara Bonilla, had been assassinated in northern Bogotá. Images appeared on the screen showing a dead gunman lying on the ground, another in handcuffs, and a white Mercedes-Benz with its back windows shot out by bullets.

The reporters were saying that, for the first time in Colombian history, a government minister had been assassinated, and I sensed that our lives were going to change for ever.

Juan Pablo came into the room and found us on our knees, crying and praying in front of the television; he must have thought it quite strange to see us like that, and at seven years old he can't have understood the gravity of what was happening. He asked what was wrong, but we only sobbed in response. Perceiving our anguish, he hugged me tight for a long time before falling asleep at midnight.

Two days later, I was heartbroken to see the minister's wife and her two children beside the coffin during the funeral in Neiva, Lara's hometown. That image has remained with me ever since.

In the solitude of the bedroom, where we would spend a sleepless night, my mother and I talked quietly about what had just happened and the consequences that the assassination would have for us, especially for me, since I was eight months and ten days' pregnant and would be giving birth very soon.

'And you're expecting a child. What are we going to do? This is the end,' my mother said, sobbing.

I hadn't seen Pablo in several days, much less had any idea where he was. I never asked him, but I found out in November 2016 when, in his second book, *Pablo Escobar in fraganti*, my son published a conversation he had with Malévolo, the person who was with Pablo at the very moment that Minister Lara was killed. According to Malévolo's account, he and Pablo were walking in the grounds of Hacienda Nápoles, accompanied by Juliana – one of my husband's lovers – and her mother. He also said that Pablo asked him to stay at the estate because it was likely that the authorities would raid it – as they in fact did a few hours later.

Very early on 3 May, one of my husband's men, Otto, appeared at my mother's apartment and told me that Pablo had sent him to warn me that it was dangerous to stay there and that I should hide out somewhere else while he made arrangements and he would then send for us.

Without thinking twice, I packed several suitcases with everything we needed for a week and took my son to the apartment of one of my decorators. Hiding there, my only contact with the outside world was through the radio and television, which continued to broadcast stories about the aftermath of the assassination and President Belisario Betancur's determination to relentlessly pursue the drug cartel capos and reactivate the extradition treaty with the United States, which he'd refused to apply since taking office.

The next day I received another message from Pablo telling me to be ready because we were leaving for Panama. Worried, I managed to make an appointment with my gynaecologist, and after the usual examination he gave me advice for getting through the final weeks of the pregnancy and provided the name and phone number of a specialist friend of his in Panama.

Given the grim circumstances, I decided to hire a nurse to be with me during the birth. One of my brothers recommended a young woman who'd looked after his children, but she was working in the United States at the time. I called her nevertheless, and she accepted my proposal. We agreed that I'd let her know where I'd be and would send her flight tickets. She told me not to worry, that she'd come to wherever I told her.

We would be leaving soon, and I felt adrift. I hugged Juan Pablo, stared at my belly, and contemplated our uncertain futures in terror. My husband had begun waging a war of unknown proportions, and we, his family, were stranded, helpless, waiting for him to make all the decisions. Of course, I never imagined the horror we'd live through soon after, and I've never forgiven myself for how numb I must have been and how disconnected from reality. I was twenty-three years old, and all I could do was put every bit of my strength and love into my seven-year-old boy and the baby who was on the way.

The departure was swift: the next morning, Otto and El Mugre showed up at the front door and said they were there to pick us up. They said we couldn't bring much weight, so I put some clothing for the baby, Juan Pablo and me in an overnight bag.

We climbed into an SUV and the driver peeled out as if someone were after us. It was agonising; for the first time in my life, I felt like a fugitive. Everything outside seemed normal as we drove through the streets of Medellín, and I wondered, 'Why is this happening to me? Why do I have to hide?' I didn't have anyone to ask. Pablo wasn't anywhere to be seen – he just sent excuses and I had to do what he said without complaining. Fearful of losing my baby if we crashed and not knowing what might happen over the next few hours, I had no inkling that nine years of horror awaited me, nine years in which I would be running constantly, nine years during which I would often open my eyes at dawn and find a rifle pointing in my face.

Half an hour later, we arrived at a pasture on the outskirts of La Estrella, where a small Hughes helicopter was waiting with its engine going. We hastily boarded – Juan

Pablo and I; Aunt Gilma, a neighbour, whom Pablo had asked to accompany us; and a doctor I didn't know but who told me that Pablo had told him to stay with me and carry the necessary equipment to take care of me in case of an emergency.

Suddenly I was sailing through the air in a helicopter, fleeing my country; below, my gaze became lost in the majesty of the vast green carpet that covered the Darién Gap as the aircraft rocked from side to side in the gusting wind. And though I'd become somewhat used to travelling by helicopter, this time was different because the pilot, to avoid showing up on radar, had to fly at such a low altitude that we could see dozens of crocodiles leaping in the swamps. It was an exotic sight but it made me afraid because the animals were obviously hungry. Aunt Gilma must have seen my fear and shouted at me to take deep breaths. Several times she asked me if we were almost there and I told her yes, though in truth I hadn't the faintest idea where we were.

After a two-hour flight that seemed interminable, the pilot landed in a jungle clearing in Panamanian territory. Almost immediately four men in a truck showed up: two of my husband's bodyguards and two Panamanians who were familiar with the routes we needed to take since we'd entered the country illegally.

The helicopter pilot was returning to Medellín with the doctor, so he said goodbye and we started what turned out to be more than a two-hour trip down unpaved roads to an apartment in a modest neighbourhood in Panama City. There we found Gustavo Gaviria, his wife and their three children, who'd arrived the same way that we had – through the jungle by helicopter.

Pablo appeared at dawn and found me dispirited and with dark circles under my eyes. We hugged each other tight, and after he asked me about the trip from Colombia and how the baby was doing, he must have sensed I was going to ask him about the minister's death because he went ahead and started offering explanations: 'The minister situation is nuts, Tata. Plenty of people were furious with him and were convinced that the fight against extradition can't be stopped. But I promise you, darling, this will all be resolved sooner than you think and we're going to enjoy our children for a long time.'

'When you talk about resolving things, what do you mean? Pablo, can't you see the situation we're in? I'm scared – I don't see a way out of this. Why did I have to leave Colombia?'

'It was just a precaution, my love. Nothing's going to happen.'

Talking with my husband was tough because he'd go off on tangents and it wasn't easy to make him speak frankly about what was going on. He was naturally evasive. And he was always suddenly saying he had to go and would be back later.

The three nights we spent in that apartment were awful. It was practically empty, and we had to sleep on mats on the floor. Pablo must have seen how angry I was and thought he could fix things by moving us to an old house in the city's historic centre. But being there was unpleasant too. It was hot and sticky and we had only some bunks with mattresses, but no bed linen or television, and everything was so filthy that I was constantly nauseated. As if that weren't enough, the shower was full of mildew and the water drained so slowly that you had to shower in flip-flops.

Furthermore, Pablo told us not to go anywhere because it wasn't safe, so that first week all we ate was grilled chicken that one of the bodyguards would bring from a nearby restaurant. The only person I visited was the gynaecologist, Edgardo Campana Bustos, who'd been recommended by my doctor in Medellín. He performed several examinations and declared me healthy, but he gave me some unexpected news: I was going to have a little girl, even though a couple of ultrasounds I'd had a few months earlier in Medellín had suggested the baby might be a boy.

We ended up getting so bored in that house that one night Pablo organised a game to name the baby. We went around and around and agreed that if it was a girl, as the doctor claimed, she would be named Manuela, as Juan Pablo suggested in memory of one of his classmates at his Montessori school.

'Grégory, it's on you if your sister doesn't like it,' Pablo told him.

But we couldn't agree on a boy's name. I proposed Daniel, but Pablo said no way: 'Tata, that's like calling your kid Hitler. Remember there was a man named Daniel Escobar who killed an entire family with an axe on a farm near Aguacatala, in El Poblado. They called him Daniel the Axeman.'

That night, Pablo also told us that before leaving Colombia he'd given instructions to deliver house keys to more than 300 families in the Moravia landfill as part of the new Medellín Without Slums project. They'd been built and were ready to be inhabited.

Finally, on 20 May 1984, we moved to another house. This one, though old, was luxurious and comfortable, similar to the residences governments set aside for prominent guests. At the entrance, we encountered an armed security guard. I later learned that the place had been provided by the strongman of Panama at the time, General Manuel Antonio Noriega, commander-in-chief of the country's defence forces. I was also told that Noriega and my husband had illegal business dealings, and that a high-ranking military officer and another man had been the ones the general had tasked with assisting us during our stay in Panama.

Luckily, at this point the nurse arrived from the United States and soon became essential company in the difficult moments to come. But despite our improved circumstances, it was clear that Juan Pablo was very lonely. At seven years old, his life had drastically changed and he now had no school, no classmates, no neighbourhood pals. His childhood was transformed so profoundly that for many years Pablo's bodyguards were his nannies, and his only companions.

Wishing to distract our son, my husband gave him a 50cc Honda motorcycle, but since there wasn't anybody to teach the boy to ride it, Pablo ordered one of his original bodyguards, Pinina, to come up from Medellín to be with the child. From then on, the bodyguard would dress all in white and go out jogging every morning with Juan Pablo riding beside him.

So things were already quite complicated on 25 May 1984, when I got up early to go to my final appointment with the gynaecologist, who'd warned me that the baby could be born at any moment. As usual, Pablo had come home at dawn and my aunt had to go to the doctor's office with me because he was sleeping. During the examination, the doctor realised I was already five centimetres dilated and told me he was sending me to Paitilla Medical Center immediately. Since we hadn't come prepared, my aunt went back home for the bag we'd packed for the baby's birth and let Pablo and Juan Pablo know what was happening.

My little girl was born at 12.45 that Friday, 25 May, and I was taken to a recovery room, where Pablo, Juan Pablo, my aunt and Gustavo Gaviria came to visit. According to them, they'd been lucky that right as they were entering the hospital lift they'd encountered a nurse who was carrying a newborn girl with a bracelet marked 'Manuela Escobar' and was heading for my room. Though I was wan and in great pain, Gustavo took a photo of the Escobar Henaos. We looked like the royal family, full of joy, and for a moment we forgot that the world was falling down around us.

The next day, Saturday, 26 May, when we started the paperwork to discharge me from the hospital, Pablo came up to me and whispered that he'd come back later because he had a meeting with a number of important Colombian politicians who'd come to Panama City. I was quite entertained with my baby, so I didn't pay much attention, especially since my husband didn't specify his intentions, though I noticed a faint smile and a gleam in his eye. I wished him luck and told him I'd wait for him at home because I'd almost certainly be discharged before he returned.

I didn't see Pablo again that day, but I was happy when I went back home to be with Juan Pablo and my little girl. It was a dream come true. The days passed, and Pablo came and went. He seemed very busy, talking with people, coming home at daybreak as usual. But I was building my world around my two children, far from my husband's activities, which seemed to be quite complex; the news that came from Colombia involved him ever more deeply in the minister of justice's assassination and the authorities had identified his capture as their number one priority.

Anything that's going badly can always go worse, as the saying goes. But what happened over the following days would go far beyond that old adage.

On 5 June 1984, two weeks after Manuela's birth, Pablo asked me if we could talk alone in the living room. Putting his arm around my shoulder, he said in a grave, dramatic tone, 'Tata, we're going to have to leave Panama for our safety. We run the risk of being arrested. We've got to send the baby to Medellín.'

'What are you talking about, Pablo? She's only just been born, I have to breastfeed her. Are you nuts?'

'No, I'm not nuts. It's necessary. I'm not sure where we're going – maybe we'll need to escape to the jungle, go hungry, be on the run, go without sleep ... We can't be on the run with a baby, Tata, it'll kill her. Grandma Nora will take good care of her in Medellín. She'll be in the best hands.'

A long silence followed. I knew my husband wasn't kidding, that my sad reality was tearing my daughter from my arms just a few days after her birth. Pablo didn't say anything else. His serious face indicated that he didn't like the decision either, but there wasn't a choice.

I wept disconsolately for a long time, and when I managed to calm down I asked about Juan Pablo. He said the boy was old enough to come with us and would be safer by our side. His decision was final. I had to suffer in silence, unable to cry out or ask for help.

Heartbroken, I went to the Colombian consulate and luckily had no difficulty getting a passport for Manuela because I wasn't yet on the authorities' radar. We set the travel date to Medellín for Friday, 13 July 1984, on a SAM flight at 1.40pm. Pablo and I signed the authorisation for my aunt and the nurse to leave the country with Manuela, and we weren't worried because my husband had 'friends' in the Panama City and Medellín airports who would make sure the immigration process went smoothly.

Once the tickets were purchased, Pablo told me he had to leave with Gustavo because things were getting complicated. He explained that they were going to Nicaragua, where they'd be met by their contacts in the Sandinista regime, which had taken power in July 1979 and was fighting to maintain control in the face of the increasing threat of counter-revolutionary groups backed by the United States. In other words, we were heading to a country that was at war. Then he told me to go to the Nicaraguan embassy in Panama City, where they'd give me visas. Before saying goodbye, he gave my aunt and the nurse some instructions: 'Make sure nobody realises my daughter is on that plane, don't talk to each other during the flight or in the airport. Make it seem like the baby is the nurse's daughter.'

Then he turned to the nurse and said gravely, 'Look, we're entrusting you with our most priceless treasure. Don't take your eyes off her for a moment. Don't tell anybody where you are going or who you're with. This is a very delicate situation.'

Their departure was fast approaching when Pablo left early one morning, warning that General Noriega's defence forces might raid the house and capture us. Juan Pablo and Manuela were sleeping. He told me to be careful and that we'd see each other in Managua.

The next day, Juan Pablo and I went to the Nicaraguan embassy, but it was an intimidating experience. It was an old, chaotic building that smelled like war. The atmosphere was military, rigid, frightening. I'd been given the number 13, and when I was called I got the strange sensation that I was going in front of a firing squad. I approached the window very slowly, fearful that they might figure out that I was Pablo Escobar's wife. I handed over the passports and noticed the workers start looking at one another and whispering. Pablo had told me they'd be expecting me, but I sensed a hostile, heavy atmosphere. They called us from one window to another and finally told me to come back the next day. The process started dragging out for days, and I breathed a sigh of relief when, the fourth time I went, they handed over the stamped passports. We were authorised to travel to Managua.

The departure day of 13 July arrived and I had to let go of my infant daughter. I cried buckets and nearly fainted, but I pulled myself together as best I could so that I didn't upset Juan Pablo, who was watching me helplessly. After saying goodbye to little Manuela, I handed her to the nurse and my aunt with a heavy heart and prayed they'd arrive safely at my mother's house in Medellín. I couldn't even accompany them to the airport because Pablo was worried somebody might recognise me or that the immigration officers might be suspicious of a baby travelling without its parents. Six interminable hours went by before they called from my mother's house to say they'd arrived, though they'd had a few scares along the way since the police and the army had set up checkpoints on the streets next to Enrique Olaya Herrera Airport. And as my husband had predicted, the immigration process leaving Panama and entering Colombia had gone off without a hitch.

But what had happened? Why, all of a sudden, did we have to leave Panama just three weeks after our arrival? The answer came via Pinina, who stayed with me and Juan Pablo when my husband left for Nicaragua. In the long hours we spent in confinement while organising the trip to Managua, I managed to get him to tell me about the high-level negotiations my husband had been engaged in from the moment we'd arrived in Panama after Minister Lara Bonilla's assassination.

According to Pinina, when my husband got to Panama, he had read in a local paper that a Colombian delegation made up of former president Alfonso López Michelsen and

former ministers Jaime Castro Castro, Felio Andrade Man-
rique and Gustavo Balcázar Monzón had been invited to
observe Panama's presidential election to be held on 6 May
1984. Spotting an opportunity, Pablo decided to try to get
an appointment with López, whom he'd met during the
1982 presidential campaign and had given substantial
funding to. He called Medellín to speak with Santiago Londoño White, treasurer of that campaign, and asked him to
set up a meeting because Pablo had a proposal to end drug
trafficking in Colombia. It worked, and López agreed to
meet with my husband and Jorge Luis Ochoa the day after
the election.

Once it was announced that Nicolás Ardito Barletta, the
Democratic Revolutionary Party (PRD) candidate, had
won the election, the former president, Londoño (who'd
come up from Medellín) and my husband met in a suite at
the Marriott in Panama City. During their conversation,
Pablo said he'd communicated with Colombia's biggest
drug lords and that they were willing to hand over their
labs, aircraft, routes and US contacts; relinquish their ill-
gotten gains; and turn themselves in to justice in exchange
for a promise that they would not be extradited.

The story of my husband's manoeuvrings in Panama
didn't end there. Pinina told me the Marriott meeting had
apparently fallen on fertile soil, and two weeks later they
received a message saying that Colombia's inspector general, Carlos Jiménez Gómez, was going to speak with them,
with the authorisation of President Betancur's administration. That was what lay behind Pablo's remark to me at
Paitilla Medical Center on 26 May, the day after Manuela's

birth, that he would be meeting with important Colombian politicians in Panama City. When I left the hospital and returned to the house where we were staying, I was so busy with my baby that I hadn't had time to ask my husband how the appointment had gone.

Pinina told me that the conversation with the inspector general had also taken place at the Marriott, and that, besides my husband, Jorge Luis Ochoa, Gonzalo 'El Mexicano' Rodríguez, José 'Pelusa' Ocampo and Gustavo Gaviria had been in attendance. At the meeting, my husband repeated the proposals he'd offered former president López and promised to send the inspector general a confidential memo detailing each proposal for dismantling drug trafficking in Colombia.

But it was all for naught because a few days later the document was leaked to *El Tiempo* newspaper, provoking such an uproar that the administration was forced to claim publicly that the secret contacts between the inspector general and the drug kingpins had been unauthorised. The Panama meeting sparked a massive political controversy that dragged on and on because everyone involved offered a different story about his role in the meetings with my husband.

Once I'd learned what had happened directly from Pinina, the man who'd been close to Pablo in those moments, I understood my husband's hurry to leave Panama. The whereabouts of the main suspects in Rodrigo Lara's assassination had been exposed, and it was very possible that the manhunt would shift from Colombia to its neighbour. There was also a risk that General Noriega, under pressure from the scandal unleashed over the contact between the mafia and the Colombian government, would betray my husband and turn him in to the DEA.

So I had no choice but to pack my bags for the trip to Nicaragua. It was a difficult time for me because I couldn't get Manuela out of my head and cried constantly. In addition, it was agonising to see Juan Pablo carrying an enormous emotional burden.

ON 20 JUNE 1984, JUAN PABLO AND I TRAVELLED ON A commercial flight and were greeted in the Managua airport by several people who identified themselves as being from the Sandinista government. They drove us in a Mercedes-Benz with official plates to a huge old mansion where El Mexicano, his wife Gladys, and four of his bodyguards were waiting.

After leaving our things in a bedroom, we took a long tour of the estate, but it struck us as a gloomy place. In a drawer I found a book that recounted the history of the area, and it described the many massacres that had taken place there in the past. In addition, the house was surrounded by ten-foot brick walls with watchtowers and heavily armed guards at each corner.

Luckily, the refrigerators were always full, and though we never saw who was bringing the provisions, it was easy to guess that someone from the Sandinista government was charged with that task.

The days passed, but the confinement was depressing. I was in the middle of changing my diet after the birth of my daughter. Though the house was large, the only place where I could talk to Pablo in private was in our bedroom, which had large, tinted windows. All we could see around us was armed men. The house was more like an encampment, with dozens of men trooping in and out of the bedrooms and with bags and camping equipment scattered all over the floor. It was a very uncomfortable situation for me, and I didn't understand why we didn't have a house to ourselves.

Pablo had noticed my irritation, but he just told me to be patient a little longer, that things were going well. He was an expert at minimising any situation, however difficult it looked. I begged him to let us go back to Medellín, but he said it was vital to wait till calm had been restored. His words made me hopeful, but it was all empty promises; the peace I so longed for kept slipping further and further away.

I remember I used to get up early with Juan Pablo and we'd try to keep ourselves entertained till noon, when Pablo would get up after coming home at dawn. The three of us would have lunch and make a huge effort to seem like a normal family, but deep down we knew that nothing was normal. Afterwards, Pablo would read the newspapers or listen to the news to keep up to date, and in the afternoons he often shut himself up with El Mexicano and several of his men in another room, where they'd talk for hours by radio-telephone. With whom and about what? No idea. I never went near them.

As the days went by, we started to grow worried about Juan Pablo, whose mood seemed to be deteriorating. He was quiet a lot, cried frequently and begged us to return to

Panama. To make things worse, there were no toystores in the city, and we'd left for Nicaragua so quickly that we'd left behind the motorcycle and other toys he'd been playing with.

We became so worried about Juan Pablo that Pablo had Pinina come up from Panama to keep him company. From then on, the boy had two new forms of amusement: listening to Colombian football games over the radio-telephone and betting with Pinina who could kill the most flies in five minutes in a room that was always full of the insects. What was Pablo thinking in having such criminals stand in as playmates or nannies for my son? Every day I prayed to God to save us from that hell.

In the meantime, I tried to look as good as possible in an effort to transcend my difficult circumstances: I wore make-up, brushed my hair and dressed up, all to boost my mood and show Pablo that his wife had the strength and courage to remain by his side. Sometimes in the evenings I'd be overcome with longing and I'd sob in my bed over my daughter's absence. The only way I could see her was to gaze at two photos my sisters had mailed me. The images of Manuela laughing kept me company, a balm that allowed me to survive in adversity. All that kept me going was the idea of seeing her soon and never being apart from her ever again.

Given our dull day-to-day reality, I sought out the pleasant company of El Mexicano's young wife, and we started getting together in the mornings to chat. Later, we would take walks with Juan Pablo three times a week and go to a hair salon that was operating in a sort of wooden hut. We were basically a couple of adolescents, a little over twenty years old, convinced that our husbands would get us out of that mess. But our excursions had to be very short because Managua was under siege by the Contras; the scars of conflict were apparent in the buildings, which lay practically in ruins, and in all the shuttered businesses.

Very occasionally I would get the chance to talk to El Mexicano, who always struck me as respectful, shy and laconic, with a friendly face and several gold teeth. He and Pablo had similar personalities – they respected each other, talked calmly, and I never heard them argue. He and my husband were very powerful, and I never noted any conflict between them. He was an unconditional friend to Pablo and even offered him all of his money for whatever he needed; the relationship they formed was so special that Pablo was the godfather to one of his children.

Since hunting flies and listening to football games weren't everyday activities, Juan Pablo renewed his pleas for us to leave Nicaragua. One morning, seeing the boy's desperation, Pablo told him all right, he'd let us go back to Medellín and he'd follow later.

I sighed with relief, but not for long because Pablo told me he was considering sending Juan Pablo back with one of the bodyguards. He claimed I'd be at great risk in Colombia and should stay in Nicaragua with him. It made me very sad to deceive the boy like that, and he clung to my skirt when Pablo told him in the Managua airport that his mother wouldn't be travelling with him, though my husband promised we'd be together in a few weeks. Inconsolable, Juan Pablo boarded the plane with Ferney, one of my husband's trusted men.

I was distraught. Overnight I found myself without my two children, in a hostile environment, surrounded by discomforts and armed men. To top it off, Pablo's absences became more frequent and there were days when I'd only see him for an hour or two before he left again.

Under those circumstances, it was obvious that something had to change, and it did. In early July 1984, I told Pablo to let me go to Panama to meet up with one of my sisters so she could bring me photos of Manuela and Juan Pablo – I wanted to see how they were doing. Luckily, he didn't realise that my true intention was to leave for Colombia because I couldn't stand being without my children anymore. After a short conversation, my husband agreed, not without first making me promise to come back. I had to choose between my husband and my children, and I preferred to be with them. I chose to risk dying so I could see them.

I WAS CARRYING ONLY AN OVERNIGHT BAG WITH A LITTLE clothing on the afternoon of 4 July when I left Managua heading to Panama City and, the next day, Medellín. I wanted to pass unnoticed and unrecognised, so I was wearing a tracksuit so it would look like I'd just been playing sports. When the plane landed in Medellín, I felt faint, but I had to pull myself together to mask my panic.

In the end, nothing happened and I reached the Altos building without any problems. There, I found my mother quite ill, depressed and four stone lighter. My reunion with my two children was an emotional one, and I hugged them tight for a long time. I was hurt that Manuela started crying when I picked her up; she didn't recognise me, having become accustomed to my mother and the nurse.

I didn't take Pablo long to figure out that I wasn't coming back, and he called to chastise me and warn that something might happen.

'Pablo, one of us has to take responsibility, we don't have a choice. I'm the only chance we've got. If they kill me, I'd rather my children know it was because I came looking for them.'

He was quiet.

'*Mister*, I promise I'll stay in my mother's house and never go out, but I have a baby who needs me. She's been without her mother for too long.'

Pablo reluctantly agreed, but he insisted that I mustn't leave Altos for any reason. That wasn't a problem: I was surrounded by my family, and my two children were a balm for my life.

I didn't hear from my husband for a long time, and from that day I strove to build a life in my confinement. The uproar over the Panama meetings had diminished considerably, and from time to time the news mentioned advances in the investigation into Lara Bonilla's death.

But everything with Pablo was a whirlwind, and on Tuesday, 17 July 1984 – two weeks after my return from Nicaragua – one of my sisters called to tell me to turn on the radio because they were talking about some very serious news. I did, and was startled into silence when I heard one of the local stations announce that the US newspaper

The Washington Times had published several photos that morning that showed Pablo, El Mexicano and several other people loading cocaine onto a plane in Nicaragua.

With my heart in my mouth and praying that the reporters had mixed Pablo up with somebody else, I waited for the nightly TV news. At 9.30, TV *Hoy* showed images in which there was no doubt that Pablo had been caught red-handed, trafficking cocaine.

The photos were devastating. They'd been taken, it was claimed, on a landing strip near Managua on 24 June by a CIA agent who'd infiltrated Pablo's operations. The news report also said that the photos proved the ties between Nicaragua's Sandinista regime and the Colombian drug cartels because one of the people who appeared with Pablo and El Mexicano was Federico Vaughan, a high-ranking official from Nicaragua's Ministry of the Interior.

I couldn't understand how Pablo could have got mixed up in so much trouble without considering the impact his actions would have on us.

Two days later, Herbert Shapiro, a judge in the Florida Southern District Court, issued an arrest warrant for my husband for conspiracy to import cocaine into the United States. It was a watershed moment for me as a wife because I knew how afraid Pablo was of being extradited. But then, if it was true that he'd ordered the assassination of a government minister, what other things was he capable of? The events that unfolded over the weeks and years to come would confirm the lengths my husband was willing to go to; as someone who was with him during that period once told me, Pablo stated several times, 'If I have to wipe

Colombia off the map, I'll do it, but I'll never let myself be extradited.'

As more and more news about Pablo came out, each bit worse than the last, it was obvious that he would have to flee Nicaragua. At daybreak one morning in late July, he showed up at my mother's apartment. It was a shock to see him. He'd never been much of a talker, but now all he said was, 'Hello, sweetheart,' and went to Manuela's room, where our daughter was sleeping deeply, and kissed her on the head. Then he went to Juan Pablo's room and did the same thing.

We sat in the dim living room and I chastised him for coming to Altos, knowing the whole world was after him. He told me not to worry, one night there wasn't going to matter. My mother heard us and got up, very upset. 'You dolt, what sort of Greek tragedy are you going to concoct now?'

'No, don't worry, everything's going to be OK, I promise.'

We fell silent. Deep down we knew that there'd never be peace in our lives again. Later, we went to lie down in Juan Pablo's room and hugged each other tight, as if we sensed that we would be together for very little time from now on. And, in fact, he got up at six o'clock in the morning, had breakfast, freshened up quickly and left with a briefcase containing a bit of clothing, deodorant, and a toothbrush and toothpaste.

I was despondent, not knowing what would happen in the next few minutes. Not the next few hours or days, let alone years. No. Minutes. That's what the war my husband had started was reducing us to. My daughter was three months old, Juan Pablo was seven, and I was twenty-three. We were locked in a spacious, comfortable place, enveloped with familial affection, and could stay as long as we wanted, but everything outside those walls was uncertain.

As I waited impatiently for a message from Pablo, I settled into a routine at Altos, starting at six o'clock in the morning, when I got up to give Manuela her bottle and fuss over her. In the mornings I had to make a big effort to show my children the value of play, even though they had to spend hours and hours with the same people in the same spaces; I had to teach them to understand that they couldn't go out onto the street, to the movies, to a park. It was a difficult situation to be in. Our only outings were to visit other floors in the building, chatting with neighbours and making sure my children interacted with the few young people living there.

Nearly a month after he left, Pablo sent Pasquín – one of his original bodyguards, and who had also gone to Panama and Nicaragua – to ask after the two children and say that Pablo was fine, not to worry, and that when things were safer he'd send for us. Intrigued, I took advantage of the bodyguard's brief visit to ask if he knew what had happened in Nicaragua and why Pablo had fallen into the trap of being caught on camera.

Pasquín replied that he'd tell me what he knew if I didn't say anything to his boss. I swore I'd keep my mouth shut, and he told me that we'd arrived in Nicaragua through my husband's contacts with the M-19, whom he'd engaged with two years earlier when the guerrilla group had kidnapped Marta Nieves Ochoa and Pablo helped rescue her. During that search, Pablo had captured some of the rebels and established lasting relationships with them.

According to Pasquín's account, when it became necessary to leave Panama, Pablo sought out the M-19 guerrilla fighters, who put him in touch with some members of the junta that was running the Nicaraguan government. The junta seemed willing to take us in in exchange for economic assistance; in return, Pablo could use some regions of the country for his trafficking operations. So Pablo and El Mexicano had travelled across much of the country by helicopter and selected a small airport near Managua to send their first cocaine shipments.

While telling this incredible story, Pasquín must have seen my eyes opening wider and wider. But it was almost over. As they were loading 1,300lbs of cocaine, they didn't realise that the pilot, Barry Seal, who'd been working for my husband for several years, was taking photos with a camera hidden in the plane's fuselage. Seal betrayed Pablo because the CIA and DEA knew he was working for the cartel and had forced him to take the photos in exchange for not indicting him and throwing him in prison. Pasquín finished his tale by saying that Pablo had been furious with Seal, and what he'd done – exposing my husband as a drug trafficker with photographic evidence for the first and only time – would end up costing him a heavy price.

GIVEN THE CIRCUMSTANCES, TENSION WAS INEVITABLE IN my mother's apartment. We were hearing all kinds of rumours that the authorities were going to raid the building at any moment. Starting at dawn, she would spend hours looking out the window, waiting for the eventual appearance of trucks full of armed men.

But the raids didn't come, and we gradually started noticing that the hunt had shifted. With that breath of air, I was able to go out, contact my wider family and direct the construction of the Mónaco building, which we planned to move into in early 1985.

On the evening of 20 September 1984, we met with Pablo at the Mónaco building to show him how the project was going and confirm that the construction matched the building designs. We went up to the penthouse via an improvised lift and started our tour alongside the architects. We were halfway through when Pablo was suddenly informed that he had an urgent call on the radio-telephone.

'Pablo, Pablo, this is El Águila. I've just been informed that your father's been kidnapped.'

'Oh no, are you serious? I'll be right there.'

Though the rest of us were startled by what we'd just heard, my husband seemed perplexingly serene. He did not leave straight away, instead staying half an hour longer and giving a few instructions. That same day, Juan Pablo and I went to be with my mother-in-law, who looked distraught over her husband's kidnapping.

We didn't hear anything over the next few days. Pablo was still a fugitive from justice and his father had been kidnapped, so it was understandable that I wouldn't know what moves he was making to negotiate my father-in-law's rescue. One day Otto arrived with a message from Pablo. Of the kidnapping, he said only that it had been carried out by four common criminals who'd already been identified, along with the vehicles they'd used.

The next day, an announcement appeared in the Medellín papers stating what Otto had told me and offering a reward to anyone who provided information about my father-in-law's whereabouts. It also revealed that the kidnapping had been carried out in two Toyota jeeps, one of them hard-topped with an official plate, 0318, and the other red with a soft top and a wooden bed, license plate KD 9964.

One weekend Pinina came to collect us and take us to see Pablo, and at the safehouse where he was staying we ran into my mother-in-law, who was looking desperate because Don Abel was still missing. Unable to take it anymore, she told Pablo, 'Don't you claim to know everything that happens in this country? So why don't you know where your father is?'

'Calm down, Mum, trust me. This is a very delicate matter and can't be resolved overnight.'

Finally, on 6 October 1984, we received word that Don Abel had been released and would be taken to a safehouse where Pablo was waiting for us. Otto came to pick me up at Altos and took me and Juan Pablo to a country house in Los Balsos, where my mother-in-law and two of my brothers-in-law were waiting.

Over the next four hours, we prayed the rosary twice. Suddenly a number of SUVs appeared and my father-in-law climbed out of one. Doña Hermilda hugged him first,

25 May 1984: Pablo and me at Panama City's Clínica Paitilla hospital with Manuela, who had just been born.

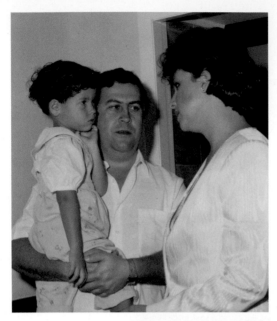

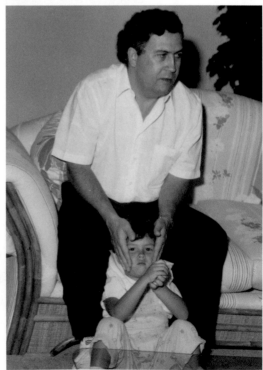

Pablo and Manuela always had a special connection. Though he was often absent because he was in hiding, she enjoyed his company. These were rare moments as a family.

Hacienda Nápoles, celebrating my daughter's birthday. Manuela dancing alone.

Manuela's room in the Mónaco building, with a mural painted by the artist Ramón Vásquez.

This is the crib where Manuela was having a bottle early in the morning on 13 January 1988, when a car bomb went off at the Mónaco building. Miraculously, she survived.

The themed parties I used to organise at the Altos building – like this one, celebrating the five-hundredth anniversary of the discovery of the Americas – were always well attended. These were periods of calm while Pablo was on the run.

This is what was left of part of the penthouse at the Mónaco building after the car bomb attack in 1988. Many works of art were badly damaged in the explosion.

Pablo and I tried to lead a normal life, but war got in the way.

This is Pablo's famous mansion in Miami. On 9 May, 1981, one of my sisters had her wedding there. The house was confiscated in 1987.

The entire family at Manuela's fourth birthday, at Hacienda Nápoles.

This photo debunks the myth of the supposed 'unicorn' that Pablo gave Manuela for her fourth birthday.

(*Above and opposite*) Manuela's birthday at La Catedral, May 1992.

This was the only Christmas we spent with Pablo at La Catedral prison. It was 24 December 1991.

Under the protection of guards from the attorney general's office, we visited the Jardines Montesacro cemetery in Medellín on the first anniversary of Pablo's death.

On 7 May 1994, five months after my husband's death, we celebrated Manuela's First Communion in the apartment in Bogotá's Santa Ana neighborhood.

The cell that Juan Pablo and I occupied at the headquarters of the
Superintendency of Dangerous Drugs in Buenos Aires, 1999.
My son was there 45 days, and I was incarcerated for 540.

Juan Pablo and his son Juan Emilio, my grandson, 2012.

then Pablo and then everybody else. He sat down in a chair with us gathered around him expectantly so he could describe his experience during those seventeen days of captivity.

'They made me walk for a long time, but luckily I'm used to walking in the mountains, or I would have died. They gave me good food and told me not to worry, nothing was going to happen to me, my son would pay my ransom.'

After the inevitable interrogation, because we were eager to know all the details, my father-in-law said he was very tired and wanted to go to his farm with Doña Hermilda.

We didn't ask Pablo what he'd done to get his father back so quickly, but a few weeks later Otto told me that the kidnappers had taken Don Abel to a farm in Liborina, a town about sixty miles from Medellín, and tied him to a bed. He was very succinct and said only that Pablo had set up equipment at Doña Hermilda's house to record any phone calls, which had swiftly led to the discovery of the kidnappers' identities, but he wanted to wait for them to demand a ransom to make sure they didn't hurt his father. After initially demanding US$10 million, the captors were flabbergasted by Pablo's reply: 'Look, brother, you kidnapped the wrong man. My father is a poor farmer who doesn't have a peso. You should have kidnapped me – I'm the one with the money.'

The kidnappers lowered their sights to the equivalent of US$400,000 in pesos, and then US$300,000, which Pablo sent with John Lada, Manuela's godfather. In the end, they got only a tiny part of the money they'd hoped to receive.

But 1984 wasn't over yet. Many things had happened over the course of the year, and in December it seemed that the waters had grown calmer. In the second week of that month, Otto and Giovanni, one of Pablo's closest lieutenants, came to pick up Juan Pablo, Nieves – our maid – and me, and took us to a country estate in the nearby town of Guarne to spend New Year's Eve with Pablo. I left Manuela with her grandmother because she was coming down with a cold.

The atmosphere was relaxed, as it generally is in December, and Pablo's men were coming and going from the estate, heading into town to buy provisions and drink beer, even though we were in a populated area and the constant movement was calling attention to us.

At dawn on one of those days, I was sleeping deeply with Juan Pablo when we were awakened by a commotion and I saw a plain-clothes police officer with the barrel of his rifle pressed against my son's belly. He must have thought Juan Pablo was older than he was because the boy was wearing an elastic device that covered his head and chin, which the doctors had prescribed for him to correct a slight misalignment of his jaw.

It was a horrible fright. My mouth went dry, I couldn't talk, and when I managed it, all I could do was ask what was happening. Though the sun wasn't yet up, I could see that one of the officers was holding Pablo's white *ruana*, a poncho-like garment, in his hand. It was clear he'd escaped, as the man confirmed when he said it had been dropped by 'one of the people who ran off'. My heart was leaping in my

chest and I held my boy tight; he was now awake and staring all around in fright.

The raid went on for almost three hours. The police
searched the estate from top to bottom and didn't let us
leave the living room. Eventually, one of them announced
that I was under arrest and would be taken down to the station for questioning.

'But why, officer? I was just sleeping with my son.'

There was no answer, and we started trying to figure out
who would take Juan Pablo to my mother's house. I also
decided to find a lawyer right away, but everything was
suddenly settled when one of the officers apologised and
said we could leave. I didn't ask why, but I imagined that
Pablo had pulled some strings somewhere. Still shaking, I
loaded my son and Nieves into a jeep and left.

Pablo had escaped, leaving his *ruana* behind. It was the
first police raid, and it wouldn't be the last. We'd got out of
that situation relatively easily but, deep down, I knew that
there were many more to come, and that our lives would be
in danger often. Nine years of anxiety awaited us.

My Meeting with Jorge Lara

We met in July 2017, but I could barely look him in the eye,
so deep was my shame. My son, now going by the name
Sebastián, had forged the path, and once Jorge Lara and I
were face to face on a small farm outside Medellín, we fell
into a powerful embrace. Then, in a moving conversation,
we shared our pain, our suffering and our sorrows, and I

repeatedly begged his forgiveness, unable to contain my weeping.

Jorge was just six years old when his father, Minister of Justice Rodrigo Lara, was murdered. He is the second of three brothers, and his life has been full of challenges.

As I listened with tears in my eyes, he talked about the pain caused by many years of exile, his mother's powerlessness and flight from Colombia with three small boys after her husband's death, the difficulties he'd faced studying in a country where he didn't speak the language.

As a memento of that remarkable encounter, I have a letter that Jorge Lara decided to write for this book. It isn't easy to grapple with its contents, which reflect the deep pain that Pablo inflicted on his family. I am immensely grateful for his words, which confirm for me once more that only forgiveness can heal us.

According to the logic of hate, I should avenge my father's death. For many years I dreamed of vengeance and thought my act would be viewed as one of heroism. According to that logic, I'd earned the right because of the monstrosities committed and orchestrated by Pablo Escobar and his accomplices and, obviously, as a result of my father's assassination. In 1984, exactly two months after the assassination, my mother, a twenty-seven-year-old widow, had to flee the country and go into forced exile with her three sons to make sure our lives wouldn't end the same way.

For several years, in exile in three different countries, we had to adapt to new customs, seek new spaces, and struggle for acceptance in societies that were completely unfamiliar to us.

In our second exile nation, Switzerland, we ended up studying just twelve miles from Pablo Escobar's family. I heard that Sebastián was studying near my school and planned to do the unthinkable. At just twelve years old, I longed for that revenge, which I planned and prepared with my best friend. Miraculously, we never scraped together enough money to carry out our plan.

The third country was France. There, at sixteen years old, after hearing the news of Escobar's death, I wanted to celebrate, but the first thing my mother told me was 'I didn't raise you that way. You aren't the kind of person who celebrates anybody's death! That man needed to be put on trial and made to pay for his crimes. But being happy about somebody's death isn't OK – it's unacceptable!' I didn't understand at first but, over the years, I realised she was right.

In 2007 I was contacted by Nicolas Entel, an Argentine film director and the catalyst for my meeting the Escobar family. It's important to acknowledge him, since he was the one, through his documentary *Sins of My Father*, who made all of this possible.

I met with Sebastián in private. There was no press, just the two of us. Our meeting was very direct, cordial and honest. And it led to a sincere friendship in which two opposite poles, seemingly destined for conflict, ended up being bound together by the history that life had fated us with.

The years passed and, in mid-2017, in the mountains of Medellín, I had a meeting with Sebastián. At the end, I said hello to some people who were there and, to my great surprise, Sebastián grabbed the hand of one of the women, looked at me, and said, 'I'd like to introduce my mother.'

It was that kind of moment where your mind sends you thousands of bits of information in a fraction of a second. Our immediate impulse was to hug: a symbol of forgiveness, acceptance, understanding and connection. We looked at each other and sat down to talk. Where did we start? I don't remember, but our conversation was honest and clear, no beating around the bush. We shared our feelings and important parts of our stories. She asked for my forgiveness, and we kept talking about different stages in life. Our encounter lasted a few hours.

It's now been almost a year since we met, and we sometimes talk to catch up and say hello. Similarly, I often talk about my father's case, which – thirty-four years after his killing – remains unsolved. I know that Pablo Escobar and his associates in the Medellín Cartel were behind the assassination, but my father didn't differentiate when condemning the infiltration of dirty cartel money into different areas of Colombian society, including sports, finance and political parties.

In this remarkable period for my country – which is undergoing a peace process, engaging in investigations of high officials, and nurturing a generation

that wants a kinder and more just future for everybody – all that is left is to build peace. We will achieve
that by breaking down barriers, paradigms, taboos,
and taking the first step.

1985

'I have to go, a problem's come up. We'll talk another time,'
Pablo told me, somewhat agitated, right as we were starting
to discuss an issue in our relationship that had driven a
wedge between us over the past few weeks.

It was 6 November 1985. We were on the farm La Pesebrera in Loma El Chocho, Envigado, where he was hiding
at the time. I had sent him several letters asking if we could
talk, until he'd finally agreed to send Otto that morning to
pick me up at the Mónaco building. My husband looked
angry, serious, and I could tell that, though he was looking
at me, his mind was elsewhere.

It took me a long time to break the ice. I told him how
the children were doing and how we'd been spending our
time but, right at that moment, just as he seemed about to
speak, Otto and Pinina came in, called him aside, and
whispered something to him. Immediately Pablo told them
to get the cars ready because they had to leave, and he
ordered some of his other men to take me back to Mónaco.

Half an hour later, back in the penthouse, I heard a commotion in the kitchen. When I entered, I found that the
domestic staff had tuned in a radio station that was talking
vaguely about an intense firefight in downtown Bogotá,
apparently inside the Palace of Justice. As the hours went

by, it became clear that Colombia was in the grip of a new tragedy: the occupation of the building that housed the Supreme Court of Justice and the Council of State, by members of the M-19 guerrilla movement.

Pablo didn't reappear or send any message, but I later learned that after saying goodbye to me at La Pesebrera, he went into hiding at a farm near Hacienda Nápoles. I remained in the Mónaco building, sick with worry. I got down on my knees – as I'd done with my mother after the assassination of Minister Rodrigo Lara – and prayed over and over and lit a candle before the image of a wooden Christ. In that moment, I was terrified by the very idea that Pablo had anything to do with what was happening in Bogotá.

The result of the events during those twenty-seven hours of horror was immensely distressing. More than a hundred people died, including a dozen magistrates as well as civil employees, members of law enforcement and civilians. But as the days passed and the country put itself back together after the tragedy, the media started reporting that the fire that had consumed much of the building on the night of 6 November had also resulted in the destruction of all of the files related to extradition requests, which had been under review in the Constitutional Chamber of the Supreme Court.

As I've stated throughout this book, I had very few opportunities to talk to my husband about the things he'd done or not done. I generally found out about them from stray comments made by his men, and I hardly ever had a full picture of events.

Regarding the occupation of the Palace of Justice, I didn't speak directly to Pablo or ask him if he'd been involved in planning or financing the operation, but over the years I've put some of the pieces together, and it's not absurd to say that my husband may have played a key role in the events that took place that Wednesday and Thursday in November 1985. And if I'd had the chance to talk to him about it, he'd most likely have given me the same answer as always: 'Sweetheart, they blame me for everything that happens in this country!'

When I say I've put pieces together, I'm referring to things that happened years ago – in the early 1980s – that I discussed obliquely with Pablo at various opportunities; with the passage of time, it has become clear that my husband and some M-19 leaders were united by disparate interests. My memory carries me back to 14 November 1981, when Pablo arrived at our house in El Diamante and told me he was very worried about the kidnapping of the student Martha Nieves Ochoa, which had taken place two days earlier on the campus of the University of Antioquia, where she was studying Economics. He also told me he'd visited the Ochoas to see what he could do to help since he valued the family, especially Martha's father Don Fabio Ochoa Restrepo and his son Jorge Luis, with whom Pablo was very close.

I replied that I hoped everything would turn out OK, but my husband started acting oddly. He stopped coming to the house, and out of the blue we found ourselves surrounded by armed men who claimed they'd been given orders to look after us. Then Pasquín showed up with instructions from my husband, who told us not to leave the house for a while until things were settled. There was one exception: they started taking Juan Pablo to kindergarten at the Montessori school in an armoured SUV; while he was in class, two bodyguards waited outside.

It was obvious that Pablo was deeply involved in the Martha Nieves Ochoa matter, which he said he'd taken on because he admired the family. Without knowing much, one day in the third week of November I chastised him when he arrived at ten in the morning, clearly having been up all night.

'Pablo, you're going to push yourself to your death for your friends. You haven't been around in days. And what about us? Are we going to get to be with you for Christmas?'

'No, my love. If I don't help them out now, then how can I ask for help later on? We have to be united on this so it doesn't happen again.'

And he left again for several days. One morning, while scanning the local papers, I realised what was going on. On one of the inside pages was a large ad that announced the creation of the group MAS, Muerte a Secuestradores (Death to Kidnappers), described the kidnapping of Martha Nieves Ochoa, and warned the M-19 in no uncertain terms that they weren't going to get a cent for her ransom.

The M-19 had kidnapped Martha Nieves? It was unbelievable. Now I understood why my husband was determined to help rescue her: in mid-July of that year, 1981, he himself had been on a list of the guerrilla group's kidnapping targets. It was ironic that the M-19 had tried to kidnap him because on several occasions my husband had mentioned his sympathy for the bold attacks the rebel group had been carrying out since it was founded, including the theft of Simón Bolívar's sword, the theft of 4,000 weapons from an army battalion, and the occupation of the Dominican embassy. Pablo had told me on multiple occasions that he liked the M-19 because those intrepid young people had become famous after hijacking milk delivery trucks and handing out thousands of bottles in Bogotá's poorest neighbourhoods.

But it was one thing for Pablo to sympathise with the M-19's propagandistic actions and quite another for them to try and kidnap him to finance their operations. So he reached out to his contacts in the security forces, and, as Pinina later told me, several members of the M-19's Medellín cell – Martha Elena Correa, Luis Gabriel Bernal, Elvencio Ruiz and Jorge Torres Victoria – were arrested in different places around the city. They were then taken to the headquarters of *Antioquia al Día*, where my husband had an office. There, Pasquín told me later, my husband informed them that he sympathised with their cause so he wasn't going to hurt them, but warned them that it was a very bad idea to get money by kidnapping certain rich and powerful figures in Medellín, himself among them.

Unexpectedly, that meeting established the foundation for a future relationship governed strictly by each party's individual interests. Over the next few weeks, Pablo gave them some money and promised to get them weapons.

But the agreement to avoid violence went out the window with the M-19's kidnapping of Martha Nieves. So it made sense that Pablo was participating actively in the search, since he already knew the members of the rebel group's Medellín cell.

After the publication of the ad announcing the creation of MAS, Pablo started coming by almost every day at eight or nine in the morning after, Pinina told me, carrying out raids with the army almost all night. Those clandestine operations ended with the capture of some twenty people, including the ones Pablo had run into four months earlier: Martha Elena Correa – a former classmate of Martha Nieves – Luis Gabriel Bernal and Elvencio Ruiz. But there was no trace of the missing woman.

As I'd feared, Pablo wasn't with us for either Christmas or New Year's Eve, which we spent at the house in El Diamante. But judging by the news, it was clear that my husband was still very active in trying to locate his friends' sister. And so, on 30 December 1981, I was surprised to see, splashed across the front page of the newspaper *El Colombiano*, the photo of a woman who'd been left outside the newspaper office, her hands bound and with a sign that said 'Kidnapper'. It was Martha Elena Correa. She'd been released only a few days after her capture, as a way of sending a message to M-19, warning them that MAS was on the kidnappers' heels.

On 3 January 1982, three weeks after the kidnapping, I spotted an ad in *El Colombiano*, published by the Ochoas, with a message that sounded more like a declaration of war:

The Ochoa Vásquez family refuses to negotiate with
the M-19 abductors who are holding Martha Nieves

Ochoa de Yepes captive. It will not pay money for her release and instead offers the sum of twenty-five million pesos [US$387,000 at the time] to any citizen who supplies information regarding her whereabouts.

Pablo's behaviour remained unchanged during that month, and the little I heard suggested that the guerrilla group had managed to escape every raid. The family's only option was to negotiate. Pablo never told me anything about it, but we were thrilled when we learned that on 12 February, 123 days after she was kidnapped, Martha Nieves had been released in Génova, a town in the department of Quindío. Many rumours have gone around about how much money the M-19 were paid to release their victim, even claims that high-level figures from several countries participated in the negotiations, but I was never able to get reliable information about that.

An outstanding witness to the Ochoa events is the Antioquian journalist Alonso Arcila, whom I called when writing this book because he had privileged access in covering Martha Nieves's release. He'd been handling the information responsibly, so Pablo called him and told him that one of his men would pick Arcila up in Envigado's park and take him to the Ochoa home known as La Loma.

'I got to that house and Don Fabio Ochoa, the father and the whole family were already there; I interviewed them and then they gave me permission to go to the airport to receive Martha Nieves Ochoa, who was coming from Armenia; she was very nervous and actually was very aloof and didn't want to make any statements, just hug her family because she was exhausted.'

In my research for this book, I spoke with several people who were close to Pablo, who told me that despite the M-19's attempt to kidnap him and their successful kidnapping of Martha Nieves Ochoa, his relationship with the guerrilla group never disintegrated and that, quite the opposite, my husband maintained close contact with Iván Marino Ospina, the second in command, and Elvencio Ruiz. My sources described numerous meetings at Hacienda Nápoles and farms around Medellín. At the time, one gift that Ospina gave to Pablo got a lot of people talking: a brand-new AK-47, which ended up in Pasquín's hands and was his weapon of choice for a long time. I also heard that Iván Marino Ospina's association with my husband meant he enjoyed certain privileges, such as being able to leave and enter the country without having his passport stamped, which worked in favour of the guerrilla leader's clandestine activities.

Their relationship must have been a close one. In late August 1985, Pablo looked downcast when he learned that Ospina had died in a standoff with the army in Cali. He didn't say anything to me at the time, but I did overhear him talking on the phone with somebody and telling them that Ospina had been a warrior, a one-in-a-million fighter.

I can't say whether my husband's interactions with the M-19 led to the occupation of the Palace of Justice, but it's quite a coincidence that Elvencio Ruiz – whose life Pablo had twice spared, first when he found out Ruiz was planning to kidnap him, and second when he learned Ruiz had participated in the kidnapping of Martha Nieves Ochoa – led the operation on 6 November 1985.

What's certain is that the collateral damage of the Palace of Justice tragedy included the destruction of the extradition files and the consequent standstill in the processing of those cases because reconstructing the files was nearly impossible. Pasquín said this lifted a weight off my husband and many other people wanted by the United States. Earlier that year the government had begun once more to send Colombian citizens to face justice in other countries, as happened with thirteen people, including Hernán Botero Moreno – president of the Atlético Nacional football team – Marco Fidel Cadavid, and the brothers Said and Nayib Pabón Jatter. I remember Pablo was very upset about those extraditions, especially Botero's, and argued that Botero shouldn't have been extradited because he was accused of money laundering, not drug trafficking.

Nevertheless, the ghost of extradition lingered on, but it shifted into the background on 13 November 1985 – a week after the events of the Palace of Justice – when another horrifying tragedy occurred: the eruption of the Nevado del Ruiz volcano, which caused mudflows that wiped out the town of Armero, Tolima, in southwestern Colombia, killing more than 20,000 people. The images of what was happening in that region were very distressing, revealing how woefully unprepared the country was for such an assault by nature.

It was agonising to witness the sad end of Omayra Sánchez, the thirteen-year-old girl who died before the TV cameras because there wasn't the technology required to rescue her from between the walls of her home. That incident broke my heart in two because even in that helpless position, the little one was telling her mother that she loved her and asking her to pray for her because she didn't want to die.

Pablo wasn't with us in those moments, but the pilot of one of his planes told me he'd sent one of his Hughes helicopters to help airlift potable water for the survivors and called his 'partners' to form a sort of aerial flotilla to transport mattresses, blankets and food.

Now that i've talked about pablo's relationship with some of the M-19 leaders, I should describe the afternoon in January 1986 when I was walking beside the pool at La Mayoría and saw my husband and Juan Pablo with what looked like a sword. Intrigued, I went over and asked what they were up to.

'Look, my love, look what I just gave Grégory: the sword of the liberator Simón Bolívar. A friend gave it to me.'

It was nuts. Bolívar's sword in my husband's hands? It looked like any other sword. Maybe it was, but maybe it wasn't. If real, it would be a historical treasure to be added to the two Bolívar belongings I'd purchased not long before: the medal he'd been awarded after his victory in the Battle of Boyacá, in 1819, and the original sketch for a sculpture of Bolívar on his horse that the governor at the time commissioned from a famous Italian artist for display in Medellín's Bolívar Square.

The last thing I heard as I walked away was this: 'Careful, son, that sword's got a lot of history. Go on, but handle it carefully and don't start messing around.'

Because of the war, the raids, the hideouts, the constant running, we'd been driven to unimagined places, constantly on the move. We lost many things and forgot others. Bolívar's sword among them. I heard about it again years later, in January 1991, when Otto and El Arete came to the safehouse known as The 40, where my children and I were hiding, with an urgent message from Pablo: he needed us to return Bolívar's sword as soon as possible.

We looked at each other in disbelief; it had been more than five years since Pablo had given Juan Pablo the sword. My son reacted, saying, 'Otto, tell my father you can't ask for somebody to return a gift. I'm not returning it, plus I don't know where it is.'

Recognising my son's determination, the bodyguard phoned Pablo so they could talk.

'Look, Grégory, return the sword,' Pablo said. 'I have to deliver it to the friends who gave it to me. They need it urgently.'

Pablo was persuasive, but finding the damn sword took several days because Juan Pablo didn't remember where he'd left it after so many years of comings and goings. The only solution was to ask all the bodyguards to search all the farms, apartments and houses we'd been in since 1985 and bring us anything they found that resembled a sword. I remember they even sent us machetes and large knives. Finally they found a sword that looked very similar to the one Juan Pablo had received and we sent it to Pablo. Before it was taken away, Juan Pablo took several photos with the sword so he'd have a memento of that significant artifact that had passed through our hands.

We didn't talk about the subject again, but some time later we understood why Pablo had asked for Bolívar's sword to be returned. Since the M-19 had completed their negotiations with the government, they needed to offer a gesture of goodwill, and what better way than to return the sword? This took place on 31 January 1991, in a special ceremony in Bogotá in which Antonio Navarro Wolff and other demobilised M-19 guerrilla fighters handed the sword to then-president César Gaviria.

Looking back at these events, I still wonder whether the sword we returned was actually the original or if somebody along the way might have kept the real one. Everything related to this episode is, to say the least, bizarre. Whatever the case, the sword the M-19 relinquished is safely held in a security vault in the Banco de la República, Colombia's national bank. Are they securing the right one? We may never know.

1986

On 25 July 2016, Juan Pablo arrived at my apartment looking very agitated. I grew worried when he said he had something to show me on his mobile phone. I was so accustomed to bad news, I thought something terrible had happened. What a relief that this wasn't the case this time.

He opened one of the messages he'd received that morning and explained that it was from Aaron Seal, son of the

American pilot Barry Seal, who'd been murdered – according to the investigations – on Pablo's orders.

Thirty years had passed since February 1986, so it was incredible that my son had received a message from one of my husband's victims, from somebody who wanted to contact him, talk about what had happened, face the past head on.

Aaron's words were astonishing:

My name is Aaron Seal and well my fathers name is Barry Seal. I'm sure you are as familiar with that name as I am with your fathers name. I had read before contacting you how you have sought reconciliation with people from your fathers past. I am very proud of you for doing that and you are a big man for doing so. I reached out to the men who actually pulled the trigger and shot my dad and told them I love them and had forgiven them. I Just wanted you to know That I long ago forgave your dad for (allegedly) paying for my fathers contract murder. I humbly come to you to request that you forgive my dad for be willing to testify against your dad and associates. My dad was just trying to save his rear end and he paid the ultimate price. Just know there are no hard feelings with me or my mother. Sebastian, I more than most can relate to how hard your life has been. My road has been rough as well but the Lord has been my rock.... I will not be offended if you choose not to reply. God bless you man, Aaron Seal

My son immediately replied, and after exchanging of several emails and a videochat, they met on 27 September of that year in Mexico City. Hours later he called and told me excitedly that the conversation had been warm; they'd talked not only about their personal stories but also about their fathers, who'd made huge mistakes that had cost them their lives in different circumstances.

The whole world knows how my husband died, but the meeting between Sebastián and Aaron confirmed a lot of things and revealed others about the factors that caused Pablo to order his men to locate Barry Seal in the United States and execute him, as they did on 19 February 1986, in a Salvation Army car park in Baton Rouge, Louisiana.

Pablo never forgave Seal for betraying him by participating in the CIA/DEA plot in Nicaragua in June 1984 and photographing him alongside El Mexicano as they were loading a shipment of cocaine into a plane piloted by Seal and outfitted with a powerful camera hidden in the aircraft's fuselage.

The moving encounter between Aaron and my son opened another door: the possibility of meeting Barry Seal's widow. At the time of writing, however, we have attempted to meet in various places in Latin America, and for one reason or another we've never been able to make it happen. I am convinced that if that moment ever happens, it will mark a turning point for us as women.

I learned many details about Seal's death during my long conversation in 2016 with Quijada, Pablo's personal accountant in Miami, whom I met with in Carmen de Viboral during a short trip to Colombia to expand my research for this book. Among many other topics, Quijada described the order he'd received from my husband to help the *sicarios* however he could in February 1986 when they travelled from Medellín to carry out the hit on Seal. This is what Quijada told me:

> Pablo called me and told me three guys were coming in for a hit. It was Guillermo Zuluaga, known as 'Cuchilla', Pedro and Bernardo. Two of them came in illegally from Mexico, and I sent somebody to pick them up and put them up in a hotel. Cuchilla asked me if I remembered Barry Seal, and I said of course, how could I forget that asshole when he's the one who ratted out Pablo. Then he told me they were going to take him out in Louisiana, where he was under protection, and explained that they had a way in and out. I didn't see them again. Later I heard Cuchilla escaped and the other two were caught on the turnpike because the taxi they were getting away in hit a deer and the driver reported the incident to the authorities. That's how they got caught.

In Colombia, Seal's death went almost completely unnoticed. At the time, far away from those events, I was organising a family gathering in the Mónaco building to celebrate Juan Pablo's ninth birthday on 24 February 1986. Wanting to give him a very special gift, I opted for something I'd bought recently planning to cherish it as a treasure: a chest containing the original love letters that Manuelita Sáenz wrote to the liberator Simón Bolívar.

Today Juan Pablo is an adult and has told me he's proud of having kept those items.

Shortly before we cut the cake, Pablo showed up unannounced, but said he couldn't stay long. We took the usual photos, and he ate a little and was very affectionate toward Manuela and Juan Pablo. Before he left, half an hour after he'd arrived, he gave the boy a letter and a hug. As always, his fleeting presence was bittersweet for me. I still wasn't used to living every moment of my life without my husband. When the party ended, I read the message Pablo had written to his son:

> You're turning nine years old today. You're a man now, and that means a lot of responsibilities. On this day, I want to tell you that life has beautiful moments, but it has tough, difficult moments too. Those tough moments are the ones that make us men. I know with absolute certainty that you have always faced the difficult moments in your life with great dignity and courage.

I was twenty-four years old at the time, and it pains me not to have realised back then that with that message Pablo was robbing Juan Pablo of his childhood, putting responsibilities on his shoulders that were beyond his capabilities. I'm angry that I didn't scold him for the contents of that letter.

PABLO DISAPPEARED AGAIN, AND OVER THE NEXT FEW months of 1986 we lived a fairly normal life in the Mónaco building. I tried hard to build a routine for my children and family. Our surroundings were important, so I decorated the apartment to emphasise colour and freshness. And since I liked the best of the best, I hired a company that would send white and red roses, anthuriums and gladioli every week from Bogotá. An expert would arrange them in nearly twenty vases distributed throughout the penthouse, including in the bathrooms.

Back then I was also very busy preparing for Juan Pablo's First Communion, which was to take place at the Colegio San José de la Salle on Saturday, 16 August 1986. The ceremony had been scheduled since the beginning of the year, and I'd been making arrangements to ensure that my son would have an unforgettable experience.

For that reason I travelled to Switzerland, since I'd heard that I'd find the best accessories for the celebration there. Indeed, in Geneva I found a store specialising in invitation cards for First Communions and ordered a hundred, on linen paper with a yellow satin ribbon. Elsewhere in the city, I found a chocolate factory that was famous worldwide for its delicious confections that came packed in a square yellow box lined with tissue paper decorated with yellow and blue flowers. A real work of art. From Switzerland I went on to Rome, to buy his First Communion suit. It was made of blue linen with grey tones, and the tie had red details that gave the suit a certain elegance and beauty. Then in Milan I bought dresses for Manuela and me.

On the appointed day, the ceremony was held at the school and Juan Pablo was accompanied by his maternal grandparents and my brother Carlos, who attended in

Pablo's stead because my husband was still a fugitive. It made me sad to see Juan Pablo with tears in his eyes while his classmates were beaming, surrounded by their parents and families.

In the evening, we held a big party at the Mónaco building. As was now his habit, Pablo came by without warning, accompanied by Fidel Castaño and Gerardo 'Kiko' Moncada. They were with us for two hours, and then left for a hideout known as El Paraíso, where they'd wait for us to continue the celebration. Hours later, my parents, my children and I went to the safehouse, served a cake and took a few photos.

Despite these few pleasant moments, we continued to be shocked by the media reports on my husband. The news described the progress of judicial processes for various crimes and the United States' extradition request.

Pablo appeared at the Mónaco building only very occasionally, and I learned of the events rocking the country through the evening news. For example, 17 November 1986 saw the murder, on the outskirts of Bogotá, of the police colonel Jaime Ramírez, who in March 1984 had headed up the occupation of the Tranquilandia coca production complex in Llanos del Yarí, Caquetá. That was the first time an official of that rank had lost his life, and in the solitude of my bedroom in the Mónaco building, I knew that the government would lash out powerfully against us.

I wasn't wrong: less than twelve hours after the colonel's murder, the army occupied the building in search of Pablo. Dozens of soldiers arrived in trucks and swarmed the seven floors, while a colonel and various underlings headed to the penthouse, where I was with my children.

What happened in that raid left me with the bitter sense that the conflict between my husband and the authorities would gradually deteriorate, to the detriment of those of us caught in the middle.

'Where is that bastard?' the colonel asked me, unable to hide his hatred for my husband.

'Colonel, he and I separated a long time ago.'

The excuse didn't do much good because right at that moment Pablo called; somebody must have told him about the raid. One of the soldiers answered the phone, and my husband must have said something really awful to him because the colonel immediately grabbed me by the arm, shoved me into the walk-in closet and shut the door.

'Go on, show me which nightgown you're going to wear tonight to look good for that murderer of cops, justices and innocent people,' he shouted, pushing me in front of a mirror.

Shaking, gripped by panic, I had no choice but to pull some lingerie out of a drawer and show it to the irate officer. The seconds seemed to drag on forever, and I begged God to make him let me go. Luckily, hearing the sound of guns and footsteps in the bedroom, he opened the closet door.

Three hours after their arrival, having searched the building from top to bottom, the soldiers left, stymied because they hadn't found a trace of Pablo. But I was shattered. My husband's increasingly violent acts, like those the colonel had alluded to – the assassination of the Supreme

Court justice Hernando Baquero; of the judge Gustavo Zuluaga; and of Coronel Ramírez (though this last murder was later proven not to have been carried out by Pablo), which had occurred in July, October, and November of that year – had a direct impact on me. In that raid, I was the one who was under threat, and I had no way to object or say anything. I could only remain silent and endure the outrage.

Hours later, Pablo called again and, sobbing, I told him what had happened. His fury was palpable, and he didn't say another word.

Several weeks went by without hearing from him, until on the morning of 18 December 1986, several of his men arrived and told me he was waiting for us in a hideout. I assumed that the sudden visit was taking place because of the chance that the authorities might raid the Mónaco building yet again, since the entire country was in an uproar over the previous night's assassination of the editor in chief of *El Espectador*, Don Guillermo Cano.

Things must have been very complicated, because for the first time Pablo's men, different men from the ones who usually came for us, said we needed to wear blindfolds because it was better if we didn't know where we were being taken.

'If you get arrested, they might force you to say where the boss is hiding,' one of them said, pulling out a few bandannas for us to use to cover our faces.

It was a new and uncomfortable situation, but I realised there was no way to go against my husband's order. We would have to cover our eyes many times over the next few years.

Two hours after leaving the building, we met up with Pablo in a small rural house, but I couldn't figure out where we were. Though the climate was warm, the atmosphere in the place wasn't terribly friendly and I was humiliated at having been forced to arrive blindfolded. I berated Pablo for the journalist's murder because the news programmes had been accusing him.

'My God, Pablo, are you nuts? Where are you going with all these assassinations? Do you have any idea what your actions are going to cost that family, and ours too?'

'You don't understand, Tata ... You don't see how corrupt the institutions in this country are.'

'And is this how you plan to teach them values and ethics?'

It was agonising to watch the events following Cano's assassination, which had occurred as he was leaving the newspaper's offices in Bogotá, unfold on TV. For the first time, the newspapers' printing presses ground to a halt, the radio suspended its news broadcast, and the TV channels stopped their news programmes.

At the time, my brother Mario was hiding in the Rosario Islands, and we spoke for a few moments by phone. One sentence of his summed it all up: 'Pablo ruined our lives with this shit.'

On one of the many days we spent in confinement, Pablo came out of our bedroom and I noticed he was carrying a hefty Larousse dictionary under his arm. He sat down on the sofa to consult it; intrigued, I went over and asked him what he was looking for. He explained that he was writing a few letters and needed the dictionary so he could use exactly the right words. Then he pulled a legal pad out of his desk and started to write. It was clear that the subject was closed.

As always, he was telling only half the truth. Later, when I talked with Neruda – my husband's consultant in writing his speeches for the Envigado town council and then for Congress – and remarked that I'd noticed Pablo consulting the dictionary, he told me that though Pablo had always been meticulous when sending written messages, he'd been taking extra care that day because he was revising communiqués for the Extraditables, a secret group whose main objective was to fight against extradition.

'Victoria, the Extraditables issued their first communiqué on 6 November, and they've already accomplished something: on 12 December, the Colombian Supreme Court ruled against the extradition treaty with the United States for the first time. But two days later, the government issued another decree reinstating it, and *El Espectador* published an editorial titled "Raining on the Mafiosos' Parade"; that's why Guillermo Cano was killed.'

Disturbed by what Neruda had just told me, I asked who the Extraditables were. He raised the index finger of his right hand, and I understood that the organisation consisted of just one individual – Pablo was the Extraditables. Worse still, I told Neruda, that meant my husband was waging a war with no way out. He agreed; little by little, Pablo had taken on the fight against extradition all by himself, though there had been a sort of syndicate supporting the cause in the beginning.

'Once, we were at Nápoles and a bunch of planes showed up with more than twenty people who met with Pablo in the dining room,' I told Neruda. 'I was playing with Juan Pablo in the yard nearby, and I heard them all offer to contribute a sum of money. He always liked being a martyr, so over time he's taken on the fight against extradition as his personal battle.'

Neruda nodded gently and ended our conversation with a challenge: 'Pablo's not going to stop, Victoria. Find out what he was going to do to Belisario Betancur after he turned over the government to Virgilio Barco.'

He changed the subject and we never talked about the matter again but, deep down, I was unsettled by what he might have meant. I only found out several years after Pablo's death, when I returned to Medellín to settle some personal affairs and met with people who'd survived the war. I asked one of them, who'd been close to my husband up until Pablo had gone to prison in La Catedral in 1991, what Neruda might have been alluding to about Betancur, and what he told me was horrifying. Pablo's wickedness had gone too far. He had no limits.

According to what I was told, Pablo wanted revenge on Betancur because, after Minister Lara's assassination in 1984, he had authorised the extradition of several people to the United States even though Pablo considered him to have promised not to do so.

My source revealed that Pablo planned to kidnap Betancur and hold him indefinitely in the jungle after the presidential succession in August 1986. To that end, he ordered Godoy, one of his men, to build a windowless cabin somewhere in the jungle between Urabá and Chocó. Godoy soon found an appropriate site and after two months of work with various assistants he completed a house that would function as a sort of prison. Pablo's men made several kidnapping attempts but, thankfully, Betancur was well guarded, and Pablo eventually discarded the idea.

1987

Hacienda Nápoles was confiscated for the first time in 1984, when the Colombian government declared war on my husband and drug trafficking because of the assassination of Minister of Justice Rodrigo Lara Bonilla. I never knew how he did it, but Pablo managed to arrange things so that we were able to remain there unimpeded for several years.

In mid-January 1987, we stayed at the estate for a few days, and on our way back Pablo decided we should travel by road because he wanted to drive to Medellín, drop us off at the Mónaco building, and then go to a safehouse. It was a huge mistake; a couple of hours later, we would go through one of the worst experiences of our lives.

Pablo was driving a Toyota SUV, and I was beside him with Manuela; Juan Pablo and Carlos Lehder were in the backseat. Two vehicles – one with Otto, El Mugre and Pasquín and another with Luigi and Dolly – drove ahead of us, and were supposed to remain in contact no more than a mile or so away so that we wouldn't lose the radio-telephone signal.

It was a sunny day, and there weren't many cars on the road; Pablo was zipping along, and when we were about halfway to our destination, Luigi warned us that he'd just gone through the tollbooth in Cocorná and had spotted a police checkpoint with four uniformed officers.

My husband kept going, and I started wondering why he wasn't stopping; I was sure something bad was going to happen.

Lehder must have read my thoughts and said, 'Pablo, I don't think we should all go in the same car, do you?'

'Yes, I know. Hang on. Just before it, there's a curve in the road on the hill right above the tollbooth, and we can scope it out.'

Pablo turned off in the curve and parked in front of a restaurant from which the checkpoint was visible. After a few seconds, he got on the radio and told Otto to park next to us so he could switch cars; he wanted me to drive the SUV to Medellín with Juan Pablo and Manuela.

Lehder climbed out of the SUV holding his rifle, Pablo followed with his SIG Sauer at his waist, and they got in the back of the Renault 18. Otto opened the trunk and put in my husband's duffel bag, Lehder's backpack and a bag of food packed in plastic containers that I'd prepared for Pablo.

I drove to the tollbooth and ended up behind two cars that were waiting to pay. Just then, in the side mirror I saw the Renault speeding toward us in the wrong lane. When it reached the tollbooth, Lehder stuck his head out the window, holding my husband's sub-machine gun, and shouted, 'We're F-2 agents! Don't shoot!'

At that, a massive gunfight began, and we were caught in the crossfire. It all happened really fast. One police officer pulled out his pistol and shot at the car's rear windscreen, while from the passenger seat Otto fired at another officer, who managed to leap into a sewer pipe. Pasquín issued a burst of gunfire. Finally we heard the squeal of tyres and the Renault 18 sped off.

I'll never forget those moments. I was trembling, fearing the worst, but I realised I had to pretend I had no idea what was happening, as if I had nothing to do with it. I turned to the backseat. Juan Pablo looked terrified, protecting his wailing sister with his body.

It was total chaos. All we could hear was screaming and cries for help. A moment later, a police officer came up and told me not to pay the toll, to just drive off, but a man in civilian clothing and carrying a pistol said no; he'd seen the men who'd caused the gunfight getting out of the SUV I was driving.

The police aimed their guns at us, ordered us out of the car, and roughly searched us. They then rounded us up with some twenty others who were at the tollbooth and took us to a small building where their offices were located. We remained there, on our feet, for nearly five hours. Manuela was crying because it was time for her bottle and a nappy change. I felt powerless as the police officers, indifferent, ignored my pleas to let me look after my daughter, who was just two and a half years old.

'You'll see what we're going to do to you, narco bastards,' the police shouted through the windows once they learned how close they'd been to Pablo Escobar.

Finally a police officer told us to go with him because he had orders to take us to the Antioquia police headquarters in Medellín. We sat in the back of the truck, and the officer who was driving spent much of the ride insulting me for having given birth to a criminal's children.

At the police headquarters, we got out of the truck. I was carrying a slumbering Manuela in my arms, wrapped in her blanket. The commander, Colonel Valdemar Franklin Quintero, was waiting there, and he snatched the nappy bag and blanket so forcefully that he almost knocked the little girl onto the floor.

'Take this goddamn woman and that bastard's children and put them in a cell,' he shouted, and his men hastened to obey. 'Please,' I pleaded, 'at least leave me the baby's blanket and the nappy bag so I can feed her. She hasn't eaten for hours, and they didn't even give us a glass of water at the toll station. Are we going to be treated that way here too?' I was sobbing, but nobody answered. The colonel just walked off with a look that showed a visceral hatred for my husband.

At 1.30am, when things had quietened down, a female police officer came up and gave me a baby bottle of formula. I was immensely grateful for her gesture, but I didn't understand why they had to be so cruel to my children because of their father's actions.

A few minutes later, Manuela was drinking her bottle when a lawyer suddenly appeared.

'Ma'am, I've come on behalf of your husband. He's fine. Don't worry, I'll get you out of here tomorrow. The most important thing right now is that I'm going to take your children to their grandmother Nora's house.'

I handed over my little girl, and Juan Pablo trailed after the lawyer, who headed to a house on the avenue known as

Transversal Superior, where Pablo, Lehder, Otto, El Mugre and Pasquín were waiting. My husband instructed them to take Manuela to my mother's house and told Juan Pablo to remain with him.

The next day, the lawyer came to get me released, and on our way back to the Mónaco building, he told me that Pablo was furious about what had happened to Manuela.

'I'll never forget the expression on your husband's face, ma'am. That's the only time I ever saw him cry. He said to me, "Who's more of a criminal? Me, who chose to be one? Or the men who hide behind the authority of their police uniforms to abuse my innocent wife and children? Tell me, who's more of a criminal?"'

Without question, that incident intensified Pablo's aversion to the police. According to the lawyer, Pablo wanted to avenge the officers' treatment of us, and especially of Manuela by denying her a bottle. His rancour had been growing for many years, starting back when he and his friends in La Paz used to throw rocks at the patrol cars as they made their rounds and shout all sorts of horrible things to the police.

TWO WEEKS AFTER THE COCORNÁ INCIDENT, ON 4 FEBRU-ary 1987, I got a call from a girlfriend from school, who told me to turn on the radio. When I did, I was very concerned to hear that the police had captured Lehder on a farm in Retiro, a town twenty miles from Medellín, and that he was to be extradited to the United States immediately.

From what I later learned, my husband was at Nápoles that day and saw a news report with images of Lehder being led to the plane that would transport him to the United States. Looking agitated, Pablo had an unexpected reaction: 'Throw yourself into the propellers! That's what I'd do! There's no way in hell I'd let them take me away; I'd rather throw myself into those blades and be killed before I'd get on that plane.'

Three days after Lehder's extradition, there was a new raid on the Mónaco building, this time by the police rather than the army. The officer in charge arrived at the penthouse with twenty armed men who lined up my two bodyguards and the domestic employees. It was six o'clock in the morning, so Juan Pablo and Manuela were still sleeping. I'd only recently got up, and the hostile attitude of the officers filled me with panic.

'Where is that monster, ma'am? You must know where he's hiding, and if you don't tell us right now, you'll be arrested.'

Juan Pablo got up when he heard the commotion and came to my side. He cried and looked very frightened; in a quiet voice, I tried to soothe him and told him not to worry, it was going to be OK.

'Captain, if you don't know where he is, with all your intelligence capabilities, how am I supposed to know, when I never see him? Besides, he's not going to tell me where he's hiding.'

The officer didn't like my explanation at all, and he ordered his men to tear the place apart looking for money, drugs and weapons.

The raid lasted almost six eternal hours, at the end of which the captain gave me a warning: 'Tell that criminal we're going to find him, since we already extradited his buddy.'

Having learned of the raid, two days later Pablo sent several of his men to pick us up, and we found ourselves in an apartment somewhere in Medellín. He looked worried, but also furious.

'Pablo, what are you going to do now?'

He didn't answer the question; all he said was that we needed to increase the security around our family.

Much later, when we were trapped in hiding for a long time, I asked Pablo if the gossip about him having been the one who'd turned Lehder in was true.

'No, Tata, I would never dream of it. Extradition isn't something to mess around with. It's true he was badly off – he did a lot of drugs and had spent almost all of his money – but we always got along and I even helped him out when he stepped in it with Rollo.'

He didn't say anything else, and I remained intrigued by his mention of Rollo, a tall man who worked for him, but with whom I'd never interacted. One of the maids, when I ran into her in Medellín years later, told me that she'd been in the kitchen of the main house at Nápoles when a commotion around the pool had caused her to hide under a table. According to her account, Lehder killed Rollo with a rifle because Rollo was flirting with a young woman that Lehder was interested in. She added that my husband flew into a rage and ordered his men to remove Lehder from the estate by helicopter and take him to another farm.

ON 27 JUNE 1987, FOUR MONTHS AFTER LEHDER'S EXTRADI-
tion, my husband came to the Mónaco building. He was
beaming. I hadn't seen him like that for ages, and he had
good reason for being in such a good mood: the Supreme
Court had just overturned extradition, so the judicial proceedings against him were no longer valid. The minister of
justice, José Manuel Arias, was forced to dismiss nearly a
hundred arrest warrants related to extradition requests,
Pablo's among them.

With the Ministry of Justice off his back, Pablo was able
to live with us for the first time in three years and nine
months. In a way, we got our home back, to the delight of
Manuela and Juan Pablo, who finally had a father who
could take them to school. Even so, during that time my
husband was surrounded by an unwieldy security force,
travelling around in a convoy of ten Toyota Land Cruisers,
each carrying four or five men armed with pistols and AK-
47s. It's odd, but Manuela, who was just three at the time,
still clearly remembers how uncomfortable she felt pulling
up at the Génesis nursery school with her father and a pack
of armed men.

Of course, that kind of deployment inevitably had its
downsides, such as what happened to Pablo and my brother
Mario one day when they were driving down a street in
Medellín. Doubled over with laughter later that night,
Pablo told me he'd been driving one of the SUVs, with
Mario beside him with a sub-machine gun under his seat,
when four cops on motorcycles stopped the convoy to
check people's IDs and safe-conduct documents. All the
bodyguards started handing over their guns, but when his

turn came, Mario had pulled out his powerful weapon and aimed it at the police officers, who were caught off guard. Then he said, 'Pablo, these fucking homos are the ones protecting you? Four cops show up, and fifty bodyguards hand over their weapons. These are the kind of lions who've got your back? You're fucked. Do me a favour, officers, and return those weapons right now, or you'll have an even bigger problem.' Half startled and half frightened, the agents gestured for the convoy to keep going.

During that period of calm, Pablo was with us most of the day, but as always he would often claim he had a business appointment in the evening, leave, and come back at dawn. It was obvious his appointments were just trysts with his lovers. I remember he would be wearing regular clothes – jeans and a button-up shirt – but he never abandoned his habit of wearing sneakers with cleats in case he had to take off running when 'the law' showed up.

But with Pablo nothing was forever. On the night of 11 October 1987 – three and a half months after he'd come to stay with us – he went back into hiding, this time because of the assassination of the former presidential candidate and leader of the Patriotic Union party, Jaime Pardo Leal.

Before leaving, Pablo told me that although he'd had nothing to do with this particular crime, the authorities were probably going to point the finger at him, so he chose to go back into hiding. And indeed, twelve hours later there was a new raid on the Mónaco building, this time by the army.

The arrival of trucks full of uniformed men became an everyday occurrence. At the peak of the war, the Mónaco building used to be raided – no exaggeration – three times a week. When they'd call up from the lobby to let me know the army was downstairs, I already knew that the block and the building were surrounded, that the soldiers had occupied the basements and were sweeping through the building floor by floor, and would soon arrive at the penthouse via the stairs and the lift. And when they did, the soldiers would herd everybody into the main living room or dining room and line them up against the wall with their hands in the air.

The army major in command would threateningly demand Pablo's whereabouts and, as always, I replied that he didn't live with us. On one occasion, a soldier suddenly shoved his rifle against the back of Sofía Vergara, the sister of Teresita, the sixty-five-year-old woman who had looked after Pablo for much of his life, and brusquely asked her what her name was. Trembling, she said it was María del Carmen Ramírez, and the soldier demanded to see her ID. Since she'd lied about her name, she assumed the worst and started to weep piteously. I stepped in and told the soldier to show her compassion, but he said he was going to arrest her. He harassed and tormented her for a long time, until eventually, late that afternoon and after six hours at Mónaco, the army major said it was time to go. After that, Sofía was known forevermore as María del Carmen Ramírez.

Pablo had been in hiding for several weeks when Pasquín showed up one day and told me my husband wanted me to prepare the apartment on the third floor because a friend of his, Jorge Pabón, was going to be staying there for a while.

It seemed odd because the original idea when we'd constructed the building had been to rent out some of the downstairs apartments to help defray costs.

I had no way of asking Pablo what was going on, so I asked the decorator to help me organise the third floor and pull some furniture out of storage.

From the start, Pabón, who was known as El Negro, struck me as unreliable and shady, and as the days went by I started seeing big, muscular, unpleasant-looking men on various floors of the building. Growing increasingly worried, I sent Pablo a message about it, and one night he came by. I was so distraught that I barely said hello.

'Pablo, who have you got living in the building?'

'Don't worry, Tata, he's a good friend, he's been really good to me.'

'Pablo, these guys are incredibly scary. One of these days they're going to kill us on the spot.'

'No, sweetie, how can you think that?'

'You're hard-headed just like my mother says. You're always running flat out like a racehorse; all we see of you is the dust you kick up. We've been living locked up here in this mansion, and we can't even take a walk outside the building or go down to play tennis.'

There was no budging him. Pablo left and El Negro stayed, despite my tears and desperation. Not long afterwards, Pablo told me he owed Pabón a debt of gratitude because in 1976, while Pablo was incarcerated at Bellavista with my brother Mario and Pablo's cousin Gustavo, Pabón had saved him from an attack when the other prisoners thought they were police plants. The two men had fallen out of touch since, but now Pabón had come looking for Pablo at a place known as La Isla, in El Peñol, and asked him for help. He was recently back in the country after spending two years in a New York prison for drug trafficking. Pablo was fond of him, so he told him he could stay in the Mónaco building till he found a place to live.

I don't know if Pablo weighed the consequences of his decision, but that man's arrival would change our lives so drastically that in short order it would trigger a new conflict that would once more leave Manuela, Juan Pablo and I caught in the middle.

1988

I was awakened by Juan Pablo's cries for help. Alarmed, I tried to move, only to realise that I was pinned between the mattress and part of the bedroom ceiling, which had fallen on top of me. My little boy was saying he couldn't breathe; worried, I started moving back and forth to get free of the weight bearing down on me. With no idea what was happening, I assumed that I'd fallen down into the basement of the building and would be trapped there for many days before we were rescued. I called to Juan Pablo to be patient, reassuring him that I was going to find him.

I pushed so hard that I fell into a hole, and when I managed to pull myself out, I looked up and could see the sky. In the distance I could hear the echoing voices of people calling for help. Amid a carpet of rubble and giant nails poking out of the fallen roof, I almost managed to reach Juan Pablo but then heard Manuela crying and rushed to see how she was. I was relieved to find her safe and sound in her nanny's arms, but when I turned around I was horrified to see that the frame of one of the aluminium windows had fallen into her crib while she was taking her bottle. I thanked God that she had only a scratch on her forehead.

I went back to Juan Pablo, who was still trapped between a concrete slab and his bed. Trying to figure out how to get him free, I discovered that a small sculpture by Fernando Botero, which was on the nightstand, had borne the weight of the roof and miraculously prevented it from crushing him. In those extraordinary circumstances, I found myself possessed of superhuman strength; I was able to lift one of the corners of the slab so Juan Pablo could wriggle free with great difficulty.

All I wanted was to get out of there with my two children, but when we found a torch and illuminated the staircase, we found it blocked by so much debris that it was impossible to go down. Suddenly the kitchen phone rang and Marina, one of the maids, told me it was Pablo.

'They've ended us, they've ended us,' I said, in pieces.

'Don't worry, Tata, I'm sending for you,' my husband said, but I replied, still sobbing, that I wanted to go to my mother's house.

When I hung up, Marina told me Pablo had already called to ask about us, but since she couldn't reach the penthouse's second floor because the ceiling of the staircase had collapsed, she hadn't been able to tell him how we were.

We were still trapped, so I shouted for help as loudly as I could, and a few minutes later two bodyguards cleared a space so we could get down to the first floor. Marina handed me a pair of shoes, but Juan Pablo had to go down barefoot and risk cutting himself on the shrapnel, twisted rebar, and broken glass scattered across the stairs. As we descended, through the windows I could see the extent of the disaster: wounded people in the neighbouring buildings and ruins all around.

Only a few minutes had passed since my son's cries had abruptly awakened me, and I still had no idea what was going on. The only thing I could think of was that a large earthquake had shaken the city.

Once we made it to the car park, we climbed into an SUV parked in the visitors' area, very close to the front door. The bodyguard who would be driving came up and told me he'd gone around the building and everything suggested that a car bomb had gone off in the rear of the building. It was around six o'clock in the morning on 13 January 1988.

As we pulled out into the street, one of my sisters, who lived nearby and had been awakened by the powerful explosion, arrived. I got out to talk to her, and the cold made me realise that we were all in our nightclothes. My sister looked very anxious; she'd thought something terrible had happened to us and had come to look for us straight away.

'Tata, when I was on my way here, you could see a black blotch all the way from Avenida Las Vegas. I was terrified that when I got here, they were going to tell me you and your children were dead.'

I told her we had to get out of there and asked her to stay to keep an eye on things and take some photos to document what had happened. Later, the architect who'd built Mónaco arrived and went through the ruins with my sister to identify any water leaks or damage to the electrical system. My sister used that opportunity to take a lot of photos that show the destruction. Years later, I met up with the architect in Medellín. When we talked about that event, he recalled, 'Doña Victoria, the sun wasn't up yet when I heard that huge boom and told my wife, "Mónaco's fallen." I raced there, worried about the structure of the building.'

In the meantime, the bodyguard drove us down the road known as Loma del Campestre and we saw that the police and several fire trucks were heading to the building. We climbed a steep, narrow trail up to the top of the mountain, to El Bizcocho, a wooden cabin known among family members as Los Viejitos. When we got to the door of the safehouse, Pablo and my brother Mario came out to meet us. We hugged, and Juan Pablo and I broke down in tears. Once inside, we found my brother-in-law, Roberto, and El Mugre, and they described how they'd been out on the terrace when they heard a loud explosion, the ground shook, and they saw a mushroom cloud rise up in the distance.

Then we sat in the living room to keep talking and drank hot chocolate with bread. They talked and talked, unaware that I was distraught because my dream of living in the Mónaco building for ever had evaporated in an instant. I was twenty-six years old at the time, and I was deeply pained to think I'd never be able to live there again.

'I assumed the three of you were dead. I knew they were going to set off a bomb against me, but I didn't figure it would be like that, against all of you,' Pablo said, visibly upset.

El Mugre was about to say something when Pablo got a call on his mobile phone and immediately answered it. His face told us it was something important, and we waited in silence for five minutes until he thanked the person for the call and hung up. Then he said, 'Those bastards called to find out whether I survived. I thanked them for their so-called support. I know it was them who set off the bomb.'

My husband's statement was enigmatic. I assume everybody else knew what he was talking about; as usual, I was out of the loop. Some time passed before I got a clear idea of the reason for the awful attack, which killed three people, wounded ten and affected another hundred.

According to several people close to Pablo, the bomb was the result of a conflict between the Cali Cartel capos and my husband because of El Negro Pabón. And the most unbelievable aspect is that it wasn't over drug trafficking or control of the cocaine market ... It was over a woman.

The story is very simple: a man known as Piña, who worked for Hélmer 'Pacho' Herrera – one of the Cali capos – in New York, had an affair with El Negro's wife while Pabón was serving his two years in the United States. Now free and back in Colombia, Pabón had looked Pablo up and asked him to talk to Cali and have them hand Piña over, since he wanted to avenge the affront. Pablo spoke to Gilberto Rodríguez Orejuela several times, but the Cali leader refused, and my husband ended up taking on his cuckolded friend's fight. The result was the bomb at the Mónaco building; the Cali guys must have known Pabón was living with us. In fact, the shock waves from the car bomb damaged a large portion of the third floor, where Pabón was staying, but he wasn't there on the day of the attack.

For the next forty-eight hours, we stayed with Pablo, who was trying to find out who'd given the order and who'd set off the bomb. I watched him silently. He looked pensive, his face furious, as if he was ready to take on all comers. It was the first time he'd been attacked like that, and his family had nearly died. I noticed a lot of people coming to talk to him and offering to back him in whatever he needed. He was in one meeting after another, but I was hurt that he wasn't paying attention to us, didn't ask me what I felt about what had happened, about the serious damage caused to his own home. Once again, he wasn't interested in material things. He could buy it all over again; as he said many times, he was a money-making machine.

He didn't ask where we were going to live either, so I made a few calls and swiftly left with Juan Pablo and Manuela for the apartment of one my sisters in the Torres del Castillo building, where we could stay for a while. We were so badly shaken by the events that we slept with the lights on for at least six months. When my children were sleeping, I would weep out of powerlessness and sorrow because my house of cards had collapsed. I couldn't even go to see what was left of Mónaco, and though we were able to remodel the building months later, the war made it impossible for me to return.

Amid all the uncertainty about our future, I became even more frightened when, three days after arriving at our temporary refuge, one of Bogotá's mayoral candidates, Andrés Pastrana, was kidnapped, followed by an attempted kidnapping and the eventual assassination of the inspector general, Carlos Mauro Hoyos. From the way the media described the events during those final days of January 1988, it was clear that Pablo might be behind them. I felt helpless in the face of the violence he unleashed; his actions were affecting more and more people as well as putting us in grave danger.

Though Pablo had recently said that we should reinforce our security, his order obviously hadn't been carried out effectively because on 21 February 1988, Juan Pablo was almost kidnapped. The boy came back to the apartment in Torres del Castillo very scared the day after his father had saved him from being snatched. He told me that shortly before he was due to participate in a motorcycle speed trial at the Bello Niquía complex, in northern Medellín, several SUVs drove right onto the track and Pablo got out of one of them. He told Juan Pablo not to worry, but they'd heard that people were looking to kidnap him, so my husband left Pinina and a few other men to look after my son while he finished the race and then to escort him home.

With the attempted kidnapping of my son, we sank into a persistent depression; it was clear that, after the bombing of the Mónaco building, the feeling of being hunted was going to be part of our daily lives. And I was terrified when the news programmes started reporting that Pablo had begun to seek vengeance, destroying the Cali Cartel's economic interests, including the Medellín branches of the drugstore chain La Rebaja, which belonged to the cartel's head capos, the brothers Miguel and Gilberto Rodríguez.

AS PABLO'S VIOLENCE INCREASED, SO DID THE PRESSURE from the authorities. But the events of Tuesday, 22 March 1988, were a huge warning bell for all of us. It was a seemingly normal day: Pablo was in hiding at El Bizcocho, Juan Pablo and Manuela had left for school at seven o'clock in the morning and I was with one of my sisters in the Torres del Castillo apartment, where we'd been living since the Mónaco attack in January.

At 7.30am the doorbell rang insistently. Nubia, the nanny, opened it to find a large number of soldiers who'd come to search the place. After shoving her to one side, the soldiers swept the entire apartment until they found my sister and me in the master bedroom. One of them asked for my ID and immediately reported it by radio: 'That criminal's wife is here.' Then he asked if the Fourth Brigade should bring me in, and they told him yes: 'Let's see if the monster shows up.'

My sister was worried I might be in danger and immediately demanded to be arrested too. They obliged, and we were locked in a cell until the next day, when we were released because I had committed no crime and was not wanted by any law enforcement agency.

I was anxious to see my children so the two of us rushed back to the apartment. When we arrived we learned that the soldiers had also gone to the Colegio San José de la Salle, Juan Pablo's school, but the headmaster had cleverly managed to keep him from being taken. One of the school sentinels had spotted the army's trucks arriving and went to inform my son's bodyguard, who removed Juan Pablo from the classroom and took him to the headmaster's office. The headmaster told Juan Pablo to hide under his desk. From his hiding place, my son watched as the soldiers came to ask about him, but the headmaster replied convincingly that he didn't know where the Escobar boy was. Once the soldiers were gone, Juan Pablo came out and didn't say another word until he was back home.

My father, who was seventy-six at the time, also fell victim to the military offensive against us. He was arrested by soldiers while he was driving in his ancient Volvo, and without offering any explanation they confiscated the car and took him to one of the Fourth Brigade's bases.

But the person who was in for the worst of it was Pablo, who was the target of an unprecedented army operation involving more than 1,000 soldiers, three helicopters, and a number of tanks sent to occupy El Bizcocho, where my husband and ten bodyguards were in hiding.

Everybody was sleeping at that hour – five o'clock in the morning on 22 March 1988 – but a couple of locals from that rural area who'd been hired to keep watch announced the military's arrival via radio-telephone. The same alert was also given by two guards on the upper part of the Las Palmas highway as they watched dozens of soldiers swarm down the mountain.

The guards' timely warnings enabled Pablo and his men to escape, but as they hurried through the mountains, they had two scares. The first was when a soldier emerged from a thicket, pointed his rifle at them and ordered them to put their hands up. Unflappable as always, my husband stepped in front of the group and told the soldier to relax, that he and his men would turn themselves in. While Pablo was talking, six of his men moved forward as if to surrender, and he, Otto and Campeón stayed back so they could make a run for it. The strategy worked. By the time the soldier noticed what had happened, they were already some distance away. He fired his gun after them, and some of the bullets came very close to hitting Pablo. A few days later, when we met up at another hideout, Pablo told me he'd felt death in that moment because the soil kicked up by the bullets hit him in the face.

The scare wasn't over. When the fugitives reached the Las Palmas highway, they came face to face with another soldier. Moving quickly, my husband pointed his pistol at him, telling him that he was from the secret police and ordering him to step aside because he was taking several detainees to the nearest station. Caught off guard, the soldier moved aside and the column of men kept going. A photographer from the newspaper *El Colombiano* who was in the area, alerted by the troop movement, captured the image of my husband and his men walking in single file.

A couple of weeks later, the army released the first wanted poster, which offered a hundred-million-peso reward to anyone who supplied information about my husband; two hotlines were set up, one in Medellín and one in Bogotá, along with a P.O. box for would-be tipsters.

Seeing the wanted poster on TV and in the newspapers made me extremely worried, but Otto told me not to worry, because Pablo had a plan to disorientate the military that was already working. When I asked him about it, he told me Pablo had paid several families in La Paz to write letters and make phone calls giving false clues about him. They'd say, for example, that Pablo had grown a beard and was hiding in a house full of armed men down on the coast; or that they'd seen him in a house with the curtains drawn, guarded by men with rifles, in Bogotá.

For months, men and women from the neighbourhood 'collaborated' in this distraction gambit dreamed up by Pablo, which also included airdropping thousands of fliers accusing police and army officials of criminal activity and human rights violations in Medellín and Antioquia. The response was immediate: one weekend a small plane dropped thousands of pamphlets with a photo of Juan Pablo, captioned, 'Would you want this kind of husband for your daughter?' Juan Pablo was treated like a criminal even though he was only eleven at the time. They persecuted him to get at Pablo. Was he going to have to pay for his father's mistakes? Surely not – but by then a conflict was looming that would drag on for years. A dirty war. On all sides.

1989

Early one morning in late January 1989, Pinina arrived at the building where we were hiding and said he had a message from Pablo.

'Doña Victoria, the boss says things are about to get really complicated and he wants you to promise that none of you will go outside no matter what. He wants you to cancel Manuela and Juan Pablo's private tutoring, and he's going to shut down the mail for a while because it's too risky.'

We were silent, with no choice but to nod our heads. Pinina left, but at the time we didn't realise how serious the warning was. Today, 1989 is remembered as one of the most violent years in Colombian history, and my husband was at the centre of it.

A couple of weeks earlier we'd moved to a spacious apartment in the Ceiba de Castilla building, known by the code name 00, which was located in El Poblado, near the Clínica Medellín hospital. Because a number of Antioquia's wealthiest families lived in the building, the authorities never came around there. I heard that one of the residents was the mother of Álvaro Uribe Vélez, who would become president of Colombia in 2002, but I never met her on the two or three times I ventured out of our apartment.

I had originally bought the apartment without telling Pablo, and told him that a girlfriend from school had rented it to me. I wanted a place where my children and I could take refuge, somewhere that the authorities weren't able to identify, and it was getting harder and harder to hide in Pablo's safehouses. The strategy worked: we stayed at Ceiba de Castilla for more than six months.

After Pinina's visit, it was clear that Pablo's instructions were being followed. We became totally isolated. None of his men came back, and we no longer heard from him. The situation was more bearable because I'd hired a trustworthy couple who not only pretended to be the apartment owners but also took care of doing the grocery shopping, paying the utility bills, and other tasks, all without even remotely dealing with anything related to my husband.

The apartment was spacious, but for a lot of the day it was roasting in there because the sun poured in from the west. Even so, it had a pleasant open terrace that helped make our long period of confinement more enjoyable.

Every day, Manuela and I would paint, watch movies, play hide-and-seek, change her dolls' clothes, and sometimes take baths on the terrace. But when I ran out of ideas, she'd cry for hours until, overcome by sadness and fatigue, she'd fall asleep. Juan Pablo spent his days shut up in the room upstairs with his friend Juan Carlos Herrera Puerta, 'Nariz', who would later offer us additional protection when we were living in the Altos building. Juan Pablo's only contact with the outside world during those six months was his bedroom terrace, where we often found him staring off at the horizon. To pass the time, he and Nariz would put together model aeroplanes and jigsaw puzzles with thousands of pieces. They came down only to share meals with us and watch the news. He created his own world amid absolute uncertainty, not knowing when the endless confinement caused by his father's actions would end.

In the golden cage of our isolation in the Ceiba de Castilla apartment, on 30 May 1989, the radio and TV announced that a car bomb had gone off in a bustling area of Bogotá, aimed at the head of the DAS, General Miguel Maza Márquez. The powerful explosion killed seven people and caused major damage around the site of the attack, but Maza was unscathed. Over the next few months, the wave of violence continued to swell; hitmen on motorcycles killed the judge María Helena Díaz and the magistrate Carlos Valencia García, and in Medellín a car bomb killed the governor of Antioquia, Antonio Roldán Betancur.

But amid these events, 18 August marked a turning point in the war. That morning, as we learned from the television news, my husband's men murdered Colonel Valdemar Franklin Quintero, commander of the Antioquia police, on the streets of Medellín. Quintero had been the officer who, more than two years earlier, had refused to allow Manuela a bottle when we'd been detained at the Cocorná tollbooth. The report indicated that six gunmen stood in front of the officer's vehicle when he stopped at a traffic light between the Calasanz and La Floresta neighbourhoods, and fired their rifles at him until they ran out of bullets.

That night, presidential candidate Luis Carlos Galán was shot as he arrived at a rally in the main square of Soacha, a town south of Bogotá. His death brought to an end seven years of conflict between him and my husband, which had begun in 1982 when Galán removed Pablo from his congressional campaign and my husband was forced to find another movement to support his aspirations to the House of Representatives.

In the research that my son did for his book, *Pablo Escobar: My Father*, he learned that the decision to assassinate Galán was made in June 1989, when, in an internal meeting of the Liberal Party during the New Liberalism Convention in Cartagena, Galán announced his intention to seek the presidency. At the same event, the political leader said that the only effective tool to combat drug trafficking was extradition.

Pablo – my son's account went on – was at the Marionetas hideout on Hacienda Nápoles that day, and those who were with him heard him utter what sounded like a death sentence: 'As long as I'm alive, he will never be president. A dead man can't be president.'

Predictably, Galán's murder plunged the country into a deep crisis. The administration of President Virgilio Barco ordered a massive offensive against the drug lords, creating the Search Bloc, a new structure within the security agencies that was to be devoted exclusively to pursuing the Medellín Cartel.

We had left the Ceiba de Castilla apartment by this time and were now staying at the Altos building, and we hadn't heard from Pablo in two months, when one of his men arrived and told us that Pablo was waiting for us in a safehouse located in a very remote, inhospitable place in the mountains around Envigado. The trip was a tortuous one; after an hour and a half by car, we had to walk more than two hours and sometimes ride mules along some impressive cliffs to a hideout on the eastern slope of the mountain. The land was adjacent to where the La Catedral Prison would be built two years later.

The worst part is that just as we arrived, exhausted, carrying food and some packages for Pablo, they notified him by radio-telephone of an ongoing police operation, so we had to eat quickly and immediately head back. Manuela was oblivious to what was happening, and Pablo told her he had prepared a surprise for her: a nighttime safari through the native forest on a litter. She was delighted by the plan, so several of Pablo's men proceeded to remove the rungs from a wooden ladder to create a stretcher similar to the ones the army uses to carry their wounded. Pablo often came up with games like that to keep Manuela from realising that we were actually running away.

When everything was ready, we settled her on the stretcher with several blankets because of the bitter cold, and four young men carried her down the mountain until we reached the car and returned to Altos. It was five o'clock in the morning, and my boots were muddy and my body exhausted. My mother got up when she heard us enter the apartment and started crying when she saw us.

'Sweetie, that man is going to get you all killed.'

'Don't worry, Mother, it was just a precaution that we came back.'

Deep down, I was terrified. Seeing Pablo was becoming a real risk to life and limb, and I felt my strength gradually ebbing. It was a huge effort, but I had to muster energy from somewhere to make sure my children had some minimal contact with their father.

Back at Altos, out of contact with Pablo once more, on 2 September 1989, I was stunned by the news that a powerful car bomb had gone off at the newspaper offices of *El Espectador*. The terrorist wave continued over the next few days with the detonation of explosives at the *Vanguardia Liberal* newspaper in Bucaramanga, at the Hilton in Cartagena and at various political sites in Bogotá.

As the war intensified, we were forced to move from place to place more frequently, with all the security risks that entailed. I was furious with Pablo, whose over-the-top actions were dragging us mercilessly along. We often had to leave in the middle of the night, with a five-year-old girl and a twelve-year-old boy, frequently in the rain, terrified that Pablo's enemies might intercept us.

On 19 September 1989, we met with my brother Mario at the Altos building. He was going to be travelling to meet up with Pablo at a farm in the Magdalena Medio region, while we, seeking a break from the pressure, were going to spend a few days with my mother, one of my sisters, my brother Fernando and Astado at the Hotel San Pedro de Majagua on the Rosario Islands.

My mother begged Mario several times not to make his trip, saying he was going to be killed and his two children would be left fatherless. We were used to her premonitions, and he told her not to worry, nothing was going to happen.

Hours later, after dinner, Mario said goodbye and we went out to the lift to see him off, but every time the door started to close, my mother would make it open again and repeat how worried she was. The fifth time she tried it, Mario wouldn't let the door open, and that was the last time we saw him alive.

At five o'clock in the afternoon on 23 September, we were sitting at a table around a tree when my mother announced, 'They've bombed Pablo in Puerto Triunfo.'

'Oh, Mum, you always bring tragedy.'

But my mother's words put us on alert, and behind her back we furtively turned on the radio and after several attempts managed to tune in to a Cartagena station, whose news programme described a massive operation against

Pablo at the farm known as El Oro, in the port of Cocorná, in the Magdalena Medio. The report indicated that my husband had escaped, several women had been arrested and one man was dead.

At five o'clock in the morning the next day, Astado, my sister, Fernando, two boat drivers and I were just leaving for Cartagena to find out what had happened when my mother came out onto her bedroom balcony and asked where we were going. We told her we were going for a little ride to watch the sunrise, and she told us not to take too long.

The boatman drove at a fast clip, and we soon arrived at an apartment in Cartagena and started calling to find out where Pablo and Mario were. Almost everybody we spoke to in Medellín and Puerto Triunfo said that my husband was fine, but that several men had died in the jungle so they weren't sure about Mario. Very worried, we went back to the hotel and were unable to contact anyone for several days, but when we returned to Medellín, my brother still hadn't appeared. Finally, we learned he'd been buried in the cemetery in Estación Cocorná, where he was identified as José Fernando Posada Mora. One of my sisters and her husband went there and managed to stealthily exhume the body and take it to Medellín, where it was cremated and buried in the Campos de Paz cemetery.

What had happened was that Pablo, Mario and two of their buddies had been at El Oro for three days with several young women who were members of the volleyball team for a public high school in the town of Caldas, Antioquia. On the morning that the helicopters showed up, while

Pablo and the two friends managed to escape, Mario was unable to get away and was shot several times from a helicopter.

My brother's death affected Pablo greatly; Mario had been his friend and perhaps the only person he really listened to. Pablo's affection for him is clear in a letter he wrote and sent to us soon after:

> Today I received the news of your death and your complete absence. Yesterday I sensed it. Though I had no knowledge of what had happened, I was unable to contain the tears that unexpectedly spilled from my eyes. I wept over your death, without knowing that you'd died. Only today have I been able to grasp how much I really loved you. What tremendously bitter tidings. What a sad, grim truth. But I promise you that our struggle will continue. I know we will triumph. They will not defeat us. I know we will overcome.

The final weeks of that fateful year would be the most difficult ones of my life. I was isolated and in hiding with my children, so, like the rest of the country, it was on the news that I first heard about two horrible attacks: the mid-air explosion of a plane with 103 people aboard on 27 November, and the detonation of a bus full of explosives at the DAS headquarters on 6 December. More than 200 people died in the attacks, which shook the nation to its foundations. I cried as I never had before, and alone in my confinement, I prayed to God to give me the strength to survive.

It was December 1989 and the war had reached a fever pitch, but Pablo couldn't have imagined that he was going to lose his most loyal lieutenant, his comrade, the man who was always ready to give his all to help my husband's cause. On Friday, 15 December, I was with my mother when somebody called to tell us that the police had taken down Gonzalo Rodríguez, El Mexicano, in the tourist town of Coveñas, on the Caribbean coast.

That was the first big blow to my husband, and for the first time it occurred to me that sooner rather than later the same thing might happen to him.

1990

In May 1990, the water was up to our necks. The war taking place in Medellín was all-consuming; the conflict between my husband, the Cali Cartel and the authorities had reached unbearable levels of brutality. Squads of armed men roamed the city, which was racked by what was practically a civil war.

After cycling through several apartments, each more precarious than the last, isolated from my family, locked up with Manuela, Juan Pablo and a maid, unable to even look out of a window, we ended up staying at a building near the Oviedo shopping centre where one of my aunts lived.

During the first part of the year, we saw Pablo only twice, on fleeting visits that lasted no longer than an hour. According to what he told me during one of those encounters, El Mexicano's death the previous December had forced him to alter his security protocols because El Navegante, the man who'd turned El Mexicano in, had learned a lot of Pablo's secrets. As a result, he had to buy new safehouses, change vehicles, reconfigure the human messenger system and even switch out his bodyguards.

Given our tumultuous existence, I was able to find out what was happening only through the television and newspapers, which narrated events as if describing the play-by-play of a football game. Early in the year, I was filled with optimism because it seemed that peace was on the horizon; the Barco administration had announced that if the drug traffickers dropped the fight and turned themselves in, it would consider lighter sentences for them.

The visit of US president George H. W. Bush in February reinforced my sense that the end of the war was possible because the Extraditables surrendered a large cocaine lab in Urabá, a school bus loaded with a ton of dynamite, and a helicopter to the government.

But the assassination, in March 1990, of Bernardo Jaramillo Ossa, presidential candidate for the Patriotic Union party, revived the conflict because the government blamed Pablo. My husband swiftly issued a communiqué denying any connection with the crime and claiming that in fact he'd supported Jaramillo because the politician had opposed extradition.

But the damage was done, and things only got worse from there. After the Jaramillo assassination, journalists exposed the fact that the government and representatives of my husband had been secretly negotiating since late 1989 to work out a legal exception in exchange for the safe return of the son of a high government official and two family members of a Medellín tycoon, all of whom had been been kidnapped by Pablo. These three people had been released in January 1990, but after the negotiations were revealed, the government said publicly that extradition had never been up for negotiation and that the only acceptable outcome was the drug traffickers' unconditional surrender.

I remember that in March 1990 Pablo sent two of his men to us with the message that the situation was about to get very delicate and urging us to remain inside no matter what. We were powerless as grim events unfolded around the country over the next few weeks, which reporters claimed had been ordered by Pablo and carried out by his men. Car bombs in Bogotá, Cali and Medellín; attacks on the Search Bloc; more than 300 police officers killed in Pablo's so-called Operation Pistol, which paid 2 million pesos for the death of each policeman ... Absolute barbarism.

Meanwhile, in our compulsory confinement, our situation had reached breaking point. My six-year-old daughter and thirteen-year-old son couldn't take any more. My husband's demented conduct and his claims that it was all for our sake had made our lives hell. The only thing I could do was seethe with rage at Pablo and wonder silently, 'When is this going to end, Pablo? My God.'

I sent message after message to my husband describing our terrible isolation, and finally he found a solution: sending Juan Pablo to the World Cup in Italy, which was due to start on 8 June 1990. That way he could kill two birds with one stone, getting the boy away from the spiral of violence and fear that was suffocating us, and offering him some distraction with the Colombian matches during the championship. We didn't say anything to the boy at the time, but Pablo told me his plan was to send him out of the country for a long time for his protection.

The trip was organised in record time, and Pablo arranged for one of his contacts to get a passport with a new identity for Juan Pablo, along with visas for various European countries. Juan Pablo would be accompanied by Alfredo Astado and by Juan and Pita, two childhood friends who later became his bodyguards.

The trip took place in late May, and we agreed that we'd communicate through an old friend of Astado's in La Paz. I was left alone with Manuela, and though I missed Juan Pablo keenly, I also understood that because Pablo's enemies had chosen my son as their preferred target, getting him out of the country was the only way to protect him.

Juan Pablo's absence gave me a certain amount of peace and I had more time for Manuela, who was impatient to go outside, see her cousins and visit her grandparents. But it was very difficult to placate her because Medellín was still a war zone; according to the media, at night the city looked like it was under curfew because the businesses would shutter at six and people would take shelter in their homes.

On Thursday, 14 June 1990, I was stunned when the TV news announced that Pinina had been killed during a Search Bloc operation in a building in El Poblado where he'd been living with his wife and daughter. I had first met him when Pablo hired him as a very young man, and my husband had often told me that Pinina was one of his most loyal lieutenants, always ready to stand by his side.

Two days before the World Cup was about to end, I travelled to Frankfurt with Manuela, my youngest sister and an aunt to meet up with Juan Pablo, Astado, Juan and Pita, who had already been informed of Pablo's sudden decision that we should all leave the country. That night we went out to eat at a restaurant and I learned in detail about the many things that had happened in their month abroad.

To start with, upon arriving in Italy, they'd had to change plans because there weren't any rooms in any of the hotels. As a result, they'd had no choice but to travel five hours by train to Lausanne, Switzerland, where they stayed at the elegant Hôtel de la Paix. Despite the uncomfortable trip, which they'd made overnight in a sleeping compartment, they'd attended the opening game between Italy and Austria at Rome's Stadio Olimpico and in the following days went to Bologna, where the Colombian national team played the United Arab Emirates and Yugoslavia. They also traveled to Milan for the match with Germany, and from there headed to Naples, where Colombia was eliminated by Cameroon. Juan Pablo said that he'd followed his father's advice to paint his face yellow, blue and red, the colours of our national flag, and to wear sunglasses so he wouldn't be recognised.

Over dinner they also talked about the big scare they'd had in Lausanne when they were having lunch at a Chinese restaurant and ended up getting arrested by the police.

'At first,' Juan Pablo explained, 'I thought something really bad was going to happen because a man came up, said a few words in French and pointed a gun at us. Then ten uniformed police officers came in and thoroughly searched us, handcuffed us and shoved us outside. In the street were a dozen patrol cars with their sirens blaring, and the area had been cordoned off. They separated us and took me to a secret house owned by the Swiss police, where they made me undress and searched me again; several hours later, they took me to another house and interrogated me for two hours. They seemed really focussed on my Cartier watch, and one of the officers asked what a thirteen-year-old kid was doing wearing a ten-thousand-dollar watch. I said my father was a big cattle rancher in Colombia, with more than 3,500 heads of cattle, and that when he'd sold some of them, he'd given me the watch as a gift.'

The explanation must have seemed convincing, because a few minutes later Juan Pablo was released along with Astado, Juan and Pita.

'The funny thing about all this is that the officers came up and, after saying they were very sorry about the way they'd arrested us, asked where they could take us. We told them to drop us off at the same Chinese restaurant where they'd picked us up,' my son said.

The explanation for what had happened was quite simple: in Lausanne they'd hired a guide who spoke seven languages and drove a Mercedes-Benz limousine, and in the past had been a favourite of the Shah of Iran. Of course they looked suspicious! Four Colombians and a Swiss driving around in that kind of car, especially when they'd arrived at the hotel late at night, stayed in their rooms almost the whole time, never went down to the restaurant and only ordered room service.

After dessert, Juan Pablo showed me a letter that Pablo had written on 30 June 1990, and that he'd received a week later, the day before I arrived in Frankfurt. I read it and was struck by the way Pablo counselled him to behave himself, study, learn other languages. In other words, he was suggesting that Juan Pablo's stay abroad would be a long one. The letter clearly illustrated the dilemmas that Pablo was experiencing at the time:

> I miss you and love you very much, but at the same time I am happy to know that you are enjoying your safety and freedom. I have decided to send your mother and your little sister to be with you because in the letter you sent you said you wanted everyone to be here when you got back, and you know the situation here has been getting a little difficult. What greater sacrifice could I make than to endure your absence? If you appear calm with your mother and little sister, they will be calm, and if you laugh, they and I will also laugh. Enjoy all of it. When I was thirteen like you, I didn't have anything, but nobody was happier than I was. But be careful: remember that you're not in your country and so you mustn't do anything that isn't legal. Don't let anybody give you bad advice. Just do what your conscience tells you. Don't try anything that isn't right.

After listening to the stories of Juan Pablo and his companions, I said I'd like to go to London to study English, but I was met with fierce opposition from Juan Pablo, who said he loved Switzerland and had no intention of leaving. I realised he was smitten with the country and ended up agreeing that we would study French in Lausanne, but first we'd visit a few German cities, including Berlin, where we arrived two days later.

I'll never forget the incredible sensation of being part of history. The city was still thrumming with the air of freedom that had begun the previous November with the fall of the Berlin Wall and the beginning of the reunification process for East and West Germany, which had been separated since 1961. I still have a few pieces of the wall that I broke off with a little hammer that somebody lent me. Many painful stories must be contained in those fragments of brick and concrete. The effects of the conflict persisted – I remember that we wanted to get something to eat, but all there was for sale were individual sausages, and there were long lines of cars waiting at all the petrol stations.

Back in Lausanne we rented two small, very expensive apartments and enrolled in an academy to study French until December. One day in late July 1990, we got a letter from Pablo, written on the seventeenth of that month, that reflected an unaccustomed optimism about our future:

I've decided to change strategy and end the war when the new government takes power. The president elect has said that he's not committed to extradition and that whether it's used depends on what the public order situation is like, so I'll make sure the public order situation is good then. The members of the National Constituent Assembly will be chosen very soon now that the people have voted, and I'm positive that the first constitutional article it will write will be one prohibiting the extradition of Colombians.

We were thrilled; for the first time, Pablo was saying seriously and decisively that it was possible to stop the bloodbath that had rocked Colombia for the past six years, since the war on drug trafficking began.

We started to believe that we'd soon be able to return to Colombia, but everything fell apart on 12 August 1990 – five days after the swearing in of César Gaviria as president – when we learned that Gustavo Gaviria, Pablo's cousin and loyal right-hand man who'd been with him from the beginning, had been killed by the police. It wasn't difficult to guess that my husband would be devastated.

Though I didn't say anything to my children, sister or aunt, I knew Gustavo's murder meant war. For ages, Gustavo had been in charge of the money, looking after the 'business'. He was the central pillar of the relationship. Pablo wasn't going to stay quiet, as became clear when we picked up the paper that arrived from Colombia a week after its publication and read in horror that on 14 September 1990, the authorities had confirmed that Pablo was holding captive Diana Turbay, daughter of former president Julio César Turbay and director of the magazine Hoy x Hoy; the journalists Azucena Liévano, Juan Vitta, and Hero Buss; and the cameramen for the news show Noticiero Criptón, Richard Becerra and Orlando Acevedo. The journalists, the article said, had been tricked into believing that they were going to interview a commander for the ELN guerrilla group, and had been missing for several days.

With the arrival of the next newspaper, we grew even more worried. It reported that Pablo was also holding Francisco Santos Calderón, editor in chief of the newspaper *El Tiempo*, who'd been kidnapped on 19 September, and Marina Montoya, sister of Germán Montoya, former general secretary for Virgilio Barco's administration.

Juan Pablo became obsessed, impatient to find out what was happening in Colombia, and especially with his father, and we were forced out of our relatively comfortable circumstances. Hell had returned. He went to the newspaper stand almost every day, which is how he learned that on 25 September a team of twenty men sent by Pablo had attacked the Cali capos while they were playing football on a farm in Candelaria, a town in the department of Valle del Cauca. Nineteen people had been killed in the intense gunfire, the newspaper reported, including fourteen players, but Hélmer 'Pacho' Herrera and other heads of the cartel had managed to escape. The article said that Pablo had attacked his Cali rivals in retaliation for a failed attack in which they'd planned to drop a powerful bomb from a helicopter while he was visiting Hacienda Nápoles.

The thought that the war was intensifying again filled my son with despair. He fell into a deep depression and even told me he didn't want to be alive anymore. I still have the image of him engraved in my memory that day when I saw him walking toward the train tracks, but I managed to persuade him to wait a little longer to see what happened.

Needing to make my children's daily lives more bearable, I had to invent a world to make it seem like nothing bad was happening. I enrolled Manuela in a horseback riding school and took her there twice a week. Luckily, Juan Pablo started getting into mountain biking, and within a few weeks he'd lost several pounds. I used to go with him up and down all the mountains; I became his friend and playmate, and I would have done anything to keep him from thinking about Colombia.

Keeping the family distracted included a two-week stay for me, my sister, Juan Pablo and Astado in the famous Clinique La Prairie, a medical retreat in Switzerland specialising in the use of cell therapy to delay aging and boost health. Disconnecting from the world gave us a bit of relief in those difficult days.

As always, events in Colombia didn't let up, and in the second week of November we read in the paper that Pablo had expanded the group of prominent people he was holding captive. According to the report, Maruja Pachón and Beatriz Villamizar had been kidnapped on 7 November 1990.

Things continued to degenerate. In the last week of November we got a letter from Pablo with news that wasn't very encouraging:

When you all left, I was really optimistic because important people were asking me to call and promising me heaven and earth. I sent a delegate, who had an audience with the important man himself for two or three hours. The important man's wife even wrote to me. But afterwards they started coming out with a bunch of nonsense, and I couldn't accept that after what they did to my partner [Gustavo Gaviria]. What happened to my partner was really destructive. They thought it would finish me off, but now they're running scared, and I know that everything's going to turn out OK.

The letter was enigmatic, but I understood that the contacts Pablo was referring to were within the upper echelons of the Colombian government.

The war had reached its peak at the end of 1990, and we naively thought we could remain in our temporary exile. We couldn't have been more wrong. Instead, we were suddenly forced to return to Colombia after we discovered that Pablo's enemies had tracked us down in Europe.

Things unfolded very quickly. One day we went out to buy plantains at a supermarket in Lausanne, but they didn't have any, so we went by car to several nearby towns and finally found some in Vevey, near Montreux. As we were leaving, Juan Pablo came up to me and said quietly, 'Mum, I think we're being followed. Sneak a look behind us, and you'll see a couple of Latino-looking guys. I've seen them everywhere we've gone looking for plantains. I don't like this.'

'Really, Juan? Are you sure?' I asked in disbelief, thinking he was so depressed that he might make up any excuse to go back to Colombia.

Even so, I sent a letter to Pablo recounting Juan Pablo's concerns, and he must have looked into it very quickly because a week later, in early December 1990, he ordered us to leave Lausanne immediately and return to Medellín. In the message he included instructions on how to avoid passport control.

Five months after departing Colombia, we returned in the middle of an upheaval worse even than when we'd left. As Pablo foresaw, we hit no snags with immigration and arrived at a spacious apartment on the seventh floor of a building on Medellín's Avenida Oriental, diagonally opposite the Clínica Soma hospital and not far from the city's police headquarters.

My first impression of the place was terrible; I could tell immediately that staying there was going to be very uncomfortable. The windows were all covered, and it was obvious there was nothing to do in the apartment. With Pablo were El Gordo and his wife, who were pretending to be the apartment's owners, as well as Popeye and La India, a dark young woman whom Chopo (one of Pablo's original bodyguards) sent to patrol outside, carry messages and buy groceries. There was no cable TV, only board games and a few books.

Over the next few days, my husband told me that the government was gradually relenting to his demands for reduced sentencing and a promise that drug traffickers wouldn't be extradited. He didn't say it, but it was clear that having ten hostages had enabled him to put enough pressure on. In the many hours we spent together, since he couldn't go out either because of the constant operations against him, I had time to understand his strategy, which seemed to be working. The previous September, the government had already issued an initial decree, number 2047, offering several guarantees to anyone who turned himself in. But my husband and his lawyers thought it insufficient, so they sent a message to the government with some additional recommendations, including the suspension of extradition and the implementation of a process in which accused drug traffickers' cases would be heard by a judge rather than going to trial.

As Pablo told one lawyer over the phone, the text was well received at the Casa de Nariño, and President Gaviria went to Medellín and publicly expressed his willingness to modify Decree 2047, noting, 'We are interested in bringing peace to the country. We are interested in having those Colombians who have committed crimes turn themselves in to face justice. For that reason, over the next week, we are going to hash out all the issues related to the decree and eventually incorporate some modifications.'

Pablo was working full-time on these matters and eagerly watched the TV news at noon, 7pm, 9.30pm and midnight, but it drove me crazy the way he was constantly changing the channel, not wanting to miss any news about himself, the decree or the hostages. Juan Pablo complained and convinced him to buy a TV with a split screen. The set arrived quickly, and that allowed him to watch both channels at once and raise and lower the volume for whichever news programme interested him.

Being with Pablo, I saw that he had a handle on things and was playing his cards in such a way that his ultimate goal of eliminating extradition wasn't out of reach. That became clear on Sunday, 9 December 1990, when he told us to watch the news for the release of the list of the seventy people who had been selected to work on rewriting the Colombian constitution starting in February of the following year. I saw him smile slyly as the journalists read the final list supplied by the National Civil Registry. 'I don't trust this decree business,' he said. 'Even if they announce the changes I've demanded, they're going to come back the next day and change it again once I'm in custody. But if it's in the constitution, they can't screw me.'

My husband was being unusually chatty; he didn't generally talk about what he was up to or who with. But since everything seemed to be going his way, he mentioned a message he'd received from his enemies in the Cali Cartel in which they offered to finance members of the Constituent Assembly who would promise to get extradition stricken from the new Constitution. 'I told them to do what they had to do,' he said, 'and I'd do my thing. They can bribe whoever they want, because I've already got some sure votes.'

On Monday, 17 December 1990, I was leafing through *El Tiempo* and saw that the paper had published the full text of a decree labelled 3030. At midday, Pablo got up and I told him the news, which clearly interested him, but he said he'd read it after his usual brunch.

Once he'd eaten, he stayed in the dining room for five hours, sunk in a deep silence as he read the paper. At one point I brought him something to eat and noticed he'd underlined almost the entire text and filled several sheets of paper with notes. He told me he didn't agree with most of the decree and was going to tell the government to issue a new one, because this one required confession in order to gain access to the judicial benefits, and that wouldn't do.

The next day, 18 December, while Pablo waited for the messenger who was going to deliver his comments on the decree, the media learned that Fabio, the youngest of the Ochoa Vásquez brothers, had unexpectedly turned himself in in Caldas, Antioquia. Pablo didn't say anything, but the expression on his face suggested that he already knew about it. The surrender process had begun, but much more was still to come.

1991

A small light at the end of the tunnel appeared on the night of 18 April 1991, when one of my sisters called to tell me that Father Rafael García Herreros had just sent Pablo a coded message through his TV programme *God's Minute*, which is broadcast every day before the seven o'clock news. The Eudist priest, who was widely celebrated at the time for the calm, clear way he talked about the word of God, broadcast the following short, enigmatic message:

> I am asking the people who are waging violence against Pablo Escobar's family members to cease at once, since we are seeking a way to him for the good of the country ... I've been told he wants to turn himself in. I've been told he wants to talk to me. Oh, sea at Coveñas, at five in the afternoon, when the sun is setting. What should I do? They tell me he's tired of his life and his struggle, and I can't tell anybody my secret.

> But I'm drowning inside … They tell me he wants to talk to me, a humble priest – not a bishop or a canon, not even an episcopal vicar. He tells me to believe in him, that he's a man of his word. I asked if he'd flee from me, from my side, and he said he would not.

I didn't know it then, since I hadn't heard from Pablo in days, but in the following weeks Father García Herreros would play a key role in my husband's surrender to the authorities. Many things happened after that, which I'll describe; in my research in Medellín for this book, I was able to put a lot of the pieces together.

Father García Herreros appeared suddenly thanks to Fabio Ochoa Restrepo, who believed that the priest, a long-time acquaintance of his, might somehow influence Pablo to cease his violent actions and take advantage of the legal guarantees that the government was prepared to offer to entice him to turn himself in.

At the time, the sense of unease was growing in the country: on 22 January the Elite Force (as we called the Search Bloc) dealt Pablo a tough blow when they killed the brothers David Ricardo and Armando Prisco Lopera in operations carried out in Medellín and Rionegro; on 24 January, four months after her kidnapping, Marina Montoya was murdered in Bogotá; and the next day the journalist Diana Turbay was killed in a messy rescue operation on a farm in Copacabana, Antioquia.

The deaths of some hostages, the release of others, and the definite possibility that something might happen to the others still in Pablo's hands – Francisco Santos among them – led Don Fabio to send an emissary to talk to my husband about Father García Herreros's renown.

According to my investigations, Pablo immediately agreed to the contact, as did the priest, who promised to do what he could. And so on that night, 18 April, he sent my husband the first coded message. When he said 'Oh, sea at Coveñas' (*O mar de Coveñas*), he was referring to Omar, the messenger who would carry the messages back and forth between them.

After that, the two were in regular touch and soon proposed meeting; *God's Minute*, too, became a communication medium between them. 'I want to serve as your guarantor to make sure they respect all of your rights and those of your family and friends. I want you to help me so I can know what steps I should take,' the priest said one night on his programme.

The complicated contact between García Herreros and Pablo took shape, but sending and receiving messages became more difficult as the Search Bloc's operations intensified. Pablo must have been worried that something might happen to us, because one night Godoy showed up at the safehouse where I was in hiding with my children, and told me that Pablo had decided to send Juan Pablo and Manuela to the United States to study English for a while. I asked him why, and he said that the boss wanted to keep abreast of everything that happened in the Constituent Assembly and with Father García Herreros. I asked about myself and he said I would go too, but later. Godoy also told me that, as far as he knew, Pablo and the priest were planning to meet in May somewhere in Medellín.

As I had no way to communicate with Pablo, I organised my children's trip. They would travel in the company of my brother Fernando, two bodyguards and Andrea, Juan Pablo's girlfriend. They left in the second week of May, and I remained with my mother in her apartment, where I felt safe.

The details of my children's trip to the United States kept me occupied for several days, so I didn't hear anything else about how the interactions between my husband and Father García Herreros were going. They hadn't met yet, but something must have happened because on the night of Monday, 20 May 1991, I heard the joyous news that Maruja Pachón de Villamizar – the daughter-in-law of Luis Carlos Galán – and Francisco Santos had been released in Bogotá.

I remained glued to the radio as the reporters put Mrs Pachón on the phone with Father García Herreros. 'You are the bravest and most generous man in the world; your love for Colombia's peace is immense,' she said, and the priest replied, 'Thank God for your return. Don Pablo is behaving exemplarily. The hand of God is visible.'

I had the chance to discuss these events with Pablo one weekend when his men took me to a hideout in the mountains outside Envigado. There he told me that the priest was very nervous about meeting, afraid he might be killed because the city was overrun with violence. He even concocted several obstacles to delay the trip, including claiming that he had lost his glasses, but they were all resolved. Finally, Father García Herreros arrived at La Loma, the farm where Don Fabio Ochoa was waiting for him, and an hour later a man known as El Médico took him to an apartment in El Poblado.

My encounter with Pablo that weekend was different, I remember; it had been a long time since I'd seen him happy and hopeful. 'Tata,' he said, 'I think the stars really are aligning now. The Constituent Assembly is going to eliminate extradition from the new constitution, and Don Fabio's contact with Father García Herreros is working. The government is listening to him.'

After that, I watched *God's Minute* faithfully every night and prayed that Father García Herreros's efforts would work to end the nightmare we were living.

Things started happening at a dizzying pace. On 21 May, a day after the captives' release, the government issued Decree 1303, which basically reiterated the demand that Pablo turn himself in. Father García Herreros remained actively involved, and on 23 May he sent Pablo a letter that I've treasured since the day I found it.

Pablo. I'm doing whatever I can to help you with everything. If you want, choose the day of the surrender. I would go to meet you with Francisco Santos, who's very grateful to you, along with Maruja and the judge of Criminal Instruction in Medellín, to the place of your choosing. I don't know if you'd rather go to Fabio Ochoa's house or wherever you say, and that way no police or judicial operation can touch you because you'll be under the national government's protection. I talked with Minister Botero [General Óscar Botero, minister of defence], and he's more or less in favour; he told me that Maza [General Miguel Maza, director of the DAS] is furious. I want to make sure you don't fall into their hands, so I'll take you to the judge so you'll be protected. I had a meeting with Santos and Maruja; they're grateful because you were good to them. Write to me quickly so we can move forward; what I don't want is for the police or DAS to catch you. Have faith in God – everything's going to turn out all right. They're preparing a place for you in Envigado where you'll be comfortable. It's the site I want to turn into the University of La Paz. First Lady Doña Ana Milena and the President are in agreement.

Thanks to the hostages' release and the quiet presence of Father García Herreros, the daily pressure let up somewhat. In late May 1991, by which time our children were out of the country, Pablo sent for me and we hid out in a humble house with mud walls located amid dense vegetation in Loma de los Benedictinos, between El Poblado and Envigado.

From then on, we remained together. Pablo was negotiating his surrender with government envoys and keeping abreast of the Constituent Assembly, which was about to finish its deliberations and release the new constitution on 19 June 1991. Despite his strong hand, he looked anxious, pensive, believing that at any moment the government might pull out of its agreements regarding his surrender.

'Pablo, what more do you want in life? Look at the opportunity they're offering you – don't think twice about it.'

As he'd already mentioned to me several times, he was sure that extradition would be removed from the new document, and that appeared to be the case one day when I saw him meeting with several people who were talking to him and taking notes. I asked an employee about it, and he told me, 'They're working on the constitution, ma'am.'

It was all set. Pablo would turn himself in once extradition was eliminated from the new constitution, and when he surrendered, he'd be tried for the crimes he'd committed over the past seven years. But those crimes would have to be proven, and he was ready to fight to show that not all of the accusations were true.

As the end of the Constituent Assembly approached, my husband was feverishly organising how he would get to the prison he'd built, La Catedral, whose construction had been entrusted, as I heard at the time, to Godoy and another young man known as El Monito.

Father García Herreros played a key role in those moments because Pablo sent him a letter via a bodyguard in which he explained his plan for turning himself in, which included a helicopter whose pilot was to be given the coordinates of the place where Pablo would be picked up, along with the names of the people who should travel in it.

On the morning of 18 June 1991, a call came in on the UHF frequency of the radio-telephone. It was Juan Pablo and Manuela, who'd just arrived in Miami after spending several days in Las Vegas, Los Angeles and San Francisco. After listening to their account of the trip, Pablo told his son that the next day he was going to turn himself in because he already knew that extradition would be removed from the new constitution. Juan Pablo expressed a number of fears, but my husband soothed him by saying everything had gone according to plan and that he could no longer be extradited. Then he spoke with Manuela, whom he told that problems were going to be a thing of the past and that it wouldn't be long before we could all live together again. Before hanging up, he told her not to be scared if she saw him on the news and in jail, since he'd chosen to be there.

Finally, at eleven o'clock in the morning on 19 June 1991, Pablo told me, 'Get your things in order so you can go home and get ready for us to meet at La Catedral. Go to the mayor's office in Envigado, and they'll take you up there.'

A strange but pleasant mix of anxiety and excitement took hold of me, and I immediately went looking for Aunt Inés, my shoulder to cry on, so she could accompany me to the mayor's office, where she was well known. Sometime after three o'clock in the afternoon, we were ready and met up with Doña Hermilda to head to La Catedral, guided by what the radio stations were saying.

As always, my mind was jumbled with questions. What kind of future is waiting for us? Will Pablo come through with the government? Will he respect the agreements? I had no answers. I asked God to give my husband wisdom in this new opportunity that life was offering him. I asked that Father García Herreros be vigilant to make sure that the black sheep – my husband – didn't stray from the flock.

Inside La Catedral, Pablo came up, gave me a big hug, and said solemnly, 'My love, I promise you're not going to suffer anymore. I promise you that. You're my reason for living, and you gave me two wonderful children who deserve to live in peace.'

Pablo must have seen that my face was pleading with him to behave himself so he could get his family back. From the deepest reaches of my soul, I wanted that to happen. I felt an immense joy for us, for the country, but at the same time I was very scared that he might be extradited. I truly believed that on 19 June we would begin a new life. I trusted that he would leave his past behind and pay for his sins. I trusted, I trusted, I trusted.

But as my grandmother used to say, a leopard never changes its spots.

THOUGH IT LOOKED LIKE A PRISON, IN FACT PABLO HAD made all the decisions about La Catedral, without any input from the government. Guards, visits, remodelling and everything else having to do with daily life in the prison was approved or rejected by Pablo.

But it wasn't long before dense black clouds appeared on the horizon. It was clear that he wasn't going to keep his word, that his promise to start a new life was just rhetoric.

When I discovered that my husband was up to his old tricks with women and started hearing about illegal activities, I pulled as far away as possible and returned only to keep the relationship between my children and their father intact. There is no point in laying out the debauchery at La Catedral or describing the luxuries in Pablo Escobar's bedroom there; in a sense, the government allowed those excesses to make sure that its number one enemy remained behind bars.

Pablo lost sight of the country and forgot his commitment to his most precious treasure: his children. He lost contact with his own life, and his efforts to recover his economic and military power drove him to madness.

1992

In mid-June 1992, my mother and I went to see Pablo at La Catedral. There was an odd feeling in the air that day. My intuition told me something was happening and that the prison was in chaos. My mother had the same sense but, unlike me, she didn't keep quiet.

'Pablo, come here. I want to tell you something.'

'What?'

'If you keep having all these people going in and out and this place continues to be in shambles, you're not going to finish out the year here.'

'Relax, don't worry. Nothing's going to happen.'

'You're so hard-headed, Pablo. You never listen.'

My mother knew why she was saying that, and so did I. And as if it were a premonition, four weeks later, our lives would change dramatically when Pablo discarded the incredible opportunity he'd been given to redeem himself and atone for his sins.

At around seven o'clock at night on Tuesday, 21 July 1992, I got a phone call from Juan Pablo, who sounded upset. He said he didn't know what was going on, but he'd just talked to Pablo, who'd told him to be on the alert because there were unusual troop movements near La Catedral. Juan Pablo told me that something bad might happen, and we agreed that Manuela and I would leave the Torres de San Michel building and go to Altos, where my mother lived.

The next twelve hours were hellish, and I had to make do with just a couple more calls from Juan Pablo, who told me that all signs indicated that his father, his uncle Roberto and about twenty of Pablo's men were going to be transferred to the headquarters of the army's Fourth Brigade in Medellín. It was an awful night, and uncertainty kept us awake. We had no idea whether everybody was dead or in an aeroplane heading to the United States. We wept and feared the worst.

At dawn on 22 July, the media reported that my husband had escaped La Catedral with his brother and nine of his main lieutenants before they could be transferred. The uproar was only just beginning.

Juan Pablo arrived at Altos that same night and told me he'd spoken to Pablo several times using a powerful broadband radio, but he'd lost contact with him when the power in the prison went out and he'd gone to wait for him in a hideout known as Álvaro's house.

My mother, Juan Pablo, and I spent a sleepless night waiting for some news of my husband, but we didn't hear a thing. The TV news programmes reported that the government was able to confirm that my husband had managed to get a twelve-hour head start because he'd cleverly made them believe he was hiding in a tunnel inside the prison with a week's worth of supplies. They also said that my husband's men had had the deputy minister of justice, Eduardo Mendoza, and the director of prisons, Colonel

Hernando Navas, tied up for hours. The government had sent the two men to the prison to notify Pablo that he was being transferred.

During my research for this book, in Medellín I found one of the guards from that period, who spent several years in prison for working with my husband. He told me that Pablo escaped at 1.30am on 22 July, when La Catedral was in darkness because he'd ordered his men to cut the electricity. He also told me that the soldiers occupied the prison at four o'clock in the morning and made the guards and the prisoners who hadn't fled lie down on the floor. Two hours later, they arrested them and took them off to the Fourth Brigade headquarters.

Reflecting on what had happened in those last months, we concluded that the occupation of La Catedral was simply a matter of time: the excesses were blatant and the prison was out of control. Laughing, we recalled a number of incidents that had occurred back then.

I already mentioned the scare I'd had in February of that year, when I had to send a suitcase of clothes for Juan Pablo because he was going to spend a couple of weeks at La Catedral after Pablo had discovered a plan to kidnap him during a Motorcycling League of Antioquia competition. My husband thought that was the only way to keep our son safe because his enemies were on the prowl.

The war between Pablo and the Cali capos did not let up, even with my husband incarcerated in La Catedral. We learned this when Pablo mentioned that he'd decided to build some cabins hidden in the bush and sleep there instead of in the prison because his enemies had planned to drop several bombs from a plane. The problem was that the few times we went to sleep in those cabins, Manuela and I practically froze.

Juan Pablo also recalled that, in turning himself in to the authorities, Pablo was supposed to confess his crimes before the prosecutors assigned to lead his cases. But my husband didn't follow through on that requirement either, practically flouting justice. According to a guard, one day when he had a meeting with justice officials, the following took place:

'Boss, it's eleven o'clock, you've got that meeting.'

'Call me when you hear the helicopters.'

'Boss, I can hear the helicopters.'

'I'm going to take a nap. Call me when they land.'

'Boss, they've landed.'

'Give them coffee and then lunch while I shower.'

Pablo would go out two or three hours later to a cabin set up specifically for court business, and when they started reading the general provisions of the law, he'd say he was getting a bad stomach ache, stand up, and leave.

On another occasion, I recalled, more than a dozen portions of seafood stew arrived at the prison, supposedly for my husband and his closest men, but nobody knew who'd sent them. Wary, Pablo suggested they give a couple to the dogs to see what happened. The dogs were fine, so they gave the food to the soldiers, who wolfed it down. They weren't poisoned as my husband had feared, and a week later my mother-in-law came to visit and asked how they'd enjoyed the stew. Caught off guard, Pablo realised what had happened and responded, 'Delicious, Mum, thank you.'

The tales of the things we saw in La Catedral were endless, but so were the things we didn't see. Soon after the escape, the media reported that the government had decided to transfer my husband because he'd ordered a hit, inside the prison, on his partners and lifelong friends, Fernando Galeano and Gerardo 'Kiko' Moncada, because of a dispute over money. I was reluctant to believe that version of events because I knew how fond my husband was of Kiko and how much he trusted Galeano. Nevertheless, it was later confirmed that Pablo had made the terrible mistake of defying not only the state and his enemies ... but also his friends.

Four days after the escape, I heard from my husband. As night fell on Saturday, 25 July 1992, Popeye arrived at my mother's apartment and said that Pablo was waiting for us at Álvaro's house, the hideout in the upper section of Envigado.

After a warm greeting, my husband told us some of the details of the escape, especially one that had been bothering him: the army had asserted publicly that he'd escaped wearing women's clothing. As an unrepentant chauvinist, Pablo was outraged by the claim and wanted to straighten things out that very night. He thought the best way to do it was to contact the director of the RCN radio station, Juan Gossaín, directly, so he asked Popeye to call the station and get Gossaín on the line.

Minutes later, my husband was talking with Gossaín, who happened to be in a meeting with the co-director of the TV news programme *QAP*, María Isabel Rueda, and with an editor of *El Tiempo*, Enrique Santos Calderón.

Though the conversation had started as an attempt to clear up a bit of misinformation, it turned into an effort to get my husband to turn himself in again. But he kept insisting on various conditions, including a guarantee that he'd be incarcerated in Antioquia and that the police would not be involved in any trial. It went on until 4am, and Pablo spoke to the journalists several times, but the exchange didn't come to anything.

Our stay at Álvaro's house dragged on, and we became restless in confinement. The first one to find the isolation unbearable was Popeye, who spoke to Pablo and told him he couldn't take being shut up inside yet again. They soon reached an agreement and Popeye was replaced by Angelito. I remember that for the first time they started keeping watch in shifts; Angelito, Juan Pablo, Álvaro – the safe-house's caretaker – and my husband switched out every four hours until dawn.

In the final months of 1992, it became clear that hiding was going to be harder this time. The news programmes started describing aggressive raids being carried out by the recently formed Search Bloc in Medellín and the surrounding area, and implied that the men who had escaped with Pablo might turn themselves in. Roberto Escobar, Otto and Popeye all surrendered to the authorities and were locked up in the maximum-security prison in Itagüí.

With war all around him, Pablo mourned the deaths of Brances Muñoz Mosquera, known as 'Tyson', and Jhonny Edison Rivera, known as 'El Palomo', two of his trusted men who'd been gunned down in Medellín between

October and November in operations conducted by the police's new team.

Álvaro's house was safe, but Pablo sensed that something was going to happen, so he told me we were going to have to be apart after his birthday, his forty-third, which we celebrated on 1 December with a small cake and a modest meal. It was a quiet evening, and we all noted a strange atmosphere of unease. Danger hung in the air. As midnight approached, I told Pablo that if it was absolutely necessary for me to take the children to Medellín, we'd do it after the Day of the Little Candles on 7 December. It was a family tradition to celebrate that holiday, and I didn't want that year to be an exception.

He agreed, and that Sunday we all gathered in the rear courtyard of the house around a little statue of the Virgin Mary, not knowing it would be the last time we'd celebrate that holiday together. I recited a prayer and Pablo and Juan Pablo listened with their heads bowed while Manuela played nearby. When I finished, we lit a candle for the Virgin Mary and one for each of us.

The next day, before he left for Altos, Pablo told me, 'Tell your brothers and sisters to move or leave the country. This is going to keep getting more and more dangerous.'

He knew that the pressure on us would intensify; Medellín was once more being rocked by exploding bombs and the selective assassination of policemen, and that meant that the authorities would turn their eyes once more to their only contact with their number one enemy: his family.

At Altos, I tried hard to alleviate the pressure, and on Friday, 18 December, I organised a sumptuous celebration for the Advent Novena. The guests had just arrived, elegantly arrayed, when a bodyguard alerted us that the Search Bloc had barged in.

After separating men, women and children into groups and searching them, the agents asked to see our papers. Juan Pablo had his ID card up in his room, so he said his name was Juan Pablo Escobar Henao, that he was fifteen years old, and that his father was Pablo Escobar. The police officer called over his commanding officer, a colonel, and told him my son's identity.

What happened from there was horrible. The officer pulled Juan Pablo to one side and told his men, 'If he even blinks, shoot him.' He then used the radio-telephone to call the Carlos Holguín School – where the Search Bloc was headquartered – and announced that he had Escobar's son and was bringing him in for interrogation. Luckily, a few minutes later we were joined by the former governor of Antioquia, Álvaro Villegas Moreno, dressed in pyjamas; he lived in the Altos building and told the colonel he wanted to make sure the raid was carried out in accordance with the law.

Villegas's timely appearance encouraged the frightened attendees, who began objecting to the treatment of their children and demanding that they at least be allowed to eat. The police acquiesced at once.

Then the colonel told Juan Pablo to follow him. My son asked where to, but two police officers shoved their rifle barrels into his stomach and removed him from the lineup. I watched them walk toward the hallway and then stop as thirty hooded men appeared. I was gripped by terror, convinced that they were going to do something to my son.

'Two steps forward! Turn to the right, now left, now turn your back. State your full name ... Speak up!' ordered one of the hooded figures.

After that, they did the same thing with each man in attendance at the celebration. Only two females were subjected to the same treatment: Manuela and me.

God is good, because at 3am, as the colonel started giving instructions to take Juan Pablo away, a representative from the inspector general's office arrived, countermanded the arrest of a minor, and told them to remove the handcuffs. The colonel kept insisting on arresting my son but, after a bitter argument with the government official, finally left the building.

Our terrifying experience that night demonstrated that the search for my husband, without question, now included his family.

AFTER THAT FRIGHTENING NIGHT AT ALTOS, CONVINCED that it was no longer safe to be there, I decided to go somewhere else. So we went to my brother Fernando's apartment in Loma de los Balsos. It was 21 December 1991, and we'd just settled in when the TV news and local newspapers reported, aghast, that my husband had personally set up two checkpoints on the Vía Las Palmas highway with fifty armed men who claimed to be DAS employees. In both places, the reports said, they stopped dozens of cars coming down from José María Córdova

Airport and, after checking the travellers' IDs, let them through.

I was startled by my husband's suicidal attitude, which I found inexplicable. I was also distraught when reporters revealed that Pablo had headed up an armed group that, at dawn on 20 December, had blown up a house that was being used by Captain Fernando Posada Hoyos, head of intelligence for the Medellín police. Having survived the explosion, the reporters claimed, the officer was then finished off.

And so, five months after Pablo's escape from La Catedral, my children and I were worse off than ever; it was getting harder and harder to find places to hide in Medellín. The war had escalated to a new high, and I was seized by an unbearable sense of impotence.

Pablo must have noticed, because on 23 December 1991, when we met up with him at a hideout in Belén Aguas Frías – where we spent Christmas and New Year's Eve – the atmosphere was heavy with worry and nobody was in the mood for celebrating. In addition, every night we had to drive down an unpaved road to a little mud-brick house, where it was easier to go unnoticed because the lights couldn't be seen from a distance. I remember all too clearly that it was a particularly difficult time for Manuela, who used to cry for hours because of the intense cold, longing to be somewhere else, with her grandmother, with her cousins. Pablo would pick her up and try unsuccessfully to explain why we couldn't leave. The war was nipping at our heels, and the future looked very uncertain. So much so, that it would be the last New Year's Eve we'd spend together.

1993

I don't think I'm wrong to say that Pablo's final hours began to tick by on 31 January 1993. On that day, the conflict with his now numerous enemies took a dramatic turn when the media revealed the existence of a secret group that would end up being deadly: Perseguidos por Pablo Escobar [Persecuted by Pablo Escobar], also known as Los Pepes.

Los Pepes made a violent entrance, destroying my mother-in-law Hermilda's farm in Peñol, a town in eastern Antioquia, and setting off car bombs in front of the Abedules and Altos buildings, where many of the members of the Escobar Gaviria and Escobar Henao families were living.

A new phase of the war had begun and made an immediate impact: Angelito came to pick us up at Ceiba de Castilla, code name 00, and took us to an apartment on Avenida La Playa, two blocks from Avenida Oriental in Medellín. My husband was there and said worriedly that if Los Pepes focussed their attacks on our family, it would be very difficult for him to protect us because his military force had been decimated.

He recalled the attack that had taken place in mid-January, when the paramilitary leader Carlos Castaño had destroyed El Vivero – the shop where one of my sisters worked – and her house in the El Diamante neighbourhood. And he noted that things were getting more complicated since in the second week of January he'd lost Víctor Giovanni 'El Zarco' Granados, and Juan Carlos 'Enchufe' Ospina, two of his most trusted men.

But now, with the emergence of a new enemy, Los Pepes, my husband said that the best thing would be for Manuela and Juan Pablo to go to the United States and then for me to join them later, once I'd attained a new entry visa for the country, since my old one had expired. After discussing the details of the journey, we agreed that the children would go with Martha, my brother Fernando's wife, their two children, and Andrea, Juan Pablo's girlfriend. Copito and Algodona, Manuela's French poodles, would go too, since she flatly refused to leave them behind.

Before leaving, Pablo warned us to be extra careful on our way to the Rionegro airport because Los Pepes were looking for an opportunity to capture our children.

By then, the dismantling of my family had begun, at Pablo's suggestion in December 1991, when the newly formed Search Bloc's operations demonstrated that attacks on us and our surroundings were now part of the strategy for hunting Pablo. Practically my entire family split apart; my siblings went in different directions and we were in touch only intermittently, with long periods of silence.

Astado, my sister and her three children, terrified, left for a small city in the central United States, and their only contact with Colombia was a small, seven-band Sony radio that they used to tune in to a Colombian station early in the mornings. They stayed there for about two years, uncertain whether the long arm of Pablo's enemies would be able to reach them. Given that they might have to flee at any moment, they bought only some mattresses, sheets, a sofa bed, and basic kitchen items. As a result, family life became difficult and the children cried constantly. My sister remembers with sadness the night they managed to tune in to a station and heard the news that Los Pepes had killed three people in Medellín, acquaintances of theirs, and left notices on their bodies accusing them of collaborating with Pablo.

Confined in our downtown Medellín apartment, I learned helplessly of my mother's seriously declining health thanks to a stroke that had left her bedridden and unable to talk. Through third parties, I heard that she was very ill and depressed.

Another of my sisters was in hiding in a distant apartment in Medellín but, one day, when she went out to run an errand in her car, she was discovered by Carlos Castaño, who followed her for a long time until she cleverly managed to slip his tail. A while later, after Pablo's death, when I had to meet with Castaño in my negotiations with the cartels, he mentioned that incident to me and said he'd been a hair's breadth from capturing my sister and killing her. He said the same of me and Manuela. It was a miracle that we escaped.

Surreptitiously, we managed to plan my children's trip to Miami, which was set for 19 January 1993. At four o'clock in the morning, I saw Manuela, Juan Pablo and Andrea off, hugging them tight because I didn't know whether it would be the last time I saw them. The previous night, we'd had to go to Andrea's house to ask her mother's permission for her to travel. I talked to her for twenty minutes, and when they said goodbye, she made a prophetic pronouncement, the kind we mothers are given to: 'Daughter, you're going off to suffer now.'

Just getting to the airport was an ordeal. The night before, a bodyguard went and left a vehicle in the airport car park and handed over the suitcases to one of Pablo's contacts. Juan Pablo and Andrea stayed at the Hotel Nutibara and took a shuttle to the Rionegro airport while Nariz and El Japonés followed along behind in a small car; everybody else went in a modest vehicle with two other bodyguards.

In the meantime, I remained alone in the apartment and prayed harder than ever, begging God to protect my children's lives. I turned on the TV, listened to the radio and waited. But at around noon I panicked when a radio station announced that they hadn't been able to leave the country. I screamed silently so the neighbours wouldn't hear me, horrified to think that Los Pepes might take my children. I paced wildly through the apartment, expecting to hear that they'd been kidnapped, but the reporters suddenly said they'd left in a helicopter, heading to Medellín's Olaya Herrera Airport. Where were they? They're going to be killed, I thought. Unable to contact them, at noon I started packing a briefcase with a bit of clothing because Pablo had told me that one of his men, Omar, also known as El Médico, would be coming to get me.

I almost went mad. More than seven hours went by before El Médico arrived and told me not to worry, we were going to meet up with my children and Pablo. We got into a car, he blindfolded me, and when I opened my eyes, Manuela, Andrea, Juan Pablo and my husband were standing in front of me. I hugged them for a long time, weeping. I won't live long enough to ever ask their forgiveness enough for the way they were forced to play Russian roulette that day because of their parents' decisions.

Juan Pablo described their terrifying adventure, which had begun when they arrived at the Rionegro airport and spotted suspicious men in several vehicles. In the international terminal, the DAS agent had only reluctantly let them through even though they had all their papers in order, including entry visas for the United States and their parents' authenticated authorisations to travel. But as they were sitting in the waiting room, Juan Pablo noticed strange movements:

'I saw hooded men in plain clothes and armed with rifles and machine guns patrolling the terminal outside the gate in groups of six. I was able to count more than twenty of them, and the airline employees, food service workers and even the janitors were looking at each other in alarm. Nobody knew who they were or what they were up to. It was Los Pepes.'

My son's account sent chills up my spine. Suddenly, several police officers had arrived, followed by four young men, employees of the Civil Aviation Authority, who were carrying the children's suitcases and said they had orders to open them. Powerless, my son watched the meticulous search, which seemed aimed at delaying them so they'd miss their flight. The gambit worked as intended. The plane took off, and there would be no other flight that day.

Juan Pablo said he'd been scared that something terrible might happen and decided to switch to the Plan B he and El Japonés had organised. The bodyguard was carrying a list of phone numbers for the regional office of the inspector general, local and national media outlets, and private lines for several prominent journalists. The code was that my son would scratch his ear as if it were itching, whereupon El Japonés would start calling to let people know what was happening. The strategy worked, and the bodyguard understood the message.

But things soon got even more complicated when the head of the airport police arrived and told them they had to leave the international terminal because they'd missed their flight. Juan Pablo started arguing with the official, but several journalists and TV news programmes suddenly showed up and the hooded men disappeared.

The original travel plan had considered how to get out of the country, but we'd never foreseen how to get out of the tight spot my children now found themselves in. In looking for an alternative, Juan Pablo discovered that a private helicopter was about to land, and that it offered a private transfer service, ferrying passengers between the Rionegro airport and Olaya Herrera. He asked someone to do him a favour and call the company to request the transfer service. It worked, and they sent an aircraft, but the guard wouldn't let them leave. Luckily, an official from the inspector general's office appeared and helped them get out to the helicopter.

When they were about to climb aboard, having left their suitcases behind because five people and two dogs were over the helicopter's weight limit, a police colonel arrived and told Juan Pablo that they weren't going to let him get away next time. The colonel punched the helicopter, but contained himself because there were some cameramen filming the encounter.

The nightmare wasn't over yet. In Olaya Herrera, Juan Pablo agreed to give a reporter from the regional TV channel Teleantioquia an interview at the Altos building, under the condition that the crew didn't stop filming. They assented, and when they reached the Altos car park my son described to the reporter what had happened. They then left through the rear of the building and crossed a small stream that led to a second building where we had an apartment and an extra car. This was the escape route Juan Pablo had previously used to escape from danger. Now that we were all reunited, we were taken, blindfolded, to a new safehouse, which seemed to be somewhere downtown. Pablo was there, but he said he would be leaving soon.

The next day, 20 February 1993, was the final blow to our frustrated trip to the United States: the US ambassador announced that Juan Pablo's and Manuela's visas had been cancelled. Pablo left after making us promise not to go out. We celebrated Juan Pablo's sixteenth birthday, but the atmosphere was so glum that we only shared a small homemade cake that I baked.

With a brutal wave of violence, Los Pepes showed that they were more than willing to destroy everything around my husband. It wasn't an exaggeration. On 27 February they destroyed the Corona estate, owned by Diego Londoño White; on 2 March they assassinated Hernán Darío 'HH' Henao, the manager of Hacienda Nápoles, whom they mistakenly assumed was a member of my family because we shared a last name; on 4 March they assassinated Raúl Zapata Vergara, Pablo's lawyer; on the 20 March Chopo was killed; and we heard on the news that Pasquín's corpse had been found, some weeks after he'd disappeared.

Los Pepes felt ubiquitous, and we were forced to move from hideout to hideout with unusual frequency. One week we'd be enduring the cold in Belén Aguas Frías; the next week, we'd be roasting on a farm in the Magdalena Medio; we'd spend others in an apartment in the Suramericana building in Medellín; and still another in a studio apartment next to the Fourth Brigade headquarters.

And so, little by little, as Los Pepes and the authorities struck at Pablo, his military and economic power practically dried up. But his family also suffered from the harshness of the conflict, because in their desire to take oxygen from my husband, Los Pepes lashed out at those who were closest to him, and those who were looking after us.

In the last four months of 1993, my husband's enemies triumphed. Legal and extra-legal forces came together to defeat him and left us, his children and wife, caught in a whirlwind from which, twenty-five years later, we have not yet managed to escape.

Chapter 9

The Fleeting Hope of Mozambique

In mid-February 1994, two months after Pablo was killed, Colombia's attorney general, Gustavo de Greiff, called my lawyer, Francisco Fernández, in Medellín and told him he wanted to see Fernández immediately because an opportunity had come up for us to finally leave the country.

Fernández immediately got on a plane, and a few hours later de Greiff introduced him to a woman of about sixty-five, with pale skin, dressed in black, very elegant, with a huge feathered hat, who identified herself as the Countess Isabela. Beside her were two black men wearing suits and ties, who seemed to be her secretaries.

The woman said in perfect English that she ran a foundation that did fundraising for the Popular Republic of Mozambique, and she explained that if the Escobars contributed to her cause, the president of that distant country in south-eastern Africa would allow us to reside there. In compensation, they would give us new identities, passports, a house in the best neighbourhood in Maputo, the capital city, and an education for my children. The countess gave the lawyer a folder with photos and information on Mozambique, and they agreed to visit us a few days later in the Hotel Tequendama, where we were still living.

Once our lawyer told us what had happened, we assessed the strange situation, but we didn't dismiss it. It had come from the attorney general himself, who was showing real signs of wanting to help us, since he more than anybody understood the difficult circumstances we were in three months after my husband's death.

It was a door that was opening, a light at the end of the tunnel. At the time, the long process of negotiating with Pablo's enemies had just begun; the capos wanted to seize all his properties in compensation for the millions of dollars they claimed to have invested in hunting him.

We didn't have many options since a lot of countries had already denied us any possibility of taking refuge there, so we invited the countess and her men over and during a long conversation they talked about the humanitarian asylum they'd offer us and the new life we'd lead in Mozambique, claiming to be, above all, defenders of human rights and aware of our dilemma. At the end of our chat, the lawyer asked the million-dollar question: how much would this 'humanitarian asylum' cost? Juan Pablo flushed with shame, but the countess evaded the question and said it was very premature to be talking about money.

When the entourage left, my brother Fernando – who was staying with us at the hotel at the time – said pessimistically that Mozambique wasn't as wonderful a country as the photos showed. Instead, he claimed, it was more like Urabá, the hot, impoverished banana-growing region on the Colombian border with Panama. And he added that the whole business sounded like a trap in order to kill us or, best-case scenario, feed us to the lions.

Even so, we continued to communicate through Attorney General de Greiff, and we slowly became enthusiastic about the idea of taking refuge in Mozambique. In Colombia, our future was pitch-dark. Any port in a storm, as the saying goes. In mid-1994, the Maputo plan became even more fully fleshed out because our lawyer had to go to Washington to work out the amount we'd have to contribute, and how, with the director of the organisation.

Amid all the chaos around us, one day Fernández, our lawyer – to whom I'll always be grateful for his unconditional support, the immense compassion he showed us, and his positive attitude in our search for the best options – came by with an idea that would be transformative in our lives: changing our names. As a lawyer, he said, he knew of an old law in the National Statute of Notaries and Registries that allowed for the correction or modification of people's names through the filing of a formal document at any civil law notary's office. According to him, it was Article 6 of Decree 999, from 1988, a modification of Article 94 of Decree 1260, from 1970.

Incredulous, we agreed and he immediately went to Attorney General de Greiff to explain that the process for changing one's identity was an easy one but would have to be carried out with the utmost discretion. The attorney general asked if he was sure a simple name change would resolve our situation, and Fernández said it would, and that we were willing to run the risk because – among other things – the attorney general's office couldn't take care of us indefinitely.

The attorney general seemed hesitant at first, until our lawyer threatened to advise us to call a press conference to denounce the evident close links between that office and my husband's enemies. De Greiff's attitude did a swift 180, and with his blessing we embarked on looking for new names in the Bogotá phone book. Our lawyer gave us clear instructions: 'Your last names need to be normal, sound like they're from good families, with no drug-trafficking connotations so they leave you alone. The idea is to be regular, run-of-the-mill citizens.'

After a long search in which we discarded dozens of options, we found the perfect names, but we decided to keep one of our original names so the change wouldn't be so traumatic. Thus, we would henceforth be known as María Isabel Santos Caballero, Juan Sebastián Marroquín Santos, Juana Manuela Marroquín Santos and María de los Ángeles Sarmiento del Valle, my son's girlfriend. My brother Fernando refused to do it, claiming it disrespected our parents. As a result, months later he couldn't go with us when we left the country for Mozambique. Once we'd selected names, we spent hours practising our signatures, which also helped us get used to our new identities.

The attorney general's office did everything it could to keep the identity-change process secret and even took care of delivering the photos we had taken in a lab on the ground floor of Residencias Tequendama to the National

Civil Registry. At last, on 8 June 1994, Andrea and I went to Medellín to sign the documents with notary 12, Marta Inés Alzate Restrepo. Because they were minors, Juan Pablo and Manuela remained in Bogotá and I signed for them.

The process of changing our identities and the possibility of leaving the country were sailing along thanks to the direct intervention of Attorney General de Greiff, so we were extremely worried when his replacement was selected: Alfonso Valdivieso Sarmiento, a cousin of Luis Carlos Galán.

The new attorney general was sworn in on 18 August 1994, and a week later Fernández made an appointment to talk about our case. Valdivieso's words surprised him: 'I'm aware of everything that's been happening with the Escobar family.'

Pleased, Fernández recounted the latest developments, and at the end of their conversation, the two men agreed that I should come see him in his office.

How could I approach him and ask for his help? Was it totally shameless? I was racked by uncertainty as I headed to his office.

My doubts were not unfounded. As I entered Valdivieso's office, I came face to face with a large photo of Galán.

'Mr Valdivieso, I don't know how to begin this conversation, how to ask for your help after everything that's happened.'

'Ma'am, what happened is very painful, but I understand your position as a mother and, for that reason, despite the harm done, I will help you.'

We didn't deserve his help, given the immense sorrow my husband had inflicted on that family, but Mr Valdivieso may have been, without realising it, the first person who showed us the value of forgiveness. He listened to me and understood my pain, our desperation to leave the country, the only way we could stay alive.

The meeting was a productive one; Attorney General Valdivieso was willing to help us. After that, we used to go to his office at least four times a week, and it became normal for them to work with us to resolve logistical problems related to our security and other issues.

The next November, when we'd finished handing over all of Pablo's assets to the drug kingpins and paramilitary leaders who were demanding them, the head of the National Civil Registry, Luis Camilo Osorio, visited us at the apartment we'd rented in the Santa Ana neighbourhood, in northern Bogotá, to give us our new citizenship papers and ID cards. Osorio arrived and sat in the dining room to issue the passports himself, with the authorisation of the Ministry of Foreign Affairs. That way, we never had to go to a government office to process our new identities; as the attorney general had promised, it was all done in private. The collaboration was so effective that the attorney general's Office of Victim and Witness Protection even made sure to pull Juan Pablo's military card to make sure the army didn't find out his new identity.

In the meantime, the negotiations with Mozambique continued and we were able to start organising our trip after depositing a considerable sum in a New York bank account in the name of a fictional government entity known as the Nut Ministry.

With our new papers in hand, we could finally leave. The first thing we did was say goodbye to my family. The last week that we were in Colombia, in early December 1994, they all came from Medellín to stay with us and share our final days with us. Not knowing when we'd see each other again, we felt immense sadness. Every so often, my mother would ask what our new names were and where we were going and, despite her insistence and weeping, we didn't tell her anything. It was very painful and even offensive to refuse to offer any information but, deep down, we knew it was best for everybody's safety. We'd found a possibility for survival, and we had to be careful to make sure it came through.

Finally, on 14 December 1994, we left the apartment in Santa Ana very early to begin the long journey into exile that lay ahead. At five o'clock in the morning, with a rented truck loaded with our belongings, we said our last goodbyes and left. Accompanying me and my children were Astado and Marleny, the maid. It was very sad because we had no idea what kind of future awaited us. At the same time, Ángeles – as my son's girlfriend was now called – and the wife and daughter of our lawyer, Fernández, would travel to Buenos Aires, where we would meet to take the plane to Africa. We would see our lawyer in Guayaquil, Ecuador.

As we prepared to leave the neighbourhood, Sebastián – as Juan Pablo was now known – got out of the car and asked Puma, the head of the CTI bodyguards, not to go with us anymore, saying that it was time for us to seek our own destiny. We later learned that Puma lost his job because he'd let us leave without finding out where we were going.

Our ride south through the country along the highway went smoothly, and we even had time to go to Palmira to say goodbye to my Aunt Lilia and then to the Basilica of Our Lord of the Miracles in Buga to ask him to protect us and remove the obstacles from our path. That night we slept in Popayán, and the next day we went on to Pasto.

When we reached the border crossing at the Rumichaca Bridge, we had trouble getting into Ecuador because we didn't have the father's signature to take the children out of the country or the permission of the company from which we'd rented the SUV. Astado, clever as always, managed to resolve the issue of my children. I didn't ask how he did it; he just said we were all set. The rental agency faxed the consent form requested by the immigration authorities, and we crossed the border into Ecuador.

After driving another 250 miles from Tulcán – the northernmost city in the country – we spent the night in a motel in the city of Santo Domingo de los Colorados, not far from Quito, the capital. The next day we traveled to Guayaquil, where we met up with Fernández, and from there we took a plane to Buenos Aires, where we would board another flight to South Africa, and then one final leg to Mozambique.

Our itinerary had us spend the night in the Argentine capital before continuing our travels. We loved the city. We stayed at the Claridge Hotel, near Calle Florida, and for the first time in a long time we were able to stroll along at ease and even had enough time to get hamburgers at McDonald's. After exploring that beautiful city for hours, I begged our lawyer to let us spend Christmas there, but he said firmly that it wasn't an option, that we couldn't take unnecessary risks, whereas in Mozambique we would be safe.

The next day we took a Malaysia Airlines flight to Johannesburg, where we changed planes to go to Maputo. From the start, we didn't like it: it was an old aircraft that looked more like a long-distance bus than an international flight. After two uncomfortable hours, they announced that we would be landing, but from the air all we could see was dusty, unpaved streets.

In Maputo's old and very run-down airport, a government delegation made up of five tall men elegantly dressed in suits and ties was waiting for us. After a polite but formal welcome, they took us to the airport's presidential lounge, a large room with dusty old furniture, all very shabby. We were stunned. Nobody dared say a word, but our startled expressions said it all. It was Sunday, and a good while later they came to pick us up in two brand-new Mercedes-Benzes and a Toyota Corolla, also fairly new. We headed up in single file toward the best neighbourhood in the city, where the embassies were clustered and where our future home supposedly awaited us. The lawyer and his family were taken to the Polana Serena Hotel, the best one in the city.

Along the route it became clear to us that we'd come to a country that had been devastated by war. The streets were dusty and lined with ruined buildings marked by bullets and rockets. The few cars that were on the streets bore the United Nations logo.

On the way, the car that Sebastián and Ángeles were travelling in was involved in a fender bender. The driver got out to look, climbed back in and kept going. When my son asked why he hadn't asked for the other driver's information so he could take it up with his insurance company, the driver responded that there weren't any insurance companies or ways to seek compensation.

The best neighbourhood in Maputo was full of modest one-storey houses, not fancy at all, very normal. We arrived at 'our' house, which looked like it was from the 1970s, a three-storey structure decorated with animal-print furniture and with bars on all the windows. And it smelled awful.

'They had us put the bars on so you'd be safe,' one of the men from the welcoming committee explained.

We soon learned that our luggage hadn't arrived and was lost, but they assured us they'd do everything they could to make sure the airline sent it as soon as it was found. So things were looking pretty dire: we were in a war-torn country, in a horrible house, with no clothes.

Even so, I tried to keep us all calm and went to the kitchen to make dinner, but there were only a few eggs in the pantry. Marleny went to a nearby supermarket and put a few groceries in her trolley, but when she went to pay she was told she could buy only half of what she'd selected because food needed to be shared among everybody. So there wasn't much to eat. 'We're off to a bad start,' I thought, and I prayed to God to give me courage.

In the meantime, Sebastián and Ángeles were waiting at a table in the garden, utterly disappointed. We ate eggs and rice, and just then Fernández's wife arrived and urged us to move to the hotel because there was food there.

'Come on, come to the hotel instead! They've even got ice cream!'

Sebastián agreed immediately, but I suggested we sleep on it and give the house a chance. But it was no use. We ended up accepting the invitation.

The hotel was like an oasis in the desert. Unlike the rest of the city, it was incredibly luxurious because the government had refurbished it to house the hundreds of UN officials who were helping to rebuild the country. There was one downside, though: despite the beautiful ocean view, the waters were infested with sharks, so we couldn't swim. Even amid that elegance, breakfast consisted of a few eggs with ham or cheese and nothing else. At lunch all they served was stroganoff.

The hotel cost a fortune, and the money we had would only be enough for two or three weeks, which could cost US$30,000. But we decided to spend the night there and decide what to do the next morning. Before going to bed I stopped by Ángeles and Sebastián's room. My son was so depressed that he said only a single sentence that filled me with worry: 'Mum, I don't know if I can stay here.'

The next day, the suitcases still hadn't shown up. I went downstairs and found a clothing store, but the only T-shirts they sold were so expensive that we decided to go out and look for a shopping centre. We ordered two taxis, and two crumbling jalopies showed up. In the street, dozens of children surrounded us, begging for coins. The poverty was overwhelming and the foul odours unbearable.

The taxi drivers took us to the only shopping centre in Maputo: a mall full of empty shops, without any merchandise. Finally, we found some flimsy blue and white T-shirts that said Maputo. We bought one each, and until the suitcases showed up two days later, the five of us looked like we were in uniform.

During our drive through the city, we decided to go to the only university we'd been told was in operation, but what we found was a house with a few desks where the only course of study was medicine. The place was also the morgue where the students practised. That was enough for us. We returned to the hotel, utterly crestfallen. Where in the world were we? We'd clearly been deceived.

To top it all off, the officials who'd welcomed us were nowhere to be found. One of them had told us to rest and that we'd discuss our future after the New Year celebrations, but at this point we weren't willing to wait until January.

It was a total nightmare. Nobody looked happy, and at night despair overcame us all. Given the tension, a serious family crisis was inevitably brewing when Sebastián, lying on the bed, took off his belt and said ominously, 'Mum, if we don't leave this place, I'm going to use this belt to kill myself. Let's go back to Colombia. I'd rather get murdered there than die of sadness in this depressing place.'

My son was clearly not joking. Knowing that things were out of control, I didn't hesitate an instant. I went out to look for the lawyer and asked him to make the necessary arrangements, informing him I'd decided to leave Maputo as soon as possible. Fernández was furious and berated me harshly. He told me to ignore the 'little prince', referring to Sebastián, because I'd made an agreement with the government of Mozambique and had paid them a substantial sum of money. He also reminded me that no other country had wanted to take us in, and said I was going to send a year of work down the drain because of a child's whim.

'It's easy for you to talk,' I said, annoyed. 'Tomorrow you're flying off to spend New Year's Eve in Paris, while I have to stay here with my children and my son's girlfriend.'

I started looking for tickets, but I had no idea where we should go, so we decided to use our return fares to Johannesburg. The problem was that the flights were only every two weeks. Fernández suggested that we stay in Maputo, saying he'd find us teachers who would give us English lessons while we looked for other options. It seemed like a sensible idea to me, so I proposed it to my children, but they flatly refused, saying they didn't want to be in Maputo a minute longer.

Things with the lawyer got so tense that he threatened to stop helping us, insisting that we should make the effort to stay at least a year and then change our identities again. But Sebastián kept saying he couldn't bear another minute in that place, especially not at the astronomical prices in the hotel, which didn't even have a TV signal.

Finally, Fernández realised we were serious and went to the airport to look for flights. He was successful and called urgently to tell us to rush to the airport; he'd found a flight that was leaving for Johannesburg in three hours. Ángeles and Manuela were playing in the pool, and they had to put on their clothes on top of their bathing suits. We crammed all of our wet, wrinkled clothing into the suitcases and raced out the door. Leaving that country was a relief, even though we didn't have an established destination.

The flight from Maputo went smoothly, and when we reached the Johannesburg airport, we stopped to look at the boards listing international departures and decided to take a flight to São Paulo, Brazil. We would think about what came next once we were there. We considered going back to Colombia, but we knew it was a huge risk. Our agreement with my husband's enemies had said that we had to leave the country and not come back.

While we were pondering our options from South Africa, in Maputo our lawyer was having problems with the authorities, who were forbidding him and his family from travelling, claiming that he'd encouraged our sudden departure. Finally, after several hours of explaining what had happened, he managed to persuade them to return his family's passports and was able to board his flight to France.

When we arrived in São Paulo, we stayed one night in a hotel. We liked Brazil, but the language barrier made things tough because we weren't really up for learning Portuguese. After discussing it endlessly and studying the pros and cons, we decided to go to Rio de Janeiro and from there to Buenos Aires, where we might be able to begin a new life. So we took the chance. I called Astado in Medellín and asked him to meet us in Argentina. That's how we ended up arriving in Buenos Aires at 3am on 23 December 1994.

Our lawyer went back to Colombia in mid-January 1995 and informed the attorney general's office that we'd changed plans unexpectedly. He asked Valdivieso several times if we were going to be all right in our new destination, and the attorney general told him not to worry. It was obvious: the Colombian government had always known where we were.

The new year, 1995, was beginning, and the road ahead of us was uncertain. How would we build a future out of the unknown? We had no idea, but together we dared to take our first steps toward finding a new identity. Argentina gave us a second chance in life, and from the first moment we were determined not to let it go to waste. We were ready to give it our all, but we would soon discover that Pablo's shadow was still present, always present.

Chapter 10

Argentina: A Second Chance

During the first break, I called home as I always did when I went to my evening life coaching class, but this time there was no answer even though my mother, Juana (as Manuela was now called), and the nurse were supposed to be there. Though it seemed strange, I decided to wait till the class was over. I couldn't concentrate; ever since the weekend, I'd been worried because of the threatening calls I was getting from the accountant's lawyers, who were claiming that if we didn't abandon Argentina and leave them everything, they'd reveal our identities.

Finally, at eleven o'clock at night, the class ended. I kept trying to call the house, but nobody picked up. A classmate offered to take me home and dropped me off outside the entrance of the building at Calle Jaramillo 2010, in northern Buenos Aires's Núñez neighbourhood, where we were living at the time. I went up to apartment 17N, but when I rang the front doorbell the maid poked her head out the side door and desperately signalled for me to leave.

I turned around and walked toward the lift, but one of our dogs slipped out of the apartment. I picked him up and went down to the first floor, frightened. In the lobby, the only thing it occurred to me to do was go into the lounge area and lock myself in one of the bathrooms. I pulled out my mobile phone and called the notary.

'Something strange is happening in my apartment,' I said, distraught. 'The maid told me to leave. I don't know who's there. Please call our lawyer and tell him to let people in Colombia know in case something happens to us. I've tried to call him several times, but he isn't answering. Please help me.'

I hung up, and in my distress I decided that my best option was to leave the building through the back door. When I reached the exit, I rang for the building concierge several times, but he didn't open the door. I kept ringing, but within seconds I was surrounded by federal police officers, who shouted, 'Freeze! Drop your weapons! Drop your weapons!'

'What weapons?' I answered in fright. 'I've got a dog and my briefcase.'

I showed them that all I was carrying was books and papers. I realised they were more scared than I was.

'Let's go up to the apartment, ma'am,' they said, still pointing their guns at me.

When I entered, I got a real surprise. Several police officers had been rummaging around for hours looking for 'something' that they couldn't actually identify. My mother, who was visiting at the time, was terrified. Juana, who'd invited a friend over to spend the night, was in her room with no idea what was happening. Ángeles and Sebastián, who'd only recently got home because they'd been invited out to eat, were watching the officers as they searched to make sure they didn't plant drugs somewhere and claim they'd found them. That had happened several times in Argentina.

I asked Sebastián what was going on, and one of the officers responded that we were under arrest for having false papers. The agents didn't really know what to do – they asked for one sheet of paper and then another, but it was clear they didn't know what the end goal was. I calmed down a little and said I was going to take a shower and change my clothes. I locked myself in the bathroom and again called the notary and my lawyer.

I gathered a little money, my documents, and my toothbrush and got ready for us to leave. A few hours into their raid, the police told me not to be scared, that it was just an inquiry. I was worried more about what was happening to my mother and Juana, and how we were going to explain a visit from the police to the parents of my daughter's friend. I thought of the accountant. He was obviously behind all of it. Can a person really be so unmitigatedly greedy that they're willing to destroy a family for money?

While that was happening, the TV was broadcasting a live news report on my arrest, melodramatically referring to me as 'the white widow'. Every channel was reporting the breaking news.

Ángeles was distraught as she said goodbye to Sebastián because the police refused to tell her where they were taking us. We headed down to the street, where they placed us in separate patrol cars and took us – driving like maniacs the wrong way down Avenida del Libertador – to the Anti-terrorist Unit of the Argentine Federal Police, at Cavia 3302 in Buenos Aires, near Avenida Figueroa Alcorta. The patrol cars were followed by numerous other cars with blaring sirens; it was like something out of a movie. Ángeles sent the maid after us in a taxi to find out where we were going.

Sebastián told me he almost jumped out of the car because he was afraid they weren't real police, since the first one who'd come up and told him he was under arrest was clearly drunk, and his police badge was of such shoddy quality that it looked fake.

After we argued with the agents about which identities they were going to put down in their logbook of the people taken into custody, they took the money, documents and toothbrush I'd brought. They wanted to force us to sign with our original names, Escobar Henao, even though my son and I told them that by law our identity was our current one, Marroquín Santos. If we signed with our old names, that could be considered falsification of documents. It was around five o'clock in the morning on 16 November 1999. They then put us in two separate large cells with bars and concrete floors.

I wasn't worried about document falsification charges. The identity change had been legal in Colombia. What's more, I was the one who'd been scammed and extorted by the accountant and his lawyers, and I'd already reported them to the authorities. We were victims, so why were we being locked up? I was positive it wouldn't take more than a few days to clear things up. I had no idea what was coming. The honeymoon that had started when we arrived in Argentina was about to end.

AT THREE O'CLOCK IN THE MORNING ON 24 DECEMBER 1994, we walked into the Bauen Suite Hotel, at Avenida Corrientes 1856, in the heart of Buenos Aires. Alfredo Astado had reserved it as soon as we told him we wouldn't be staying in Mozambique. I found the place desolate and dark. Later, I found out why I hadn't liked it: it had once been the clandestine centre of operations of the Secretariat of State Intelligence (SIDE).

I decided we weren't going to stay. After a day and a half of travelling from Mozambique, and despite the late hour, Sebastián and I went off to look for something better. We got in a taxi and asked the driver to take us to a well-located apartment hotel. A while later he dropped us off on Calle Guido, in Recoleta, across from an elegant old building where we found a place with a small living room, a kitchenette and two bedrooms. It was just what we were looking for. We paid for a month up front. We had a safe place at least for the next thirty days, which sounded like an eternity to us. We'd been living like nomads for a decade, never knowing where we'd be the next night.

Now all together, we slept the entire day until Astado called at five o'clock in the afternoon. Because of the time change, we thought 24 December was over but, no, it was Christmas Eve 1994. It had been a year since Pablo's death, and we felt a deep sadness. We exchanged Christmas cards, a family tradition, a ritual we maintain even today. Despite our grief, we went out to walk around the decorated city and entered the Buenos Aires Design shopping centre, which was bustling with happy people. Nobody would ever have suspected that Pablo Escobar's family was there. We sat down at a table on the terraces and had dinner. I used the little energy and love I had left to offer my support amid all the uncertainty and in the end were able to spend some pleasant, caring time together. We stuck to our motto in life: one day at a time.

The first two months in Buenos Aires, we all slept a lot. We were finally feeling the accumulated fatigue of all those years, all those anxieties and fears, persecutions, raids and attempts on our lives. Astado would come to the hotel at noon and tell us to go out and get to know the city, but we didn't feel like it. All we wanted to do was close our eyes and forget our reality.

The few times I went out in the street, I took all the fliers people were handing out offering all sorts of classes: singing, dancing, philosophy, art history, cooking ... The idea was to start building a life. Sebastán used to complain about the clutter of paper everywhere, but my priority was to set up a normal life, which wasn't so easy since we'd never had one.

Despite everything, Argentina seemed like paradise to us. We were unaccustomed to the feeling of ease in the streets. We tried to embrace the sense of peace, the greenery and the magnificent parks. But we were still plagued by uneasiness. Whenever I saw a police officer, I crossed the street. We were plagued by the question, 'How long will this last?'

Before the end of summer, I got busy looking for a school for Juana. I visited a number of them and finally enrolled her in the Escuela Jean Piaget. She had to take catch-up classes to make sure she reached the right grade level, so I took her twice a week without fail. I used to wait for her outside so she wasn't alone for even a moment; adapting to a new country and a new name was very hard for her. In the meantime, Sebastián and Ángeles started looking for a university and taking computer classes.

When we left Colombia, the soap opera *Café, con aroma de mujer* was all the rage, so we decided to use it as a foundation in putting together the story we'd tell people. When they asked, we'd say we were Colombian, originally from Manizales, who'd been coffee growers but had been forced to leave the country because of kidnapping threats and the death of my husband, Emilio Marroquín, in a traffic accident.

We used to get together every night and gradually recreate our history, fleshing it out with more details. In Argentina people ask a lot of questions, and that made us uncomfortable. Colombians are more reserved. That was one of the first culture shocks we experienced: everybody asked why did you come here, where from, who with, for how long, and so on. That frightened us. Given how paranoid we all were, we took it personally. So we had to do a lot of intense preparation to refine our new identities.

But Argentina was also where we had to put our feet on the ground. The era of luxury and unrestrained spending was over, and now we had to take care of the money we'd been allowed to take from Colombia. Like anybody else, we had to find ways to earn money to cover our day-to-day expenses. In addition, at that time Argentina was one of the five most expensive countries in the world because the peso was one-to-one with the dollar. It was like living in Switzerland.

It was in Buenos Aires that Sebastián learned to ride a bus for the first time in his life. Ángeles took care of pretty much everything – grocery shopping, paying the bills, Juana's school supplies – because we no longer had a team of employees. When she moved out to live with Sebastián, I had to do it all by myself, and I admit that I still find it difficult.

Sebastián and Ángeles finally decided what they wanted to study. He enrolled in an industrial design programme at the Instituto ORT, and Ángeles studied marketing at the University of Belgrano. Before they and Juana started classes, I found an apartment to rent, but it was impossible to get approved because we didn't have bank accounts or credit cards to back us up.

Luckily we met Ingrid, an Argentine woman who rented us a very small apartment for a couple of months and then helped us sign with a real estate agent. And so in March 1995 we rented an apartment near the intersection of 11 de Septiembre and Juramento, in Belgrano, where we lived for two years. It had two rooms and a study into which we crammed two beds and a desk, a black sofa, and some armchairs that folded out into beds. We used a kitchen table as a dining room; it was the only piece of furniture the owners had left us. We opted to leave everything just as we found it, remembering how, back when we were living in safehouses, every time we'd started decorating, we'd had to flee.

The only things we bought were three bicycles, which lasted only two months because a neighbour stole them from the parking area. Not wanting to draw attention to ourselves, we didn't say anything, much less report him to the police.

Adjusting to Argentina included one incident that falls somewhere between comedy and drama. One day I got on a bus, and when we were halfway between Belgrano and Santa Fe, the driver made a stop and passengers started getting on and off. Just then I heard a noise that sounded like a bomb or a machine gun, and all I could do was squeeze my eyes shut tight. I thought I was dead. I waited a long time, and eventually the driver came up and asked me what stop I was going to, thinking I'd fallen asleep. I looked around and couldn't figure out why I wasn't wounded. I got off at Avenida Juramento, a block from where I was living, and was sobbing by the time I got home. Only when I told my children what had happened did I realise that the noise I'd heard had been produced by trains rumbling on a viaduct over the street, which is common in Buenos Aires.

Juana had a really hard time adjusting to our new life. She came home from school several times asking why she couldn't be named Manuela like she used to. Though I tried to explain it was because of the threat of kidnapping, it was very hard for a ten-year-old to understand. Sometimes she cried all afternoon and got very depressed, so at school they recommended that I send her to music therapy classes. I did, and they worked. Thanks to her singing voice, she was able to participate in a number of recitals and concerts for children, which restored a bit of her happiness and enabled her to make a few friends and enjoy a somewhat normal life for a while.

Nevertheless, she once came home very frightened because one of her classmates had read in the paper that their school had received bomb threats because it was a Jewish institution. At around that time, Ángeles picked her up from school one afternoon and the teacher told her that during an evacuation drill Juana had become really upset, perhaps because she wasn't used to things like that; but when they left the school, Juana asked Ángeles if the threats were because of her.

Despite our efforts to find a place in this world, things weren't going very well. In our tiny apartment, there was constant tension in the air and we fought a lot. The pressure got so bad that one day Sebastián announced that we needed to leave our 'acute Escobaritis' behind and focus instead on the new life that lay before us.

For that reason, I decided we should start seeing a psychologist, though it would be very odd as we would only be able to talk about the fictitious life story we had invented, an approach that Sebastián questioned several times. But I didn't see it that way. Between the lines, there were things in my life that I could work on trying to heal, like my grief over losing Pablo. We finally took the plunge, though first we made sure our story was coherent. An hour before the appointment we went to a cafe to review the details: we were from Manizales, my husband had died in an accident, etc., etc. Sebastián entered the psychologist's office reluctantly and scowled the whole time, looking like he wanted to take off running. But it served some purpose in the end.

THAT FIRST YEAR IN BUENOS AIRES, WE HAD A REALLY hard time adjusting. We didn't have a car, we led a fairly simple life and we missed Colombian food desperately, among other things. We used to search every produce shop looking for tropical fruits and some vegetables, but we couldn't find them anywhere. One day I walked into a Jumbo supermarket and got so excited when I saw plantains that I bought six boxes. It had been more than a year since I'd seen one. I fried so many slices for freezing that they didn't fit and I had to make friends with the building concierge so I could ask him to store some of them in his freezer.

At the beginning of 1996, my mother and Isabel, one of my sisters, came to visit. As a precaution, they travelled to another country first and bought tickets to Buenos Aires there. For a long time, my relatives didn't take direct flights from Colombia to make sure they weren't followed, and they sometimes had as many as three layovers in different places before landing in Argentina.

Whenever they visited, the name issue was a huge mess because we had to change their last names too. The time that Isabel came, one of my friends, perplexed, asked why my mother had given us both the same name. Of course, we hadn't noticed the problem until that moment and had to make up a story and an additional name for her.

During one of my mother's stays, there was one funny incident that illustrates how hard it was to adapt to another culture. One Saturday night a few friends invited me out to a club, and my mother agreed that she and Isabel would look after my children. In Buenos Aires it's common to start the night at midnight and go to several hotspots. We were in a popular club when an employee brought hot chocolate and pastries to the table. Surprised, I asked why, and the response left me speechless: 'The sun's coming up, María Isabel.'

I couldn't believe it. I went out into the street and, indeed, the sun was already shining. Knowing my mother, I immediately thought how furious she'd be, since in her view a widow should never stay out all night. I raced home, but the more I hurried, the higher the sun rose, the brighter it shone. It was nine o'clock when I arrived home. I took off my shoes and climbed the stairs very slowly, but she was waiting for me on the second floor. I tried to explain, but she didn't let me say anything.

'I don't want to hear a word. You're shameless!' she shouted, and closed her bedroom door.

I may have been thirty-five years old, but I was still afraid of my mother. Luckily, half an hour later Dr Hebe San Martín arrived with a colleague for a family therapy session I'd set up. Having heard what had happened, they focussed the conversation on the lack of values and respect for one's children. They explained to my mother that in Argentine culture it was normal for people young and old to come home at midday after being out having fun all night. Just in time, too, because my mother was so furious that she was considering going back to Colombia that very day.

In our apartment on 11 de Septiembre and Juramento, I also had one of the biggest scares in my life when the intercom buzzed one day and a federal police officer asked for Sebastián.

'I'll be right down,' I replied, very frightened, and immediately told my son to hide in the parking area while I found out what was going on.

I went down in the lift, overwhelmed with panic, and all I could think was that we'd been found out.

'Good afternoon, sir,' I said to the officer.

The policeman saw that I was pale and my voice shaky, but he clearly didn't know anything because he simply explained that he'd come to collect on a bill that Sebastián and a friend had failed to pay at the Federal Shooting Club, where they'd gone for target practice. The policeman left the bill and I assured him I'd settle the debt as soon as possible. I felt my heart start beating again. After the scare was over, I told Sebastián he needed to be careful because any thoughtless act could expose us and ruin what we were trying to build. It was the first time he'd gone to the club, and he did it to satisfy a friend who'd invited him several times, but we'd agreed it would be the first and last time because it wasn't good for people to see him handling weapons, even if it was just for sport.

We moved religiously every two years to change neighbours, relationships, and everything else to avoid being found out. To correspond with our family, we created a mail route that went first to the United States, then to Canada and from there to Colombia. In each place people would remove the stamps and apply new ones to erase our trail. In addition, we rarely called, and always from payphones. We were trying to disappear from the world, and every step we took sought to protect our big secret.

One of the things we had to be most careful about was keeping our temporary status in Argentina up to date, so every three months we would cross the border into Uruguay and re-enter with a new tourist visa. But those trips were risky too, so we decided it would be better to start the immigration process and get residence permits. My therapist recommended the lawyer Tomás Lichtmann. But we discovered that the immigration process was going to be very complicated for us because the documents we were requesting from Colombia would be useless if they didn't have our new identities. We were able to process some of them with the authorisation of the Colombian attorney general's office, while for others, like my children's school grades, we had to send a copy of the public record of the identity change to request that they be discreetly amended. In addition, every time we stood in line to take a document to a civil office, we were always terrified somebody might recognise us or that when we gave our fingerprints a red alert would go off in the Interpol databases. Even so, we took the risk. We were determined to request residency and put down roots in Argentina.

That's what we were doing when one day my mother called from Medellín, sounding desperate; my brother Fernando's drug addiction, which had been a forty-year struggle, was out of control. I'd always felt very guilty about his addiction and the hell it caused him and his family. I'd accompanied him to rehab facilities several times, and I knew the horrors that such people suffered through.

Without hesitating, I told my mother to send Fernando to Argentina to see if we could help him, and I immediately got in touch with the renowned psychiatrist Eduardo Kalina, who'd rescued the football player Diego Maradona from drugs. Dr Kalina told me to bring Fernando in, and that he'd help him get through it.

My brother arrived a few days later and we went to Dr Kalina's office. The doctor ordered a series of tests to prepare for checking him in to the clinic. But it all went south when Fernando found out he was going to be hospitalised. Hearing us discuss that option, he fell apart and flew into a rage, ranting wildly. Out of his head, he tried to talk to the doctor, and thoughtlessly revealed that his sister was the widow of Pablo Escobar.

Immediately, Dr Kalina called me in and told me what my brother had said. The only reason I didn't collapse to the floor in a faint was because I was already sitting. I knew the situation was very dangerous. Fortunately, the doctor was compassionate and listened to my explanation: 'Doctor, my brother tells everybody that we're related to the president, we're involved with the guerrillas, we're members of the wealthiest family in Colombia ... It's the drugs, and we don't know what else to do.'

Dr Kalina watched me weep piteously, and when I paused he said, 'Don't worry, ma'am. If you're not actually Escobar's widow, don't worry about it, let him talk.'

I left the clinic, called Colombia, and, in desperation, told them to come and get Fernando because he might reveal our identities. Three days later, one of my sisters and her husband arrived and took him to Havana, Cuba. Things didn't work out there either, so he ended up returning to Medellín.

With that danger past, a little while later somebody recommended a psychologist and trainer who ran an institute called Life School on Avenida Independencia. I'd always liked psychology, so I enrolled in a coaching programme. At first it wasn't easy because I had to reflect on a life that I couldn't make public and could only talk in front of the other participants using invented facts. It was very taxing. People noticed that I spoke very little and very quietly, and mentioned it to me. They said I seemed absent from the world, and they were right. Out of fear, I avoided engaging with my emotions, even though I was thirty-five years old. My terror that somebody might recognise us was real, but despite all that I completed a certificate in leadership and ontological coaching.

As the months passed, I was also forced to find work and earn an income so we could live more comfortably. My lawyer at the time, Tomás Lichtmann, advised me to apply for residency as an immigrant with capital. For that, I needed to invest US$100,000 and develop a project that would create jobs for Argentine citizens. It was then that Lichtmann introduced me to the accountant, who also owned a small real estate company, to take care of the accounting that I needed, by law, as part of the paperwork for seeking residency.

The accountant started to take us around, and through his real estate company I looked for a place on the outskirts of the city. I sensed that my family needed a place of our own to be far from the noise of the big city and find a bit of peace in nature. I kept telling them, 'Invest in health, invest in health,' while they stared at me with no idea what I was talking about. And so, I bought a house at the Las Praderas de Luján country club, where we spent a couple of summers and every weekend for two years. Sebastián used to ask me what the hell I was thinking buying a house outside the city when I didn't even have a car to get there, but I didn't care. At first we would rent one for the weekends, and then we bought a small Mazda 121 into which we'd cram four dogs and more people than the law allowed.

Buying the house wasn't free of deception, a lamentably all-too-common practice to which we have fallen victim many times in Argentina. I'd arranged with its previous owners that they'd sell the house furnished, and we came to an agreement and marked a few objects that they'd take with them, but the rest of the furniture was to stay, including a black Steinway & Sons grand piano. But the couple replaced it with a Chinese-made piece of junk that didn't even look like the original piece included in the price. However much I complained, the owner was so disrespectful, rude and nasty that once the sale was finalised, I decided to focus on enjoying my family in the new space.

With his generous manner and his commitment to helping a foreign family, the accountant gradually won our trust and friendship and we started consulting him at every step we took. We used to invite him to our home with his wife, daughter and two employees, and he soon became part of our inner circle. Juana in particular became very fond of him, which later, when the problems started,

became a huge mess because he would manipulate her easily, knowing that she was young and naive.

Because the immigration office was demanding that I
present an investment plan for Argentina, I started looking
at business options with the accountant and decided to
buy a lot that didn't appear to have a future because it was
in an area full of homeless people, cardboard-pickers and
truckers that nobody wanted to go to. I always felt I had a
knack for real estate, and I could already tell that in a few
years the supply of lots in nearby Puerto Madero was going
to dry up because of the boom in luxury condos, restaurants and corporate offices that was making the area the
most desirable place to live in the city near the River
Plate. I knew it was the best place to buy, and over time I
was proven right. I bought the smallest lot on the
block, just 2,400 square feet, on the corner of Avenida Ingeniero Huergo and Calle Estados Unidos. I paid around
US$200,000, and later found out that the accountant had
jacked up the price so he could take an extra cut in addition
to his sales commission.

The money we had was enough to buy the property, but
not to develop the project the immigration office was calling
for, so we put it on the back burner until 1998, when we
decided to sell. It was at that point that we started negotiating
with the Shell Corporation, which sent a letter of intent
expressing interest in purchasing it for US$500,000. But just
as things were coming together, advertising started to appear
around the city for a documentary on the life of Pablo Escobar
to be broadcast on the People + Arts channel. We panicked,
afraid that our faces would appear in the TV special.

Amid that commotion, the accountant arranged for us to meet up one night at the restaurant Clo Clo, on the river-front, with the pretext that he wanted to talk to me. To my surprise, during dinner he raised his voice and said aggres-sively that we'd tricked him and that he knew who we were; he added that he'd found out when he spotted an interview we'd done years earlier at the Hotel Tequendama in Bogotá that was published in an Argentine magazine.

At his words, I went cold and excused myself to the bathroom. I called Sebastián and said we didn't have a choice, I would bring the accountant to the apartment. Once there, my son told him our entire story, in thorough detail. The accountant became very emotional, cried along with me, and assured us that he'd help us no matter what.

A few days before the documentary about Pablo was broadcast, we decided to close up the apartment and move our furniture into storage, concerned that anything could happen. We told the few friends we had that I was going on a trip with my mother – who was visiting at the time – my two children, the dogs and the family luggage, and that we would be staying on the coast till the end of summer. Once again Ángeles had to take care of the move all by herself because we felt we needed to be far away from the city for safety reasons. She would arrive once everything was settled.

During those hours of uncertainty, before we left for the coast, I made one of the worst mistakes of my life: I gave the accountant power of attorney and signed blank docu-ments so that, through his real estate company, he could move forward with selling the lot and the house in Luján. I had no idea at the time that his intentions weren't noble and that he was actually working on a strategy that would leave him with everything.

On the coast, we rented a small house in Cariló, 225 miles from Buenos Aires, a little way back from the beach, and went to spend New Year's Eve there to make sure our acquaintances didn't associate us with Pablo's story. Luckily, my mother came with us. For my children it was a gift to be able to spend time with her; she had a great sense of humour and liked playing cards, and during that short period we had a lot of fun, cooking, taking walks in the woods, playing with the dogs and waiting to see if anything was going to happen. The little house didn't have cable TV, so we didn't know what had happened with the documentary, but we did watch the news in case they said anything.

But those idle days were cut short by an unexpected visit from the accountant, who came to talk to Sebastián and me. It was then that his corrupt intentions were revealed, as he demanded a monthly payment of US$20,000 to 'take care' of us and of himself, given the danger he could be putting himself in by working with a family like ours.

'You know I don't have access to that kind of money. What are you thinking? Plus, there's no need for you to take care of me – I changed my identity so I'd be safe,' I replied.

The accountant said not to worry, we'd talk about it later, and left. He was speculating that our new identities were fake, unaware that the legal procedure through which we'd acquired them was our only protection. But time passed and he was nowhere to be found – he didn't answer the phone and was impossible to track down. I was immensely worried. Our money was in his hands, so I decided to go in person to look for him at his office. There, his partners and accomplices said he'd had a nervous breakdown and was in the hospital, in no shape to see anybody. Dejected and about to leave, I had the bright idea of asking if I could use the office phone and called the accountant's mobile phone. He answered. It was all a lie.

'Weren't you supposed to be in intensive care?'

'María Isabel, please understand, I'm just taking precautions until things are straightened out. Talk to Lichtmann, the lawyer.'

'Give me my things, and I don't want to see you again; you've only been doing our accounting for a few years, so I have nothing to fear.'

Even so, I got in touch with Lichtmann, but he was absolutely unwilling to help me, given who we were. I went to his office, I cried, I begged for him not to leave me alone, since I had two teenage children and a little girl to take care of, but he said he wanted nothing to do with us, even though he'd recommended the accountant in the first place, introducing him as a good guy.

Despite the tense situation, on 25 May 1999, I decided to throw a party to celebrate Juana's fifteenth birthday. Sebastián, my mother and my siblings objected. They couldn't believe I was going to organise a gala while the accountant was issuing his threats. I thought that after so many years of sorrow and worry, it could be a good idea. So with a few friends and some family members who came from

Colombia, we celebrated my daughter's birthday at the Círculo Italiano social club. Resigned, Sebastián had spent
hours and hours learning to dance the waltz, and it was
very moving to see him dancing with his sister. Juana also
sang during the party. For a few hours, the approaching
storm died down a little.

I remember that Juana's music teacher was good
friends with the heads of the symphony orchestra at the
Teatro Colón, Buenos Aires's most prestigious theatre
and, thanks to her, I was able to get them to play the waltz
at a very reasonable price. The director of the group told
me that nobody in the city had ever hired them to play
that classic, and since he didn't have any daughters, he'd
never organised a quinceañera and given anyone that
pleasure.

In the middle of the celebration, I had another huge
scare when at midnight a policeman appeared at the door
of the Círculo Italiano. An aunt who'd come from Colombia came up and whispered for me to come because a police
officer needed me. As I walked to the door, my heart was
pounding in my chest.

'Good evening, ma'am. I'm here to advise you that some
of the cars here are parked illegally.'

That was all. The celebration ended peacefully, but seeing Juana growing up and knowing that at her age I was
already married to Pablo was an emotional shock. How
could I, as just a girl, have had a relationship with a man
who was so much older? I used to stare at Juana and was
startled by her innocence, her way of talking, of acting. All
of a sudden, I understood my mother's objections, my

rebellion and the pain my parents had felt upon seeing me in that relationship so young.

THINGS WITH THE ACCOUNTANT GREW WORSE. FOR MUCH of 1999 I tried to negotiate with him, with the lawyers acting as intermediaries, but he ended up changing any agreement we reached. Every day he wanted more and more. In the end, it was all for naught. Though I'd done everything I could to protect the new life we'd built so carefully and prevent our true identities from being revealed, the accountant made things so difficult that one night I talked to Sebastián and Ángeles and told them, 'We've got two options: leave the country or report the accountant. What do you think?'

'Mum, are you prepared to go to prison?' my son asked.

'Yes, Sebas, because we haven't done anything illegal. We're not going to go to prison for that.'

The next day I went to see my lawyer and asked him to accompany me to the courthouse. I took the plunge, and in October 1999, at courthouse 65 in Buenos Aires, I filed suit against the accountant and his partners. In discussing the suit with a judge, I revealed to her that I was Pablo Escobar's widow, that the Colombian government had changed our identities, that for the past eleven months I'd been receiving threats from the aforementioned parties, and that they'd stolen several properties from me.

I also recounted how, from the moment he'd learned who we were, the accountant had worked to cut off my relationships with the people around us. The first thing he did was talk to the mothers of Juana's schoolmates and, after telling them my story, warn them that I was dangerous and they should stay away from me. Then he visited the notary, Susana Malanga, and terrorised her so aggressively that she fled. I also said that in a moment of desperation I'd bought a telephone that could record calls so I could prove that the accountant was using all kinds of ruses to frighten me, including claiming that his primary clients were drug traffickers who were willing to testify against me. I stored recordings of all the crazy things he said to me in sealed envelopes and then took them to two notaries in Buenos Aires to make an official record of what was happening. In response, the accountant hired a lawyer who was infamous in Argentina, and he threatened several times to reveal our identities if we continued to demand what was ours.

While all this was going on between us and the accountant, the authorities got wind of it. According to the justification given in the case file, in early October 1999, Roberto Ontiveros – a mid-ranking police officer – claimed he'd recognised me by chance, at a traffic light at the intersection of Cabildo and Juana Azurduy, from photos he'd seen twenty years earlier at the Federal Police's Superintendency of Dangerous Drugs that identified me as Victoria Eugenia Henao, the wife of Pablo Escobar. The investigation says that Ontiveros wrote down the license plate of the vehicle I was driving and then looked up who it belonged to: the Uruguayan company Inversora Galestar S.A., which I own, which led him to my name, María Isabel Santos Caballero. He therefore suspected that I'd changed my identity illegally. From there, Ontiveros, who happened to be near my apartment, was able to confirm that a Colombian woman lived there with her daughter and a young couple.

Having gathered this information, Ontiveros reported back to Jorge 'El Fino' Palacios, his boss, the head of the Argentine Federal Police's Department of the Antiterrorist Investigation Unit, who in turn notified federal judge Gabriel Cavallo of the news. The judge then started reviewing the legal basis for the investigation, which sought to pursue 'all investigative processes that tend to corroborate the existence or nonexistence of illegal activities, especially in terms of money laundering or other activity laid out in the Narcotics Act'.

The case file indicates that Cavallo decided to arrest Sebastián and me on Monday, 15 November 1999, when he learned that a TV programme was planning to reveal that night that Pablo Escobar's widow was living in Buenos Aires. The operation was carried out by Palacios along with fifteen other officers.

So Sebastián and I ended up in custody. For the first two weeks, they took us to several jails around the city, and it was clear they didn't know what to do with us. One night they left us in the Palace of Justice, a dirty old building that was full of rodents. They didn't allow us to bathe. I begged the judge to let somebody bring us clothing and food, and he agreed. On another night they put me in a huge cell by myself, and at two o'clock in the morning I was able to bathe with ice-cold water, which restored my spirits considerably.

At about four o'clock in the morning, several women began to arrive, each one more frightening than the last. In the midst of the rage and insults they were shouting at the guards, they started relaying their reasons for being there: *I killed my husband because he was with another woman, I stole from so-and-so, I stabbed what's-his-name … The stor-*ies got worse and worse. I listened in horror and thought, 'My God, what story am I going to tell when it's my turn?' Fortunately, the guards appeared and took me to a hearing at the federal courthouse on Calle Comodoro Py.

The cells were smaller there, with floor-to-ceiling iron bars and a concrete slab that served as a bed, though it was impossible to stretch out because they were only about four feet long. We would sit there all day, waiting to be taken to testify. On several days they offered me *mate*, a tea that is common in Argentina, but I refused it. In the afternoons they gave us hamburgers, but the meat looked rotten and purple. It was horrible. I tried to only drink water, but eventually out of hunger I accepted some *mate* and bread. Sebastian didn't eat a bite for four days because he was afraid he might be poisoned. When he couldn't stand it anymore, he asked for water, which the guards served him in an ashtray. Every interaction involved shouting, and every time we moved to a new cell they wanted us to sign documents with our old names, which we always refused to do; these endless, awful arguments made us feel like ani-mals every time.

It was a desperate situation. I pleaded with the judge not to send us to the regular prison because our lives might be in danger. I noted that if anything happened to us there, he would be the one to blame, and that our lawyers would make sure to the tell the media as much. I was so persistent that the judge agreed to send us to the Superintendency of Dangerous Drugs on Avenida Belgrano, near the Congress building in Buenos Aires.

For the first three months, I wasn't allowed to leave my six-by-five cell, which had a two-foot-wide cold concrete bench and a latrine. The crumbling walls were marked with words written by clearly desperate people. During my captivity, the lights were on all the time to keep an eye on my movements and probably to undermine my mental state – who can rest with an intense white light glaring on them?

The atmosphere was tense and depressing. At first I was treated really badly and insulted. My son experienced the exact same thing; I was able see him and talk to him through a small rectangle in the door that the guards used to check on prisoners during their rounds. It was as if my cell contained Pablo Escobar himself, not me. Those first months, many police officers and city officials came through to 'look at us'. Pablo Escobar's widow behind bars was a can't-miss spectacle. When they observed me, I felt like a zoo monkey in its cage.

Growing increasingly restless in confinement, I proposed to the guards that they let me clean the cells that were left empty when inmates were transferred to other prisons. Luckily, they agreed. So at about eleven o'clock in the morning I would come out of my cell, go to a bathroom to get buckets of water and then scrub each cell with soap. I sometimes made as many as fifty trips, but I didn't care because the work kept me busy for three hours. I was grateful not to be locked up. Plus, when I finished they'd let me take a shower, which I tried to drag out for as long as possible.

The intense work allowed me to get to know the guards, who gradually realised I wasn't crazy or a criminal and started to see me as a human being. When Sebastián was incarcerated along with me, I used to go up to the window of his cell and urge him to help me with my work so he wouldn't be locked up, but he said no, he was fine reading.

'Mum, you're the one who offered. I'm not going to clean this place when we've been put here unjustly.'

While I was trying to survive my difficult circumstances in prison, things outside were very, very complicated. The Argentine press beat upon us mercilessly. The media published all kinds of slander and false news stories, and nobody in my family was prepared for it.

The person who was most deeply affected was Juana, who was being looked after by Ángeles and my mother; it was through a press report that she learned that her 'millionaire coffee-growing family' was actually the family of a drug lord. Naturally, we'd never told her what her father had done. Within days, her schoolmates started bullying her and the parents demanded she be kicked out or they'd pull their children from the school. Juana's teachers even refused to let her in their classes because she was Pablo Escobar's daughter. She was expelled from the school without compassion. My daughter went into an emotional crisis. She didn't understand why the adults were rejecting her. Juana didn't know her own story – she'd been in hiding for years at her parents' request, but she'd never asked why she had to hide. She just obeyed. She was very young when Pablo set our tragedy in motion. The adults' cruelty caused her a great deal of emotional distress.

Juana went into a severe depression, and things became so dire that the psychologist asked the judge to let me receive calls from her. After that, we talked as many as five times a day. Sobbing, she would berate me, telling me how stupid I was and asking how I could have married a man like that, why I'd lied to her for so many years. I didn't know what to do. All my life I'd tried to protect her and keep her from finding out the truth, and now I realised what a terrible mistake I'd made. To be honest, I'd never been brave enough to explain to her the terrible truth of our life in Colombia.

Our family situation teetered on the edge of crisis. Ángeles had to deal with Juana and my mother until two of my sisters came from Colombia to help out. My mother suffered from diabetes and had had several strokes, and the stress of our daily lives didn't help. Because of the media pressure, Ángeles lost her college friends. People ran away from us.

Even the four dogs – French poodles that we'd brought from Colombia so Juana wouldn't get so depressed – were dying of sadness. On the vet's recommendation, I slept in T-shirts and then sent them home so the dogs could smell my scent.

As the days passed, the judicial process continued. Sebastián and I submitted to questioning for many hours, explaining one by one the documents that the police had seized on the day of our arrest; most of them were pamphlets for buildings I'd visited so I wouldn't lose contact with the architecture and interior design world, but the judge suspected I owned the properties, subpoenaing all the builders and architects named on the fliers I'd been given on the street.

Every time Judge Cavallo called me in to make a statement, he'd use my old name, Victoria Eugenia, making me feel as if I were a liar and had a fake name. He never called me María Isabel. He used to say that if I told him about my bank accounts in Colombia and other countries, he'd release me. I felt more and more helpless as I listened to his requests. I couldn't give him that information because it didn't exist. He said that if I reported any corruption, he would first release my son and then me.

The days dragged on, as did the lawsuit. My sister Isabel came to see me, but she couldn't bear being in the cell and we had to move to a tiny room set up for receiving visitors. I'll never forget her horrified face when she entered. My mother also visited me a few times before she returned to Colombia. One day she was with me and I recorded a cassette so she could take it to Juana's psychiatrist, but I talked for more than an hour, and when she left the guards confiscated it because they thought the recording contained information that could be used against me. To top it all off, one of my lawyers thoughtlessly commented that my sisters might be arrested. As a result, one of them fled to Colombia and took my mother with her.

A month and a half after our arrest, we finally got some good news: on 29 December 1999, Sebastián was released from jail. It was more than fair; he never should have been there in the first place. He never worked with the accountant in any fashion. It was very hard for him to leave me alone in that place. We cried together for a long time. I hugged him and told him to be brave, saying that everything was going to be OK. I added that the best gift he could give me would be to bring me his student ID from starting an architecture degree at the University of Palermo. He asked how he could possibly study with all the problems we had. But one day he made me immensely proud by showing up with his student ID in hand.

I talked to Ángeles, who has been like a daughter to me, about how important it would be for her to enroll in the coaching programme to learn to muster strength in difficult moments like the ones we experienced, and also to expand her circle of friends. She offered the same objections as Sebastián, but in the end she agreed.

The skills I had acquired in the coaching programme also allowed me to establish more amicable relationships with the guards. I used to ask them about their lives and listen attentively, so at a certain point I shifted in their eyes from criminal to counselling therapist. Thanks to that closeness, I was able to move down to the second floor, to a larger cell that had a decent bathroom, a small utility sink and a kitchenette; in addition, I could put my mattress on the floor. Things became more bearable.

Because of my confinement and the challenging emotional circumstances, I was eating at an astonishing rate. I was always asking Ángeles to bring me more food. Five months in, I weighed more than seventeen stone. Worried,

Ángeles told me one day that if I didn't stop eating, the next clothing she'd bring would be sheets to wrap me in because I wouldn't fit into anything else. I started to acknowledge the serious harm I was doing to my health, and luckily a prisoner in the cell across from mine gave me a recipe for a soup that boosted weight loss. Between that soup, drinking *mate* and doing yoga every morning and night when they let me watch TV, I was able to lose almost half of the weight I'd gained.

Since the light in the cell was always on, I read and wrote a lot. And I did whatever I could not to be locked in. I volunteered to paint the cells, bars and all, wash the curtains and sometimes even cook meals for the guards. At night, when they finished doing the rounds to make sure everybody was accounted for, they would invite the commissioner and sub-commissioner to eat. I would help the female guards with their make-up when they had a special event after work. After a while, my cell ended up looking like a therapist's office. At the end of the work day, agents from the Superintendency of Dangerous Drugs, the Argentine equivalent of the DEA, would come to ask me all sorts of questions.

In the meantime, the tumultuous judicial case against me was progressing very slowly. The investigating prosecutor Eduardo Freiler learned via a phone call from his wife that he'd been named prosecutor on the case; the Argentine attorney general's office contacted its Colombian counterpart requesting all information regarding our identities. The response arrived quickly and was conclusive: the name change had been legal and had been carried out so that we could leave the country. And the media claimed that the governments of the two countries had made an agreement so that we could enter Argentina in secret. That wasn't true, of course.

The winds of truth started blowing in our favour. Freiler studied the confiscated documents and our statements and notified Judge Cavallo that he had not found sufficient evidence to move the prosecution forward and requested that it be dismissed. Under pressure, Cavallo asked the federal court to review the case to see if he could continue the investigation and, if so, replace Freiler.

And so, in record time, my case passed through the hands of seven prosecutors. The prosecutor Carlos Cearras advanced the case to an oral hearing, but with serious reservations, which he laid out in writing, about the major inconsistencies and the lack of inculpatory evidence. For that reason, he altered the charge against me, no longer considering me the head of an illegal association. As a result, on Friday, 5 April 2001, Cavallo ordered my release.

The events that followed were immensely beneficial to us. The renowned prosecutor Jorge Aguilar not only endorsed our innocence before the three judges of Federal Oral Tribunal 6, but he asserted that we had been the victims of illegitimate deprivation of liberty, abuse of power and prevarication. He argued that our civil rights had been trampled.

One of my lawyers, Ezequiel Klainer, called Sebastián to tell him the good news, just as my son was on his way to the university to withdraw from his classes and devote himself entirely to my case. But the lawyer explained that my bail had been set at US$200,000, and if we couldn't produce it, I'd be stuck in prison. To that, my son replied gratefully that at least I'd been granted release and that he'd look into how to come up with the money.

Thrilled about the news but worried about the bail money, Sebastián called the prison several times, but he wasn't able to get in touch with me because the line was always busy.

The day went by as usual until a guard suddenly informed me that I had a call from Medellín. It was Astado, who wanted to congratulate me on my release. Surprised, I asked, 'What release, Alfredo? Nobody's said anything to me.'

Everything was up in the air, but since I didn't know anything officially and the press didn't seem to have found out, for the time being I distracted myself with two colleagues from my coaching programme who'd come to study with me.

In the meantime, the hours passed and we still didn't have the bail money. But according to what Sebastián told me afterwards, on the courthouse steps he providentially ran into Ricardo Solomonoff, another of my lawyers, who'd just returned from southern Argentina to Buenos Aires.

My son told him it had been impossible to come up with the bail money, but Solomonoff told him not to worry, that he'd loan us the money.

'Sir, please know that if you lend me the money, I have no way to guarantee that I can pay it back, and I would hate to let you down. This is about my mother's freedom, and anybody would accept the offer without a second thought,' he said, aware of our economic reality.

'You mother's getting out today, Sebastián; otherwise, someone will come up with another crime on Monday to keep her locked up. Wait here and we'll go get the money together,' Solomonoff replied without a moment's hesitation.

But my lawyer was initially told that he couldn't pay the money that day because it was Friday and it couldn't be left in the office. Furious, Solomonoff wrote a handwritten letter demanding that the court instruct the National Bank of Argentina to receive the money, or else he'd sue for illegitimate deprivation of liberty. The court agreed and requested that the bank's primary offices open outside of regular hours in order to deposit the cash in a security box once it had been counted.

At ten o'clock that night, the lawyer and my son arrived at the Superintendency of Dangerous Drugs, where I was being held. They looked exhausted. I couldn't believe it. Sebastián hugged me and we wept together, overwhelmed by powerful emotions. Then he told me to get dressed and pack my things because we were leaving. I prayed. I gave thanks to God.

I then had the chance to tell Solomonoff that a representative had come to my cell to quiz me about where the bail money had come from. The lawyer flew into a rage, unable to believe the injustices I'd been subjected to, even as I was on the verge of being released.

The paperwork took more than two hours. At last I signed the form that gave me my liberty. I stepped out of my cell, looked at it for the last time, closed the door, replaced the padlock, and left. Yet another confinement was now behind me; though it had been very different from the one I'd experienced at Pablo's side, it was perhaps the most painful one I ever faced.

I remained on conditional release until 14 November 2005, when the case was dismissed, and on 31 August 2006, the National Chamber of Criminal Appeals in Cassation confirmed the ruling. And it had all happened because somebody had tried to trade our anonymity for money. I had endured the most agonising eighteen months of my life. I was punished without ever being convicted of a crime and deprived of my liberty just for being Pablo Escobar's widow.

Most ironic of all, nobody seemed to care about the psychological assault I felt I had suffered at the hands of four men: a lawyer, an accountant and two employees. For ten months I experienced intimidations because I was obviously extremely vulnerable, with a little girl and two young people to care for. On top of that, out of foolishness and naivety, I'd signed the blank documents that allowed them to take everything from me. They extorted me, threatened to kill me, gave me a matter of days to leave the country and promised to plant cocaine in my cars so that we'd be arrested ...

The accountant ended up in prison too, accused of money laundering. They sent him to the Devoto Prison, where the other inmates nearly lynched him for having dared to steal from the widow of Pablo Escobar. He had to be transferred to the building where Sebastián and I were, but one floor up. It was very unpleasant to know he was in the same place as us.

One day I had to go upstairs, and I saw he had bloodshot eyes because he smoked a lot, and his face reflected his distress about the situation. I had no wish to speak to him. I was very hurt and felt a lot of resentment; I still didn't understand how he could have gone so far. What I am sure of, though, is that he never dreamed he'd go to prison. He thought that because he'd turned in the widow of Pablo Escobar and her millions of dollars, nobody would touch him. When my supposed fortune failed to materialise, he was arrested himself.

The accountant used the same strategy I did to avoid being shut in all day and volunteered to paint the walls. Fortunately we never crossed paths or said anything to each other. He ended up being in prison for almost two years and got out two months after I did. A while back I saw him on my way out of a supermarket, and though he called to me, I turned my back on him and kept walking.

As for what happened with the supposed fraud and scam, the Argentine government returned two properties that the accountant and his partners had taken from us.

The night I was released, I returned to the apartment on Calle Jaramillo. I was under the same roof as my children and my four dogs once more. I hugged Juana for a long time. Sebastián was so worn out from everything he'd had to deal with day after day that he could barely stand. Several friends came by the house to say hello. I received a million calls from Colombia. That night I decided not to go to bed because I hadn't seen the sunrise in nearly two years, so I patiently waited for the sun to come up. As day broke, I took photos of the landscape and thanked God for being free again. Still, it felt very strange to be home and to be able to sleep with the lights off.

Chapter 11

Pablo's Ghost Continues to Haunt Us

'María Isabel, go on the Internet, read the article in *El Tiempo*, and we'll talk later.'

An icy chill ran through my body when I heard my editor's serious tone; it was clear that it wasn't good news. It was noon on 22 October 2017.

I went to the Colombian newspaper's website and saw an upsetting headline: 'The "narcotransfers" ensnaring Escobar's widow and "Chicho" Serna. Argentine millionaire accuses soccer player and capo's heirs of receiving money from José Piedrahíta.' The article was illustrated by a photograph of my son, Sebastián, and me.

I've never objected to making public the truth about Pablo's life and that of his family. That's why I decided to delve into my own story to recount it in this book; that's why I waited a quarter of a century before I dared say a word about my husband's responsibilities and those of his family. But my total silence has also enabled many of the world's media outlets to write lies about me and my family.

The tone of the article written by *El Tiempo*'s investigative unit was all too familiar; it wasn't the first time the press had drawn conclusions that strayed far from the truth.

The article claimed that the Argentine businessman and lawyer Mateo Corvo Dolcet, who was in police custody, had confessed to paying us a hefty sum of money for introducing him to José Bayron Piedrahíta, a prominent Colombian cattle rancher and businessman who'd been arrested on 29 September 2017, at the request of a US court, for allegedly bribing a federal agent to expunge his criminal record. The publication also asserted – citing one of the prosecutors for the new case – that we must have known who Piedrahíta was and where the money had come from. It also claimed that in the next few weeks an Argentine judge would subpoena us for interrogation and that we were sure to end up in prison.

They even trumpeted 'the dossier that took down the Escobars. Audio recordings and documents prove they were part of a money-laundering operation with a powerful capo.' But after Sebastián made a complaint, they corrected the later editions, saying that there were 'zero recordings of the widow: *El Tiempo* found that there are no intercepted calls as originally claimed. In fact, the Escobars' numbers do not appear among the nine mobile phones tapped by the authorities.'

On 14 May 2018, when Sebastián and I were called in for questioning, we decided that our best course of action was to make our statements in writing.

Your Honour, my purpose here is to explain who I am, how I have conducted myself since my arrival in

Buenos Aires twenty-five years ago, and my complete lack of involvement in any criminal activity, whether related to Mateo Corvo Dolcet, José Bayron Piedrahíta Ceballos, or any other person, as I have never participated in any illicit action or omission, here, in Colombia, or in any other place, not even during the few years I lived with the man who was my husband, Pablo Emilio Escobar Gaviria. I also wish to demonstrate the non-existence of any money-laundering activity.

It is regrettable that I am being forced to defend myself by going back to my cruel, bitter, and devastating past, not only because it means reopening badly healed wounds, the trauma of which I have not yet overcome, but also because that connection, being the 'widow of …', has already subjected me to unpleasant experiences with this country's federal courts, during a proceeding in which I was unjustly incarcerated merely for that, for having been married to Pablo Escobar.

This descriptor, Your Honour, has stripped me – as this lawsuit clearly demonstrates – of any other identity beyond that label, to such an extent that even the press release from the judiciary's news agency through the Centre of Judicial Information, which published my summons to this hearing, is titled 'Judge Barral has summoned the widow and son of Pablo Escobar for questioning …'

Even now I awaken in the middle of the night, gripped by fear caused by everything we lived through in Colombia, and that is one of the many reasons I feel such immense gratitude toward Argentina. Living in this country made it possible for us to live again, and has opened doors so I could educate my children to help them grow and become upstanding adults. We have studied and worked here, and I have been honoured by becoming a grandmother. Part of my daily struggle, which has led me to undergo a nearly unbearable re-examination of the worst years of my life, is to make sure, as far as I can, that my grandson is able to be a happy Argentine boy of Colombian extraction and not 'the grandson of ...'

Ever since we settled in Argentina, I have worked here like any other citizen to make ends meet. I never inherited the millions of dollars that the legends about my husband claim. In fact, the Colombian government confiscated nearly 100 per cent of the assets and properties belonging to my husband. Another portion of his assets were relinquished to my husband's enemies.

Had that not been the case, the Colombian government would never have protected me and my children despite the barbaric acts perpetrated by my husband. Your Honour, we, too, were unquestionably victims of his atrocities.

At the urging of the Colombian government, as a symbol of peace, I met with the other cartels to work toward bringing an end to the war begun by Pablo Escobar against the Colombian state and the cartels in a power struggle over his criminal activities. These meetings were essential for Colombia to avoid further bloodshed, and they saved the lives of many Colombians, including lawyers, friends and family members. Your Honour, please be aware that on 13 January 1988, my children and I survived an attack in which my husband's enemies detonated 1,500lbs of dynamite right next to us.

When Pablo Escobar started the war, I heard that it was with the Cali Cartel. When he died, forty cartel heads from around Colombia, whom I'd never heard of, appeared and I was forced to negotiate with them for a year, under government protection but, nevertheless, with our lives constantly at risk. Even as I recount these events, Your Honour, please know that in those cartel meetings, I never, ever met Mr. José Piedrahíta; he never sat at the negotiation table; he never made himself known; nobody ever attempted to collect money in his name; nobody ever mentioned him. I met José Piedrahíta fourteen years after my husband's death, quite separate from any context related to the world of drug trafficking or my husband's activities.

Ever since, I have worked to support my children. Both finished their schooling and became professionals with university degrees. Sebastián, in particular, has devoted his every effort to becoming a successful professional. He is a devoted, caring son and brother and has become our emotional support.

In 1999 I was extorted by an accountant to whom I'd trustingly revealed my previous identity. I received constant threats urging me to leave the country and that he was going to plant cocaine in my cars. History, I am sad to say, is being repeated in this trial.

I didn't see Mateo Corvo Dolcet again for several years. I graduated from an organisational coaching programme and have held various domestic and international roles in that field. I live an austere life. Every day, like any other citizen, I get up and start working. For the past twenty-five years I have been renting the various apartments where I've lived, because I do not have the money to purchase a property. The only asset I had was sold, declared to the government, and the proceedings given to my children so that they could move forward in their lives, as the Argentine Treasury is well aware, thanks to my own sworn declarations.

As I said, it's been thirty-five years since I lived with Pablo Escobar (I lived with him only between the ages of fifteen and twenty-two). He died twenty-five years ago, and I've been living in exile in this country for twenty-four. I've lived for thirty-five years without his physical presence, yet am still haunted by his actions.

I have been investigated by the Colombian government for years, while my husband was alive and also since, by the DEA, the CIA and Interpol, merely for being married to Pablo Escobar. The only conclusion that all of these entities came to was that I am, and have always been, far removed from all criminal conduct. I have no criminal record either in this country or in any other place in the world. I have only been a mother and, now that I am in Argentina, also studied and worked.

Pablo left us only horror and war as an inheritance. Nothing else. The Colombian government seized almost all of the assets we had, and the rest went to my husband's enemies as spoils of war.

I've kept a low profile, living like an ordinary citizen, but never hiding. My son, Juan Sebastián Marroquín, is now forty-one years old. Ten years ago he was strong enough to show his face to the entire world, to ask forgiveness for the horrors his father committed. He has written two books, *Pablo Escobar: My Father* and *Pablo Escobar in fraganti*, now translated into fifteen languages, which relate the complicated twists and turns of his life. He made two documentaries: *Sins of My Father* and *Escobar Exposed*, as a result of which he was invited by the United Nations to celebrate World Peace Day in 2010. For the past five years, he's been giving talks about drug trafficking around the world, showing young people that it's a path they should not follow. He once had 6,200 young people in attendance at a single lecture, showing them the price he's paid for his father's actions; to date, in Mexico alone, more than 100,000 young people have heard his testimony. He has learned that lesson and would never dare follow Pablo's unlawful path. At the end of his book, he thanked his father for having shown him which path not to take.

My daughter Juana, thirty-three, remains paralysed by the past. She has been unable to escape the pain that the war left this family; she has lived side by side with horror since she was in my belly. Regrettably, today she still feels that she has no place in this world despite her upstanding behaviour, because people's biases prevent her from growing and pain follows her like a shadow.

I have conducted my real estate activity through a corporation, Nexo Urbano S.A., which I set up for that purpose because my name was widely known and might harm a project's commercial image by associating it with 'the widow of ...'

When I started out in that business, Sebastián was already fully devoted to his professional career as an architect. The project which we first worked on together was one he'd created for the lot I owned at Avenida Ingeniero Huergo 913/5, at the corner of Calle Estados Unidos in Buenos Aires. This had been restored to my possession by judicial order when the case against me was dismissed; over the years, despite having been purchased for a paltry amount, it had increased in value thanks to the development of the Puerto Madero neighbourhood.

In that context, I think in about 2007, I ran into Mateo Corvo Dolcet at a real estate event. He told me that he'd retired from his career as a lawyer and was now focused on the real estate market, especially on developing his own project in Pilar.* With his characteristic politeness, he asked about Sebastián. I told him about my son's achievements, and we agreed to stay in touch since it seemed we could join forces in our business activities. Mateo told me specifically that he would need investors in order to carry out an ambitious real estate plan in Pilar.

Halfway through the year, I thought it would be fruitful to hold an event in Medellín, my native city, where I could make use of contacts through my family, to find investors interested in taking advantage of Argentina's attractive real estate market. I was looking for financing for Sebastián's project on my lot on Avenida Ingeniero Huergo and was also interested in acting as an intermediary for any other projects.

Sebastián's professional activities as an architect and his outstanding work have led him to forge a close relationship with the renowned architect, then president of Argentina's Central Society of Architects, Daniel Silberfaden. I invited Silberfaden to participate in the Medellín event and to promote his activities and projects, and he accepted.

When I travelled to Colombia, I stayed at my family's home, as I've always done ever since I've been able to return to that country, while Silberfaden stayed in the hotel where we would be holding the

---

* A suburb of Buenos Aires.

event. Once the event began, Silberfaden and I held three meetings a day for three days.

The structure was a daily meeting organised around a breakfast and an afternoon session with an invitation to a tea. Each meeting was attended by about fifteen people. Several of these developers had fifty years of real estate experience. There were a total of six gatherings attended by approximately sixty people, including architects, developers, businessmen, and bankers. As each session finished, people came up to say hello and ask us about specific real estate opportunities in Argentina.

As one of my sisters explained in her testimony, Piedrahíta attended the event with his wife on her invitation. I met him there, where he introduced himself as the manager of Frigorífico Subagauca, a meat-processing company.

His affluence and his substantial business interests were widely known in Colombia, and almost everybody who participated in the event knew him. Piedrahíta congratulated us on the presentation and showed interest, requesting our contact information.

I didn't see him again until late 2007 when he visited Argentina for a cattle show, whereupon he called me and we met for an hour. He let me know that he was interested in investing in the country and requested that I explore options, which he would review in the following months when he returned. He did so in early 2008, with his entire family.

In preparation, I looked for several investment options, among which I included Sebastián and Silberfaden's project for my lot in Puerto Madero, projects by Daniel Silberfaden, the Corvo Dolcet project, and various others.

When Piedrahíta arrived in Buenos Aires at the start of 2008 with his family, I introduced him to my son and we shared a number of family lunches. In the meantime, Piedrahíta demonstrated his economic capabilities and seriousness by making it clear that he wanted to make the investments in his own name and had liquid assets set aside for that purpose, and, indeed, that he had not discarded the idea of settling or having a second residence in Buenos Aires.

Piedrahíta even told us about many of the philanthropic endeavours he was involved in back home, all of them in his own name.

And so I accompanied him to look at a variety of projects. I did so always acting as a real estate agent, a role that, as I said, I carried out through the company Nexo Urbano S.A.

I first showed him the project that Sebastián and Silberfaden had devised for the lot I owned on Avenida Ingeniero Huergo, but unfortunately it was not to Piedrahíta's liking. I then introduced him to a prominent local developer, who unsuccessfully proposed a number of projects that he was helming at the time.

Finally, I put him in touch with Mateo Corvo, with whom I set up a meeting in the hotel district of

Puerto Madero, where Piedrahíta was staying with his family. That was carried out by Sebastián at my request, since when we'd visited Mateo Corvo Dolcet on previous occasions, the two of them had always enjoyed their conversations. In addition, once Mateo and I met again, when I learned about his projects, I encouraged the relationship between Mateo and Sebastián because I thought it would provide my son with career opportunities. In fact, the two of them were in close contact during that period, especially after the introduction of Piedrahíta, because of matters that had nothing to do with him or me and were related only to projects from Sebastián's architecture studio.

Obviously, before the meeting I made it clear to Corvo that connecting him with this or any other potential investor was part of my job as an intermediary and that if it proved a fruitful alliance, my commission would be at the market rate, somewhere between 4 and 5 per cent at the time. Corvo agreed without hesitation. He and Piedrahíta met and quickly became interested in doing business together.

As I mentioned, because of the affluence that Piedrahíta exhibited, his personability, his particular devotion to his family, and the way he put all his expenses on a credit card, I never dreamed he was linked to illicit activity. In fact, he used to talk about how hard he'd worked to build his cattle company, which was clearly successful. He decided to invest in the project in Pilar. I knew absolutely nothing about the details of that investment, which were handled by Corvo Dolcet and Piedrahíta.

Corvo explained that it would be a gradual investment and that as Piedrahíta sent his payments, Corvo would give me a portion equivalent to my commission. We agreed that I would receive 4.5 per cent of any investment that Piedrahíta might make in Argentina using Corvo as an intermediary.

Here I must pause a moment. Your Honour, despite the popular image, our family lives off the earnings from our jobs. My primary interest was that the renowned, successful Colombian cattle farmer, whom I had met in Colombia during a trip with the president of Argentina's Central Society of Architects seeking investors, would buy my land. That way, I could give part of the money I would receive to my children so that they could buy their own homes. I managed to do so years later when I sold that lot to another party. But when the deal fell through, I attempted to interest Piedrahíta in other real estate opportunities in which, as is standard, his developers recognised my participation as an intermediary.

So was Piedrahíta the only party interested in investing in the Corvo Dolcet projects that I introduced? Well, no, I introduced several people who, for various reasons, didn't end up investing, but they were seriously interested in doing so. The Court should recall that Sebastián was working as an architect and industrial designer at the time, so when my work put me in contact with people I thought might further my son's career, I tried to connect them.

During that period, my son had cultivated a close friendship with another foreign student, the Ecuadorian architect Rafael Carrasco, with whom he set up his architecture studio Estudio-Box, later named BOX Arquitectura Latinoamericana. Through Carrasco, we met the head of a company in New York, who, at my suggestion, met with Mateo Corvo to discuss investment possibilities, though ultimately the deal fell through, for reasons unknown to me.

Once I'd introduced Piedrahíta and Corvo Dolcet, I hardly interacted with the former and, feeling cheated by Corvo, stopped communicating with him. The reason for my falling out with Corvo Dolcet was simple: he never offered a clear accounting of the percentage we'd agreed on, nor did he reveal whether Piedrahíta had made other investments because of contacts Corvo had provided.

Specifically, he gave me small payments of money that never surpassed US$5,000, with increasing reluctance over time. I had no dealings with Piedrahíta, and it would have been tacky to contact him to inquire about his investments, so I had to trust the information provided to me by Mateo Corvo.

Corvo Dolcet never gave me any money spontaneously; it was always as a result of my repeatedly calling or emailing him about it. In some cases, I would copy in Sebastián or forward the replies because the payments were being given more and more grudgingly. At the time, Sebastián was still trying to move forward with an architecture project for homes for the elderly on the lot in Pilar.

It is for that reason that, though he had no connection with Nexo Urbano S.A. or the commission itself, Sebastián became involved in demanding that Mateo pay me the balance he owed. Unfortunately, I find that I am still unduly influenced by the chauvinistic notions that prevail in Colombia, so I thought that if I involved Sebastián, not only would I bolster the possibility that he might get architectural work, but also that, being a man, he would have Mateo's respect and make him pay me. This criminal proceeding illustrates how wrong I was on both counts: Corvo gave me only a small portion of the money he owed me from Piedrahíta's investments in his projects, and, had I not involved my son, he would not have been summoned to testify.

I admit to having grown insistent, and in early 2011 my relationship with Mateo Corvo was broken beyond repair. Because of Sebastián's efforts, and his and Corvo's interest in moving forward with the architecture project he had designed with his partner, Corvo Dolcet gave me a 'rough' accounting of what Piedrahíta had invested and told me that 4.5 per cent of that investment equalled US$101,950. He initially pressured me to accept that sum in the form of shares in the company Ínsula Urbana, which I absolutely refused.

I kept pushing and was finally given the full amount at the beginning of 2011. As I said, thanks to this process I learned, through Corvo's own statements, that the remittance was not proportional to Piedrahíta's investment. Corvo then told Sebastián that he wanted a formal record of that payment, so he drew up the document that Your Honour found at his home, which only Sebastián signed because I was not present. That document should not, in fact, have been signed by my son since he had not participated in the intermediation that led to the commission, but it seems that Corvo asked him to do so as a sort of guarantee that no further claims would be made.

That is as far as my participation went, lawful in every way. I am unable to describe the events in greater detail because it has been more than ten years since I introduced Corvo Dolcet and Piedrahíta. After the events described above, I lost contact with Corvo. Sebastián kept in touch a little longer, trying to move his project forward, and when that proved impossible, he too ceased to have contact with Corvo. Around the same time, he began his work as a writer, lecturer, and documentary producer, which has given him so much success, influence and personal satisfaction that he abandoned his career as an architect.

My real estate work was not very lucrative for me either, so Nexo Urbano S.A. became defunct. From there, I began to specialise in coaching, and in October 2016 I signed a contract with Editorial Planeta to write my first book, which also allowed me to begin my work as a lecturer.

It was an unpleasant surprise to see the press reports about my involvement in this criminal proceeding. Nevertheless, I trust that Your Honour will be able to review the facts and note the absence of any condemnable behaviour on my part.

Once again Pablo Escobar's 'widow' and his 'millions' are in the news. As time passes, the news has less and less to do with reality and has become unfit even for a movie script, since the truth always comes out, which is that I work day in and day out.

The summons to testify at the request of the Public Minister also highlights an 'independent' event that took place between 2011 and 2012, the purchase of the property – a 1,100-square-foot apartment – where my son and his family currently live.

My son, Sebastián, will provide the exact information about that purchase, which will lay out the sequence of events, as I did not take part in the purchase; he acquired the property with his earnings and my financial assistance. It is true that before the acquisition I gave him two gifts of money, one when I received funds from a bill of sale and the other when I registered a deed. In both cases they had to do with the sale of my lot at Avenida Ingeniero Huergo 913/15 in the city of Buenos Aires.

The gift has been classified as justifying the criminal charge, with the claim that there is no legal documentation backing it up. Without question, in light of my account, this is the case only because Your Honour and the prosecutors consider me to be, above all else, the 'widow of Pablo Escobar Gaviria'. Otherwise, common sense would find it quite unremarkable that a single mother, upon selling her primary asset, would divide the money obtained from that sale into equal parts to help her children and aid them in acquiring their own first homes.

I have no doubt that, given the importance of family for the residents of this country, gifts from parents to children are extremely common. Whereas for my fellow citizens, enabling one's children to have their own homes is understood as fulfilling the dream of home-ownership and produces a sense of pride, fellowship, and joy, that same gift being given within 'the family of ...' is seen as an assumedly criminal act.

I am completely subject to the jurisdiction of the Court, but I cannot fail to object that this summons has been issued to me merely for being 'the widow of ...' Because of that label, it is assumed that I knew more than ten years ago that a real estate investor, known to all as a prominent livestock tycoon, was a drug trafficker, when at the time nobody suspected it.

Because of that label, it is thought that my son used illicit funds to acquire his properties. Because of that label, my behaviour as a mother is looked at askance, when I gave my children money to help them acquire their homes.

My previous dealings with the federal judiciary, though they ended with a just outcome that was consistent with the truth, have only subjected me to increased stigma and harm. I come before this court with the hope that achieving a just finding in this proceeding will be less costly to my health. I therefore hope that my account will be assessed impartially, that the evidence I offer here to clear my name will dispel all doubts, and that, in judging me, Your Honour and the entire world will evaluate the behavior of 'María Isabel Santos Caballero' completely apart from any label or prejudice based on my past and the family ties I have left behind.

Once the news was published, we swiftly became fodder for the Argentine press, and by the following day journalists from various outlets were posted outside the building where I live. The nightmare was starting again. And though I knew we had committed no crime, I was terrified to think how all of this would affect my five-year-old grandson. I panicked. I thought that at any moment Argentina's federal police were going to raid my apartment and arrest me.

Pablo's ghost continues to haunt us. This new charge brought other consequences that were equally painful. I have been actively involved in raising my grandson, Juan Emilio, doing craft projects, making costumes and telling stories at one of the children's groups he was part of. But it is astonishing how many adults prefer to believe blindly, and instantly, news reports that once again depict me as someone I am not.

For twenty-five years I have silently and respectfully endured the scorn of the public for having the irrevocable title of being 'the widow of ...' As a result, I have often had to surrender my rights as a woman. I wonder: how can I show my children anything good if I continue to resign myself to surrendering those rights? The brutal force of prejudice made me realise again that though I have never been convicted – indeed, have never been part of any criminal trial nor even called in for questioning – I was not welcome in a group of women that came together with the shared purpose of loving our grandchildren. These displays mean not only being ostracised from society myself, but seeing my innocent young grandson being rejected too.

I feel compelled to protect him, hiding from him the previous reality that is such a deep wound for me, because it is as unfair as the persecution to which I and my son, Sebastián, are victim today. What can I teach my grandson if I continue to be absolutely silent? Would that be a good example for him? I remain committed to his growth in many ways, and I will not surrender my rights as a grandmother to give him all my love and respect and to share with him my life experiences, so he can grow up with the same human values and respect for life with which I raised my children.

Once I had discussed the news of the investigation with my daughter-in-law, we decided to get in touch with Sebastián, who at the time was in Cannes, France, attending MIPCOM, a trade show for TV and movie producers. After trying repeatedly for more than an hour, Ángeles managed to track him down. He was very worried and upset, because he's always chosen to be an upstanding man who – despite his father's bad example – abandoned any desire to become wealthy for the second time in his life by unlawful means. He has learned the lessons of his father's deadly past better than anybody. Today he devotes his life to encouraging young people and adults at his lectures around the globe not to repeat Pablo's history.

Even so, my son decided not to break off his trip. He was scheduled to travel to three other French cities to present the French translation of his first book, *Pablo Escobar: My Father*. He then decided to travel to Barcelona to meet with the heads of his publisher, look them in the eye and explain the details of the case. From there he went to Mexico City to give talks to more than 5,000 students at several schools.

The uproar produced by the press reports caused other collateral damage: the Banco Caja Social closed Sebastián's savings account, which contained nothing but the royalties for his two books. I still remember my son's disappointment and indignation; he doesn't know what else he can do to avoid being compared undeservedly to his father's illegal activities. It would seem that the banks are trying to force him to act like a delinquent; what future awaits him if he doesn't have the right to hold a savings account? How will he be able to live within the nation's legal structures when he is unable to use its banks?

After fulfilling his obligations abroad, Sebastián returned to Buenos Aires. He had asked us not to go to the airport to pick him up since reporters might be lying in wait or, in the worst case scenario, he might be detained by immigration officials. I waited with my heart in my throat, afraid he might never come home. He said it was the longest, most painful and agonising flight of his life, but, thank God, he had no trouble entering the country and the press were nowhere to be seen. Once he was home, he cried for a long time in Ángeles's arms and thanked the Lord for allowing him to see his son.

As I write the end of this book, it has been eight months since they announced the charges against us. During that period, in a manner I've never observed before, my son has been unable to hide his irritation. Even his face has changed. Maybe he feels it more acutely now because he is a father. I understand. It didn't take long for his old fears about the possibility of becoming a father to come out. Pablo's criminal saga has reached Juan Emilio, Juan Pablo's only son.

Since the Argentine prosecutors announced the investigation, several of our friends have pulled away, but the vast majority have supported us. Still, it has been painful.

Sebastián has also had several of his foreign lectures cancelled, which worries me since it is one of his sources of income and this new accusation has meant paying for legal counsel, an unforeseen expense that is having an impact on his family's plans. People continue to believe that we have millions of dollars, which could not be further from the truth. My children and my daughter-in-law work and live off their earnings, like everyone else. The greatest favour that Pablo's enemies ever did his family was to take away that toxic inheritance but, even though it is in other people's possession, every once in a while, fantasists and fools pop up who still believe that for decades we've been hiding a fortune that we don't actually possess.

This new injunction by the authorities, which has garnered a great deal of attention in the media, has destroyed our peace of mind and our privacy. What my daughter experienced on 24 April 2018, is infuriating. A local magazine published photos of her leaving my apartment. The headline was outrageous: 'Obese and depressed, Manuela, Pablo Escobar's daughter, re-emerges.' Enrique García Medina, who took her photo, also tried to take mine by flinging himself across the hood of my vehicle; this is unquestionably reprehensible behaviour, and shows a lack of respect for a family that only wants a place in this world.

Little is publicly known about Manuela because she has tried to keep her life private, as she has every right to do. She hopes that people will understand and allow her to live in peace. Yet there are always opportunistic reporters or writers trying to make money by publishing false tales about her life. So many lies have been told about her that maybe this is a good time to tell a few truths.

Manuela was a child we very much wanted and sought to have. Before she was conceived, I had four miscarriages and an ectopic pregnancy, and Pablo and I underwent various fertility treatments that required time and consistency. In September 1983, I finally became pregnant.

But eight months and fifteen days into the pregnancy, I had to flee the country because of the death of the minister of justice, Rodrigo Lara Bonilla. Manuela was born on 25 May 1984, in Panama, and within a few days Pablo forced me to send her to Medellín because it was very dangerous to have her with us. I was reunited with her only two months later, but she did not recognise me at all. Because of the time we were separated, she refused to let me hold her or to take a bottle from me.

For her first two years, Manuela did not have daily contact with her father because he was in hiding. I was living with my mother, perpetually on edge because of the constant unannounced police and military raids. These events are forever engraved on my children's memories.

In 1985, when we moved to the Mónaco building, we baptised Manuela in the Santa María de los Ángeles church, but, as would happen on so many other occasions in my daughter's life, Pablo was not present. The few times he visited we ate together as a family, then he lay down in Manuela's crib with her and told her stories until she fell asleep. Afterwards, he'd play with Juan Pablo for a while before leaving again.

My husband managed to live with us for three months in 1987 because all legal proceedings against him had been lifted, and he took our little girl to nursery school every day. For Pablo, Manuela was his guardian angel, his dancer, his singer, his princess, as he used to call her. And he was able to keep her in a sort of glass bubble because he never told her what he did or who he was.

In 1988, things changed drastically when my husband's enemies set off a car bomb outside the Mónaco building and we had to leave for good. Manuela was three and a half at the time. From then on, we saw Pablo only sporadically because he was a fugitive from justice, and his lovers and affairs also took up a good deal of his time.

In 1989, we celebrated Manuela's fifth birthday at Hacienda Nápoles. Pablo attended the party for a while and gave her a black mare and her foal, but the child was unable to enjoy them because we were constantly having to go into hiding. A false story has emerged about that birthday that has captured people's imaginations and that many still assume to be true. I am referring to the famous unicorn that Pablo supposedly gave his daughter. How absurd. People claimed that Pablo ordered his men to nail a horn to the forehead of a white horse and staple on wings so it would look like a unicorn. They also said that the animal died when the resulting wounds became infected. I don't know where that horrifying story came from, but it certainly never happened.

Manuela and Juan Pablo grew up surrounded by fear. Pablo's circumstances, thanks to the manhunts and raids, had a direct impact on our children, who had to behave in ways far beyond their years. In Manuela's case, for example, Pablo gave her instructions on what to do if anybody asked her something. He didn't explain anything, just told her, 'If a policeman or anybody else asks you something, just tell them, "Ask my mother". Never tell them anything.'

Even after all this time, she still obeys that order, and when anybody asks her anything, however trivial it may be, she always replies, 'Ask my mother'.

My goal in telling part of my children's story is to show that their road has been a rocky one. It is to be admired that they have managed to rebuild their lives so honourably. For that reason, it is all the more painful that we are currently being subjected to an investigation, because my children, and now my grandson, are in the middle of a storm that shows no signs of abating.

In the meantime, Ángeles has been very strong throughout this new trial, as she has many times in the past. She came into our lives when she was just twenty years old, and she chose to be with my son at a tumultuous time. Today I wonder: what caused her to board a sinking ship? Why didn't she leave? She has been my guardian angel. We have shared our lives for thirty years, and we share the same goals. She is a wonderful human being who has accompanied me in my sorrows and has shown me my own strength.

It seems appropriate to say here that Sebastián refused to have a child for many years, afraid that any child of his might be subjected to the same suffering that he and his sister endured. He was terrified that a new member of the family might be touched by his grandfather's criminal career. But after thinking about it for a long time, he and his wife decided that their desire to be parents could overcome any challenge. Juan Emilio was born on 21 December 2012, and our family has been full of light and hope ever since.

Juan Emilio has meant that I have reconciled myself with life; he offers me my most genuine contact with joy. When I am with him, I connect with his innocence, his snuggles and his whims. I am very present, showing up for every moment I can. When he stays at my house, we lose track of time. And when his parents call to say they're coming to get him, he tells them, 'No, please, don't worry about me! I'm fine!'

But reality is merciless and cannot be postponed. He is growing up rapidly. Ángeles talks to her son about the books his father has written; Sebastián shows him photos of his grandfather, and he does not intend to hide the truth when the moment comes. I am determined to tell my grandson who the man I married truly was, but to do so while following his parents' lead. It will be a difficult undertaking for all three of us.

As the days pass, talking to Juan Emilio becomes more complicated. Like the day we were driving along in my car and he asked, 'Grandma, how did my grandpa die?'

I froze. I didn't know how to answer, and I didn't want to lie either, so I texted Ángeles and Sebastián to ask what I should do. He asked again, and I said the following: 'That's a very painful memory, sweetheart … Wait a little bit and I'll tell you.'

Just then I got a message from Sebastián, who suggested I tell him that his grandfather had died on a rooftop. I did so, but Juan Emilio had a new question: 'But how, Grandma?'

'Sweetheart, it makes me really sad to have to remember that.'

And I changed the subject.

In these two years of reflection while writing this book, I have become fully aware of the pressure that Juan Pablo and Manuela were subjected to both physically and mentally. Only now do I realise that I have many conversations still to engage in, many apologies to make for the terror, the confinement, the not being able to go to school, the isolation that prevented them from having contact with other

children and with their own family. Today, despite everything, my children are still betting on life and imploring
society to view them as the human beings they are. I only
pray that my grandson does not suffer the consequences of
this new trial by fire and that Pablo's ghost leaves us in
peace at last.

Epilogue

The Secret I Kept for Years

I had to reconnect with my story and delve into the depths of my soul to find the courage to reveal the sad secret I'd been keeping for forty-four years.

One night, rocked by emotions my writing had stirred up and with my deadline for this book bearing down on me, I decided to open my heart to Sebastián, my son. Learning this secret was devastating for him, since he'd had the mistaken impression that his father and his mother had enjoyed a rather less cruel relationship than the one I revealed. Ever since, the bond my son once felt with his father has not been the same.

Very likely the reader will have a similar experience and will feel contradictions if they contrast the following revelation with the Pablo I have described up to this point. I have written it as I experienced it and felt it. Only as I was finishing this book have I felt the need to share this secret, to tell this truth that will certainly damage even further people's perceptions of the man my husband was.

I told Sebastián that at the time I was fourteen and Pablo, my boyfriend, was twenty-five. One day he hugged me, kissed me, and I felt paralysed and frozen with fear. I wasn't ready; I didn't yet feel sexual desire; I lacked the tools to understand what that intense, intimate contact meant. Three weeks went by, and though I was unfamiliar with the side effects, I quickly realised that something strange was happening to me. But I never dreamed I might be pregnant.

A few days later, Pablo came looking for me when I was walking near the house and asked me how I felt. I said I was fine and he asked me to come with him to a woman's house. I didn't see anything unusual in his manner, and a little while later we reached a house in a distant, impoverished area of Medellín.

An older woman, hardly saying hello, told me to lie down on a cot and then inserted several plastic tubes, the kind they use for IVs, into my uterus. All she said was that they'd serve as a preventive. Naively, I asked, 'To prevent what?' and she replied, 'To keep you from getting pregnant.' Then the woman told me to be very careful and when I started bleeding, to take out the plastic tubes.

I can't really describe that moment clearly, but I had no idea what was going on. I simply obeyed in silence. After the 'intervention', Pablo dropped me off at home and asked me to follow the woman's instructions to the letter and let him know if anything happened. But it wasn't so easy to deal with that situation. I had seven siblings and there was only one bathroom in the house, so we couldn't dawdle in there. For the next few days I lay with those strange objects inside of me, racked by intense pains, but I couldn't tell anybody anything. I just prayed to God for it to end soon.

After I told Sebastián, I hesitated a lot over whether I should tell Manuela. Over the course of our lives, I had hidden many things from her to avoid causing her even more pain, but I thought the moment had come. Manuela's reaction was very intense. She asked several questions that I was unable to answer about why Pablo had done what he did without asking me and why he hadn't warned me of the risks of performing an abortion in those conditions. She found Pablo's behaviour all the more reprehensible because he could have put my health and even my ability to have more children in jeopardy.

My woman-to-woman conversation with my daughter became even more difficult when I was unable to explain why I'd let so much time pass before telling my children. I said that I'd never talked about the subject with anybody, not even my best friend, because even today an abortion is classified as an unforgivable sin. I'd planned to take this secret to the grave.

In revealing what happened to me, my aim is to face up to my past and accept responsibility; I don't feel comfortable portraying myself as my husband's victim because of the great respect I owe his other victims. There were many questions I didn't dare to ask, that I had to swallow, because my parents made no room for dialogue, for revealing things like what had happened to me, because of cultural and moral conditioning. Out of ignorance, they transferred that burden to me, but I do not judge them. They were only doing what they knew.

I admit that all of this happened because I was totally disconnected from reality. In the trauma-focussed therapy sessions I attend regularly, I asked my doctor about it, and he replied that what had happened to me could be considered rape. In that era – the 1970s – we lived in a social context in which having sexual relations with one's boyfriend was considered a terrible transgression and was viewed very badly, especially in a family with deep religious conviction. I was expected to behave like a teenager with no right to have opinions, to be silent and submissive with my future husband, and, most of all, to still be a virgin when I entered matrimony.

To cope with what had happened to me, I turned to science, seeking a professional analysis that would help me face and untangle that part of my private experience. And of course the diagnosis took my breath away:

> We starkly see the beginnings of the career of a psychopath, a manipulator. It is clear how Pablo Escobar conceives of romantic relationships: the woman is his property. He can make use of the woman's body, both to have sexual relations and to impose an abortion, without considering her opinion or even informing her of what the procedure is. He puts the woman's life at risk, coolly endangering her in front of her family. Over time, these characteristics become heightened and intensified.
>
> That fourteen-year-old girl can be considered to have been abused (technically, there must be a five-year age difference between the perpetrator and the

victim for the act to be considered abuse, and in this case there is an eleven-year difference). On the one hand, the victim is in thrall to a spell that takes possession of her will. The abuser isolates her from external reality, making himself her only point of reference, thus manipulating her psychological reality. On the other, the complement to that isolation is fear: fear of confronting him, and of the consequences that might result, which could even include death (as occurred in other cases).

In the grip of these two elements, the victim is wrapped in a psychological reality that clouds her understanding and cloaks reality. Her behaviour is guided more by the abuser's internal state than by her own emotions or judgement, in an attempt – often futile – to appease him, to avoid provoking his abusive reaction.

It is not easy to talk about all these secrets, which opened wounds I have not had the courage, the desire, the emotions or the strength to re-examine and heal before now. Only today, very late in the game, am I able to grapple with what Pablo did to me, first as my boyfriend and later after becoming my husband.

I want you all to know that despite everything, at the time I did not feel coerced, or I did not want to see it that way, or maybe I simply found no other way out. But I forgive Pablo because I feel that in the end one thing turned out well: we have two children who were born from that union, with which we honour their lives. I am grateful for them because they give me the strength to keep on living.

I wonder, deep inside, whether the unconditionality of my love for Pablo has to do with my personal reaction to all the violence he subjected me to at fourteen years of age, or if, on the contrary, that essence was always present in my relationship with him.

At the end of the painful story I am sharing here, I feel I have been able to relive Pablo's cruelty and ponder whether what bound me to him was fear or love.